PSYCHOANALYSIS
AND FEMINISM

PSYCHOANALYSIS AND FEMINISM

A Radical Reassessment of Freudian Psychoanalysis

With a New Introduction by the Author

JULIET MITCHELL

BASIC
BOOKS

A Member of the Perseus Books Group

First published by Allen Lane 1974
Published in Pelican Books 1975
Reprinted in Penguin Books 1990
Reprinted with a new Introduction in Penguin Books 2000

Published by Basic Books,
A Member of the Perseus Books Group

A CIP cataog record for this book is available from the Library of
Congress.
ISBN 0-465-04608-8

00   01   02   03—10   9   8   7   6   5   4   3   2   1

For my mother

Contents

Acknowledgements

The author and publishers gratefully acknowledge permission to quote from the following works: James Strachey, ed., *The Standard Edition of the Complete Psychological Works of Sigmund Freud*, Sigmund Freud Copyrights Ltd, The Institute of Psychoanalysis, and The Hogarth Press Ltd; Simone de Beauvoir, *The Second Sex*, 1968, Jonathan Cape Ltd and Alfred A. Knopf Inc; Eva Figes, *Patriarchal Attitudes*, 1970, Faber & Faber Ltd and Stein & Day Publishers; R. D. Laing and Aaron Esterson, *Sanity, Madness and the Family*, 1964, Tavistock Publications; R. D. Laing, *The Divided Self*, 1960, and *Self and Others*, 1969, Tavistock Publications.

. . . in his medical school a doctor receives a training which is more or less the opposite of what he would need as a preparation for psychoanalysis. His attention has been directed to objectively ascertainable facts of anatomy, physics and chemistry . . . His interest is not aroused in the mental side of vital phenomena; medicine is not concerned with the study of the higher intellectual functions, which lies in the sphere of another faculty. Only psychiatry is supposed to deal with the disturbances of mental functions; but we know in what manner and with what aims it does so. It looks for the somatic determinants of mental disorders and treats them like other causes of illness.

Psychiatry is right to do so and medical education is clearly excellent. If it is described as one-sided, one must first discover the standpoint from which one is making that characteristic into a reproach. In itself every science is one-sided. It must be so, since it restricts itself to particular subjects, points of view and methods. It is a piece of nonsense in which I would take no part to play off one science against another. After all, physics does not diminish the value of chemistry; it cannot take its place but on the other hand cannot be replaced by it. *Psycho-analysis is certainly quite particularly one-sided, as being the science of the mental unconscious.*

(Freud, 'The Question of Lay Analysis', 1926, Standard Edition, Vol. XX, p. 230–31 [my italics]).

Introduction, 1999

A year or two ago, while throwing out some old papers, I came across a proposal I had submitted to a publisher in 1968 for a book on the social history of the twentieth-century Western family. Finding this confirmed a sense of absurdity that I had lived with ever since the publication of *Psychoanalysis and Feminism* in 1974 – for this was the book that emerged. There was no mention of psychoanalysis anywhere in the proposal. As far as I was concerned, a very generous publisher[1] had simply accepted a substitute – a completely different book. For my book on the family I had intended to read a few articles of Freud's on 'femininity' and, with that in mind, had entered the British Museum reading room at the start of a university long vacation. I emerged at the end of the summer having read all twenty-three volumes of the standard edition of Freud's complete works. The projected work had changed and something in me had done so also. I had been deeply marked by my reading Freud, and probably it is this that carries the book; twenty-five years later, I am no less impressed by Freud, although somewhat more independent of him. Due to the energy generated by my respect for Freud's work, the centre of gravity in *Psychoanalysis and Feminism* shifted from the family to psychoanalysis, and the title reflects this.

Yet, when more than twenty-five years later I reread *Psychoanalysis and Feminism* for this new edition, I was surprised: though not the book I had originally planned, in a sense it is a book about the family.

If the book changed between its conception and execution, it changed again – through its reception – after publication. The book I wrote here was altered by its subsequent history. Thus, neither at the time of publication nor at any time since, did anyone really notice the sections on Wilhelm Reich and R. D.

Laing. Yet I had selected Reich and Laing precisely because of their attempts, in the first case to extend left-wing discussion of the family away from economics and into ideology and sexuality, and, in the second, to move clinical analysis of the psychology of the nuclear family outwards into the larger public sphere. I had also used Jacques Lacan's now famous 'return to Freud' in conjunction with his interest in Louis Althusser's suggestive ideas about psychoanalysis and ideology and Claude Lévi-Strauss's about psychoanalysis and kinship alliances. The Lacan that was subsequently picked up by Anglo-Saxon feminism gave pride of place to his introduction of linguistics to psychoanalytic theory. The family was left by the wayside.

As a result of this shift of interest my introduction of psychoanalysis to feminism was never perceived as carrying the family with it, so not only the sections on Reich and Laing but also the rather flamboyant reflections about kinship in the last section of the book were largely ignored. My intention had been to bring psychoanalysis to bear on the position of people in their kinship networks – how that context unconsciously 'creates' them and they it. In fact, the intention of this book suffered from a more general fate, for, already by the 1980s, after a flurry of excellent feminist anthropology, any study on kinship had been largely dropped from academic curricula and the family itself had been completely demoted from its position as an important target of political change and analysis. Interest in both is now returning.

Psychoanalysis and Feminism used the experience and literature of the women's movement and also the writing of (and to some degree about), in particular, Freud, Reich and Laing, Althusser, Lévi-Strauss and Lacan. When the book was finished I felt a strong need to root these latter (male) writings in experience. Until I left my university post in 1970, I had been teaching English literature. I decided to retrain as a psychoanalyst. In 1978, I qualified as a psychoanalyst, trained largely in the British (or Independent) School of Object Relations. There was only one centre of training for psychoanalysis of adults in Britain – the London Institute of Psychoanalysis. However, within this one institute there are three orientations – Independent Object Relations, Kleinian Object Relations and

Anna Freudian (now called Contemporary Freudian, which is more focused on drives and defences). Where Freud's and Anna Freud's theories are known as 'one-person' psychologies, Object Relations, particularly of the British School, is a so-called 'two-person' psychology. The first emphasizes the drives, desires and fantasies of the subject and the second stresses the unconscious interactions with a crucial other person, the so-called object – in particular, the subject's mother. All three branches of training were powerfully dismissive of Lacan, whose 'return to Freud' had so impressed me. However, despite the immense importance of my training and my earlier interest, the conjunction of kinship, ideology and psychoanalysis continue to concern me.

Thinking back raises two obvious questions. Why, firstly, did psychoanalysis have such a renaissance within feminism? And, secondly, why did the relationship between these develop the way it did, that is, largely away from an interest such as mine in understanding the construction of sexual difference within ideology (or sexual difference *as* part of ideology), together with the interaction of the individual psyche and the kinship system? The intention behind *Psychoanalysis and Feminism* was to indicate that psychoanalysis seemed to offer some way into the question of how, along with all social changes, something persists that is incommensurate with the real social situation. For, while it is true that women may be socialized into assuming the position of the second sex, this conscious, deliberate socialization is inadequate to explain the structure of sexual difference and the inequalities that always arise from it, despite the fact that there is enormous diversity of social practice.

So, the original project was to use a dimension of psychoanalytic theory to forward an understanding of how, beyond the biophysical–chemical–anatomical–constitutional factors and the social learning behaviours of sexual difference, we live ourselves as subjects which are sexually differentiated, or, in today's idiom (with which I have always disagreed), 'gendered'.[2] The question had arisen out of an omission in my earlier essay on the family, 'Women: The Longest Revolution' (1966), in which I had tried to intervene in those accounts of the family that presented it as a unit, either functional (as with 1950s accounts typified by Talcott Parsons) or dysfunctional (as with the 1960s assaults on it typified by R. D. Laing). Such a unity echoed rhetorical positions and froze the concept of the family in any given time. Instead, I proposed that there were three major familial structures – reproduction, the socialization of children, the sexuality of the couple – and a fourth – the overall social economy – within which the first three were all embedded. In any particular situation, one or other of these could change without the others changing. What I came to feel was left out of the account was how such structures were lived in the heart and in the head and transmitted over generations. The transmission of ideas also seemed to have a degree of autonomy, as conditions alter but attitudes may not – or vice-versa. This was the problem I raised in the last chapters of *Women's Estate* (1972) and then turned to more fully in *Psychoanalysis and Feminism*. The project was not without its difficulties. *Psychoanalysis and Feminism* was written at the height of a political movement, the so-called 'second-wave' of feminism; its polemical certainties as part of a political dialogue to an extent obscure the exploratory and tentative nature of its enterprise. This enterprise, however, seems to me still to involve questions that have not – and perhaps will not – be resolved, but which nevertheless still need to be asked.

The extended notion of 'ideology' that Louis Althusser introduced – that it is the equivalent to 'how we live ourselves' as subjects, both in general and in our own particular social world – had an obvious appeal. Ideology, in all the unsatisfactory vagueness of Althusser's sense of it, seems crucial as an issue. Why, despite massive social, economic and legal changes, is there still a kind of underwater tow that makes progress regress on matters of 'gender' equality? This is not a tide that after going out returns more or less completely to the same spot; we do not revert exactly to the status quo ante – but nevertheless feminism seems always to be rowing against a current that is ultimately the stronger force. There is an inherent conservatism at work in the psycho-ideological living of sexual relations that any feminist progression ultimately encounters. The crucial point, however, is that conservatism actually seems inherent in the very construction of sexual difference – as though the difference itself has in its constitution insisted on stasis. This is not to say that the two terms of sexual difference – femininity and masculinity – and the content of their relationship do not also vary greatly.

There is a drive for change but also a drive to stay put. The family is always changing its social and economic form and function, yet ideologically it is conceived of as though it were the still centre of a moving world. This is all too visible in contemporary protests about changing kinship modes such as single parenthood, childfree couples, same-sex parents. Although everyone is partly conservative, it is 'women', in terms both of their socio-economic position in the family and of the psycho-ideological construction that predisposes them to that location, who become the ascribed repositories of that human conservatism. Feminism is confronted with the task of pursuing emancipation in the heart of darkness. The conservatism enjoined on, and practised by, the family and the women therein is not simply a matter of rhetoric – though it certainly is that – it is also the result of the generational transmission of a certain kind of thought about concepts like masculinity and femininity. This 'kind of thought' is, of course, partly conscious, deliberately chosen and enacted. However, it is primarily an unconscious process. Such an unconscious process is the object of both psychoanalytic theory and its clinical practice.

On page 315 of this book I quote from Freud's *Totem and Taboo* (1913), a highly problematic mythological reconstruction of human prehistory, but one that despite this goes to the centre of the difficulty. The thrust of the book's story is that in man's prehistory a primal father kept all the women for himself. In time, the sons ganged up and murdered him. Society was inaugurated when these brothers next realized that they could end up fighting amongst themselves, each against all, and instead they instituted restrictions on which brother could have which woman. This was the taboo on incest. Freud's mythologies such as 'Totem and Taboo' play an important organizing and explanatory role in his thinking. In this case, however, he summarizes his thoughts with a caution:

Before I bring my remarks to a close ... I must find room to point out that though my arguments have led to a high degree of convergence upon a simple comprehensive nexus of ideas, this fact cannot blind us to the uncertainties of my premises or the difficulties involved in my conclusions.[3]

He cites two major examples of these uncertainties and difficulties: first, his thesis needs the hypothesis of a collective mind; and second, he has observed that there is an unconscious sense of guilt felt by most people, even though they have not actually done wrong. His story rests on these two notions – guilt and a collective mind – which in their turn are needed to explain his clinical observations. With reference to them both, Freud concludes:

It must be admitted that these are grave difficulties; and any explanation that could avoid presumptions of such a kind would seem to be preferable.

Nevertheless, he goes on with regard to the first:

Further reflection, however, will show that I am not alone in the responsibility for this tested procedure. Without the assumption of a collective mind, which makes it possible to neglect the interruptions of mental acts caused by the extinction of the individual, social psychology in general cannot exist. Unless psychical processes were continued from one generation to another, if each generation were obliged to acquire its attitude to life anew, there would be no progress in this field and no development.[4]

Freud's rare references to a collective mind must never be confused with Jung's notion of a collective unconscious. Whereas Jung postulates an innate original symbolism that we all share, Freud simply points to the fact that humans must have some mental experiences in common that are transmitted rather than re-experienced afresh each time. It was for his notion of the inheritance of acquired characteristics that the naturalist Jean-Baptiste Lamarck, whose ideas were already outmoded at the time of *Totem and Taboo*, continued to hold interest for Freud. In the field of psychology, Jean Piaget proposed that specific intellectual abilities might be genetically transmitted. Freud does not offer a scientific explanation of how this transmission takes place – all he says is that he knows it happens. As a mode of explanation, he uses his mythology in place of a scientific theory. What he insists on – and it would still be insisted on – is that he is observing phenomena and these phenomena demand some hypothesis such as that of a collective mind. The problem persists for us today and, contained within it, is one aspect of the acquisition of a knowledge (and a persistence of that knowledge) of the difference between the sexes. No one particular social change necessarily deflects the force of a largely unconsciously acquired history. For instance, it is not only that, perhaps because of biological instinct, and certainly because of the environment of school, street and media, a child raised by two parents of the same sex nevertheless may make a 'normative' adjustment to heterosexuality for itself, as seems to be the case. Something other than the actual situation has intervened. Unconscious thought processes are an important contribution to these instances of normalization. Through deciphering such processes one finds the second example that Freud raises: humans feel guilt without necessarily having committed a crime. A child who has been raised in a very uncritical home environment nevertheless feels at fault, self-attacks and thinks he has done something wrong. This is, in part, why children (and others) are always insisting, 'It's not my fault' – they fear it is, when it isn't.

'Unconscious thought processes' are mostly ordinary thoughts turned into ones of which we are completely unaware. It is the process of transformation from awareness that makes for their bizarre appearance when they become manifest once more – as they do in dreams, neurotic symptoms, psychotic behaviour, jokes and the many psychopathologies of everyday life. But on being made unconscious, ordinary thought processes seem to 'meet up with' something that is already there. Within psychoanalysis explanations for this vary. After the First World War, Freud posited an unconscious 'id' that is, an 'it' within us. Within the id, are the psychical representatives of the drives. The thoughts excluded from consciousness meet up with these psychical representatives of the drives which impel our minds to do some work by demanding the satisfaction of a release from the tension which would build up if there were no discharge. These psychical representatives of drives force us to work to this end, to find ways, for instance, of getting some food, or an object for our rage. For Melanie Klein, the neonate brings with it primitive unconscious fantasies which are also different in appearance from conscious fantasies; for Wilfred Bion and others, there is a 'nameless dread' – an overwhelming anxiety that can haunt us against our better rational judgement. At one stage in their thinking, for Jean Laplanche and Jean-Bertrand Pontalis primal fantasies offered mythological answers to a primary questioning about life, that is, questions that the small child cannot formulate – Where do I come from? What is the difference between the sexes? – but to which its imaginings offer an answer. For Jacques Lacan, the unrepresentable Real is traumatic but we are born into 'the Symbolic', an ordering within which we must find our position.

In all these diverse hypotheses there are explicit or implicit postulations of a 'collective mind', a primary condition that all humans share. Because we are born prematurely, and thus with less developed instincts than other animals, we are more dependent on our carers and so the impact of our helplessness in the face of the world is all the greater. Whatever there is in the neonate's unconscious has probably been brought about by a trauma that initiates human life – the world breaks in on us violently and its impingement is registered as a 'trace'. The trace on the psyche of a primary experience attracts to it the repression of later wishes that would otherwise endanger the individual. From clinical experience psychoanalysts know beyond doubt that unconscious thoughts may be communicated between people, and even through people, across generations – but this is only inexplicable if we deny a shared mental terrain. If it were the case that we had nothing in common, then observed unconscious communication would have to be either magical or absurd. The transmission through unconscious processes of 'ideas' and 'ideology', in the widest sense of that term, overlap.

When *Psychoanalysis and Feminism* was written, the search in those days of early second-wave feminism was for what qualities women had in common across the many huge divides of class, race, ethnicity, family ties . . . The question was: What differentiates women, not from each other, but from men? It was a necessary strategy for forming a political movement. It is not, therefore, without irony – or poetic justice? – that the use of psychoanalysis to further this quest offered the very sword which cut it apart. Post-structuralism and post-modernism, deploying the understanding at the heart of Freud's theory – that the human subject is not identical to herself – assaulted what it saw as the essentialism and universalism of the feminist project. In part it was correct to do so; in part, incorrect (for, despite reproductive technologies, we are still all universally conceived by one mother and begotten by one father); in part it erected straw women. Thus, I for one contended in this book that we should examine a specific situation and only from the particular see if there are any more general observations to be made (see pp. 364–5). Kinship and the family, and the reasons for using psychoanalysis to investigate their processes, were the fall guys: the questions raised about ideology and kinship/the family were omitted or reprimanded as naively universalizing and essentialist.

Thereafter, feminist deployment of psychoanalysis bifurcated. The branch that used a part of the theory (Object Relations) in which the transformational effects of thought processes becoming unconscious is not highlighted, persisted. In this theory, originally associated with the British schools of psychoanalysis, the focus is on fantasies, identifications and behaviours, not symptoms. Unconscious processes are regarded as though they follow the same logic and appearance as consciousness. This perspective arises from the analysis and observation of children in whom the differentiation into unconscious and conscious/preconscious is not yet marked and where disturbed *behaviour* is more prevalent than bizarre *symptoms*. Nancy Chodorow, who first published with the feminist anthropologists, used psychoanalytic Object Relations theory to explain sex/gender division as arising from processes of differential identification. Likewise, Dorothy Dinnerstein and Jessica Benjamin explored inter-relational processes, with the additional deployment of self-psychology. I think we should see their ideas as complementary to, rather than as alternatives of the Lacanian interpretations of Freud's theories. In Freud's concept there is an economic dimension, the human drive wants satisfaction and the release of tension – it is indifferent as to the object through which this is attained. Object Relations proposes that there is an urge towards a particular human object, such as the mother, or part thereof, such as the breast ('object' so called because it is the object of the child's drive). It seems to me that both processes go on – the mistake is either to confuse them or to use one to eradicate the other – and that both are crucial. Chodorow's subtitle to her first book, *The Reproduction of Mothering* (1976), was 'Psychoanalysis and the Sociology of Gender'. This is an accurate description, for here the Anglo-Saxon feminist meaning of 'gender', as socially inscribed by learning and identification, both unconscious and conscious, is a term appropriate to a sociological use of Object Relations theory. A girl identifying with her mother who in turn identified with her mother is one important aspect of the transmission of gender roles. Such a realistically based identification is the basis of the proposition associated with these theorists, that if we had shared parenting there would be less gender differentiation. But, on this reading, a child reared by same sex parents should likewise be homosexual and this is just not the case. The question not addressed by a reference to identificatory processes is: Why is something that is not realistically encountered – for instance, Freud's observation that a sense of guilt does not necessarily relate to an actual crime – nevertheless a transmitted, common and necessary experience? If identification were all, it would simply take too long for a child to acquire human meaning and thus for cultures to become established. This is a simple point, but one that still needs addressing.

The other branch of feminism, from the latter part of the 1970s, used psychoanalysis in a diametrically opposite way. In this second trend, everything was considered unstable, displaced, never identical to itself, in a process of constant slippage. The use of psychoanalysis here contributed to the rise of deconstructionism and post-modernism; there was an explicit and intentional move away from the question of ideological transmission (in conjunction with family/kinship). We might characterize this tendency as leading to the imperialism of the unconscious. Consciousness and preconsciousness were consumed by 'the unconscious' which, following Lacan, was the only proper object of psychoanalysis. This unconscious was equated absolutely with the repression of sexuality – to read the one was to read the other. There is, of course, an intimate relation between the two, but they are not the same. The death drive was also considered important, but Lacan's re-emphasis on Freud's point that its unconscious manifestations are the effect of the castration complex bound the death drive to sexuality, too. This is the perspective I am arguing in *Psychoanalysis and Feminism*. However, my original intention was not to augment our understanding of sexual difference through sexuality, but to map an area where we might begin to chart the transmission of unconscious 'ideas' of sexual difference. I now think I might have made this clearer if – still staying with Freud – I had referred to the more general feature of the id, the unconscious drive for mental work in order to relieve tension. The equation of the unconscious and sexuality was partly a misreading of the work of those of us who were interested in the question of ideology, and partly an intentional redirecting of that work. The redirection of the enterprise is exemplified in an early comment of Jacqueline Rose's. In an interview with the journal *m/f* in 1984, she claimed:

It will have crucial effects ... whether psychoanalysis is discussed as an addition or supplement to Marxism ... or whether emphasis is laid on the concept of the unconscious. For while it is indeed correct that psychoanalysis was introduced into feminism as a theory that could rectify the inability of Marxism to address *questions of sexuality* [my italics], and that this move was complementary to the demand within certain areas of Marxism for increasing attention to ideological determinants of our social being, it is also true that undue concentration on this aspect of the theory has served to cut off the concept of the unconscious, or at least to displace it from the centre of the debate.[5]

The original project had indeed been to bring psychoanalysis to bear on issues of ideology – by making use of an approximate equation of unconscious processes and aspects of ideology through unconscious processes. A key feature of this equation concerned the transmission of the meaning of sexual difference. In misreading the use of psychoanalysis as *for sexuality* and then denouncing the interest in ideology, we can see in Rose's comment one example of the move away from any transmission of ideology and the politics of the family – which could be in part understood through an analysis of unconscious processes.

At the time of writing *Psychoanalysis and Feminism*, 'patriarchy' and 'oppression' were interim operational terms being
deployed by the then politically active Women's Liberation
Movement. 'Oppression', as with struggles for independence in
the then-named 'Third World', was a term used to distinguish
the mode of subjugation from 'exploitation' which, in the
Marxist sense, had a precise meaning – the extraction of, and
profit from, surplus labour. 'Oppression' never achieved precision as a concept. 'Patriarchy' was to suggest a structure of
oppressive social division other than that of social class or race.
It was in the analysis of 'patriarchy' – the rule of the father (as
more specific than the sexism of men) – that psychoanalysis was
turned to as a possible source of understanding. The question
of ideology and the transmission of unconscious ideas and
effects of sexual difference linked up with the notion of patriarchy. Patriarchy was what was most emphasized by Lacan's
'return to Freud', which privileged the concept of the castration
complex and what he punningly called the *'nom/non du père'*.
The prohibition on an incestuous relation with the mother is
common to all cultures; however, according to this psychoanalytic reading, such prohibition emanates from the position of
the father – either the father's name or his utterance of the law.
In this theory, the resolution of the castration complex institutes the meaning of sexual difference. It is this part of Lacan's
return to Freud that my book makes use of.

Subsequent feminist work which deployed Lacan, because it
ignored the possible relationship of ideology and unconscious
processes in favour of the absolute equation of sexuality and the
unconscious, was more interested in Lacan's other formulations. Offering the insight that the unconscious is structured
like a language (not that it *is* a language, which is a mistaken
reading on which some textual analyses came to be based),
Lacan saw the phallus as standing, not for an object (the penis)
but for what is missing. It is missing in women, and it is this
absence that established the phallus as the primary signifier
which institutes language as a chain of signifiers instead of as a
system in which a sign is related to what is signified. A sign
refers to something present; a signifier is instituted by something that is not there and hence only means something in the

context of other signifiers. 'Phallic' can describe a penis, but it can also indicate a church steeple or a powerful 'phallic' mother. The explanation of the phallus as the primary signifier was both liberating and problematic for feminism – the penis was demoted but the phallus instigated all language. The emphasis on the structuring of language facilitated the move into using psychoanalysis to read sexual difference within cultural texts. An interest in patriarchy, the father and kinship was displaced. The move to texts and representations of sexual difference pulled almost the entire feminist use of a Freud–Lacan orientation in tow. The new focus entailed a stress on the imbrication of sexuality, language and textuality. In the process 'the unconscious', in so far as it related to the question of ideology and patriarchy, as explored in this book, either became absorbed into something else or was dismissed. Here I want to argue not against this literary work but only for the importance of a return to the original project of using psychoanalysis to help understand the transmission of sexual difference within 'ideology'. Through what slippages was this project misunderstood and displaced?

Psychoanalytic theories are always models of conflict. Indeed, all Freud's theories take conflict as their base. Neurotic symptoms express conflict; the symptoms express one (or more) wish to do something and also the prohibition against such wishes. Both wishes and prevention appear in the symptom: a dream may reveal only the wish, a dream is a dream of fulfilling that wish, but the fact that the wish can only be realized in a dream indicates that it is not allowed into daily consciousness, and therefore that the formation of the dream involves a conflict. Freud, in what is known as the first metapsychology, made the distinction between the conscious, the preconscious and the unconscious. The theory was that the two forces of the conflict were a sexual drive and a drive to preserve oneself; one represses any wish to sexually possess the parent (the Oedipus complex) in order to protect oneself from punishment for the imagined offence.

After the slaughter of the First World War and the psychological issues that arose from it, after also a realization over years of clinical work that the process of cure was difficult and, on the patient's part, a drive not to get well was prevalent, Freud, while never really abandoning his first formulations, superimposed on them new concepts and a new metapsychology. The prohibition on incest became a law (the castration complex) which symbolized the metaphorical 'death' of the subject if broken. This was taken up into the proposition of a 'death drive' as the other force in conflict with sexuality. In the new post-war account, the sexual drive was retained but transformed into a larger 'life drive', in which there was more emphasis on a model of reproduction – it became a drive to form ever more new unities. The death drive, by urging towards stasis, opposed the forward movement of the life drive. The notion of a death drive is behind an observed phenomenon such as the compulsion to repeat something – in particular, to repeat the experience of a traumatic event – and thus to be psychically stuck. Freud next superimposed on the system, conscious, preconscious and unconscious, the metapsychological formulation of the superego, the ego and the id. The latter is the repository of the representations of the drives and absolutely unconscious, but aspects of the superego and ego are likewise unconscious. 'The unconscious' gives way to the notion of unconscious processes that pervade any part of the mental apparatus. The concern is also to explain the transmission of 'ideas' down the generations. The shift to the new metapsychology is important. On page 330, I quote Freud's autobiographical reflections on its significance:

Since I proposed a division of the mental personality into an ego, a super-ego, and an id (1923), I have made no further decisive contribution to psychoanalysis. What I have written on the subject since then has been either inessential or would soon have been supplied by someone else.[6]

Ego psychology, which came to dominate American psychoanalysis, took its departure from this second metapsychology. When Lacan inaugurated his famous return to Freud it was in virulent opposition to American ego psychology, which favoured the therapeutic task of enlarging the conscious part of the ego to enable it to take control. To Lacan, such a unified ego was a complete impostor. For him, the analyst's task, instead of facilitating such illusions of unity, was to emphasize the points of rupture and division in psychic life. Thus Lacan, like Freud before him, although with a more systematic intent, emphasized the intimacy of the disruptive death drive and the divisive castration complex. Freud had argued that the infant cannot experience death, and so concepts of death were derived from the cataclysmic separation from the meaning of one's subjecthood which took place under the threat of castration. Lacan reformulated the first part of this contention into the fact that birth (one person being born from another) and death (someone dying so that the next generation can live) are the two events that cannot be symbolized. Instead, Lacan's 'Symbolic' is constituted by the castration complex, which situates all subjects as either man (living under the threat of castration) or woman (already castrated). Feminism took over this Lacanian perspective, with highly creative results but to the detriment of using psychoanalytic insight into the transmission of 'gendered' thought.

Lacan refuted accusations that he only used the early Freud in his return and, with his stress on the death drive (which was formulated by Freud as late as 1920), it is clear that he did not. Nevertheless, in another way, the accusations were accurate, for Lacan read the death drive into Freud's earlier metapsychology of conscious, preconscious, unconscious, not the superego, ego, id to which it led. Reading back on my book twenty-seven or so years after its inception, I see that, as with the subliminal red thread of the family, another of its features has changed colour. The book was praised originally for introducing Lacan to Anglo-Saxon feminism, then, somewhat later, as the use of Lacanian and post-Lacanian psychoanalysis spread like wild fire, it was criticized for mistakes and misunderstandings in this area. In particular it was said that I had not properly situated Lacan's work within his main triumph – the introduction of linguistic theory to psychoanalysis. Until now, this accurate criticism seemed simply to refer to inadequacy on my own part – to something I had not grasped. Undoubtedly that was part of the reason, but I now see that there was another force at work. The aspect of Lacan's emphasis on the phallus that I took up was the phallus, not as the primary signifier in a chain of signifiers, but rather in relation to Lévi-Strauss's stress on exchange as the basis of society. I wrote: 'Lacan suggests that [the phallus] represents the very notion of exchange itself, but it represents the actual value of exchange or the absent object of exchange. Obviously symbolic exchange. The phallus is the very mark of human desire ...' In other words, I was taking from Lacan something other than the use of linguistic theory that subsequently became so popular; I was taking up the question of ideology, through Althusser's account, and linking it to the theories of Lévi-Strauss. My concern at the time of writing *Psychoanalysis and Feminism* (along with that of many other feminists) was for women to produce a feminist anthropology of kinship in advanced industrial societies and for a 'matching' production that described how this was unconsciously (as well as, of course, consciously) lived and transmitted as 'femininity' (or masculinity). My approach was in part, then, a wish to hijack Lacan for an anthropology of the family.

However, problems also arose as a result of getting stuck in a trap set up by Lacan's welding of the castration complex and the death drive on to the first, superceded metapsychology of '*the* unconscious'. Althusser, whose concern to root ideology in a psychoanalytic reading of transmission through the family I found helpful, got stuck in the same trap. In a letter criticizing his own article entitled in English 'Freud and Lacan', Althusser wrote of 'the discussion of the forms of *familial ideology*, and the crucial role they play in initiating the functioning of the instance that Freud called 'the unconscious', but which should be rechristened as soon as a better term is found'.[7] Of course, 'a better term' (or terms) of superego, ego and id had been found in the second metapsychology, but Althusser's psychoanalytical thinking was embedded in Lacan's polemic against American ego psychology and could not escape the equation of ideology with 'the unconscious' of the first metapsychology. What would have helped was the notion of unconscious processes manifest in the ego and superego and the concept of the id. Of the superego, Freud wrote: '[M]ankind never lives entirely in the present. The past, the tradition of the race and of the people, lives on in the *ideologies of the superego* and yields only slowly to the influences of the present and to new change ... [my italics]'.

Freud's id – that 'better term' for the unconscious – was what
Georg Groddecks had called the 'it', an enormous part of our
generic selves where the representatives of a biological drive
that forces us to think meets that which culturally we are not
allowed to think about. The id continues all the earlier characteristics of the system unconscious. There can be no negation
within its modality; contradictions exist side by side.
Condensation and displacement (Lacan's metaphor and
metonymy) and symbolization are how it works. But it is also
the place where the representatives of the drives reside. The
superego, with its transgenerational transmission of rules and
laws; the id, where drive representatives meet what has been
repressed; the ego, which comprises countless other egos – all
are concepts which offer a way forward into thinking about
ideology as 'how we live ourselves' as sexually differentiated
beings. Above all, it is within the terms of this second metapsychology that the early, influential psychoanalytic writings on
female sexuality and femininity are situated. Freud's own brief
essays into the subject of femininity take place within the
framework of this second metapsychology. There is no need to
subscribe to the subsequent development of ego psychology if
we merely return to this starting point.

In *Psychoanalysis and Feminism* I argue that, although these
notions produce a difficult reading of femininity for feminism,
it is this difficulty which is precisely the point. Why, despite
enormous social, economic, legal progress, does feminism have
to keep coming back to challenge the resistance to change in the
'gender' status quo? Freud's account opens up ways in which
we can think about why 'gender' conservatism persists in the
face of change; why, indeed, the other side of progress seems
always to be reaction.

Lacan's rereading of Freud, even as it is used by feminists, is
in some ways more dismal for feminist politics than is Freud's
original version. Not really interested in the superego, Lacan
gives no place to the possibility of change; there is no twitching
of the heavy hand of the past as it is set up within us. There is
no diachronic account. Males and females must, in the very
construction of their sexual difference, take up different positions in relation to the threat of castration. This allows for opti-

mism in terms of shuffling positions – a boy can take up the position of 'being castrated' and the object of desire, while a girl can be a subject who is only in danger of castration; but these are individual possibilities, the law of sexual difference is in itself inviolate. If any reversals of 'gender' position are undertaken unconsciously, then they are pathologies – if they are pursued consciously, then they constitute political choices. This may be one reason why the feminist use of Lacan for the sexual text of the subject opened the way for gay studies and queer theories to focus on the proliferation of sexual bodies even if Foucault's anti-psychoanalytic work was their main impetus; why, too, as one can deliberately enact different stances, the space was cleared for today's vogue of political practices of 'performance' and 'performativity'. All these offer current variations of stance. Structuralism and post-structuralism opened up post-modern possibilities of fluidity and flexibility, but did not look for ways of providing for any account of historical change, or therefore, of a political practice that might promote such change.

A return to the question of kinship (and within that the question of work and the division of labour – for the two are interconnected) is to ask for an account that allows for historical change and cultural variation. This was the reason for my use of Lévi-Strauss for kinship and of Freud/Lacan for a kind of internalized anthropology of kinship. The project is limited and specific; it is within the family that the initial construction of living as a gendered subject, not as a gender-neutral human-being, has taken place. It is within the first few years of life that the human infant-becoming-child exceeds her individual capacity to learn and somehow acquires the meaning of a social life beyond her actual situation. It is here, in the network of kinship and subsequently of work (the division of labour), that sexual difference in all its certainty and uncertainty is first constructed.

Mary Jo Buehl has documented how feminism has tried to make use of psychoanalysis from its very outset – demanding in particular that its phallocentric model be remedied to understand female sexuality. Looking back at this history, something else now strikes me: Freud did not get fully engaged with an exploration of feminine sexuality, not only because of his sexist prejudices and his chronic cancer, but also because there is an intellectual problem inherent in the exercise. The pathological indicates the 'normal' with which it is on a continuum. Psychoanalysis deals above all with symptoms. However, femininity and masculinity are not symptoms, and nor are they pathologies. When one comes to practice psychoanalysis as a clinician with a long history in feminism, it is almost a shock to reflect on one's work and realize that the question of femininity and masculinity crop up relatively rarely.

Psychoanalysis and Feminism (written before I became a psychoanalyst) sets out the terms whereby we can use psychoanalysis in the context of kinship rules and relations to understand the construction of sexual difference. After it was finished I turned to pursuing the same questions through the *symptoms* of hysteria – an apparently 'gendered' illness. Hysteria was the condition that led to the foundation of psychoanalysis and much later it became a preoccupation of second-wave feminism. More than twenty years later, my reflections on our universal proclivity to hysteria brought me back to what I see as the great theoretical omission of psychoanalysis – the significance of lateral relationships. Vertical, descent relationships and their prohibitions (the Oedipus and castration complex) are crucial, but so too are horizontal, collateral and affinal ones (siblings, peers and partners). I can remember the feeling of tension in my body as my mind sensed a contortion when on pages 370–76 of this book I quoted Lévi-Strauss and commented:

The brother (maternal uncle) must give his sister in marriage and not desire her incestuously, both he and the sister whom he gives away are as close as one can get to being each other. The distinction between them is minimal and the prohibition on their union (the incest taboo) establishes that smallest of differences which is necessary to inaugurate society.

My tension was due to the fact that there is no place for this prohibition on sibling incest in any of the theories of psychoanalysis.

When the infant is thrust from its position of imagining it is all to the mother by the birth of (or expected birth of) a sibling or by recognition that an older sibling was there before it, it wants its mother with the full flow of total possessiveness and wishes to displace absolutely any rival. First it aims to displace the sibling, then the father who made the other child with the mother. There are fathers *and* siblings. In patrilineages, fathers give away daughters; in matrilineages, brothers exchange sisters. By and large, the status of women in matrilineages is higher than in patrilineages. The minimal differences are between brothers and sisters, not between fathers and children. The infant catastrophically experiences another sibling (or potential sibling) as having apparently identical claims on the mother to whom it may have turned. Siblings are in the same position to the parents but they are also different from each other. To establish this difference, their incest must be prohibited. This prohibition sets up a minimal difference between the subject and the other. Twins are so disturbing – regarded as magical for good or ill – because they appear as doubles, not differences.

This minimal difference moves languages from a system of equivalencies or signs, where the sign relates directly to what is signified, into language as a system in which signifiers relate to signifiers – words have meaning in relation to the differences they show from each other.

In the 1980s, developmental psychologists and emergent family therapists started to look at sibling relationships. There had been interest in the subject in the inter-war years, but the post-war reconstruction of the family had suppressed an interest in siblings in favour of the overwhelming importance of mothers and fathers. Judy Dunn and Carol Kendrick, in starting their interview/observational-based research on sibling relationships, commented that observing young siblings highlighted aspects of human growth that may simply go unnoticed if development is studied solely in the context of parent and child.' Until then, the focus on the father had been supplemented by a focus on the mother, but sibling interaction without the polar pull towards the parents had not been studied. It is likewise startlingly absent from psychoanalysis, both in theory and in practice. Developmental and social psychologists can study sibling interaction on its own; for psychoanalysis it needs to be brought into conjunction with parents. Both Freud and his followers saw normal development as starting with children relating to their parents and then only secondarily moving out to siblings and peers. In fact, although there is undoubtedly a relationship to the mother from birth, a full social relationship which demands three (or more people) from the outset is not only instituted by the father but also (perhaps even more so) by siblings or other children. It is these that make the mother into a social being towards whom the infant's feelings thus become Oedipal. If we bring the relationship towards siblings (or their substitute peers) into conjunction with the relationship to the mother, a different dimension of that Oedipal moment is also uncovered – what in *Mad Men and Medusas* (2000) I have called the 'parthenogenic complex' – the giving birth from oneself alone.

When feminism followed Lacan in welding the death drive (and with it the castration complex) on to the first metapsychology and, in particular, the unconscious, it missed an opportunity for introducing historical change into the construction of sexual difference. It also strengthened the patriarchal prejudice within psychoanalytic theory, making patriarchy both timeless and necessary and keeping mothers and matriarchies as pre-Symbolic, pre-history.

The absence of the object is what links symbolization, the production of the signifier, the castration complex and the death drive. The emphasis on this entailed the death drive being given pride of place so that the significance of the superimposition of the life drive on the earlier formulation of the sexual drive was largely ignored, or used only illegitimately as a means of making sexuality unimportant.

Feminism that followed Lacan's emphasis on the significance of absence for the construction of the laws of the Symbolic order only elaborated the area dominated by reproduction and mothering by making it exist outside the Symbolic order (in what Lacan designated 'the Imaginary'). This pre-Symbolic place of maternity coincides with the area of infant–mother relations that is the preoccupation of Object Relations theory. Feminism that used Object Relations theory followed that theory's emphasis on the importance of the mother but was uninterested in any underlying laws. For Object Relations theory, both symbolism and sexual difference are developmental processes. So both tendencies consider the mother as important, but not within the framework of cultural laws. We have a great deal of rich work on mothering, but no place for the mother within the laws of the human order. Furthering the project of *Psychoanalysis and Feminism* through the observations of my clinical practice, my 'research' interest in hysteria and my continuing concentration on unconscious transmission of ideas and effects, led to my seeing what I would tentatively describe as 'the law of the mother'. This prohibits parthenogenic fantasy. As with the castration complex, it comes into operation not in the earliest period, but when the child is sexually active in its Oedipal fantasies, in its auto-erotism and its play with peers and siblings.

As with all psychoanalytic work, a problem in the present day symptoms or practices of the adult (or older child) leads to a hypothesis of what must have taken place in the past. We see in the perverse violence of an adult sexual abuser of a child, or (the area I have worked on more fully) the fantasies, symptoms and enactments of the hysterical parent, that there is an inability to recognize the 'otherness' and the boundaries of the abused child. This seems to me to result from a continuation of a general desire which exists in everyone's childhood of being able to produce a baby – but to produce one from oneself. For this reason I have called it the 'parthenogenic complex'. I suggest that the prohibition on this fantasy emanates from the place of the mother. It is as though the mother said to her child – boy or girl – 'No, you cannot be pregnant and give birth to babies, that is the position to which I have acceded.' If, however, the child accepts this prohibition and acknowledges the loss or absence of what they so badly want (if they mourn the death of a desire), then a girl can one day accede to the place of the mother, but a boy must accept that he is, and always will be, in the position of the one who cannot do so. (This is equivalent, in reverse, to the castration complex.) The abusive parent or the hysteric is someone who has not accepted the law of the mother – his or her child is psychologically a child's child, parthenogenically produced. The pillorying of single mothers in most societies is testimony to the strength of this childhood wish. The single mother is no more and no less likely to consider that her offspring were parthenogenetically conceived than is any parent in an apparently normal 'two up and two down' heterosexual marriage. In fact, the denigration of the single mother probably, in part, comes from society's wish to disown the parthenogenetic fantasy and project it on to a scapegoat.

If we bring together the two issues of reproduction and sibling relationship, we may have a preliminary sketch of the complexity and the changes within the construction of sexual differentiation that can have taken place. Rereading *Psychoanalysis and Feminism* twenty-five years after its publication makes me want to suggest that we need to go back to the drawing board. There is, I believe, still a place for using psychoanalytic theories in alliance with kinship studies to give us more access to some understanding of sexual difference.

In the Western world, where in the last two decades there has been a major increase in mothers working, siblings and peer groups have become crucial as they always are in developing countries. Our developed world, with its ever greater emphasis on the equality of women, the prevalence of practices such as prolonged statutory childhood and adolescence through schooling, the rise in single parenthood, may be becoming more like matrifocal/matrilineal societies (which perhaps should be redesignated 'sibling societies') in which there is the minimal difference as between a brother and sister, not the maximal distinction as between children and parents. Therefore, the 'difference' that marks 'gender' may be based not only on the differential effects of the castration complex but on the construction of a distinction between brother and sister.

Psychoanalysis and Feminism aimed to introduce the meeting point of psychoanalysis and kinship studies to feminism at the point of the differentiating moment of the castration complex. In this no child can make babies with the mother – but the prohibition is different for those who will take up a masculine from those who will take up a feminine position. Patriarchies are still very much in place. However, although feminism developed psychoanalysis in extraordinarily fertile and subtle ways, the thrust of the project initiated in this book got left behind and, with it, the possibility of seeing a more complex picture. The unconscious processes of the second metapsychology and sibling relationships must now be added to my initial portrait to pursue what seems to me is still an important project of how we live ourselves, affectively, cognitively, ideologically, unconsciously, as sexually differentiated beings.[8]

New Haven, Connecticut.
November, 1999

Notes

1. André Schiffrin, then running Pantheon Books, now the founder of the New Press, New York.
2. See D. Hay and J. Mitchell, 'Sex and Gender' in *A Textbook of Social Psychology* (Polity, forthcoming). For a psychoanalyst, 'gender' must be constructed through sexuality.
3. S. Freud, *Totem and Taboo*, 1913 (1912–13). S. E., Vol. XIII, pp. 157–8.
4. Ibid., p. 158.
5. J. Rose, 'Femininity and Its Discontents', *Feminist Review* 14, 1983, p. 8.
6. S. Freud, 'An Autobiographical Study', 1926, S. E., Vol. XX, Postcript 1935, p. 72.
7. L. Althusser, Letter concerning his article 'Freud and Lacan', 1969, *New Left Review* 55, p. 48.
8. My thinking in this introduction owes a great deal to the extremely perceptive and interesting critique of my work in Julia Swindells and Lisa Jardine, *What's Left?* (Routledge, 1990).

PART ONE

PSYCHOANALYSIS AND FEMININITY

Freud:
The Making of a Lady, I

1 Psychoanalysis and the Unconscious

No understanding of Freud's ideas on femininity and female sexuality is possible without some grasp of two fundamental theories: firstly, the nature of unconscious mental life and the particular laws that govern its behaviour, and secondly, the meaning of sexuality in human life. Only in the context of these two basic propositions do his suggestions on the psychological differences between men and women make sense. It is necessary to make sure of their meaning before any specific theses can be comprehended and assessed.

It is also, I would suggest, a characteristic of most attacks on Freud's work that, though the criticism *seems* to be over specific issues, what is really being rejected is this whole intellectual framework of psychoanalysis. Most hostile critics pay tribute to Freud's discovery of the nature of unconscious mental life and of infantile sexuality, and of the importance of sexuality in general. Most politically revolutionary writers would outbid Freud in their stress on the final indivisibility of normality and abnormality, forgetting that this was one of Freud's starting points. There is a formal obeisance to Freud's theories, yet behind most criticism of details there lies an unacknowledged refusal of every major concept. Time and time again, one dissident after another has repudiated singly or wholesale all the main scientific tenets of psychoanalysis.[1] For the same reason that these critics unconsciously deny the unconscious, it is difficult to offer an explanation of it: it *is*

1. Here I am only going to refer to points of psychoanalytic theory that seem to me to be persistently denied or misunderstood by those critics of Freud whose theses on the psychology of women concern me. Thus I am omitting many crucial concepts, an understanding of which would be essential for a less specific use of psychoanalysis.

unconscious. But, obviously, it would be worse than inadequate just to suggest that we take Freud's word for it, that we just *believe* in its existence. Although we *can* have a subjective knowledge of our own unconscious mental life, it is only in its random expressions that we can recognize it. Symptoms of the unconscious manifest themselves in latent dream-thoughts, slips of pen and memory, etc., and these are all we can ever know of it in this subjective sense. But Freud, in systematizing these manifestations, offers objective knowledge. We can see how it works and understand the need for it to exist to explain what is happening in the symptom. In one sense, Freud found the unconscious because nothing else would explain what he observed – and he certainly tried everything anyone could think of first. Once, after much doubt, he had postulated its existence, he set out to determine how it worked. This makes the process sound too sequential: an instance of how it worked, of course, would also help convince him of its existence. In other words, unlike the poets and story-tellers to whom he always gave credit for their recognition of the unconscious, Freud could not *believe* in the unconscious, he had to *know* it. To be convinced of his knowledge, we cannot believe it either, but if the laws by which he claimed it operated can be shown to have an internal consistency, then we can give up a faith for a science – imperfect as it may be.

The unconscious that Freud discovered is not a deep, mysterious place, whose presence, in mystical fashion, accounts for all the unknown; *it is knowable and it is normal.* What it contains is normal thought, utterly transformed by its own laws (which Freud called the primary process), but nevertheless only transformed and hence still recognizable if one can deduce the manner of the transformation, that is, decipher the laws of the primary process to which the thought is subjected. For instance, an unconscious wish originating in infancy becomes attached to the wish in the present time which has evoked it, but if it is unacceptable to consciousness, it is pushed down (repressed) into the unconscious where it is transformed and where it remains – until re-evoked, or until it breaks out (as a symptom), or until it is analysed. The point for our purpose here is that unconscious thoughts are repressed and thus transformed 'normal' ones, and that they are always there, speaking to us, in their way.

It is within the understanding of the unconscious that all Freud's observations are made – even those that seem not directly to impinge on it. Leaving aside again those questions that relate to his other great discovery, the role of sexuality, what he is therefore saying, for instance, about the nature of femininity, relates to how femininity is lived in the mind. If we take in advance an illustration from the heart of the feminist opposition to Freud, we can see how crucial is this framework of the concept of the unconscious. In a number of places, Freud refers to his statement that for the woman the baby is a substitute for the missed penis; I will give the version that tends to offend most:

> So far there has been no question of the Oedipus complex, nor has it up to this point played any part. But now the girl's libido slips into a new position along the line – there is no other way of putting it – of the equation 'penis–child'. She gives up her wish for a penis and puts in place of it a wish for a child: and *with that purpose in view* she takes her father as a love-object. Her mother becomes the object of her jealousy. The girl has turned into a little woman[2].

The process being discussed here can be re-described within the terms of the mental structures outlined above. Accepting for the moment the assertion that the girl wants a penis, the desire for one is incompatible with actual possibilities. It is therefore repressed into the unconscious, from whence probably on many occasions it emerges transformed. The only legitimate form (or the only form legitimated by culture) is that the idea (the representation of the wish) is displaced and replaced by the wish for a baby which is entirely compatible with reality. The

2. Freud, 'Some Psychical Consequences of the Anatomical Distinction Between the Sexes', 1925, S.E., Vol. XIX, p. 256. See also pp. 101–4 below for a further discussion of this. Throughout this book, quotations from Freud's work are from the *Standard Edition of the Complete Psychological Works of Sigmund Freud*, translated and under the general editorship of James Strachey in collaboration with Anna Freud, assisted by Alix Strachey and Alan Tyson, London, The Hogarth Press and the Institute of Psychoanalysis, 1964 edition. For all references to this edition I have used the abbreviation S.E.

two wishes are in fact one, and will continue to be active in different parts of the mental apparatus: the penis-wish will remain repressed in the unconscious, the baby-wish will be consciously expressed. When, as probably in later life, the woman actually comes to have a baby, the emotions she feels will also have attached to them the repressed unconscious penis-wish; the actual baby will therefore satisfy a very deep-seated, unconscious desire and if it is a baby boy the reality offered will give even greater satisfaction as it will coincide still more pertinently with the unrecognized wish. I know that for the moment we are leaving aside what is for the anti-Freudian feminists the massive stumbling-block of the original wish for the penis – but I think the main problem arises because the suggestion is taken outside the context of the mechanisms of unconscious mental life – the laws of the primary process (the laws that govern the workings of the unconscious) are replaced by these critics by those of the secondary process (conscious decisions and perceptions), and as a result the whole point is missed.

Most hostile critics of Freud implicitly deny the very notion of an aspect of mental life (expressed in its own 'language') that is different from conscious thought-processes. Other psychologies are about consciousness, psychoanalysis is dealing with the unconscious – this was a point on which Freud had to insist even before the first of the important breakaways that came within the psychoanalytic movement. Thus, in 1907, when they were still very much colleagues, we find Freud rebuking Alfred Adler for not realizing the distinction and for offering an analysis of mental life based only on conscious thought-processes. In the light of Adler's penchant for Marxism and future foundation of a school of sociological psychology, it is an interesting rebuke.

Freud's discovery of the unconscious was, of course, completely bound up with his attempts to understand neurotic disturbances, in the early days most particularly the symptoms of hysteria. When he first began to realize that the bodily symptoms of hysteria (paralysis, contortions and so on) were physical expressions of mental ideas, he started to listen more carefully to what the patients had to say.

Studying hysteria in the late eighties and nineties, Freud was stunned to hear women patients over and over again recount how, in their childhood, their fathers had seduced them. At first he gave an explanation in which the repressed memory of *actual* childhood incest was reawakened at puberty to produce the neurosis. He then realized that the whole thing was a phantasy.[3] And in essence this is the step that, pertinently here, neither Reich nor his feminist critics will take with him, nor allow him to take. Freud found that the incest and seduction that were being claimed never in fact took place. The fact that, as Freud himself was well aware, *actual* paternal seduction or rape occur not infrequently, has nothing to do with the essential concepts of psychoanalysis. Once Freud had acknowledged that he must abandon what he called the 'trauma theory' of actual incest, the notion of phantasy was bound to come in. Whatever the facts and figures of the situation, the desire was far more prevalent than the act. From the notion of unconscious phantasy, Freud's theories moved in one direction to the formulation of unconscious desire and, in another direction, to an understanding of infantile sexuality. Psychoanalysis deals with aspects of the drive: the repression of its psychic representation and its expression in demands, wishes, desires and phantasies – with the interaction of the unconscious, the preconscious and the conscious. Desire, phantasy, the unconscious or even unconsciousness are absent from the social realism of, amongst others, Reichian and feminist critiques. These criticisms are, therefore, in this respect not so much anti-Freudian as pre-Freudian.

In the symptoms of hysteria (and with variations, those of the other two neuroses – obsessionality and anxiety) what is

3. O. Mannoni (*Freud*, Pantheon, N.Y., 1971) points out how Freud preserved the trauma theory (as this hypothesis came to be called) for himself by dreaming that he as a father desired his own daughter, Mathilde (not vice versa which would have entailed the notion of infantile sexual desire and its 'return' in the symptoms of his hysterical patients). Writing of the dream to Fliess, Freud said, 'The dream of course fulfils my wish to pin down a father as the originator of neurosis and put an end to my persistent doubts.' Letter to Fliess, 31 May 1897, *The Origins of Psychoanalysis*, Imago, London, 1954, p. 206.

being expressed in another language is the repressed sexual idea which some crisis has re-evoked; a symptom is an alternative representation of a forbidden wish which has broken through from the unconscious, whence it was banished, into consciousness – but in an 'unrecognizable' form. Condensed into the symptom are all the energies of the sexual drive and those that were used originally to repress it: it is both the thoughts attached to the drive and its denial. It can be seen why Freud said that the neuroses were the negative of perversions: perversions are the acting out by the adult of one or other of the undirected, hence polymorphously perverse, sexual drives that the child manifests, neurotic symptoms are the failure of the effort *not* to thus act out such drives and desires. As Freud further pointed out, a man has more opportunity to engage in so-called sexual perversion – a woman, whose sexual activity is more restricted by society, must content herself with a neurotic symptom. As we shall see later, it was because the desires of the child want satisfaction in socially forbidden ways and have to be repressed when, at the time of the Oedipus complex, and the closely connected castration complex, he or she desires either or both parents (incest), that Freud claimed that this moment was 'the nucleus of the neurosis' – it is the resolutions and irresolutions of the Oedipus complex that are re-expressed in the neurotic symptom. (The formation of psychosis is somewhat different; this will be discussed in the chapter on R. D. Laing.) Because some people resolve the Oedipus complex – the entry into human culture – more thoroughly than others, there is an unequal chance of a later neurosis. (Freud did refer to the possibility of constitutionally determined unequal strength of the drives – but this, he stated firmly, was a question for biology, not psychoanalysis.)

There is, however, obviously, another tenet behind many hostile criticisms of Freud's work. It is claimed that Freud was prescribing a correct 'normal' pattern of behaviour. Yet time and again, during his life, Freud had to point out that so-called 'normality' is only relative and is itself 'neurotic', 'pathogenic', 'psychotic' and so on. Indeed, the very nub of his work was the elimination of an absolute difference between abnormality and normality.[4] Cases of neuroses gave him the clues to normal mental formations, dreams were everybody's everyday, or every night, psychoses: sexual perversions or inversions were both widespread and could constitute a choice. In 1905, Freud wrote in his 'shocking' case-study of a young hysterical girl, Dora: 'The less repellent of the so-called sexual perversions are very widely diffused among the whole population, as everyone knows except medical writers upon the subject',[5] and in 1935, to a mother so overwhelmingly distraught by her son's inversion that she could not bring herself even to mention it:

... Homosexuality is assuredly no advantage, but it is nothing to be ashamed of, no vice, no degradation; it cannot be classified as an illness; we consider it to be a variation of the sexual function ... Many highly respectable individuals of ancient and modern times have been homosexuals, several of the greatest men among them ... It is a great injustice to persecute homosexuality as a crime – and a cruelty too ...

By asking me if I can help you, you mean, I suppose, if I can abolish homosexuality and make normal heterosexuality take its place ...

What analysis can do for your son runs in a different line. If he is unhappy, neurotic, torn by conflicts, inhibited in his social life, analysis may bring him harmony, peace of mind, full efficiency, whether he remains homosexual or gets changed ...[6]

4. Normality should mean corresponding to whatever norm is being discussed. But normality is frequently equated with health. If we want a rough definition of the signs of a state of mental health: health is the uninhibited quest for knowledge, mental illness the painful pursuit of secondary ignorance – a need not to know, though the knowledge will insist on making its presence felt. Platonists believe that the soul's progress through the world is the search for knowledge; early on in his career Freud contended that an aspect of the psychoanalytic 'cure' was the release in the patient of the ability to work at intellectual and creative pursuits, and the regaining of the curiosity which had been repressed by the difficulties of the Oedipus complex. This regaining could not be innocent, it had to acknowledge and know all that had happened. Nor, of course, can health ever be absolute – for psychoanalysis likewise, it is a platonic ideal.

5. Freud, 'Fragment of an Analysis of a Case of Hysteria', 1905 (1901), S.E., Vol. VII, p. 51 (otherwise known as 'The Case of Dora').

6. 9 April 1935, *Letters of Sigmund Freud, 1873–1939*, ed. Ernest Freud, Hogarth Press, London, 1961, p. 419–20.

'Normality' is a useful marker on a continuum, no more . . . 'a normal ego . . . is, like normality in general, an ideal fiction . . . Every normal person, in fact, is only normal on the average. His ego approximates to that of the psychotic in some part or other and to a greater or lesser extent . . .'[7] The notion of normality is neither tenable for psychoanalytic theory, nor is its attainability a desideratum of analytic practice:

> Our aim will not be to rub off every peculiarity of human character for the sake of a schematic 'normality', nor yet to demand that the person who has been 'thoroughly analysed' shall feel no passions and develop no internal conflicts.[8]

It is not just Freud's liberal benevolence speaking through these statements: any other conception would have prevented his foundation of psychoanalysis. Only if we can see that the same mechanisms operate in psychotic, neurotic and normal states (in differing degrees and ways, of course), can we see that normal life, like the other two conditions, is a compromise with reality. Feminist criticisms of Freud claim that he was denying what really happens, and that the women he analysed were simply responding to really oppressive conditions. But there is no such thing as a simple response to reality. External reality has to be 'acquired'. To deny that there is anything other than external reality gets us back to the same proposition: it is a denial of the unconscious. Such a denial also affects the concept of the child. Without the notion of an unconscious mind, there are only three possibilities for a presentation of infancy. The child can be a miniature and perfectly rational adult, correctly appraising social reality. Or it can become the absent centre of a world of other people: it is seen only as others relate to it. Or, finally, the child can simply vanish from the story. In this

7. Freud, 'Analysis Terminable and Interminable', 1937, S.E., Vol. XXIII, p. 235, or: '. . . a healthy person, too, is virtually a neurotic . . . The distinction between nervous health and neurosis is thus reduced to a practical question and is decided by the outcome – by whether the subject is left with a sufficient amount of capacity for enjoyment and of efficiency.' *Introductory Lectures on Psychoanalysis,* Lecture XXVIII, 'Analytic Therapy', S.E., Vol. XVI, 1916–17 (1915–17), p. 457.
8. Freud, 'Analysis Terminable and Interminable', op. cit., p. 250.

last case we have an instance at the conceptual level of 'infantile amnesia' – the problem that, as Freud discovered, we forget our early childhood.

Freud, on the other hand, proposed that the new-born infant was dominated by what he eventually designated 'the pleasure-principle' – a process in which pleasure is striven for and unpleasure withdrawn from. The infant in the earliest infant–mother nexus lives almost entirely within the terms of the satisfaction or otherwise of its needs. If its wishes are un-satisfied it expresses unpleasure and then hallucinates the satisfaction it has been denied (as in later life, we fulfil our wishes in dreams). But repeated non-satisfaction leads to the abandonment of hallucination and the registration of what is *real* – in this case real deprivation. This is the introduction of the reality principle. But the reality principle by no means takes over entirely from the pleasure principle, nor is its introduction uniform and unbroken; it hardly seems to touch some aspects at all. For instance, the pleasure principle remains dominant as a means of translating reality, in phantasy, in children's play, in adult day-dreaming. Nor does the reality principle maintain a strong hold on the sexual drives which, because they can achieve their pleasure in auto-eroticism, are not at first very dependent on external reality. All people not only retain the pleasure principle but also, and this goes with it, are constantly engaged in unconscious processes, both in their untenable desires and in their frequent flights from and refusal of reality, their daily acts of repression. (Unconscious processes and the pleasure principle behave in much the same way.)

The strangest characteristic of unconscious (repressed) processes, to which no investigator can become accustomed without the exercise of great self-discipline, is due to their entire disregard of reality-testing; they equate reality of thought with external actuality, and wishes with their fulfilment – with the event – just as happens automatically under the dominance of the ancient pleasure principle. Hence also the difficulty of distinguishing unconscious phantasies from memories that have become unconscious. *But one must never allow oneself to be misled into applying the standards of reality to repressed psychical structures*, and on that account, perhaps, into undervaluing the importance of phantasies in the formation of symptoms on the ground that they are not actualities, or into tracing a neurotic sense of guilt back to some other source because there is no evidence that any actual crime has been committed. *One is bound to employ the currency that is in use in the country one is exploring* – in our case a neurotic currency [my italics].[9]

We shall see later how radical feminist critics have told Freud he is a fool for not applying the standards of reality to repressed psychical structures; by doing so, they have misunderstood his language. Freud found that an understanding of neurotic mechanisms gave him an understanding of normal mental processes (in other words, they were not different); because both the symptoms of neuroses (in particular in the early days, hysteria) and the normal-psychoses, in other words, dreams, were his 'royal' road to the unconscious (though he used the phrase only of dreams), it was their language they had to use – this was the currency of the land he was mapping.

The snag with Freud's presentation of his discoveries and, therefore, of any attempted simplification and re-presentation of them, is that a description *reverses* the analytic procedure. Freud was listening to the *recollected* history of his patients, he reconstructed infantile life from the fragmentary stories the patient told in which time past and time present are one. He read the history of the person *backwards* – as it is always essential to do; but in retelling it, he describes it as a march forwards, a process of development where it is in fact a multi-level effort of reconstruction. This distinction becomes very important when, as I believe, post-Freudian analysts of femininity continued to describe a process and forgot the historical nature of the events – their work is thus developmental, not analytical. This was a dilemma too, faced later by child analysis. Again, what can be forgotten is that at every moment of a person's existence he is living and telling in word, deed or symptom the story of his life: a three-year-old child has a past that he lives in his present, just as does the octogenarian. It is the crucial acquisition of the story of his life that that person is undergoing at the Oedipal moment, and that repeats itself in different ways throughout

9. Freud, 'Formulations on the Two Principles of Mental Functioning', 1911, S.E., Vol. XII, p. 225.

his time on earth – or rather within his days in human culture. Freud's discovery of infantile sexuality, and of sexuality as a key factor in mental life, is a perfect example of this difficulty: the person *does* develop and change sexually, but not with ruthless sequential logic and never so that the past is 'past'; even a person's account of his change is a coherent story of himself, it is the way men and women and children 'live' themselves in the world.

2 Sexuality

The way unconscious mental life operates provides the terminology, the fundamental system of thought within which Freud's specific theses have to be understood. Freud's other major discovery, his discovery of infantile sexuality, is of a different order; it does not provide the language and theoretical framework of psychoanalysis, it is not a new mental vocabulary that we have to learn here. But the general theory of infantile sexuality is also essential for an understanding of Freud's arguments about femininity.

Everyone knows that Freud 'discovered' what he admitted every nursemaid already knew: the sexuality of children. What is far less popular, even today, is the implication of this. By implication, naturally, I do not mean that we won't acknowledge that every little three-year-old is a sex maniac but, simply the implications not for the child but for the nature of sexuality as such. Despite Freud's work, the temptation is still to see sexuality as interpersonal sexual relationships, and sexual phantasies or auto-eroticism as perverse. Thus in some ways it has been far easier for homosexuality to be accepted than, say, fetishism. In other words, sexuality, to be 'decent', must have an object. This implicit predilection for object-directed sex necessitates a return to pre-Freudian methods of classification of types of sexuality. The achievement of Freud's contemporary sexologists, such as Havelock Ellis, was to categorize the different modes of sexuality, as though there was one essence which could be channelled off into other branches. This implied a number of things: a certain fixed, static quality to sexuality, an alternate either/or to the various modes available, normality versus abnormality, and adult sexuality alone. One essence then, which had the possibility of getting trapped into diverse tributaries, a pool of normal sexuality *from which* various more or less abnormal channels could run. The object-orientation of our present-day assumptions obviously does not imply quite the same theory, but nevertheless something very close to it. While formally acknowledging infantile sexuality, it, too, takes its stand from the position of conventional adult sex and involves the notion of a 'given', a complete sexuality which may, it is admitted, take different forms. In fact, the basic difference between popular contemporary ways of perceiving sexuality and Havelock Ellis's method of classification amounts to little more than the compulsory tolerance of the former.

Freud's theory of sexuality is completely different. Instead of accepting the notion of sexuality as a complete, so to speak ready-made thing in itself which could then diverge, he found that 'normal' sexuality itself assumed its form only as it travelled over a long and tortuous path, maybe eventually, and even then only precariously, establishing itself. (Incidentally, this surely constitutes a more radical undermining of the notion of normality than the vagaries of any *de rigueur* tolerance?) In other words, Freud put the stress entirely the other way round: instead of the pool which released itself in different ways, Freud asked from what sources was the pool formed. He realized that instead of a pool from which tributaries ran, the tributaries were needed in the first place to form the pool; these tributaries were diverse, could join each other, never reach their goal, find another goal, dry up, overflow and so get attached to something quite different. There is no nostalgic normality, nor (implicit in such a notion) any childhood bliss when all is as it should be. On the contrary, in childhood all is diverse or perverse; unification and 'normality' are the effort we must make on our entry into human society. Freud had no temptation to idealize the origins with which he was concerned.

[In childhood] The excitations from all these sources are not yet combined; but each follows its own separate aim, which is merely the attainment of a certain sort of pleasure. In childhood, therefore, the sexual instinct is not unified and is at first without a sexual object, that is, auto-erotic.[1]

1. Freud, *Three Essays on the Theory of Sexuality*, 1905, S.E., Vol. VII, p. 233.

Freud first officially formulated this notion that sexuality was composed of a number of 'component elements' in the *Three Essays on Sexuality* (1905). It is impossible to overstress the importance of the distance involved here between conceptions of sexuality as a monistic essence (Havelock Ellis et al.) and the Freudian notion of it as a complex unity. What, then, caused Freud to arrive at his theory? His shift away from the trauma theory of the occurrence of *actual* incest took a long time and was a painful, reluctant move (just as its inauguration had likewise been most hesitant). A combination of factors forced it on him – the unlikelihood of the prevalence of incest being the least important of these factors. The first hints were negative. General opinion maintained that childhood was innocent; furthermore no one remembered ever experiencing any sexual desire within infancy. Nor had any hysterical patient ever previously recollected any of the sexual traumas that Breuer's and Freud's 'cathartic' (or earlier hypnotic) methods of treatment somehow summoned forth. (Freud had good reason, not only because of his own and Breuer's integrity but also because of the efficacy of their treatment, to know that these sexual memories were not imposed by the analyst, and even if they were it would not have mattered because it would have only indicated a shared willingness on the part of the patient.)[2] Amnesia, then, was an important manifestation of hysteria; but amnesia about nearly all aspects of infancy was likewise an expression of normality. Tentatively, following what was to become a central tenet of his theory – the notion that neurotic behaviour was the clue to normal behaviour, or an exaggerated manifestation of the same mental process – Freud drew the obvious conclusion: amnesia in both instances was no accident, nor was the coincidence arbitrary. Furthermore, his 'patients', of whom he was soon to become one himself, also revealed the nature of their desires in the very utterances of their

2. As Freud says in a later footnote to the *Three Essays*: 'In this connection I cannot help recalling the credulous submissiveness shown by a hypnotized subject towards his hypnotist. This leads me to suspect that the essence of hypnosis lies in an unconscious fixation of the subject's libido to the figure of the hypnotist, through the medium of the masochistic components of the sexual instinct' (ibid., p. 150 (added 1910)).

accusations. 'Anna O' (Bertha Pappenheim), the very important patient whose case Breuer discussed at length with Freud, gave an early example of what was to become much later the central notion of transference: she passionately wanted to seduce her doctor as she claimed her father had seduced her. Whatever her father had actually wanted, she revealed in this reversal of roles her own original infantile desire. Later, when it was no longer necessary, Freud had his theories of childhood sexuality confirmed by direct observation. 'Little Hans', a five-year-old boy, had a phobia, as his father reported it to Freud, of an unmistakably sexual nature. Although the connection between the child's dread of horses and his sexual desires had to be analysed, the framework in which the fear was set was from the outset explicitly sexual, for the father recounted the many sexual conversations of the child. (Probably this was the first time, for a long time that is, that a child had been really listened to – previously such stories were all too often put down to the scurrility of lower-class nursemaids.)

If a study of neuroses thus led Freud inexorably to the notion of infantile sexuality, it no less inevitably led him to his theory of the nature of sexuality. A child's sexuality quite evidently could not be exactly the same as an adult's, and, furthermore, why had his neurotic patients had to suppress it – many of them were after all fulfilling the criteria of respectable married people? Indeed, why would anyone have to forget their childhood desires, if they were 'acceptable'?

... psycho-analytic teaching ... shows that it is by no means only at the cost of the so-called *normal* sexual instinct that these symptoms originate – at any rate such is not exclusively or mainly the case; they also give expression (by conversion) to instincts which would be described as *perverse* in the widest sense of the word if they could be expressed directly in phantasy and action without being diverted from consciousness. Thus symptoms are formed in part at the cost of *abnormal* sexuality; *neuroses are, so to say, the negative of perversions.*[3]

The symptoms of the neuroses revealed their content as being both infantile and sexual and the sexuality they exhibited was

3. ibid., p. 165.

perverse as well as normal. In other words, though in the present some particular sexual frustration might trigger off a neurotic symptom, it was not only this visible sexual misery that the neurosis expressed. If the 'forgotten' sexual desire was perverse, then infantile sexuality must itself be 'perverse'. The logic of this thought is presented by Freud in the arrangement of the *Three Essays* – a book written, obviously, after he was convinced of his findings. First he sets out all the types of sexual aberration both in well-known perversions and those revealed in the psycho-neuroses, then he deals with infantile sexuality (later he added the section on puberty); the point is that an analysis of the neuroses showed him the way to childhood sexuality and – by the structure of the book – he lets it do so for the reader. (The account in the *Three Essays* entirely omits the progress of the other side of Freud's initial discovery: the role played by ideas and desires, the notion of sexual phantasies. This realization resolved itself in this connection most fully in the concept of the Oedipus complex. But my account follows Freud's in this omission because it is of such all-importance as to necessitate separate treatment.)

It has often been claimed that Freud's understanding of what is sexual is so large as to be too vague and all-inclusive for the demands of scientific precision. In fact this all-inclusiveness is, on the contrary, a characteristic of analysts who came to disagree with him. For there is nothing general or vague in Freud's theses on sexuality. To replace a simple unity (the Havelock Ellis notion) by a complex unity is to define more *precisely*, not more loosely, its constituents. Those critics who say we might as well name what Freud calls sexuality or 'libido' simply general life-energy are inverting his investigations to produce a banality. What Freud did was the opposite – he said that 'life-energies' (if that is the term we must use) are sexual. A reversal of Freud's contention does not amount to the same thing – in fact it is an absurd restatement of the incomprehension Freud had to try and decipher. Freud showed how those acts which convention regarded as 'innocent', deeds apparently free from pleasure and the desire for pleasure, were in fact sensual acts. When, as he frequently does, Freud comments that he means sexual in the broadest sense of the term, what he is referring

to are *all* the components of the sexual drive and all the manifestations of the drive, perverse and normal, which are much
more numerous than anyone had previously been inclined to
believe. On the other hand, we must be careful not to go
overboard in the other direction, for having accepted the fact
that to say 'life-energies' are sexual is not the same as to say that
sexuality is just life-energy, is no excuse for trying instead to
say *everything*, everywhere, is sexual. Against this pan-sexual
reaction to his discoveries Freud fought no less hard than against
the denial of infantile sexuality. Freud's whole theory of mental
life is a theory of *conflict* – if everything were sexual where would
the conflict be?

Freud's theory of sexuality as a complex unity involved also
a redefinition of what sexuality 'itself' is. Prior to Freud it was
conceived of as one of the 'instincts', and therefore, as with
instincts in animals, it implied a pre-adaptation to reality. Freud
humanized it, seeing that because of its ideational mental character, as it manifested itself, it existed only within the context of
human culture. In the *Three Essays* he wrote that by an 'instinct'
'is provisionally to be understood the *psychical representative* of
an endosomatic, continuously flowing source of stimulation . . .
[my italics]'.[4] Later works stressed that the question was still
an obscure one and clearly one of the dilemmas was always the
balance and relationship of the endosomatic source and the
psychical representation, in other words, the tension between
the physical and the mental – a difficulty which Freud also
expressed more than once by saying that the concept of an
'instinct' was 'on the frontier between the somatic and the

4. ibid., p. 168. I have followed a habit that is to be found in
American, but not English literature on Freud, of translating '*Trieb*'
as 'drive', not 'instinct', except within the quotations, which are all
taken from the English Standard Edition of Freud's Works (see above,
p. 7, note). Since no one talks of 'drives' in animals, the use of this
translation seems to me therefore somewhat more felicitous, for what
Freud was trying to define was something human – I have, however,
retained the use of the term 'instinct' when discussing Reich's work in
this field. Reich himself used 'instinct' in his American writing and it
would in any case seem to me to sum up precisely where his concept
and Freud's differ. Reich's was no 'frontier' concept between psychology and biology but a biological one. Reich's man certainly
shared his instincts with the animals.

mental'. But what is really important is that for Freud the drives are *always psychic entities*. It is as these that we have to conceive them, and so far, because this exposition has stuck to the explanations of the *Three Essays*, it has failed to take this into account. Before we do so, however, we should look briefly at Freud's notion of sexual stages and erotogenic zones.

Within the precision of his explanation, even at the time of the *Three Essays*, Freud was also importantly imprecise. One of the later imprecisions was the duration of the pre-Oedipal phase of infancy. This was an important imprecision, coinciding with his increasing stress on moving from a chronological, 'time'-dependent notion of 'stages' of development to a theory of imbrication, parallels, simultaneity, and diachronology: a description that tries to break with the developmental implications of his earlier formulations. In his earlier notions, Freud often makes it sound as though a child grows like a plant: root, stalk, leaf, bud, flower, fruit – where there is overlap it is completely predictable. Life is a journey through the 'stations' of the cross (or railway track): orality, anality, 'phallicity', latency, genitality, procreativity, death. A preceding 'stage' might erupt into another – but it shouldn't. The task of life is to leave each behind, a discrete sedimented layer in the rock that is to become our life. In this system we methodically build our memorial to ourselves as we go. But in particular, Freud's later works (freed from the necessity of the first exposition), though never altogether losing the chronological presentation of these early theories, posit a fluidity, a multifariousness, a complex 'time' of space, not a simple 'time' of place, an awareness verbally expressed, that every moment is a historical one – a summation of a person's life.

For the moment we can present Freud's early formulations on the first few years of life quite schematically or emotively: projectively experiential – pretending artificially to relive the experience ourselves, ignoring relationships, re-creating the sensuality. The baby born into full sexuality passes through three roughly sequential stages where one after another erotogenic zone first dominates and then becomes dormant. (1) *The oral stage*. The baby sucking at the breast reveals more than the self-preservative instinct for nourishment. 'Sensual sucking', the taking and giving of the nipple, the rhythmic movements, the suffusion of the whole body (long after need is fulfilled) with total somatic satisfaction, the first self-sufficient, unrelated smile, reciprocity that leaves you content with yourself alone . . . together; sleep. Mother and child, cameo of love, the prototype of sexual intercourse as a later reunion. But the breast must be lost, the mother-breast leave the field of vision from time to time. What can compensate? (2) *The anal stage.* This has a self-sufficiency, a discreteness that is almost a 'so there' to the absent mother. 'I can do it alone – I don't need you.' (Indeed the persistence of this 'stage' in the anal obsessional adult is precisely this: a refusal to let things touch, meet, be joined.) If the lump of breast is not there, in that sensitive hole, the mouth, then there are faeces which can be as warm as milk or made solid and forced to move likewise in rhythmic contractions in another sensitive hole: the anus. Like the nipple they can be retained or released with the same omni-erotic glow of satisfaction as a result. The baby, filled with milk or emptied of faeces, experiences an analogous contentment: the relaxation after the tension of the to-fro movements of bowel and mouth. But the mother who withdrew the breast now demands her own control of the baby's defaecation. From now on the baby gains only the highly *non*-somatic joy of pleasing another: feeding and excreting to *her* time and pleasure. What now can it discover for itself from itself when even the bodily convulsions of screams (the stomach pulsating like mouth and bowels), the milk-faeces-tears are not approved of? (3) *The phallic stage.* A lump that like the faeces can be hard or soft; stimulated, like the nipple it can rise and fall: penis and clitoris. But where to put it? Before, the 'lump' was the undifferentiated mother's, the sensitive hole the baby's, or the faeces insensitive and the anus alive. Now it is the other way round. The 'androgyneity' of the body that provided both receptacle and vehicle is lost, the boy cups his hand and the girl presses and rubs together the lips of her genitals: new hollows for new solids, back-forth contractions, tension, release. But when even this ingenious, inventive masturbation is condemned by adults, what is there left? No wonder the child gives up. (4) *Latency.* An 'innocent' child. A boy. A girl.

The initiation of each stage has two characteristics: the deprivation of the self and a new awareness of the other. The self and the other. But also the self *as* the other. That earliest of questions 'where do babies come from?' is 'Where do I come from?' 'Who am I?' (The baby, having no 'I' to formulate the question in either of the last two ways – if it had it wouldn't need to ask, it would already be too late, tautologous – proposes it in terms of an object, a third, 'babies': as it will refer to itself by name rather than by the personal pronoun 'I'.) Each answer parallels the sexual stages (the fact that they may not coincide does not in any way alter this). They are 'answers' to the sexual drive which is lived verbally as an ontological question. The baby wants to know where he is to fit in, in this ever growing nexus of *different* people. The answers that he finds for himself tell him nothing; they maybe reassure him that though he is depriving himself of his bodily satisfactions in order to become one among others, he will get his reward and his own back when the time comes for him to allow himself to dream of realized satisfaction, when he has given up enough to become adult, then he can have all that he has lost back again – or so he will think, in order for the time to come. The answers to 'Where do babies come from?' suggest too that the question also means 'Mummy, Daddy, how do you get your pleasure? When can I have mine again?'

Freud's theories of a baby's theories of birth and sexuality tell us as much and no more than his description of the three sensual stages:

1. *The Omnipresent Penis*   Both sexes are thought by both boys and girls to have a penis. They do not apparently conceive of a vagina, though the assertive urge to thrust and penetrate into *something* is there. But the need for a receptacle only makes the child produce the second theory: a baby is a lump of excrement. Both men and women can give birth. The baby-faeces

2. *The Cloacal Theory*   comes out of the body and is given

3. *The Sadistic Theory*

up, to another. Husband and wife *give* each other a child. However, the recollected possible sight or imagined sight of sexual intercourse and basic aggressive urges also suggest the baby's third theory: sexuality is a battle, the stronger male wounding the weaker female.

In the first infantile theory the world is the baby, in the second the baby makes the world, in the third the baby is excluded from the world. But, in fact, all these notions are about the baby's relationship to itself. Presented like this, these theories can tell us only two things. First they confirm Freud's description that in this pre-Oedipal phase, sexual ambivalence or 'bisexuality' persists. Children want everything. Five-year-old Hans will not relinquish procreativity to women.

FATHER: But only women have children.
HANS: I'm going to have a little girl...
FATHER: You'd like to have a little girl?
HANS: *Yes, next year I'm going to have one ...*
FATHER: But why isn't Mummy to have a little girl?
HANS: Because *I* want to have a little girl for once ...
FATHER: Only women, only Mummies have children.
HANS: But why shouldn't I?
FATHER: Because God's arranged it like that.
HANS: But why don't *you* have one? Oh yes, you'll have one all right. Just you wait.
FATHER: I shall have to wait some time.[5]

No pleasure, though abandoned and the desire for it repressed, is ever completely given up. Just as the girl will wait for her clitoris to grow into penile activity, so the boy will wait till he can have a baby. But the theories have an interest beyond the flexibility of their gender. In each case the theory is transformed *because something is missing*: the self-sufficiency of the first egocentric experience. The child who first finds all he

5. Freud: 'Analysis of a Phobia in a Five-Year-Old Boy', 1909, S.E., Vol. X, pp. 86–7. (Father, who reports the conversation, is 'I' in the text; I have substituted 'Father' for clarity.)

requires in his own body and its extension in his mother's breast gradually has to come to terms with the notion of alternatives: if you have one, you cannot have the other, above all you cannot have everything. So, comparably, the transition from one sexual 'stage' to another is achieved and necessitated through deprivation: loss of breast, loss of faeces, loss of penis; fears of castration. However, it is obvious that the nature of these losses is by no means identical.

But by this point, as at every point, we are at the Oedipus complex, without which none of this or anything really makes sense. Let us first make one thing clear, which takes us back to our objections to the majority of Freud's hostile critics. All these 'stages' are important only within the context of the child's efforts to find itself, that is to say, to find where it fits into the scheme of things – it is, so to speak, looking for itself. The child has to discover his place first via his relation with objects, then as himself an object for other people. In doing this, the child does not pass through stages, he tries them on, they are part of his history, even as he enacts them:

> To put it briefly, the instinctual stages, when they are being lived, are already organized in subjectivity. And to put it clearly, the subjectivity of the child who registers as defeats and victories the heroic chronicle of the training of his sphincters, taking pleasure throughout it in the Imaginary sexualization of his cloacal orifices, turning his excremental expulsions into aggressions, his retentions into seductions, and his movements of release into symbols – this subjectivity *is not fundamentally different* from the subjectivity of the psychoanalyst who in order to understand them, tries his skill at reconstituting the forms of love which he calls pregenital.

In other words, the anal stage is no less purely historical when it is lived than when it is reconstituted in thought, nor is it less purely founded in intersubjectivity. On the other hand, seeing it as a momentary halt in what is claimed to be a maturing of the instincts leads even the best minds straight off the track . . .[6]

A point that is being made here, amongst others, is that the notion of a maturing of instincts, and the popular way of reading

6. Jacques Lacan, *The Language of the Self, The Function of Language in Psychoanalysis*, trans. Anthony Wilden, Johns Hopkins Press, Baltimore, 1968, p. 24.

the 'stages' of drives, is false and evolutionary. What Freud intended was the opposite: once again, you can only read a person, as you can only read history, backwards, you start from last things first. And as I said earlier, even as they happened, they were part of the *history* into which the child was born. The above writer, Jacques Lacan, suggests that the inadequacy of Freud's 'theory of instincts' is precisely an indication of Freud's contempt for its significance. Leaving aside Lacan's theoretical reasons for this assertion, even the repetitious nature of Freud's definitions and evident lack of concentration on the problem would make this seem most likely. Lacan contends:

> In any event one has only to go back to the works of Freud to gauge to what secondary and hypothetical place he relegates the theory of instincts. The theory cannot in his eyes stand for a single instant against the least important particular fact of a history, he insists, and the *genital narcissism* which he invokes when he sums up the case of the Wolf Man shows us well enough the disdain in which he holds the constituted order of the libidinal stages. Going even further, he evokes the instinctual conflict in his summing-up only to steer away from it immediately . . .[7]

Freud's achievement was to transform the biological theory of instincts into the notion of the human drive, then to trace its possible expressions and to relegate them to their place within the person's history of subjectivity. Above all, Freud's case-histories show that there is little justification for treating the 'stages' either as absolutes or as even separate and sequential; and a theoretical essay, 'Instincts and Their Vicissitudes' opens with the statement that the 'instinct' is a borrowed concept on which psychoanalysis, for the time being, has to lean, but which can be regarded as no more than a convention. Freud reminds us that the greater advance of knowledge will not 'tolerate any rigidity even in definitions'.

In discussing Freud's concept of infantile sexuality, it has been necessary briefly to introduce his theory of drives, but in doing this many crucial features have been omitted, most importantly the distinction he draws between the aim of a drive and its object. Every drive is active (it is from this that many critics, in particular those with a feminist orientation,

7. ibid., p. 26.

derive their mistaken notion that Freud thinks the sexual drive or libido is the prerogative of the male – certainly he calls it 'masculine' but this is precisely because of his attempt to define masculinity as activity – a feature both sexes can and do share, as we shall see). For the activity of the drive Freud posited an energy theory to which Reich returned. Psychoanalysis is not in the least concerned with the physiological process that probably provides the source of the drive – it was this preoccupation which was left to Reich, and we shall see whither it led him; psychoanalysis is concerned with the mental representations and hence the drives can only be known by their aims. The drive's aim, however, can be passive or active; that is to say it can express itself as the desire to be in a passive or active relationship to another, for the aim is always and only the satisfaction of the desire.

The question of the object displays another essential feature of the sexual drive – its flexibility. Freud defines the object thus:

> The object of an instinct is the thing in regard to which or through which the instinct is able to achieve its aim. It is what is most variable about an instinct and is not originally connected with it, but becomes assigned to it only in consequence of being peculiarly fitted to make satisfaction possible. The object is not necessarily something extraneous: it may equally well be a part of the subject's own body. It may be changed any number of times in the course of the vicissitudes which the instinct undergoes during its existence; and highly important parts are played by this displacement of instinct.[8]

It is simpler to leave it at that for the moment. It should be re-emphasized that the drive has no *natural* object and hence that what is regarded as normal sexuality (which is always only relative) has to develop from the many component drives that compose this complex unity, which is human sexuality. Each component, either alone or together, can become fixated at a certain point, or each can be regressed to – the result of either occurrence is perversion or neurosis, in any case none is ever entirely given up. So that even in normal sexuality there will be a residue of perverse impulses which can also find expression in various ways, as 'minor perversions' within the normal

8. Freud, *Papers on Metapsychology*, 'Instincts and Their Vicissitudes', 1915, S.E., Vol. XIV, pp. 122–3.

sexuality, or if repressed and inadequately so, as neurotic symptoms, or, reacted against as disgust, shame, morality, its energies can be redirected into 'higher' spheres. The degree to which the latter takes place (and in our culture it always does to a vastly varying extent), is the basis for the all-important act of sublimation which in its turn contributes to character formation, virtue, artistic achievement and so on. But that is another subject.

3 Narcissism

It is often thought that psychoanalytic theory proposes that the human being is impelled and determined only by sexual drives which originate in an untamed infancy. But, on the contrary, Freud's discussion of infantile sexual stages was only one dimension of his work. The new-born baby has also to direct its energy to discovering itself; where auto-eroticism is a physical expression of this preoccupation, 'narcissism' is the term given to the all-important wider psychological implications of this moment.

Most people tend to forget the place of Echo in the mythological life of Narcissus.[1] What we remember is the lovely boy, looking in the pond and falling for his own image. For Narcissus there was no way out of this circular fate – he couldn't possess himself, and so, driven by his frustration to the point of despair, he finally died. After death he was transformed into a flower. But Echo, who was the voice of Juno's punishment, loved him. Juno had condemned Echo, who was too loquacious, never to speak in her own right, but only as the response of another. In such a predicament, clearly the worst thing possible happened to her – she fell in love with the original narcissist, who was so absorbed in himself that he couldn't speak to her. In her frustration she, too, pined away in body and died, though her punishment is still heard to speak in endless echo.

Echo is not directly mentioned by Freud either, but the implications of the whole story are certainly present in his adaptation of the term 'narcissism'. He first referred to the concept in a footnote added to the 1910 edition of the *Three Essays*. The mention is part of a brief explanation of some of the

1. I am indebted to a friend, Vickie Hamilton, for the reminder of the role of Echo in the Greek legend of Narcissus and the suggestion of Echo's place in the psychoanalytic myth of narcissism.

mental processes involved in homosexuality, a subject to which this new concept was later to contribute a great deal. There is a pleasing pertinence in this first use by Freud, for, I would suggest, it is this concept (if one can isolate it for a moment from the elements into which it was fused) that did most to transform the implications of the *Three Essays*. It is not that it corrected these, but rather that it decisively located the drives, and the 'stages' in the context of the person's history of subjectivity. Octave Mannoni calls the *Three Essays* 'the book of the drive', and *The Interpretation of Dreams* 'the book of the desire'; the concept of narcissism seems to me to have submitted the former, irrevocably, to the latter. It is from this point onwards that Freud really demonstrates how unimportant the notion of a 'pure instinct' is to man, how far psychoanalysis has separated itself from biology and – what is to some extent the same question – how far man has come from the animals and what has been done to his animal nature.[2] He explicitly announces the total inadequacy of any biological theories of instinct. It is this submission of the drive to desire, and the subsequent sexualization of even the knowledge of the self, that makes the 1914 essay *'On Narcissism'* such a landmark. Ernest Jones and, following him, the philosopher-critic Richard Wollheim, present it as a crisis in Freud's theory of the instincts; their argument maintains that Freud, fascinated by dualism, had hitherto opposed the sexual instincts to the ego- or self-preservative instincts (hunger, etc.); now he found that even the latter could be sexualized, so for some years afterwards he had to look around for another polar element to enable him to reassert his dualism, and finally

2. It is interesting that in this essay 'On Narcissism' (1914) Freud writes as though announcing the possibility of this future development of his work: 'I try in general to keep psychology clear from everything that is different in nature from it, even biological lines of thought. For that very reason I should like at this point expressly to admit that the hypothesis of separate ego-instincts and sexual instincts ... rests scarcely at all upon a psychological basis, but derives its principal support from biology. But I shall be consistent enough [with my general rule] to drop this hypothesis if psycho-analytic work should itself produce some other, more serviceable hypothesis about the instincts. So far, this has not happened.' Freud, 'On Narcissism: An Introduction', 1914, S.E., Vol. XIV, pp. 78–9.

(helped no doubt by the holocaust of the First World War) he thought up the death-drive. There is no doubt that Freud's formulation of the death-drive owes a great deal to his earlier concept of narcissism – but this supposed despair about dualism is not the primary feature of the relationship between the two, nor is it the main significance of the 1914 essay, 'On Narcissism'.

Freud was first led to his thoughts on narcissism by his preoccupation not with the neuroses but with the psychoses, in particular with what he called the paraphrenias – paranoia and what has since inaccurately come to be labelled schizophrenia.[3] Freud establishes what is from his standpoint a crucial difference between psychoses and neuroses (a subject that is to be of central importance in our discussion of Laing's work, see pp. 358 ff.).

A patient suffering from hysteria or obsessional neurosis has also, as far as his illness extends, given up his relation to reality. But analysis shows that he has by no means broken off his erotic relations to people and things. He still retains them in phantasy . . . It is otherwise with the paraphrenic. He seems really to have withdrawn his libido from people and things in the external world, without replacing them by others in phantasy. When he *does* so replace them, the process seems to be a secondary one and to be part of an attempt at recovery, designed to lead the libido back to objects.[4]

In psychoses such as paraphrenia, then, the libido is drawn away from objects back into the self. This, Freud proposed, coincided with an obviously observable phase of childhood – infantile megalomania – when the child believes it only has to wish for something for it to materialize, its own 'magic' controls the world.

3. 'The designation chosen by Bleuler for the same group of forms – "schizophrenia" – is also open to the objection that the name appears appropriate only so long as we forget its literal meaning. For otherwise it prejudices the issue, since it is based on a characteristic of the disease which is theoretically postulated – a characteristic, moreover, which does not belong exclusively to that disease, and which, in the light of other considerations, cannot be regarded as the essential one. However, it is not on the whole of very great importance what names we give to clinical pictures.' Freud, 'Psycho-Analytic Notes on an Autobiographical Account of a Case of Paranoia (Dementia Paranoides)', 1911, S.E., Vol. XII, pp. 75–6 (otherwise known as the 'Schreber Case').

4. Freud, 'On Narcissism', op. cit., p. 74.

Thus we form the idea of there being an original libidinal cathexis of the ego, from which some is later given off to objects, but which fundamentally persists and is related to the object-cathexes much as the body of an amoeba is related to the pseudopodia which it puts out.[5]

In other words, at first, the self loves the self (or the ego), only later does it 'put out' some of this self-love on to other objects. It is this primary narcissism that re-expresses itself in psychosis, and it was this that was hidden from psychoanalytic investigation whilst it concentrated on the neurosis whose problematic attachment (but attachment none the less) to objects other than itself obscured this situation.

In the absence of adequate case-study material on psychosis (psychotic conditions being so much more serious, they end up not in the analyst's consulting-room but in psychiatric hospitals), Freud had to approach his theory by a series of 'obvious' observations. I have already mentioned his remarks on children's megalomania; now he goes on to notice the withdrawal of libido from the world to the self in cases of physical illness and, more complexly, in hypochondria, and then, most interestingly from our point of view, in cases of love between men and women or inter-sexual love. Freud proposed that in instances of hypochondria and paranoia-schizophrenia, the return of the libido on to the self involves also a stifling or 'damming-up' of it there, as in neurosis a damming-up (and consequent failure of expression) occurs with its object-directed libido. This imprisonment of libido is bound to be experienced as unpleasurable, and this unpleasure is therefore likely to be, at least in part, responsible for the necessity to turn outwards from this self-absorbed state into that of love of others; so narcissism, which is a crucial stage of building the ego, has to be moved on from if the person is not to end up in the vicious circle in which Narcissus found himself:

A strong egoism is a protection against falling ill, but in the last resort we must begin to love in order not to fall ill, and we are bound to fall ill if, in consequence of frustration, we are unable to love.[6]

So love can be of two types: that which fits the narcissistic

5. ibid., p. 75. 6. ibid., p. 85.

type, or that which displays the fact that the sexual drives
become attached to the ego instincts and have chosen another as
their object. Freud further broke down these two positions so
that the latter had two possibilities for original love-objects.
The other object could be: (a) the woman who feeds the baby;
(b) the man who protects him. The first, the narcissistic type of
love, had four possibilities of love available to it: (a) the person
he himself is; (b) what he, himself, once was; (c) what he,
himself, would like to be; (d) someone who was once part of
himself. Many aspects of these last possibilities occur in the
normal course of events and Freud cites as an instance of the
satisfaction of both (b) and (d) the love of parents for their
children:

> The child shall have a better time than his parents; he shall not be
> subject to the necessities which they have recognized as paramount
> in life. Illness, death, renunciation of enjoyment, restrictions on his
> own will, shall not touch him; the laws of nature and of society shall
> be abrogated in his favour; he shall once more really be the centre
> and core of creation – 'His Majesty the Baby', as we once fancied
> ourselves. The child shall fulfil those wishful dreams of the parents
> which they never carried out ... Parental love, which is so moving
> and at bottom so childish, is nothing but the parents' narcissism
> born again, which, transformed into object-love, unmistakably
> reveals its former nature.[7]

Narcissism can be normal in heterosexual love relationships. In
particular it is seen in the woman's wish to be loved; it is likewise
found in the 'deviant' developments of perversions and homosexuality. In the case of inversion, Freud's earlier case-studies
had already suggested that the homosexual was choosing not
another of the same sex, but himself in the guise of another.

The normal occurrence, then, is for the narcissistic libido to
be damped down and transferred to objects; but some of it
clearly remains. To this remainder Freud devoted his attention
in the proposition of the third possibility with which narcissistic
desires are confronted: the love of the self as one would like
it to be. It is a fundamental psychoanalytical thesis that a
person will never wholly give up what he has once enjoyed.
Among other things he is obviously unwilling to abandon his

7. ibid., p. 91.

infantile notion of his own perfection. So rather than renounce it altogether – in response to the demands of the real situation – he transforms his self-attachment into an attachment to what he would like to be – an ideal self or an ego-ideal: 'What he projects before him as his ideal is the substitute for the lost narcissism of his childhood in which he was his own ideal.'[8] Unlike sublimation which consists of a redirection of libidinal drives (*not*, as is often popularly thought, a repression of them) into what are officially non-sexual pursuits (involving therefore a change of aim), idealization does not in itself involve this diversion from sexuality; it engages, rather, in an overestimation of the object (such as happens in romantic love) or in increased demands on the ego to be as perfect as the subject would like to be. From this point of departure, Freud presented the possibility of what he called a special agency, which he was, a few years later, to name the super-ego; here is the idea at its genesis:

It would not surprise us if we were to find a special psychical agency which performs the task of seeing that narcissistic satisfaction from the ego ideal is ensured and which, with this end in view, constantly watches the actual ego ... Recognition of this agency enables us to understand the so-called 'delusions of being noticed' or more correctly, of being *watched*, which are such striking symptoms in the paranoid diseases ... Patients of this sort complain that all their thoughts are known and their actions watched and supervised; they are informed of the functioning of this agency by voices which characteristically speak to them in the third person ... This complaint is justified; it describes the truth. A power of this kind, watching, discovering and criticizing all our intentions, does really exist. Indeed, it exists in every one of us in normal life.[9]

Large amounts of necessarily homosexual libido are drawn to the ego-ideal which will be formed by various identifications, first with the image of the self, then with parents, and later with teachers, fellow-men and public opinion in general, and which is to be incorporated in the super-ego, the agency split off from the original ego for this purpose. In his ego-ideal the person fits in with the social system. He cannot conform to this *ex nihilo*, but only in obedience to the ideals of 'a family, a class or a

8. ibid., p. 94. 9. ibid., p. 95.

nation'. But ideals periodically fail and the predicament of Narcissus takes over.

The next year, writing on the problems of mourning and its relation to melancholia, Freud extended the implications of narcissism to explain aspects of these normal and psychotic conditions.[10] In normal mourning, a necessary withdrawal of libido from the loved object (who is lost) takes place. In cases where the lost person cannot be given up and grief is excessive, this failed mourning can become psychotic: the person cannot withdraw his libido and thus hallucinates compensatory objects. But this latter development is not typical; in typical cases both who and what has been lost are quite consciously apprehended by the bereaved person. In melancholia, as distinct from mourning, this conscious factor is missing; the melancholic person cannot know consciously what he has lost – for it is an aspect of himself. At least, that is what he presents it as, and so in a sense it is, but not the sense to which he lays claim. The melancholic accuses himself of the utmost unworthiness, he has apparently the greatest sense of failure in enacting his ego-ideal, he displays himself as a person beneath contempt, but one whom you must nevertheless take good notice of. It turns out that there is little real humility in this noisy self-abasement. Freud found that listening to the self-accusations of people in a state of melancholy revealed that they were in fact making attacks on others:

The woman who loudly pities her husband for being tied to such an incapable wife as herself is really accusing her *husband* of being

10. In this whole area of thought Freud was very indebted to the work of his colleague, Karl Abraham. Already in a letter to Abraham in 1910, Freud expresses his belief that he has 'solved' the difference between paranoia and schizophrenia (still then referred to as dementia praecox), and furthermore that he is moving towards the notion that megalomania is a sexual over-estimation of the ego (clearly a foreshadowing of the concept of narcissism) but he adds that he realizes that Abraham has already expounded that theory and that he, Freud, is merely a plagiarist. As Abraham's enthusiastic reception of Freud's draft of the Narcissism essay four years later makes clear, Freud had added a lot of original ideas. However, Abraham's work in this field was crucial; it was also the spring-board for Melanie Klein's later theories on the nature of this entire pre-Oedipal moment. Klein contended that 'melancholy' was, in the words of Burton, its seventeenth-century anatomist, 'an inbred malady in every one of us'.

incapable, in whatever sense she may mean this. There is no need to be greatly surprised that a few genuine self-reproaches are scattered among those that have been transposed back. These are allowed to obtrude themselves, since they help to mask the others and make recognition of the true state of affairs impossible . . . The behaviour of the patients, too, now becomes much more intelligible. Their complaints are really 'plaints' in the old sense of the word. They are not ashamed and do not hide themselves, since everything derogatory that they say about themselves is at bottom said about someone else.[11]

What has happened is that when, for some reason or other, the love for someone has ended, the libido that is withdrawn does not pass to another object, but reattaches itself to the ego – in a very specific way. This is not a straightforward replenishment of narcissism as in physical illness, but instead the released libido is employed in such a way that it causes the ego to identify with the abandoned object: 'Thus the shadow of the object fell upon the ego, and the latter could henceforth be judged by a special agency, as though it were an object, the forsaken object.'[12] The ego becomes the object of its own love, but through transferred, or secondary, not primary, narcissism. In the case of the complaining woman self-love is then disguised by self-hate so that the reproaches can safely be made.

Is it significant that Freud's illustrations are from marital situations, where there may be a literal impossibility either of finding another object or of openly withdrawing on to oneself – in other words, where the prescribed situation makes it highly likely that the woman will identify with the husband whose love she no longer has or for whom she feels no love? It is clearly significant, but important only in the sense that this marital predicament confirms a certain likelihood to which the woman's psychological history has prejudged her; for at the centre of this melancholic experience is the fact that there must have been in the first place a rigid fixation on the loved object. However, at the same time, though it was a fixation, its force was weak because it was based on a narcissistic love, rather than an

11. Freud, 'Mourning and Melancholia', 1917 (1915), S.E., Vol. XIV, p. 248.

12. ibid., p. 249.

object-attachment, hence from the outset it was liable to undergo this process of identification: the subject loving itself in the form of another person. Of course, all the ambivalence of the original love comes into force, so that in apparently condemning himself, the melancholic can exercise all the revenge he wishes. and thus express his sadism. Turned round on himself, however, vengeance takes the form of a tendency to suicide. The lost object thus, both in love and in death, has completely mastered the ego. Melancholia frequently alternates with euphoric mania, and Freud was dissatisfied with his explanations of this. One thing, however, was clear: again the decisive factor was the regression of libido from the lost object to the ego. When melancholy has exhausted its work, the libido, hitherto attached, even if by self-denunciations, to the self, is free for manic delights – a sudden release of narcissistic energy, as Keats (a narcissistic poet, if ever there was one) thought, although he put the states of melancholy and mania in the opposite order:

> She dwells with Beauty – Beauty that must die;
>   And Joy, whose hand is ever at his lips
> Bidding adieu; and aching Pleasure nigh,
>   Turning to poison while the bee-mouth sips:
> Ay, in the very temple of Delight
>   Veil'd Melancholy has her sovran shrine,
>   Though seen of none save him whose strenuous tongue
>   Can burst Joy's grape against his palate fine;
> His soul shall taste the sadness of her might,
>   And be among her cloudy trophies hung.[13]

Narcissus, who loved only himself, was unreachable by any other voice – no one could call him forth from his solipsistic reverie; Echo was the all too appropriate witness to his fate, as he was to hers. Narcissus never believed that what he saw in the pond's mirror was himself, and because there was no one there to tell him where he got off, he died in love with himself as

---

13. Keats, *Ode on Melancholy* – Keats's poetry is veritably obsessed with his refusal to accept the lost object. Perhaps it is none too soon to point out that describing Keats as a narcissistic poet is no adverse criticism.

though he were another person. Narcissus was for ever grasping his shadow which was the object of his own desire, but what eluded him was himself: the mirror did not give him himself, because the only one in the world he had to tell him where he was, was Echo, the absolute *other*, to whom none could get attached because she would not listen and who did no more than repeat the words of Narcissus' own self-fascination. But no one could have done any more; for Narcissus is confined in intra-subjectivity.

Narcissus, or the baby, has to find out where he stands and hence who he is in the eyes of other people. While the megalomaniac moment of the neonate when the baby and the world are apparently indistinguishable goes on, another search is also being undertaken – the baby is looking for itself in others. D. W. Winnicott[14] sees this as the baby's search for itself in the responses of the mother's expression, the mobility of the facial moods in which she reflects for the baby his own behaviour; or it could be seen as this but also as the baby's more general fascination with human faces or human beings who are harmonious wholes at a time when the baby is unable to control its own movements. It is a question of finding the self-image in the image of another, and of constituting the self in that discovered image. This first rooting of the self is remote from any notions we might have of 'reality' – it is, and it must be, an imaginary construct. The helpless human baby, fascinated by the complete human faces and forms that he encounters, imagines his own future, and thus enters into a primary identification with the human form. Freud (and interpreting him, Lacan, whose reformulations of this phase are so important) thought that this characteristic of the human baby was due to its premature birth – organically in evidence – and its consequent long period of helpless dependence. The infant's response to the human forms around it is not a sign as yet of an inter-subjective relation-

14. D.W. Winnicott in 'The Mother as Mirror', in *The Predicament of the Family*, ed. P. Lomas, London, 1968. Here Winnicott states that this theory is a transposed derivation of Jacques Lacan's concept of 'the Mirror-phase'. My subsequent account of Freud's notion of narcissism is conducted within a schema deduced from this central Lacanian theory.

ship, in fact it is comparable to the child's response to its own image in the mirror where the child really grasps itself for the first time as a perfect whole, not a mess of uncoordinated movements and feelings. Narcissus became stuck in his desire for this supra-real object (his reflection) and he could not accept that it was imaginary – consequently he sank into fits of alternate melancholia and mania till he died, a virtual act of suicide, to become symbolized, even in apparent 'death', by the circularity he had never escaped – a flower which grows from itself, for the narcissus needs no cross-fertilization, it grows and fades with the repetitiousness of the seasons; no more than its mythical originator does it know the intervention of another either as a person or in death.

It is this original identification of the ego in the inverted and perfect whole of the other that is the basis for all later identifications – for example, those of inter-subjectivity, such as the child's later identifications with its parents. But this first identification with the image clearly suggests that it is not only the mirror that is a reflection, but also the very 'identity' the child forms. This identity is an imaginary construct based not on a true recognition, but a mis-recognition; the self is always like another, in other words, this self is constructed of necessity in a state of alienation: the person first sees himself in another, mother or mirror.

Freud's essay on narcissism hence claimed: 'a unity comparable to the ego cannot exist in the individual from the start; the ego has to be developed'. This developed ego is that which is created in the mirror image. But Freud here, and in 'Mourning and Melancholia', also indicated the way out of the impasse of an adult ultra-subjectivity, a way which still bears the marks of its narcissistic origin, though it has managed, for the time being, to escape the fate of Narcissus. The way out is the ego-ideal, later the superego.

However, the narcissistic construction of the ego provides a model for further acts that strictly speaking come outside its terms of reference. Thus the primary narcissistic identification whereby the ego is originally imagined on an identification with its own image is the base for secondary identifications with other people, for what Lacan calls the 'dialectics of identification'. The ramifications of the 'mirror-phase' spread beyond the strictly narcissistic moment, the moment of intra-subjectivity and the constitution of the ego for the infant in his own reflection. For the moment it is necessary to plunge backwards into the question of what has happened to the theory of infantile sexuality once it has been subjected to the concept of narcissism.

4 Masculinity, Femininity and Bisexuality

The baby, then, possesses a sexual drive which is a complex structure of different component parts and which can have diverse aims and can be active or passive in its direction. Initially the baby satisfies his urges within himself – auto-erotically, or from his mother's body which seems to be experienced as an extension of his own. But the growing awareness of his incompleteness and of his separateness is forced on him by his acknowledgement that all satisfaction does not come from within, or that, as a prime example, the breast that nourishes him comes and goes. Later, Freud added to his account of this period the notion of narcissism – the means whereby the infant forms an imaginary notion of himself. The very young child moves from his auto-erotic body self-satisfaction to a self-satisfying image of his own body or self; thus the ego becomes gradually and fluctuatingly differentiated from the unconscious, so that though much of the ego must itself remain unconscious a part will, through the essential agency of perception, be conscious. This, to use Lacan's terminology, is the Imaginary relationship of the self to itself – it is crucial that this first notion of identity is not *real* but imagined – the baby has been 'given' himself by his mother's or another's responses or by the inversion of a mirror which has much the same effect. Within this framework, the answer to the question 'Who am I?' is therefore 'another' – which is one way of interpreting what Melanie Klein described as this primary paranoid-schizoid position within which all human infants temporarily rest. So far, however, we have learnt nothing about the distinction between girls and boys. The question is, is there as yet anything to learn? Is there any differentiation within either this area of sexual drives, or, secondly, within this level of the Imaginary relationship, epitomized (though not completed) by narcissism? Let us look more historically at Freud's theses – or, rather, regard them from the point of view of their own chronology, not, as we have been until now, from the standpoint of the subject's history.

One of Freud's earliest hunches and lasting convictions was his notion of bisexuality. He was convinced that the human infant was at first bisexual, and though the idea was to have much more important dimensions later, at the time of the *Three Essays* and indeed considerably later, it no doubt contributed to his belief that the difference between the sexes did not really emerge properly until puberty. Though also it is probable that a reluctance to subscribe to his own discovery of infantile sexuality influenced him in the general direction of retardation. In fact it is fair to say that the more Freud's theories advanced, the earlier in date were his preoccupations. At first, he thought that though their formations originally arose from the diverse resolutions of the Oedipus complex, puberty was the time when femininity and masculinity properly emerged. He then detected crucial differences within the formation of the Oedipus complex and finally he was left asserting the central importance of, among other things, sexual differentiation within that dark continent he had hardly begun to explore – pre-Oedipality. As his work progressed Freud became more, not less, aware of the problems. Land he thought already mapped was now found to have been done so through a mist. In one after another crucial area, Freud came to find his discovery of the mist the clearest sign of his progress. But the premature light, the flashes of clarity, were valuable, they showed him that now he saw through a glass darkly. In 1925, critically ill with cancer, Freud urged psychoanalytic researchers to struggle back into the period of remotest infancy; there could be no danger of the work becoming mechanical because there were regions as yet unsignposted '. . . everything that is to be seen upon the surface has already been exhausted; what remains has to be slowly and laboriously dragged up from the depths'.[1] If he retained his earlier schematization it was with an awareness of its excess clarity; yet if the pattern was now less stark the original lines were accurate

1. Freud, 'Some Psychical Consequences of the Anatomical Distinction Between the Sexes', op. cit., p. 249.

enough to serve their purpose. Nowhere must this implicit self-critical attitude of Freud's be more thoroughly appreciated than in his writings on pre-Oedipal childhood. On three issues, the old Freud seems to have felt the obscurity most clearly: the death-drive, the emerging distinction between the unconscious and consciousness in the post-natal child, and the differentiation between the sexes. These issues all urged him to look further and further back into the pre-Oedipal history of the individual and of society.

In looking at Freud's theories, for the moment, chronologically we are up against a specific problem in this area. Re-using Octave Mannoni's assertion that *The Interpretation of Dreams* (1900) (the book of desire) and the *Three Essays on Sexuality* (1905) (the book of the drive) represent the two poles on which Freud's theories were built, there is one (actually there are several, but for our purposes here, one) important further distinction to be made between them. It seems to me important that in the first book Freud was exploring completely new territory. Although, of course, he did not 'invent' words, there is a freedom in his use of terminology to describe the processes of the unconscious which cannot be found, for obvious reasons, in the *Three Essays*, nor in any of the works that deal more specifically with questions of sexual drives. In this last field Freud was making a revolutionary extension of conventional knowledge – but an extension nonetheless; it would have been impossible to invent words, borrow them from diverse disciplines or what have you. So what we see is not Freud coining language from within the domain of his work – neurotic currency as he called it – but champing at the bit of enforced restriction. Freud felt free to change the language used to describe mental structures as his ideas developed – so unconscious, preconscious and conscious have added to them the new concepts 'superego', 'ego', 'id'; but Freud's sexual vocabulary did not change – however, and this is the difficulty, the notions they described, to some extent, did do so.

The new formality of the terms 'superego', 'ego' and 'id', and the elusive characteristic of the concept of a second drive, the death-drive, a theoretical construct, suggest the same thing: Freud's search for a new language to chart his terrain. Often, as he compared his work to the natural sciences, in particular to physics and chemistry, he could not avoid a profound difference. Unlike an electrical current or a sliver of protoplasm, the object of his study was human experience and it confronted him, not only with its own laws, but with its own means of communicating these laws. His own imported concepts had to come to terms with those they met *within* the subject matter. There is a movement in Freud's language so that the terms he used late in life, though they *coincide* with ones used earlier, had quite often, I believe, somewhat different connotations. This factor is particularly important in any discussion of sexual theories. Furthermore, the concepts of 'superego', 'ego' and 'id' were devised by Freud only after 1920; his sexual terminology dates from his first exploration into the neurosis, it dates from his own pre-analytic days, it is in no way 'his'; though his precision was never the greatest, he could not change these terms and maintain the necessary consistency which revealed the development of his thoughts. In fact, however, his language was moving away from its early descriptive quality (where word matched observation) to a more symbolic role in relation to his material, a more self-sufficient system. It is clear that where Freud borrowed the descriptive words of his society he was increasingly uneasy about them. The terms 'masculine' and 'feminine' are a case in point.

It was as though at first, for Freud, there were only boys until the Oedipal moment established a distinction between the sexes. But he was always worried by the terms 'masculine' and 'feminine'. In his pre-analytic days he played with the current belief that sexual desire was itself 'masculine' (in the limited sense of appertaining to the male) and repression, 'feminine' (of the female) – this he already repudiated in letters to Fliess and in a draft for his paper on 'The Aetiology of Neurosis' in 1893. In his *Three Essays on Sexuality* (a work which, though first published in 1905 Freud went on altering until 1924) he explicitly states that he does not find the terms particularly useful. Biologically they are adequate to describe the strictly anatomical differences between the male and the female, but popularly speaking they usually represent 'activity' and 'passivity', in themselves tricky concepts, but nevertheless of some use for the purposes of psychoanalysis. At this point, Freud felt an early sexual distinction between boys and girls could be detected, a distinction which he left unexplained: though the girl in her clitoral activity is a 'little man', yet in masturbation she does not use the same methods. The boy's use of his hand to stimulate his penis 'is already evidence of the important contribution which the instinct for mastery is destined to make to masculine sexual activity'.[2] Only the sexuality of the male contained aggressiveness, the biological significance of which was the wish to overcome the resistance of the sexual object (the female), by means other than wooing. Freud was not to be allowed to let such unsubstantiated notions rest. Perhaps Adler's full exploration of this very notion helped Freud to drop the idea.

At this point, when he thought that the true sexual differences were linked to reproduction and thus emerged only at puberty, Freud also implied that they were thereafter to be the most important factor in shaping human life. Yet in early childhood the distinctions were there; again, at this stage, largely unworrying to Freud, unexplained and unresolved. We can see that in this model he is still overly tied to functional biological development. He observes that a girl develops a sense of shame, disgust and pity with far less resistance than a boy, she more readily represses her sexuality, and in general her sexuality takes a passive form. If libido as such is not the sole prerogative of the male, it would still, from the early active sexuality of both boy and girl, Freud contends, be fair enough to call it 'masculine', meanwhile stressing that it occurs indifferently in both sexes. It is clear that Freud later felt the confusion he had got into and which was a correct response to two concepts – masculine and feminine – that defy strict scientific utility, but nevertheless must be used. In a footnote added in 1915 to his *Three Essays on Sexuality*, Freud clarified their uselessness, though even this is not his last word on the subject; he returned to the erroneous terms with the fascination of a man who could not see his way through them as terms, though I believe, he had come to an understanding of their meaning which surpassed them:

It is essential to understand clearly that the concepts of 'mascu-

2. Freud, *Three Essays on Sexuality*, op. cit., p. 188.

line' and 'feminine', whose meaning seems so unambiguous to ordinary people, are among the most confused that occur in science. It is possible to distinguish at least three uses. 'Masculine' and 'feminine' are used sometimes in the sense of activity and passivity, sometimes in a biological, and sometimes, again, in a sociological sense. The first of these three meanings is the essential one and the most serviceable in psycho-analysis. *When, for instance, libido was described . . . as being 'masculine', the word was being used in this sense, for an instinct is always active even when it has a passive aim in view.* The second, or biological, meaning of 'masculine' and 'feminine' is the one whose applicability can be determined most easily. Here 'masculine' and 'feminine' are characterized by the presence of spermatozoa or ova respectively and by the functions proceeding from them. Activity and its concomitant phenomena (more powerful muscular development, aggressiveness, greater intensity of libido) are as a rule linked with biological masculinity; *but they are not necessarily so, for there are animal species in which these qualities are on the contrary assigned to the female.* The third, or sociological, meaning receives its connotation from the observation of actually existing masculine and feminine individuals. Such observation shows that in human beings pure masculinity or femininity is not to be found either in a psychological or a biological sense. *Every individual on the contrary displays a mixture of the character-traits belonging to his own and to the opposite sex; and he shows a combination of activity and passivity whether or not these last character-traits tally with his biological ones* [my italics].[3]

Freud, in attempting to bite through the restraining bit of 'masculine' and 'feminine' to find some psychological meaning for them, or to establish their meaninglessness, fell back on his own obstinate retention of the notion of bisexuality. The concept originates in one of his euphoric responses to his friend Fliess's fascinating but bizarre theories: '. . . bisexuality! I am sure you are right about it . . .'[4] Freud wrote back, ecstatically.

With the concept of 'bisexuality' we find the same sort of somewhat anxious link-up with biology as Freud made, more deprecatingly, in the case of masculine and feminine. But its psychological importance is central to Freud's writings in this area. Like so many of his revolutionary notions it originated as a

3. ibid., pp. 219–20 n.
4. 1 August 1899, *The Origins of Psychoanalysis*, op. cit., p. 289.

hunch, was questioned, cross-questioned, modified, found wanting and finally re-established as an essential concept. In the
course of its history it moved from its biological origins to a psychoanalytical meaning. As with 'masculine' and 'feminine', the
word remained the same but the significance shifted. Indeed, the
three words are a part of one concept and only the changing use
of each enables us to envisage *precisely* what this concept means.
As Freud says, the biological and conventional meanings – and
even the connotations of 'activity' and 'passivity' – are not
enough. In this instance we have to examine the development
of the terms from their beginning to their final form.

   Freud's great initial discovery was, of course, the sexual
sources of the neuroses. The first major published work he produced was, in the days before his full founding of psychoanalysis,
'a series of studies on hysteria' in which he collaborated with
Breuer. Most of his patients – and all whose case-histories he
wrote up – were women. And although Freud staked his reputa-
tion on his support of Charcot's revolutionary idea of male hysteria,[5] most hysterics were women. His subject matter, hysterical
neurosis; his material, women; his discovery, the omni-import-
ance of sexual ideas. It seemed an accidental linkage, and
Freud's first efforts at interrelating the elements were to demonstrate that hysteria was 'feminine' – though emphatically to be
found in men. His last result was the conclusion that 'the feminine' (being a woman in a psychological sense) was in part a
hysterical formation. Put elliptically like this, we can see the
logical similarity between the initial task and the final result.
Why did Freud need twenty or more years to get from (a) to
(a)? But the statements, 'hysteria is a disorder found mainly in
women', 'hysteria is a neurosis with feminine characteristics',
and 'femininity is linked to hysteria', are, in fact, obviously
fundamentally different propositions. Again, as with bisexuality,
Freud reiterated his primary 'hunch', but a return to something
is always a return. Despite the saying, an old man does not

   5. It had previously been assumed that hysteria – the rising of the
emotions of the womb – could only be found in women. Charcot,
whose lectures in Paris Freud attended, demonstrated that men were
also hysterics. That Freud later found hysterical neurosis 'feminine'
is an analysis on a completely different level of understanding.

become a baby again, he only seems to do so to us in our oblivion of the one and ignorance of the other state. Notions, borrowed from an 'outside' source (here biology and convention) and superimposed on empirical observation, become, when they are revalidated intellectual light-years later, something else: they are new theories. The coincidence of Freud's first and last terminology in this field is very confusing. But it is essential that having admitted that the end supersedes the beginnings we do not forget those beginnings as they apply to an analysis of women. For popular psychology and social conventionality (as well as the case that is made by most feminist opposition to Freud) continue to offer us those beginnings as though they were Freud's conclusions. It is natural that they should do so, as they, themselves, *are* those very beginnings from which Freud started. Such is the danger of coincidence. These beginnings are the conventions and ideologies which he found inadequate and which in *apparently* confirming by trying to understand, he overthrew.

That at first Freud regarded all small children as though they were little boys, in fact, did no harm: in later challenging his assumption he had to see *why* it was not true and in doing so he discovered its truth – in the new sense he gave 'masculinity' and in a new dimension too to bisexuality. Again it was a case of coming back at the end of his life to his original hypotheses, and confirming them with a different understanding that amounted to a new meaning.

Bisexuality is met at every turn in Freud's analyses of his patients. As it moved away from being a largely biological postulate, it became a disposition faced with various possibilities; it ended by being the unsolved crux of the matter – both in theory and practice.

In 1938, in his final, and posthumously published, survey of the crucial concerns of his life work, Freud wrote:

At this point [that is at the point of the Oedipus moment] we must give separate accounts of the development of boys and girls (of males and females), for it is now that the difference between the sexes finds psychological expression for the first time. We are faced here by the great enigma of the biological fact of the duality of the sexes: it is an ultimate fact of our knowledge, it defies every attempt to trace it back to something else. Psycho-analysis has contributed nothing to clearing up this problem, *which clearly falls wholly within the province of biology*. In mental life we only find reflections of this great antithesis; and their interpretation is made more difficult by the fact, long suspected, that no individual is limited to the modes of reaction of a single sex but always finds some room for those of the opposite one, just as his body bears, alongside of the fully developed organs of one sex, atrophied and often useless rudiments of those of the other. For distinguishing between male and female in mental life we make use of what is obviously an inadequate empirical and conventional equation: we call everything that is strong and active male, and everything that is weak and passive female. *This fact of psychological bisexuality, too, embarrasses all our inquiries into the subject and makes them harder to describe* [my italics].[6]

Post-Freudian analysts, as we shall see, have all too often interpreted 'this great antithesis' between the sexes to mean an absolute distinction between men and women for whom, indeed, therefore, anatomy was the *only* destiny. Nature had made the sexes essentially different and in social life thus diverse they must go forth. Obviously, on the contrary, what Freud meant was that *both* sexes in their mental life reflected this great antithesis; that in the unconscious and preconscious of men and women alike was echoed the great problem of this original duality. Without distinction, both sexes are preoccupied with the great distinction: in different ways they both flee from its implications. Both men and women live out in their mental life the great difficulty that there are men and women. Only in their wildest dreams can they resolve the dilemma as Aristophanes does with his laughing seriousness in Plato's *Symposium*, where an original hermaphrodism solves the problem as all of us both desire and dread.

If bisexuality is the unsolved figure in the carpet of the theoretical problem, it is also the irreducible nub of the practical exposition of personality, the necessary frustration to which the analytic 'cure' must be liable. Again, in one of his very last essays to be written, 'Analysis Terminable and Interminable', Freud, stressing the obstacle which physiological and biological

6. Freud, 'An Outline of Psychoanalysis', 1940 (1938), S.E., Vol. XXIII, p. 188.

barriers caused to the progress of therapy (he had, as he wrote four years earlier, 'never been a therapeutic enthusiast'), placed a heavy weight on the two crucial expressions of bisexuality in mental life – penis envy and the castration complex, the two sides of the same coin. I shall discuss these two concepts later; for the moment we should note that Freud considered they were never utterly resolvable. In his last word on the subject, Freud returned, though critically, to his first inspiration for bisexuality. But in the forty-six years that had elapsed since its first introduction, the concept has undergone a crucial development. In 'Analysis Terminable and Interminable' Freud says that though the presence of two sexes is a fact of biology, the mental experience of this is a matter for psychology: it does not *cause* our mental life, but our mental life has to take it into account – indeed it is the most fundamental and difficult problem it has to face – on a par with only one other dilemma: where do we come from and how do we fit in? In taking into account the biological 'great antithesis' between the sexes, we are psychologically bisexual; each of our psychologies contains the antithesis. The change the concept of bisexuality has undergone corresponds to a shift in Freud's way of reading its event: instead of starting with the baby and following its evolution (a tendency of the method of presentation in the *Three Essays*) he has done what he had undertaken with every other concept and reversed direction – as he has always done in his discoveries. He has this time presented his reading backwards from the experience of the adult in analysis to the problems of the infant. In changing direction, the concept of bisexuality has moved from being a simple notion, a postulate of a sort of infantile unisex, to being a complex notion of the oscillations and imbalance of the person's mental androgyny. It is this dilemma, in which the subject is still resolving the precise point of the place he occupies in the world, in terms of his (and her) wish for it not to be the feminine place, which is the only, and ever-present, alternative to where anyone really wants to be – in the male position within the patriarchal human order.[7] If I

7. An interesting confirmation of Freud's manner of working through the phantasies of neurotics to uncover also the structures of

am not a man, then I am being a woman. Bisexuality has become
linked to the crucial psychoanalytic tenet of the castration complex. In a footnote Freud points out that the man's castration
anxiety does not, of course, prevent his passive relationship to a
woman, just to another man – as we can see, for example, in the
implications of homosexuality so central to the follow-the-leader/
father position. Masochism and passivity of a man before a
woman imply no danger of loss of manhood as it is in that very
role that the mother accepted him. In other words, the feminine
predicament, for *both* sexes, applies only in the relationship to
men.

The very young infant, auto-erotically satisfied, with a
bisexual disposition, finding itself in an image given to it by
another; this would seem the halcyon condition of human prehistory. Everything Freud writes confirms that there is no
important psychological sexual differentiation in this pre-Oedipal
situation. But this situation is not a stage, not an amount of time,
but a level. At another level, the culturally determined implication of the sexual difference is always in waiting.

---

normal mental life can be evidenced in what we might call the halfway-
house stage of this shift in the implications of bisexuality. In 1908
Freud published a very brief paper entitled 'Hysterical Phantasies and
Their Relation to Bisexuality', in which he claimed that hysterical
symptoms manifested two sexual phantasies, a masculine and a feminine
one; or, one could say, the symptoms had homosexual and heterosexual implications. Often in analysis one would be resolved but the
other would persist undetected. 'The bisexual nature of hysterical
symptoms, which can in any event be demonstrated in numerous
cases, is an interesting confirmation of my view that the postulated
existence of an innate bisexual disposition in man is especially clearly
visible in the analysis of psychoneurotics' (1908, S.E., Vol. IX,
pp. 165–6).

5 Pre-Oedipal Sexuality

So far the analysis that we have learnt from Freud suggests that there is no important distinction between boys and girls in the pre-Oedipal phase, yet, what happens next, the Oedipus complex, is so profoundly different for the two sexes that it alters the meaning of what has gone before. Although, then, within the pre-Oedipal period there is no great distinction, yet the period comes to have a very different meaning – it becomes, in a sense, vastly more important for a girl than for a boy.

The pregenital erotic stages, the finding of the self within narcissism, are sexually undifferentiated, but although they are pre-Oedipal, they take place within the shadow of the Oedipus complex and it is this that casts its mark back over their whole meaning. What we have so far learnt from Freud about infantile sexuality, narcissism and bisexuality has to be seen in the context of this Oedipally determined, pre-Oedipus phase.

It is in the *Three Essays* that Freud offers his first discussion of what is by now the notorious notion of the polymorphously perverse sexual disposition of early childhood. All this means is that there is nothing to stop the multifarious and multitudinous aspects to the drive that comprises sexuality from going off in any direction wished for. Any irregularity can occur in the absence of the restraining might of the cultural inhibitions of shame, disgust, morality. (There is nothing either but the acquisition of this 'culture' to prevent polymorphously perverse adulthood – it isn't a state you grow naturally out of, it is a condition you learn to reject.) Anyway, children reveal scopophilic (pleasure in non-perverse sexual looking), exhibitionist and cruel tendencies all of which (though independent at first) can become attached to genital activities. Pregenital sexuality, with its oral urge to incorporate the object (which is an important basis for later modes of identification) and its anal phase with its sadistic overtones, is neither predominantly masculine nor feminine – and neither sex responds more strongly to one than to the other – variations are individual and accidental. The third and phallic phase is initially as impervious to gender differences as the oral and anal phases, though it is within this area that Freud said the choice of recognition has to be made, the recognition that the phallic power of another is bigger and better than one's own: in the boy's case, that of the father, in the girl's, that of all men. In the reaction to the recognition, as we have seen, Freud located the diverse expression of the same shock: penis-envy for women and castration anxiety for men – in one, they want it, in the other they could lose what hopes they have. But sunk in narcissism and polymorphously perverse, the male at least takes himself for the model of the universe: everyone is constructed in the image he is finding of himself. At first one feels as though Freud has neglected to follow through the logic of his own insights and assume that if, in this brief moment, the boy takes the world to be male, the girl must likewise take it to be female. He has indeed been castigated time and again for this failure – a failure that as we shall see, Karen Horney and Ernest Jones made good to the entire detriment of the psychology of femininity. Later, Freud, after doubts and questions, remained convinced of his hypothesis.

Girls *do* transfer to men, women and boys their notion of their own sexuality; but at this stage it is clitoral genitality alone that they experience and as the clitoris is homologous and analogous to the penis, they too assume a phallic world.

In the *Three Essays*, Freud does not discuss the implications of the fact that for both sexes the first sexual object is the mother's breast and then the mother who cares and cuddles. The mother's role in this is certainly outlined but the lack of symmetry for the two sexes is not seen as significant; the mother-and-child idyll (the baby is always a boy) indicates merely that Freud thought there was as yet no important distinction. The first love for the mother (or mother's breast) has to be reacquired as a necessary part of the Oedipal moment; it is this reattachment (and the girl's analogous attachment to her father) that persists through the later choices of sexual objects made by adults. In the boy, of course, the first and second mother (the pre-Oedipal and Oedipal mother) are fused, so that in papers written before Freud realized the crucial importance of the pre-Oedipal situation, there is no clear distinction evident in his writing, either. It was the elision in the case of boys, echoed in his own theory, that Freud was to eliminate when he first directly tackled the question of the distinction between the sexes:

> In examining the earliest mental shapes assumed by the sexual life of children we have been in the habit of taking as the subject of our investigations the male child ... With little girls, so we have supposed, things must be similar, though in some way or other they must nevertheless be different ...
>
> In boys the situation of the Oedipus complex is the first stage that can be recognized with certainty. It is easy to understand, because at that stage a child retains the same object which he previously cathected with his libido – not as yet a genital one – during the preceding period while he was being suckled and nursed.[1]

Only now, in 1925, after the reformulation of the structure of the mental apparatus in *The Ego and the Id* (1923), did Freud explicitly direct himself to the question of the pre-Oedipal mother-attachment. His work on the psychoses and his theories of narcissism had all perforce dealt with this period – but it was only in regarding the complexities of the Oedipal situation and its different manifestations for the two sexes that Freud was forced to reconsider the significance of the pre-Oedipal love-object – the mother. Even then he was tentative, only finally stressing the crucial nature for the girl of this earliest mother relationship (a relationship with someone of the same sex) in his 1931 essay 'Female Sexuality'. Of course, hitherto in his case-studies, it had forced its presence on him – but I would suggest that the nature of the case-studies themselves prevented him seeing its importance. Indeed, after 'Dora', a case of hysteria, published in 1905, Freud only reported two more detailed case-histories of women – one in 1915, a brief case of paranoia, and the other a case of female homosexuality in 1920. An instance of female homosexuality would be likely to present a crucial, and ambivalent, mother-attachment, and paranoia, as one of the

1. Freud, 'Some Psychical Consequences of the Anatomical Distinction Between the Sexes', op. cit., p. 249.

psychoses, would likewise assume this because of the importance for it of the pre-Oedipal period of narcissism.[2] But it seems that the symptomatology – in the inversion and in psychoses – that presupposed a mother-attachment obscured its significance; the observation acted as a screen to the development of the theory. Furthermore, the premium Freud placed on the Oedipus complex as the 'nucleus of neuroses' held him back for some time from acknowledging the awareness he clearly already had of this earlier pre-Oedipal period. This is not to deny that hitherto Freud had always had a male archetype in mind – indeed he constantly acknowledges this fact himself – it is just to suggest that there were also other considerations than male chauvinism standing in the way of his comprehension of female sexuality.

In his first explicit reference in 1925 to the importance of the pre-Oedipal mother-attachment, Freud commented that psycho-analysis had covered the surface of mental life and now it had to explore the depths; in 1931, in his paper on 'Female Sexuality', he makes the same point but deploys an image from his favourite field of archaeology: 'Our insight into this early, pre-Oedipus, phase in girls comes to us as a surprise, like the discovery, in another field, of the Minoan-Mycenaean civilization behind the civilization of Greece.'[3] Freud didn't altogether like what he found there. As the mother is the first nurturative, caring love-object for both sexes, the mother-attachment would be expected to be a loving one; but not a bit of it. *Preceding* any rivalry the little girl might feel with the mother in her demands for the father in the positive Oedipal stage, there is already considerable hostility to be found in her attitude. A generalized rivalry with siblings and father certainly causes a good deal of the jealousy and resentment, but this primary hostility is something else again. It

2. The same considerations would, of course, also apply to 'Dora' as a hysteric. See, for instance, Freud's observation in 'Female Sexuality': 'Among these [new ideas] is a suspicion that this phase of attachment to the mother is especially intimately related to the aetiology of hysteria, which is not surprising when we reflect that both the phase and the neurosis are characteristically feminine, and further, that in this dependence on the mother we have the germ of later paranoia in women.' ('Female Sexuality', 1931, S.E., Vol. XXI, p. 227.)

3. Freud, 'Female Sexuality', ibid., p. 226.

would seem to arise from the fact that there is no bottom, none, to a child's boundless love and demand for love, there is *no* satisfaction possible and the inevitable frustration can cause violent feelings. The mother simply cannot give the baby enough. And then, of course, finally, there is the situation in which the girl blames her mother for the fact that she is a girl and therefore without a penis (this we will consider later). Probably at some time the girl blames her mother for the social restrictions placed on her sexual life – but this would become particularly true only at puberty when there is far greater control of a girl's freedom than of a boy's. As later love patterns are built on this primary love-relationship, all this hostility can be transferred in the final event from the mother on to the husband – who thus really replaces the *mother* in the girl's affections. Freud comments:

... we noticed that many women who have chosen their husband on the model of their father, or have put him in their father's place, nevertheless repeat towards him, in their married life, their bad relations with their mother. The husband of such a woman was meant to be the inheritor of her relation to her father, but in reality he became the inheritor of her relation to her mother.[4]

More important, however, than all the innumerable reasons a girl might have, or might later conceive of (as rationalizations), for her hostility to her mother, is the general tendency towards ambivalence: the very primacy and intensity of this relationship makes it liable to contain hate as well as love – the girl, unlike the boy, cannot make a separation of these emotions and transfer the hatred to a rivalrous father, because she must soon come to take this same father as her love-object.

In describing the nature of this first mother-attachment, Freud comments that for both sexes there are active and passive aspects. In this instance he stresses the girl's active desires through all phases – oral, anal and phallic. We can easily see how the child always tends to convert a passive impression to an active reaction, it struggles against dependence, wanting to do things instead of having them done to it. In the girl this can be evidenced in her mastery of the situation through play, in particular she

4. ibid., pp. 230–31.

'mothers' her mother as a child, she enacts games with dolls in the endless ingenuity of do-as-you-are-done-by. Other phantasies of active wishes towards the mother tend to be obscured by the later transference to the father; but Freud asserts that all those previously thought to be characteristic only of boys are also to be found in girls. There is a fear in both sexes of being killed by the mother and so there is a shift to activity in an aggressive death-wish against her. Both also wish to give the mother a baby, or, with the mother, to have produced the newly-arrived brother or sister, just as Little Hans would have liked it. Little Hans wanted his baby sister to belong to him and his mother, he also looked after his doll, Grete, as though she were his baby. Now Freud points to the fact that girls do exactly the same. It is only when the full force of her hostility towards her mother comes to bear on the little girl that these active urges (along with many passive ones) undergo repression. As she pushes aside her active desire, the girl, thoroughly fed up with her lot, may well repress a great deal of her sexuality in general. But she makes use of what is left of her passive aims and tries to take her father as her new love-object.

In all the passions of the first mother-attachment the little boy and little girl are alike – it is only with the necessity for her mother-*det*achment that the girl gets going on the path to femininity. As we shall see 'castration', frustration and the demands of heterosexual custom all set this hostile detachment in motion.

When the *Three Essays on Sexuality* were first published in 1905, Freud considered that the psychological distinction between the sexes only really set in with the second phase of man's diphasic sexuality, in other words after the latency period with the onset of puberty, when the menstruating girl recognizes the role of her vagina and the boy is able to produce semen, when full genitality arises for the first time and is inevitably linked with reproduction. (Freud devoted a section of his work to this adolescent period, but really it had to wait for Anna Freud's more thorough investigations into adolescence thirty years later.) In the 1905 study, the three important concepts which were decisively to change Freud's thesis were missing: the Oedipus complex, though postulated some nine years earlier, was omitted, and the castration complex and its feminine correlate penis-envy were only added in subsequent editions. If the concept of narcissism was to inaugurate a re-reading of the pre-Oedipal phase, castration and the Oedipus complex (indissolubly linked) were to provide the framework for a reinterpretation of infantile sexuality as a whole. One 'stage' of the sexual drive was filtered through the glass of narcissistic desire, the next through the desires whose configuration comprises the Oedipus complex. The relative simplicities of the baby's self-preservation urges and sexual drive are now, because of these two concepts, seen through the complexities of the subject's history of wishes, repressions, denials, desires ... In Freud's work the interpretation of the distinction between the sexes will never be the same again. Gone is the logical thesis that it is with the reproductive powers of puberty that the male and female take on the attributes of masculine and feminine; psychological development does not follow the neat path of physiological evolution, and though others retained this link, Freud himself became more and more concerned to make a break.

Reinterpreted through the history of the subject's desire, the distinction between the sexes can be seen to be established in an ever more primary fashion; it can likewise be seen to be ever more important. In the very last, and unfinished, idea that Freud published, it is the prime significance of this question that preoccupies him, for this issue, above all, seems to be at the root of the formation of the ego, in other words the ego takes on its creation within a world culturally as well as biologically divided into two sexes. This acknowledgement caused Freud to think that at the eleventh hour he might be on to a new theory of the ego. He had previously recognized that the ego was in part created as a divided self – an *original* split necessitated by its very formation within the alienation of the mirror-image; but now his observation of a further instance of a split in the example of fetishism makes Freud link it closely to castration and hence it would be connected with the distinction between the sexes.[5] This is a long way from the analogous and parallel development ascribed to girls and boys in the *Three Essays*, though it is foreshadowed in the earliest psychoanalytic concepts of the Oedipus complex

5. See 'The Splitting of the Ego in the Process of Defence', 1940 (1938), S.E., Vol. XXIII.

and bisexuality (the latter a concept which, as we have seen, Freud had to remould in psychoanalytic terms). It is a long way, too, from Freud's cavalier assumption that the little girl's first sexuality was 'male' and there. was an end to it – it was 'masculine', but now that was only the beginning of it.

6 The Oedipus Complex

Writing 'prematurely' of paranoia, melancholia and mourning, and of the death-drive in 1897, Freud wrote, 'It seems as though this death-wish is directed in sons against their father and in daughters against their mother',[1] and five months later, reporting on his analysis of himself to his friend Fliess, Freud recollected a screen-memory (a trivial childhood memory that covers an important one) of his mother at the time of her confinement with his sister Anna (Freud was two and a half years old at the time) which he was to use later in *The Psychopathology of Everyday Life*. He went on to say:

I have found, in my own case too, falling in love with the mother and jealousy of the father, and I now regard it as a universal event of early childhood ... If that is so, we can understand the riveting power of *Oedipus Rex*, in spite of all the objections raised by reason against its presupposition of destiny ... the Greek legend seizes on a compulsion which everyone recognizes because he feels its existence within himself. Each member of the audience was once, in germ and phantasy, just such an Oedipus, and each one recoils in horror from the dream-fulfilment here transplanted into reality, with the whole quota of repression which separates his infantile state from his present one.[2]

1. Draft N., Notes, III, 1897, S.E., Vol. I, p. 255. 'Prematurely' in the sense that he had not yet formulated his theories of them. This 'death-wish' is by no means the same as the psychoanalytic concept of the 'death-drive'; however, as the editors of the Standard Edition suggest, this reference may well be the beginnings of the idea of the Oedipus complex.

2. Freud, Letter to Fliess, No. 71, 15 October 1897, S.E., Vol. I, p. 265. For those who would charge Freud with the perversions of subjectivity, one should note his statement in another letter to Fliess in November of the same year. 'My self-analysis is still interrupted and I have realized the reason. I can only analyse myself with the help of knowledge obtained objectively (like an outsider). Genuine self-

In a comparable context of dreams of death-wishes against those of whom the dreamer is consciously fond (under the category 'Typical Dreams'), Freud reiterated his insight in *The Interpretation of Dreams* where he gave further examples of disguised or direct dreams that illustrated the material. At this stage, the concept was only descriptive – but descriptive of a universal situation. Gradually, however, by relating it to the other foundation-stone of psychoanalysis – the unconscious – Freud gave it its dynamic role in the history of mental development. It is *only* this combination that gives meaning to the Oedipus complex.[3]

The first full case-histories after the *Studies in Hysteria* – Little Hans, Dora and the Rat Man – deciphered the operations of the Oedipus complex before it was fully formulated as a theory. So in the 'Dora' analysis, in which he unravels the tissues of sexual desire in an eighteen-year-old girl (Dora's repudiated heterosexual wish for her father and her homosexual attachment to her father's mistress, Frau K.), Freud introduces the psychical complex that he is to reveal by the sort of sociological comment on families that would warm the heart of many a radical therapist today:

It follows from the nature of the facts which form the material of psycho-analysis that we are obliged to pay as much attention in our case histories to the purely human and social circumstances of our patients as to the somatic data and the symptoms of the disorder. Above all, our interest will be directed towards their family circumstances – and not only, as will be seen later, for the purpose of inquiring into their heredity.[4]

---

analysis is impossible; otherwise there would be no [neurotic] illness. Since I still find some puzzles in my patients, they are bound to hold me up in my self-analysis as well.' (No. 75, 14 November 1897, ibid., p. 271.) Of course, as Octave Mannoni explains, Freud had his analyst in Fliess, the recipient and, in a sense, originator, of Freud's letters. This letter confirms the point that psychoanalysis is a process of helping the analysand to know himself – neurosis is a mark of man's estrangement from himself and, for good reasons, his refusal of knowledge.

3. To ignore this connection is common and fatal: see both Reich and the particular feminist critics discussed later.

4. Freud, 'Fragment of an Analysis of a Case of Hysteria', 1905, S.E., Vol. VII, p. 18.

Freud certainly gives a social portrait of the operations of a nuclear family, but the important implications of these 'family circumstances' are the phantasies and repressed desires that, re-evoked in adolescence or later, are witnesses to the infantile Oedipal drama. (Freud was only later to realize the import of the *combined* homosexual and heterosexual aspects of this scene.)

In Little Hans, Freud had his first unnecessary but fascinating confirmation of a child's sexual phantasies from a direct record of infancy. Little Hans wanted a baby with his mother, fell ill to retain her exclusive love which was threatened by his sister's birth, and transferred the fear of his own death-wish against his father to horses, which thus became the expression of his phobia. In this way he ensured a double advantage – he converted his violent hostility into a fear of someone being hostile to him and he then transposed this fear of a person – his father – on to a neutral animal, a horse. He would not go out for walks in case he saw a horse, so he stayed at home with his mother who thus gave her frightened child more of her attention – the 'purpose' of the phobic illness in the first place. The feelings the boy has for his mother and father are neat expressions of the Oedipus complex as it is lived within the nuclear family. Sometimes Hans resolves the triangular dilemma in which he is placed; then 'The little Oedipus had found a happier solution than that prescribed by destiny. Instead of putting his father out of the way, he had granted him the same happiness that he desired himself: he made him a grandfather and married *him* to his own mother too.'[5]

In the history of the 'Rat Man' Freud heads a section of this case of severe obsessional neurosis, in which the intense ambivalence of the young man to his now dead father is revealed, 'The Father Complex'. Only gradually did the term 'complex' come within psychoanalytical writings to indicate the totality of *repressed unconscious* ideas that surround an emotionally coloured event. (Previously it was used without the all-important connotation of unconsciousness.) The Oedipus complex is the *repressed* ideas that appertain to the family drama of any primary constellation of figures within which the child must find its place. It is not the *actual* family situation or the conscious desire it evokes. In

5. Freud, 'Phobia in a Five-Year-Old Boy', op. cit., p. 97.

the case of the 'Rat Man' we can see Freud bringing the Oedipus complex (though here it is not actually named as such) under the sway of the concept of the unconscious and giving it its full psychoanalytic meaning:

> The uniformity of the content of the sexual life of children, together with the unvarying character of the modifying tendencies which are later brought to bear upon it, will easily account for the constant sameness which as a rule characterizes the phantasies that are constructed around the period of childhood, irrespective of how greatly or how little real experiences have contributed towards them. It is entirely characteristic of *the nuclear complex of infancy* that the child's father should be assigned the part of a sexual opponent and of an interferer with auto-erotic sexual activities; and real events are usually to a large extent responsible for bringing this about [my italics].[6]

What *actually* and specifically happens is nowhere near as important as what is *expected* to happen in man's general cultural history.

From now onwards, the Oedipal situation became the 'nuclear complex' of neuroses and a cornerstone of psychoanalytic theory. It had always been this, but the delay with which Freud favoured its realization is important. It is often said that only the discovery of his own Oedipal desires made Freud recognize the fact of infantile sexuality, but clearly that is not the whole truth. In one sense, of course, it was part of the same realization, in another the implications of the Oedipus complex had to be developed and infantile sexuality reviewed through the light they cast on it. The Oedipus complex is the nucleus of neuroses, not because of the incest wishes that it reflects – but because of the *repression* of these. The Oedipus complex is not a set of *attitudes* to other people, but a pattern of relationships between a set of places – actually occupied, or otherwise. (As Freud says in the passage just cited, real events and people are *usually, but not necessarily*, present.) The first intrusion of the idea of the Oedipus complex into Freud's thought – in a dream – necessitated his removal of the notion of a *real* occurrence (the literal seduction by the parent

6. Freud, 'Notes Upon a Case of Obsessional Neurosis', 1909, S.E., Vol. X, p. 208 n. (otherwise known as 'The Case of the Rat Man').

of the child) and the substitution, instead, of the theory of phantasy. Thus, the Oedipus complex *was* a part of the general recognition of infantile sexuality, but a special part and one that was to have different consequences.

For a long time, the Oedipus complex can really be said to have been a major, but nonetheless relatively simple notion. The substance of its complexity is revealed in the case-histories; the numerous consequences of it, such as the universal feelings of guilt (resulting from desired incest and hence desired parricide), are mentioned in theoretical contexts. A macro-cosmic expression of it is conceived within the mythological anthropology of *Totem and Taboo* (1912–13), but the first full abstract presentation of it, in the Introductory Lectures of 1916–17, remains descriptive. At the level of theory, the concept had not yet fully transcended the days of its first suggestion in the letter to Fliess. (Perhaps we could take as an indication of this point the fact that Freud, up to and including this Lecture, nearly always explains it by re-telling Sophocles' version.) But in the next year the publication of another case-history – that of the Wolf Man – prepared the way for an elaboration of the concept that was to enforce its shift from an acknowledged cornerstone of psychoanalytic observation to a realization of what had always been implicit within it or had been previously expressed over-simply – that is to say its highly complicated role as the instigatory moment for the individual of human culture. Again, except in the resumé, the Oedipus complex of the Wolf Man is not mentioned by name – but its newly perceived elaborations are clearly manifest. Freud was concerned with the infantile neurosis of his patient, this time a rich young Russian who, at the age of four, had succumbed to an anxiety hysteria expressed as an animal phobia (fear of wolves) but later replaced by obsessional neurotic features. The 'Wolf Man' was the child of parents whose wealth and ill-health left him in the care of a nurse and then a governess. His Oedipal attachment had all been directed to his first old peasant nurse, his 'Nanya', who after being devoted to him in earliest infancy rebuffed him and threatened his masturbatory activities with castration. This experience was later repeated, with variations, with a young housemaid whom the boy desired. Nevertheless, in the patient's phantasies, it was his father and not the housemaid or Nanya who was the castrator:

> Although the threats or hints of castration which had come his way had emanated from women, this could not hold up the final result for long. In spite of everything it was his father from whom in the end he came to fear castration. In this respect heredity triumphed over accidental experience; in man's prehistory it was unquestionably the father who practised castration as a punishment and who later softened it down into circumcision.[7]

Though in his conclusion Freud cautioned against assuming a phylogenetic heritage and stressed that it must only be postulated *after* it had been read back through the individual, he nevertheless pointed out how when, as for instance in this case, the real experiences fail to fit the standard Oedipal schema, they are remodelled to do so and the mother and/or nurse are fused and the father replaces the woman as castrator. The adult re-experiences his infantile entry into his own history in terms of the correct mythological convention. This is the significance of an inherited culture. But of greater import here than this was the fact that in presenting this case of repressed homosexuality Freud was led to the first descriptions of a 'negative' or 'inverted' Oedipus complex which was to become a concept of momentous, if transitional, import for the Oedipus complex of women, which had hitherto been suppressed from the theory on the pretext that it was the same as the male version – merely the other way round. The case-history of a man revealed this 'inverted', feminine Oedipus complex and was, paradoxically, a step in the direction

7. Freud, 'History of an Infantile Neurosis', 1918, S.E., Vol. XVII, p. 86. Freud was explicit here on the significance of phylogenesis. 'I fully agree with Jung in recognizing the existence of this phylogenetic heritage; but I regard it as a methodological error to seize on a phylogenetic explanation before the ontogenetic possibilities have been exhausted. I cannot see any reason for obstinately disputing the importance of infantile prehistory while at the same time freely acknowledging the importance of ancestral prehistory. Nor can I overlook the fact that phylogenetic motives and productions themselves stand in need of elucidation, and that in quite a number of instances this is afforded by factors in the childhood of the individual.' (ibid., p. 97.)

of getting rid of the notion that had hitherto accounted for the Oedipal situation of girls on an exclusively masculine model.

Although the study was only published in 1918, Freud had been working with the Wolf Man in 1914 – the year of his seminal essay on narcissism. The Wolf Man presented Freud with a conflict between passive and active aims and a struggle over the adoption of a feminine or masculine position. Freud had to present this dilemma without falling into the Adlerian trap of suggesting that this conflict of bisexuality (or of masculine protest against femininity) was itself the source of neuroses. All the ego is concerned with, is repressing offensive sexual demands – its interest is its self-protection and the preservation of its narcissism, be it of a predominantly masculine or feminine variety. Nevertheless, conflict of masculinity and femininity in this case presented Freud with some thoughts that were to become extremely important for his later efforts at deciphering the psychological consequences of the distinction between the sexes. The Wolf Man had been early seduced to sexual activity by his elder sister, and this experience had conflated with a dream of white wolves – hence the 'Wolf Man'. On interpretation the dominant image in the dream stood for the father and was in its turn a re-expression of an even earlier witnessing of the 'primal scene' – in this case anal intercourse between the boy's parents. The patient oscillated throughout his early years between a passive, homosexual wish for his father and an active identification with him in which he made his nurse and then the housemaid into his sexual objects; there then came a secondary homosexual desire for the father, and so on. The history is immensely complicated and here I only want to show the significance of Freud's interpretation for the development of the Oedipus complex and sexual differentiation:

[The Wolf Man's] last sexual aim, the passive attitude towards his father, succumbed to repression, and fear of his father appeared in its place in the shape of the wolf phobia.

And the driving force of this repression? The circumstances of the case show that it can only have been his narcissistic genital libido, which, in the form of concern for his male organ, was fighting against a satisfaction whose attainment seemed to involve the renunciation of that organ [that is, if he took his *mother's* place]. And it was from his threatened narcissism that he derived the masculinity with which he defended himself against his passive attitude towards his father.

We now observe that at this point in our narrative we must make an alteration in our terminology. During the dream he had reached a new phase in his sexual organization. Up to then the sexual opposites had been for him *active* and *passive*. Since his seduction [by his sister] his sexual aim had been a passive one, of being touched on the genitals; it was then transformed, by regression to the earlier stage of the sadistic-anal organization, into the masochistic aim of being beaten or punished. It was a matter of indifference to him whether he reached this aim with a man or with a woman. He had travelled, without considering the difference of sex, from his Nanya to his father; he had longed to have his penis touched by his Nanya, and had tried to provoke a beating from his father. Here his genitals were left out of account; though the connection with them which had been concealed by the regression was still expressed in his phantasy of being beaten *on the penis*. The activation of the primal scene in the dream now brought him back to the genital organization. He discovered the vagina and the biological significance of masculine and feminine. He understood now that active was the same as masculine, while passive was the same as feminine. His passive sexual aim should now have been transformed into a feminine one, and have expressed itself as 'being copulated with by his father' instead of 'being beaten by him on the genitals or on the bottom'. This feminine aim, however, underwent repression and was obliged to let itself be replaced by fear of the wolf.[8]

In the Wolf Man the femininity was repressed and he only began to lose his apathy and develop social interests when, during analysis, it 'became possible to liberate his shackled homosexuality'. In his case he had retained his identification with his mother's sexuality; but it was the fear of castration that he could not resolve except with an unacceptable loss to his narcissism; the *masculine* narcissism attached to the genitals came into conflict with an already existent homosexual aim which was an expression of an early inverted or negative Oedipus complex. If this illustration shows Freud struggling to reveal how passivity becomes connected with femininity and activity with masculinity, it also shows how neither are connected with the biological gender, but with the *situation* of the subject.

8. ibid., pp. 46–7.

Freud's next important case-history in this connection was 'A Case of Female Homosexuality'. From our point of view here, ironically, it is interesting for what it doesn't do. Instead of the Wolf Man's repressed homosexuality and femininity – the passive attitude to another man – we have here a quite conscious choice: the young woman's absolutely *un-neurotic* resolution of her adolescent dilemma. With the vocal revival of the Oedipus complex at puberty, this girl had turned all her desires towards her father. Yet it was precisely at this point that her mother, to whom she was a great rival, managed to get pregnant. Furious at her father's betrayal of her love, she turned away from men as love-objects and instead 'she changed into a man, and took her mother in place of her father as her love object'. The revived mother-love was actually attached to a series of mother-substitutes (at first to mothers of her friends), and in this way by her final blatant attachment to a 'society lady', who was alleged to be both bisexual and promiscuous, she effected her revenge on her father most satisfactorily – he was unduly scandalized by her blatant lesbianism. The revived secondary nature of this homosexuality kept hidden from Freud the significance of the pre-Oedipal mother-attachment. Though he was fully aware of the problem he so to speak misinterpreted it or mis-recognized it.

As with the Wolf Man, Freud's thought in 'A Case of Female Homosexuality' was dominated by the influence of bisexuality on the Oedipus complex – a factor that was already making this 'nucleus of the neuroses' a far more complicated structure than originally postulated. 'In all of us, throughout life, the libido oscillates between male and female objects ...' and as the Wolf Man had unconsciously repressed his femininity, so this young girl had intentionally and consciously assumed her masculinity.[9]

9. We should note, however, that Freud was only finally prepared to designate her *sexual* behaviour 'masculine' (for want of a better term, as he acknowledged); on other issues he took his distance from such descriptions: 'Some of her intellectual attributes also could be connected with masculinity: for instance, her acuteness of comprehension and her lucid objectivity, in so far as she was not dominated by her passion. But these distinctions are conventional rather than scientific.' ('The Psychogenesis of a Case of Homosexuality in a Woman', 1920, S.E., Vol. XVIII, p. 154.)

As we have seen with the Wolf Man, Freud constantly warned against sexualizing repression (repression is the repression of the associated *ideas*, not of sexuality itself) and creating sexual-gender conflict as in any way determinant (rather than possibly illustrative) of-pathological outbreaks. Such an interpretation would be nothing more than a transposition of a kind of vulgar Manichaeism (the great biological antithesis of male and female) to mental life, and despite Freud's supposed preoccupation with dualities, this is *not* what he had in mind.

Freud now 'theorized' the stage to which he had been led in his case-histories. In *The Ego and the Id*, he formulated his new conception of the mental apparatus, as he had done once before in *On Narcissism*. With his new analysis of the nature and structure of the ego, Freud pointed out that: 'The intricacy of the problem is due to two factors: the triangular character of the Oedipus situation and the constitutional bisexuality of each individual.'[10] The coming together of these two theses resulted, as we have glimpsed, in the new notion of the 'inverted' or 'negative' Oedipus complex. What Freud now called a *complete* Oedipus complex (as distinct from his earlier *schematic* concept based almost literally on *Oedipus Rex*) revealed the twofold nature of the situation: the boy would also respond in a feminine way and take his father as his love-object and hence identify with his mother with all the ambivalence of rivalry (e.g., the Wolf Man); so too, sometimes, the girl, after having had to abandon her father as a love-object, identifies with him instead and thus makes 'masculinity' dominant (e.g., Freud's 'Female Homosexual'). At the dissolution of the Oedipus complex, all four possibilities will be represented with varying degrees of strength (that is both parents as objects, both parents taken in identification). But the consequences of this influence of bisexuality on the Oedipus complex are far more important than this mere postulation. Indeed, Freud was not preoccupied with bisexuality in this thesis, but with the formation of the ego.

Reverting, with amplifications, back to the theories of *On Narcissism*, Freud points out how in the very first moments of an infant's life, when it feels at one with the mother's breast, there can be no real distinction between object-love and identification.

10. Freud, *The Ego and the Id*, 1923, S.E., Vol. XIX, p. 31.

But there is first an increasing need for objects to satisfy erotic needs, then there is the necessity of relinquishing these objects – for they are not always present and their possible absence must be recognized. The way in which the love-objects are partially abandoned as love-objects is that they are incorporated into the ego, or self. The ego is thus formed by this setting up of objects inside itself. It is also an important method of identification, so that it can be said that the ego is created by identifications.

The ego, thus forming itself from relinquished love-objects, also, of course, helps to make itself a lovable object – and here we are back at the centre of narcissism. But the identifications with the father or mother that result from the dissolution of the Oedipus complex are not necessarily formed as a sort of compensation for the lost object (though in the negative dimension of the Oedipus complex, they are just this). As the positive Oedipus complex of the boy is shattered, he gives up his *mother* as object, but identifies with his *father* – this new type of identification must be distinguished from the earlier (or simultaneous) ones that replaced a lost object. Freud suggests a new term for it – the 'superego'. The superego stipulates that the boy *must* be like his father, but not *too* like him – i.e. he must not wish to take his place with the mother.

The child's parents, and especially his father, were perceived as the obstacle to a realization of his Oedipus wishes; so his infantile ego fortified itself for the carrying out of the repression by erecting this same obstacle within itself. It borrowed strength to do this, so to speak, from the father, and this loan was an extraordinarily momentous act. The super-ego retains the character of the father, while the more powerful the Oedipus complex was and the more rapidly it succumbed to repression (under the influence of authority, religious teaching, schooling and reading), the stricter will be the domination of the super-ego over the ego later on – in the form of conscience or perhaps of an unconscious sense of guilt.[11]

The earlier identifications were made by a series of 'ego-ideals'. The new Oedipal identification contains the power of the authoritative father, which is the special characteristic of the superego. One gets the feeling in this and similar passages in *The Ego and the Id* that although Freud makes token statements to the effect

11. ibid., pp. 34–5.

that, in reverse, the same is true for the feminine Oedipus complex, he is in fact already half-realizing that this cannot be the case. Though he offers a hesitant footnote elsewhere to substitute 'parents' for father, his choice of the father as the repressive agent here is more than an accident of male bias. As he was soon to realize, it *is* the father and not the two parents who play this particular role.[12]

The superego, formed by a complex identification with the objects to which the libidinal impulses of the id were most attached and the prohibition of these desires, can, though transformed, contain the most strenuous of unconscious impulses. It is its unconscious aspect, its profound relationship to the id and the internal psychical world that it represents, as well as its historic role whereby parental stances and the law of the father are transmitted, that makes the superego the heir to the cultural acquisitions of mankind. The individual ego makes the general human culture his own; he learns thus to be an acceptable human being. And to the question that if it is the id that can be inherited, and yet it is only the individual ego that can reflect the external world, how is culture thus acquired and transmitted, Freud answers that the distinction between ego and id is not rigid (the ego being only a differentiated part of the id), and hence:

The experiences of the ego seem at first to be lost for inheritance; but, when they have been repeated often enough and with sufficient strength in many individuals in successive generations, they transform themselves, so to say, into experiences of the id, the impressions of which are preserved by heredity. Thus in the id, which is capable of being inherited, are harboured residues of the existences of countless egos; and, when the ego forms its super-ego out of the id, it may perhaps only be reviving shapes of former egos and be bringing them to resurrection.[13]

We are each huge and contain multitudes – multitudes in whose names we create ourselves and together with whom we continue

12. Melanie Klein's 'combined parent-figure', though it referred the question to an earlier moment in the child's history (which is also represented by her wish to pre-date the Oedipus complex), misses the significance of Freud's selection of the father which is so crucial for an account of patriarchal culture, or, as Freud would put it, for culture which is patriarchal.

13. ibid., p. 38.

our cultural heritage, passing on to others the way of our lives in the language of our unconscious. The energies of the Oedipal desires will continue in operation in the formation of the superego. Conscience, the sense of guilt, social sense, religion, culture itself, all thus originate for the individual in his specific inheritance of his civilization. Having finally brought to fruition the concept of the superego, Freud realized that the Oedipus complex was with good reason the cornerstone of psychoanalysis – its overcoming was the single most momentous sign of human culture.

The concept of the Oedipus complex needed to be supplemented by the notion of bisexuality for the range and implications of different cross-sexual identifications to be apprehended and the more generalized ego-ideal to become specified as an earlier system of identification which preludes the way to the most significant identification with the Oedipal father and the formation of the superego. One more crucial concept had to be brought into line (or rather, it had always been there, but its import could only be realized by its far closer association with the Oedipus complex): this concept – to prove the turning-point in Freud's final comprehension of the psychological effect of the anatomical distinction between the sexes, and really his last word on the history of human subjecthood – is 'castration'.

7 The Castration Complex

The Freudian concept of the castration complex is one of the most difficult to accept. Integral to the theory there is an explanation for this, but here I only want to raise a few questions about this widespread repudiation.

One of the most common objections made is that, unlike in the nineteenth century, permissive child-rearing nowadays freely allows masturbation and a child is almost never threatened with the cutting off of his penis or offensive hand. But as we have seen in other instances, immediate social reality of this kind is not altogether relevant. The *actual* threat can be absent, but the *idea* of it still there. Furthermore, other factors than a literal threat enter into the castration complex: the anatomical distinction between the sexes and the cultural law of patriarchy play their parts.

While it is common to utterly repudiate Freud's theory of a castration complex and of penis-envy, it is also common to use bowdlerized versions of them in popular psychology. How often is a woman told she wants 'to wear the trousers' (and shouldn't), a man that he is unsure of his masculinity? Our frequent use of these notions calls in question our rejection of Freud's theory, as it was precisely one of the points of the concepts (as of all concepts of psychoanalysis) to get at the meaning behind the common social habit.

The castration complex is the third and intimately related concept that together with bisexuality and the Oedipus complex forms the essential background to Freud's later development of his theories of femininity. It finally marks the psychological distinction between the sexes.

Paradoxically, that most egalitarian of notions – bisexuality – spelt death for the Oedipal equivalence of the sexes, to which Freud had clung so pertinaciously. Hitherto he had thought that the prepubertal differences had been due largely to social conditioning – greater sexual repression and inculcation of shame in little girls. The different love-object, father as opposed to mother, had simply been the other side of the same coin. Castration, threatened in the case of the boy, already consummated or already constituted as a 'lack' in the case of the girl, had always held an important place, but its main accountability was for the inferior regard in which women were socially held. Though all its features were already grasped in the early part of the century, it had somehow remained only loosely connected with the Oedipus complex, to which it was crucial – joined by a rope but not integral to it. In fact, the two concepts only realize their full meaning together.

Although Freud already refers to the significance of the castration-threat in *The Interpretation of Dreams* (1900), he does so outside the context of the Oedipus complex – in fact both are mentioned in that work, solely in the description of their respective Greek myths which are re-lived in contemporary dreams. Zeus, favoured by his mother, and thus able to take revenge on Kronos, his devouring father, emasculated him. As Freud was to point out in *The Psychopathology of Everyday Life*, this is only a partial version – Kronos originally likewise castrated *his* own father, Uranus; however the recent death of Freud's own father and the profound feelings this brought to the surface in Freud, hid this detail of the story. Freud, as his dream of desiring his young daughter Mathilde had already revealed (see page 9 n. above), found it more acceptable to be the father than the incest-desiring or rival-castrating son – as do most men. But Freud was to realize that castration had a place *within* the Oedipal legend, just as it has a place in its daily resurrection in the Oedipus complex: an analysis of dreams demonstrates that blinding is a metaphor for castration; after the discovery of his crime, Oedipus blinds himself as a punishment. The Zeus-Kronos-Uranus myth went to supplement the Oedipus legend in Freud's re-creation of man's phylogenetic and ontogenetic history.

When in 1908 Freud first formulated the 'castration complex' it explained all there was to know about the difference between the sexes – it defined the girl and made the boy abandon his incestuous wish for the mother. The girl felt totally inferior, because she lacked something, and the boy felt temporarily inferior to his more phallically powerful father. The castration complex ended the boy's Oedipus complex and therewith his infancy. It seemed to lie behind all neuroses, to dominate all dreams and perversions, to account for the social inferiorization of women because they were without a penis and for the glorification of men as the proud possessors. Freud then qualified and modified its role – largely in response to Adler giving it primacy as a fundamental organically based 'masculine protest' in which an original deprecation of women and a wish to be a 'real' man are the basis of all future development. Freud criticized Adler for hopelessly confusing the biological, social and psychological meanings of 'masculine' and 'feminine': but from the very strength of his criticism he perhaps stepped overboard when he wrote, 'I know of cases of neuroses in which the "masculine protest" or, as we regard it, the castration complex, plays no pathogenic part, and even fails to appear at all.'[1] Twelve years later in answer to a question from the analyst Dr Edoardo Weiss, then working in Italy, Freud replied:

Your question, in connection with my assertion in my paper on Narcissism, as to whether there are neuroses in which the castration complex plays no part, puts me in an embarrassing position. I no longer recollect what it was I had in mind at the time. Today, it is true, I could not name any neurosis in which this complex is not to be met with, and in any case I should not have written the sentence today. But we know so little of the whole subject that I should prefer not to give a final decision either way.[2]

He continued forcefully to condemn Adler's simplified notion in which castration *on its own* initiated both character development and neurosis; yet ten years later, Freud reasserted its centrality in relation to the all-important Oedipus complex. To say that he 'generalized' the meaning of castration is not to suggest that he loosened it or made it vaguer, rather that he made it more complex. His generalizing only echoed its own function, as a nodal point stretching back and forth from birth to death, summarizing within its instance the totality of loss.

1. Freud, *On Narcissism*, op. cit., pp. 92–3.
2. ibid., editorial footnote, p. 93.

Castration can be pictured on the basis of the daily experience of the faeces being separated from the body or on the basis of losing the mother's breast at weaning. But nothing resembling death can ever have been experienced ... I am therefore inclined to adhere to the view that the fear of death should be regarded as analogous to the fear of castration ...[3]

Castration – or the threat thereof – is, so to speak, the high point of the psychological fear of loss and hence of danger. But before it reached this central role, the concept of castration underwent a number of important vicissitudes. It is as though, as elsewhere, whilst he worked out the full significance of an idea, Freud 'forgot' he had already stated it.[4] In *On the Sexual Theories of Children* (1908) Freud makes the observation that young children attribute to both sexes a penis. At first the boy doesn't believe what he sees – the girl will grow a penis. At this stage, Freud called this 'falsifying perception', later it became the all-important technique of disavowal. The assumed presence of a female penis also acts as a handicap in the child's postulating the presence of the vagina; the strict comparability of genitals that it proposes thus prevents an accurate notion of sexual intercourse. However, reality has to impinge when the boy's own manual masturbation is threatened with punishment. Of course neither the sequence nor the particular occurrence are as significant as the general rule. So, for instance, threatened punishment for masturbation can precede the sight of female genitals – it doesn't matter, *both* must collide for the idea of castration to take hold. And what of the little girl? Just as her sexuality is at this stage phallic (clitoridal) and her attitude active and 'masculine', she must have the same response to the high merits of the penis:

It is easy to observe that little girls fully share their brother's

3. Freud, 'Inhibitions, Symptoms and Anxiety', 1926, S.E., Vol. XX, pp. 129–30.
4. It is for this reason that so many of the theses offered in Freud's letters to Fliess in the nineties seem premature – in many cases it was only at the end of his life that he returned to them and gave them their full import. Castration is no exception – except in that, interestingly, it does not seem to occur in the Fliess letters. Freud himself was also obviously resistant to any acknowledgement of a passive attitude on his own part to another man.

opinion [of the penis]. They develop a great interest in that part of the boy's body. But this interest promptly falls under the sway of envy. They feel themselves unfairly treated. They make attempts to micturate in the posture that is made possible for boys by their possessing a big penis; and when a girl declares that 'she would rather be a boy', we know what deficiency her wish is intended to put right.[5]

Freud wrote his paper on the sexual theories of children commensurately with his work on Little Hans – the child who really provided Freud with the material for this abstract version. Hans thought his mother and his sister Hanna had penises, that boys as well as girls gave birth to babies, anally, and so on. But more importantly, the case of Little Hans is a monument to the importance of castration.

Hans's sexual theories predate the onset of his phobia of horses. By the time this takes place he has accepted that women do not have penises. His phobia is inaugurated by an anxiety-dream in which his mother has left him (over a decade later anxiety and castration are to be profoundly connected in Freud's revised theory of the former). When awake, Hans became frightened to go out for walks and it was found that this was due to a fear of horses which had originated when he saw a horse fall down in the street. The large horse, and another daydream of a big, strong giraffe and a crumpled giraffe were seen to represent his father's superiority and his own defeated (crumpled) strength. In the language of the phobia, his love for his mother was intensified and his fear of his father found expression. We have already seen the implications of the Oedipal love, but with the analytic resolution of Little Hans's animal phobia, Freud stressed the other side of the Oedipus complex in a new and crucial way:

With Hans's last phantasy the anxiety which arose from his castration complex was also overcome, and his painful expectations were given a happier turn. Yes, the Doctor [Hans's mother had threatened he would be the agent of castration to stop Hans's masturbation] *did* come, he *did* take away his penis – but only to give him a bigger one in exchange for it.[6]

5. Freud, '*The Sexual Theories of Children*', 1908, S.E., Vol. IX, p. 218.

6. Freud, 'A Phobia in a Five-Year-Old Boy', op. cit., p. 100.

Here is introduced – unelaborated as yet – the crucial notion that castration bears the transmission of culture. By submitting to its *symbolic* role, the boy learns that one day he will come into his paternal heritage with a bigger and better penis. By realizing that one day he will be a father in his own right, Hans more or less resolves his infantile fear of castration. The Oedipus complex, then, is not the trinity it is so often envisaged as – mother, father, child – but a relationship between four terms of which the fourth and the determinant one is castration. But, again, it was some time before Freud fully realized what he had said.

Death and castration are near-allied, as the 'Rat Man' realized (and as castration's role in the Oedipal situation makes essential). In his consulting-room notes on the 'Rat Man's' obsessional neurosis, Freud records his own confused remembrance of his patient's story of his sister's death. Freud forgot some details as a result of his own complexes.

... once when he was very young and he and his sister were talking about death, she said: 'On my soul, if you die I shall kill myself.' So that in both cases it was a question of his sister's death ... Death was brought close to him, and he really believed that you die if you masturbate ...

Secondly, and this seemed to him far more important, twice in his life, on the occasion of his first copulation (at Trieste) and another time in Munich ... this idea occurred to him afterwards: 'This is a glorious feeling! One might do anything for this – murder one's father for instance!' This made no sense in his case, since his father was already dead.[7]

The Rat Man's phantasy life welds together death, castration, copulation and the role of the father. But with the formulation of the death-drive in *Beyond the Pleasure Principle* (1920), this descriptive account whereby the fear of castration provokes a death-wish took on a new significance: death-wishes against the father (always an aspect of the Oedipal situation) gave way to a more complex association of castration as an indication of death. A new theory of the structure of mental life separates the death-wish already proposed in the letters to Fliess and in *The Interpretation of Dreams* from the death-drive of 1920 and beyond. *The Ego and the Id*, the book in which Freud first

7. Original Record of the Case, S.E., Vol. X, pp. 264–5.

formulates this new schema, gives us a hint of the significance to which the notion of castration had been tending, but which needed the proposition of the death-drive to bring it into being. In this book Freud presents a complicated account of the ego forming itself in a struggle between the demands of two external worlds – the 'real' world outside and the equally real world inside (though external to the ego from which it is formed), the world of drives, demands and needs (the id) and a third world that the ego itself has created from the id in its attempts to deal with it: the superego. Incidentally, for those convinced of Freud's perpetual dualism, this is a very dialectical construct. As it is placed midway between the id and 'reality' and midway between the id and the superego, the ego, while it does its utmost to get into a position of control, is also inevitably in a position of dependence. And now, given the two conflicting drives of the id – the death-drive and the libido – the ego is in further difficulty. As it overcomes the libidinous demands by the processes of identification and sublimation (the formation of the superego), it helps the aggressive urges of the id – but by so doing it becomes, itself, vulnerable to them. The superego (initially, largely the internalized father and the culture he represents) is aggressive; to create it and then to ward off the danger of its creation, the ego has to itself become lovable. (The child from lusting after one or other of its parents has to want to be loved by them.) Thus threatened on all sides, the ego is the originating point of all anxiety. Anxiety is the warning sign of possible danger. The nature of the anxiety that the ego experiences in relation to the superego is what concerns us here:

... we can tell what is hidden behind the ego's dread of the super-ego, the fear of conscience. The superior being, which turned into the ego ideal, once threatened castration, and this dread of castration is probably the nucleus round which the subsequent fear of conscience has gathered; it is this dread that persists as the ear of conscience.[8]

It is not just that one might wish one's father dead and find to one's horror that he has the instrument of execution firm in his superior power, but rather that in the very internalization of powerful authority, the death-drives of one's own id are given

8. *The Ego and the Id*, op. cit., p. 57.

full play. Of necessity one turns one's violence against oneself. Fear of castration, then, leads one to identify with the castrating agent and, with the aid of one's own aggressive drive, incorporate him into one's own personality as an internal authority-figure, a judging superego whose severe criticisms one is then endlessly anxious about.

But the connection between death and castration is tighter still. Fear of death suggests that the ego must have abandoned all its narcissistic self-attachment (here Freud makes a sharp distinction between realistic anxiety – say a bull-charge – and neurotic anxiety as in melancholia, but the same internal mechanism is probably at work). Melancholia, as it had done earlier, may provide a model for 'normality'. The ego feels hated (instead of loved) by its own superego and fears death from it. Living is equivalent to being loved by the superego, and thus being protected by it. As the ego once feared castration from the father, it now again feels an equivalent threat from the superego that was formed out of an identification with him. Freud comments:

These considerations make it possible to regard the fear of death, like the fear of conscience, as a development of the fear of castration. The great significance which the sense of guilt has in the neuroses makes it conceivable that common neurotic anxiety is reinforced in severe cases by the generating of anxiety between the ego and the super-ego (fear of castration, of conscience, of death).[9]

In reformulating his theories about anxiety, Freud, without ever abandoning it, changed not the nature but the connotations and scope of the theory of castration. Anxiety precedes the fear of castration; it is a red-light warning of a possible danger. The first anxiety would seem to be birth. Freud wrote 'Inhibitions, Symptoms and Anxiety', among other reasons, in the effort to sort out his disagreements with Otto Rank's argument that the birth-trauma and not the Oedipus complex was the nucleus of the neuroses. Freud's examination shows that this cannot be the case. A child's anxiety-potential *in*creases, not decreases after birth. Thinking of the obvious instances of childhood anxiety: the dark, being alone, a strange instead of a familiar person, it would seem that the child's fear crystallizes around an absence – that of

9. ibid., pp. 58–9.

the loved and longed-for person. The child is dependent on its mother (or her substitute) for the satisfaction of his needs – her absence means growing internal tension because the needs cannot be satisfied, and the baby is helpless. It is this situation which re-creates or rather creates *a posteriori* the so-called anxiety of birth. The child learns that the presence of the mother can save it from this birth-like danger, hence the loss of her means danger to which the child gives the signal of anxiety, an act of self-preservation as it is intended to prevent her loss. The biological separation of the act of birth is replaced and reinterpreted by the psychical relationship with the mother. But then the baby has to learn to master the absence of the loved and needed object.

Here we can revert to the momentous observation, which Freud had made seven years before, as he had watched a small, preverbal child master the painful situation of its mother's comings and goings by acting out the situation symbolically in play: the child incessantly threw away and then regained a cotton-reel, uttering each time 'da' (there), 'fort' (gone). The anxiety caused by the mother going can be resolved by understanding that she will come back (the immensely significant gain of comprehending *absence* is, for the moment, another issue). The point is that this anxiety does *not* (any more than does the anxiety of birth), involve socially unacceptable ideas. On the other hand, the incestuous desire for the mother that then arises *does* involve the forbidden. Now, anxiety comes into play to suggest fear of castration if these incestuous ideas are not abandoned. Anxious that he will suffer castration from his father, if he does not give up his desires for his mother, the little boy represses the idea of incest. If the castration complex is not adequately resolved – and that means if the possibility of castration is not *symbolically* accepted, then the Oedipus complex is not shattered and aspects of its irresolution will recur in later neurosis. Little Hans finally 'resolved' his castration complex in a paradigmatical way by realizing that he would one day be heir to his father's rights, if he gave up his own desires in the infantile present. If symbolic castration is accepted, and the Oedipus complex thus dissolved, the next stage of anxiety must be fear of the superego, which has replaced the threatening father. Again this anxiety is normal, and only in its exaggerated forms neurotic. In the right degree it amounts to socially correct moral anxiety.

With the depersonalization of the parental agency from which castration was feared, the danger becomes less defined. Castration anxiety develops into moral anxiety – social anxiety – and it is not so easy now to know what the anxiety is about.[10]

The anxiety here only relates to the superego which on the resolution of the Oedipus complex replaces the previously over-loved and over-feared parents. Later, additions will be made to it from their more generalized social representatives – teachers, preachers, policemen ... The superego, later, re-projected on to various agents of destiny, becomes the ultimate expression of 'normal' anxiety, the fear of loss of love, of ultimate punishment – fear for life, death. The superego threatens its own ego, from which it in part arose.

Once again this chronological presentation obscures the fact that, though there is a developmental aspect, each anxiety can coexist, change order (backwards or forwards), persist, elicit responses appropriate to a later or earlier situation and so on. But of all these anxieties it is the castration fear that lies deep at the heart of the resolution of the Oedipus complex; despite his new theories of anxiety, it therefore retains its primacy in Freud's theories of man's mental life.

The concept of castration is the link between narcissism and the Oedipus complex. In the move from auto-eroticism to object-love, the phallus, which symbolizes the ability to connect with the loved object (the mother), is the bridge. The threat to the phallus is, therefore, the greatest threat to the ego's narcissism and it is the greatest threat to the child's object-relations. Fear of castration is thus both pre-Oedipal *and* the cause of the end of the Oedipus complex. We shall see how, in the case of the girl, the pre-Oedipal recognition of castration is all-important, and how, in the case of the boy, the heir of the patriarchal law, it is the acceptance of symbolic castration which ends the Oedipus complex that is crucial.

Freud explicitly referred to the fear of castration as a 'primal phantasy'; but its twofold nature made him reflect on it in ways

10. Freud, 'Inhibitions, Symptoms and Anxiety', op. cit., p. 139.

that can seem contradictory. Thus in *On Narcissism* Freud claims that the castration complex cannot be determinate of neuroses but later he stresses its centrality in precisely this role. The difference is that the later reference places castration in the context of the Oedipus complex and the earlier one refers to its pre-Oedipal narcissistic significance alone. Little Hans provided a model of a resolved castration complex; many are not so successful. In his last writings Freud stressed that an unresolved castration complex was the greatest of all obstacles to a full therapeutic 'cure'. An inadequate acceptance of symbolic castration is evidence of an inadequately dissolved Oedipus complex. The attempts made to stave off acknowledgement of castration take a number of forms: two of these are fetishism and 'doubling' (reduplication of an image). The theories are both crucial for Freud's later work on the psychological distinction between the sexes.

In *The Interpretation of Dreams* Freud records dreams in which a doubling or multiplication of a frequent symbol for the penis indicates an effort to ward off the fear of castration. (We can see the significance of this for women, as dreams of a repeated number of children – 'little ones' – are given the same import.) Much later, Freud detects this mechanism as an underlying cause of the 'uncanny' sensations produced by notions of one's double. It is also the primal fear that lies behind the anxiety attached to losing other organs (hands, eyes, teeth, etc.) and its exploitation in these and other disguised forms can again – in fiction – be used to create scaring and 'uncanny' impressions. Many phantasies of castration converge on the mythological symbol of Medusa's head. But from our point of view, the most fruitful single theme that Freud investigated under this rubric at this time was fetishism.

There were certain issues whose refutation mattered to Freud. Though the centrality of the idea of castration took longer to be established than other concepts of commensurate importance, doubts cast on it called forth strong responses from Freud. Thus in one footnote he sarcastically comments on the triumph of oversight that therapists who claim never to have noticed it have achieved. His theory of fetishism was also some time in the making, in that though its crucial aspects are pinpointed quite early, the synthesis comes only in 1927 – and it is re-deployed fascinatingly in 'The Splitting of the Ego' in 1938. The theory had the incidental value of 'proving' castration:

> An investigation of fetishism is strongly recommended to anyone who still doubts the existence of the castration complex or who can still believe that fright at the sight of the female genital has some other ground – for instance, that it is derived from a supposed recollection of the trauma of birth.[11]

The instance of fetishism indicates (as does, incidentally, that of the Medusa's head) the other dimension of the castration complex: fear of the mother, or rather of the mother's genitals – that first proof that castration can occur. The fright sustained by this shock is too much for some to recognize, so they disavow the sight of their own eyes or ears, if someone is trying to tell them about it. Instead of acknowledging this evidence of castration they set up a fetish which substitutes for the missing phallus of the woman, but in doing this fetishists have their cake and eat it: they both recognize that women are castrated and deny it, so the fetish is treated with affection and hostility, it represents the *absence* of the phallus and in itself, by its very existence, asserts the *presence* of it. Instead of accepting the possibility of symbolic castration – with hopes of bigger and better things to come – the young boy disavows the possibility of its occurrence by denying what he has perceived of women's genitals and thereby keeps his own penis safe for his own use – his masturbation can continue unhampered. The fetishist displaces the valued object to another part of the body. The symptoms that result from the creation of a fetish bear witness to the fact that the boy does indeed know of castration, yet simultaneously does not. There is always this oscillation between disavowal and acknow-ledgement; the ego has split itself as a means of defence, but somewhere, somehow, even here the fear of castration seems to break through, expressed in one or other symptom.

There is, of course, an alternative way of not resolving the castration complex: the choice of homosexuality, the result of an inhibition at the Oedipal stage. This is the development of a feminine position – by men. Senatspräsident Schreber (whose

11. Freud, 'Fetishism', S.E., Vol. XXI, 1927, p. 155.

autobiography Freud analysed) had phantasies of becoming a woman on whom God could beget a new world, he thus provided a full picture of this feminine predicament. The 'negative' aspect of the Oedipus conflict – the boy's love for his father – here predominated and God (who replaced the father) was to carry out the action – that is, the castration (the making into a woman) that was indispensable for this love to be realized (Schreber referred to this act as 'soul-murder'):

> Senatspräsident Schreber found the way to recovery when he decided to give up his resistance to castration and to accommodate himself to the feminine role cast for him by God. After this, he became lucid and calm, was able to put through his own discharge from the asylum and led a normal life – with the one exception that he devoted some hours every day to the cultivation of his femaleness, of whose gradual advance towards the goal determined by God he remained convinced.[12]

Instead of waiting, like Little Hans, for big things to come, Schreber opted to accept not the symbolic possibility of castration, but the supposed *actual* castration (in phantasy) that is the mark of femininity. Unlike Judge Schreber, the Wolf Man found the knowledge of women's apparent castration an unsustainable blow to his passive love for his father – he had violently to suppress his feminine attitude towards men. The active form of the Oedipus complex and the inverted (passive) one can both come to grief through the castration complex.

Thus the choices for men are: fetishism, acknowledged or denied homosexuality, or – 'manhood', which is itself only a makeshift resolution of the other possibilities, all of which are contained within it.

Acceptance of the possibility of castration is the boy's path to normal manhood. The practice of circumcision – a watered-down version of castration – was the acknowledgement the Jews made, at Moses' behest, to the power of God, the Father. They agreed to wait, bowing to His Supremacy; they would be the chosen people, bearing the mark of His Power, accepting castration temporarily, for better things to come. But there is, inevitably,

12. Freud, 'A Seventeenth-Century Demonological Neurosis', S.E., Vol. XIX, 1923 (1922), p. 92.

another implication to their choice: as, in some way castrated unlike other males, they are feared and despised – like women.

Castration, or rather the reaction to the idea of it, comes to be the crucial dividing line between the sexes:

... while the child is at the highest point of its infantile sexual development, a genital organization of a sort is established; but only the male genitals play a part in it, and the female ones remain undiscovered ... *At this stage the contrast between the sexes is not stated in terms of 'male' or 'female' but of 'possessing a penis' or 'castrated'*. The *castration complex* which arises in this connection is of the profoundest importance in the formation alike of character and of neuroses [first italics, mine].[13]

From the point at which boys and girls were more or less alike until puberty (except for the effects of social pressures), back through the notion of their parallel Oedipus complexes, Freud has now moved to an assertion of a crucial difference at the very centre of the ego as it makes and takes up its place in the world. The moment of this difference is the castration complex.

At the phallic stage, the girl realizes she is without the phallus and proceeds to envy it. The boy, seeing the female's lack, fears the possible loss of his own. This is the distinguishing moment between the sexes. Made to feel *originally* deprived, through what seems like a fault in nature, not, like other deprivations, a culturally demanded necessity, the woman bases her future demands on this lack no less than the man denigrates her because of it. She becomes – through penis envy – envious as though 'by nature'; she demands privileges and exemptions ('pedestal treatment') to compensate her for her supposed biological inadequacy. The 'masculine' clitoris is abandoned as inferior and must not be reactivated at puberty, it must 'pass on' its sensitivity to the previously unawakened vagina – the preeminently 'feminine' genital, the centre of receptivity and reproduction. As this transference from the clitoris to the vagina often fails to work, and as, in any case, the path to womanhood seems to offer few social attractions, many women hanker back to their clitoridal days, or, in their envious way, want to be men.

13. Freud, 'An Autobiographical Study', S.E., Vol. XX, 1925, p. 37.

Freud was quite clear that, though the loss of the breast in weaning or the giving-up of faeces in toilet-training foreshadowed castration in that they accustomed the child to deprivations, they were not, as some analysts suggested, to be equated with it. As we shall see later, Freud gave a number of reasons for the value attached to the phallus – here it is only the effect of that value that concerns us. Having incorporated it into the concept of narcissism – its ownership is crucial to the nature of the ego being formed, or rather its loss would be an immense blow for the narcissistic ego – Freud had to recognize the distinction between the sexes in this respect. This recognition, and the diverse role of the castration complex, led him, in the second half of the twenties and the thirties to a reassessment of the Oedipus complex and from there to the development of his theories of femininity and the pre-Oedipal, narcissistic stage.

The castration complex and the Oedipus complex were finally welded together in a short paper: 'The Dissolution of the Oedipus Complex' (1924). Freud opened this article with the statement that though the Oedipus complex had long been known to dissolve and that this inaugurated the latency period and ended the first phase of mankind's unique diphasic sexuality, yet the cause of its dissolution had hitherto been inadequately appreciated within the theories of psychoanalysis. The cause of that dissolution, he now asserted, was the danger of castration. Neither the punitive threat of castration (actual or imagined), nor the previous weaning or toilet-training are adequate to make the boy realize the dangers that ensue from desiring his mother; only the sight of female genitals can bring into operation the idea of the castration that was already feared. (This time-lag between the narcissistic valuation of, and hence fear for, the genitals, and the later castration complex activated at the moment of the Oedipal crisis, Freud designates a 'deferred' effect.) The idea of castration shatters both the negative *and* positive aspects of his Oedipus complex – to want his mother means getting rid of his rivalrous father, who proves to be more powerful and a castrator to boot; to want to *be* his mother and hence win his father's love likewise means being, like her, castrated: 'both [attitudes] entailed the loss of his penis – the masculine one as a resulting punishment and the feminine one as a precondition'.[14] So, in 'ideal' cases, narcissism triumphs, the penis is retained and the Oedipal desires thoroughly put down – for the time being or hopefully 'for ever'. The difference between 'time being' and 'for ever' is the difference between inadequate repression and the successful destruction of the complex and hence is the difference between the normal and the pathological. Of course, the former is only an ideal and the Oedipus complex is never utterly or entirely disposed of.

At first the little girl just thinks she personally has done rather badly – later on her clitoris will grow. In other words she, too, accepts that her mother is phallic. Gradually she has to accept the applicability of castration to all females – of which she is one. Just as with the boy, this must bring to an end her sexual object-love for her mother. But at this point, Freud was still a bit confused or confusing as to what happened, when it happened and how it happened – and he acknowledged as much. So before we examine the importance of this necessarily different response to the same situation – the castration complex – within the terms of its differential effect on the Oedipus complex and hence on the psychological meaning of the distinction between the sexes, let us look for a last moment at some of the consequences of castration-acceptance itself.

The fear of castration in boys is expressed as an outburst of anxiety on the part of the ego (this is often contained in animal phobias, such as that of 'Little Hans'). In fending off the forbidden libidinal desires of the Oedipus phase, the ego, threatened by castration, may disavow them or institute a regression to an earlier, pre-phallic phase, or it may undertake massive acts of repressing the drive and, in doing so, will to some extent desexualize itself (the latency period) *and* partially suppress the very activity which is definitional of masculinity. At this point, having so-to-speak nearly established it, Freud wrote,

14. Freud, 'The Dissolution of the Oedipus Complex', S.E., Vol. XIX, 1924, p. 176. (The editors of the Standard Edition say that this paper is only an elaboration of some passages in *The Ego and the Id*; but that is not strictly correct, for it is really in this paper that for the first time Freud brings indissolubly together the castration and Oedipus complexes.)

. . . is it absolutely certain that fear of castration is the only motive force of repression (or defence)? If we think of the neuroses in women we are bound to doubt it. For though we can with certainty establish in them the presence of a castration *complex*, we can hardly speak with propriety of castration *anxiety* where castration has already taken place.[15]

But a full utilization of his account of anxiety went on to take care of this dilemma; as we have seen, there are various related reasons for the production of anxiety, all to do with separation. Birth ('There is much more continuity between intra-uterine life and earliest infancy than the impressive caesura of the act of birth would have us believe')[16] is a separation from the mother with whom the infant is as one, then there is the object-loss of the mother in her temporary absences in infancy (the '*da*' and '*fort*' of the cotton-reel game), then the fear of the loss of the phallus, the response to which is the latency period. (Each anxiety can overlap, persist, be given up or coexist.) In 'normal' women the middle position (that is, fear of object-loss, though, of course, 'phallicized' with the entry into the Oedipus complex) seems to have held most sway or been reverted to; just as it has in cases of hysteria, in contradistinction to obsessional neurosis which is so strongly linked to the last phase – castration anxiety. Freud, always preoccupied by what he called the 'choice of neurosis', made this all-important connection between hysteria and femininity:

It is precisely in women that the danger-situation of loss of object seems to have remained the most effective. All we need to do is to make a slight modification in our description of their determinant of anxiety, in the sense that it is no longer a matter of feeling the want of, or actually losing the object itself, but of losing the object's love. Since there is no doubt that hysteria has a strong affinity with femininity, just as obsessional neurosis has with masculinity, it appears probable that, as a determinant of anxiety, loss of love plays much the same part in hysteria as the threat of castration does in phobias and fear of the super-ego in obsessional neurosis.[17]

With this suggestion of the 'femininity' of hysteria, Freud returns to his earliest case-studies, the women whose fears, dreams

15. Freud, 'Inhibitions, Symptoms and Anxiety', op. cit., p. 123.
16. ibid., p. 138.   17. ibid., p. 143.

and phantasies he first listened to with Breuer in the eighties and nineties. At that time prevalent medical opinion held that only women were hysterics, but, following Charcot, Freud denied that. He never needed to reverse his opinion, or rather it became so obviously incorrect as never again to need his refutation. But in showing how bisexuality could find psychological responses of a masculine or feminine nature, in both men and women, he nevertheless found hysteria a 'feminine' neurosis. Women are supposed to be feminine, but this gives them no more exclusive rights over hysteria than it does over femininity.

Freud:
The Making of a Lady, II

8 The Castration Complex and Penis-Envy

The question of the path to 'normal' womanhood, just as of that to 'normal' manhood, subsumes the specific subject of female sexuality, which is nevertheless clearly a crucial part of it. In its turn the issue of clitoral or vaginal orgasm, which has become a focal point of the repudiation of Freudian psychoanalysis, is really only a very small part of the whole question of female sexuality.

At the outset, all infants believe that everyone has a penis, and the girl that hers will grow. The boy discovers the fear of castration through threats to his masturbatory practices and through the disappearance of the penis in coition if he witnesses it, but more importantly at the sight of female genitals – or rather, as it seems to him, at the sight of the absence of them. The girl only has to look at herself. The apparent absence will never return, the lack cannot be made good, and, hence, because this is a *real* (not phantasied) situation, it cannot finally constitute either an absence or a lack. But castration, and the different meaning of it for the two sexes, is the crucial concept. By this point – not necessarily in time, but in mind – the infant in our society is inserted in the nucleus of its family: itself, its mother and its father. The boy and the girl who both thought all had a penis, who both were attached to the mother as the only important 'other', must part ways, never to coincide again except in neurosis or psychosis, except in perversions, and except in all those perpetual neurotic, psychotic and perverse moments that lie behind normality. In these moments there is unleashed an aspect of the psychological sex one might have been were it not for culture's interpretation of the different places to be assigned to the two sexes.

On the plane of object-attachment, the boy as he enters into his phallic heritage can at first preserve the mother as the

focus of his lust. The girl must shift from her mother-attachment to a sexual desire for the father. This interprets what
seems to be her biological fate. Having only a clitoris, she can
no more physiologically possess her mother than culturally she
must ever be allowed to wish to do so; although, hitherto, like
the boy, she has clearly wanted to with full 'virile' aggression,
just as the boy (though he has neither womb nor vagina) has
wanted to be possessed by the mother, bearing her a child.
This is pre-Oedipally, when, because sexual roles are in no
way fixed, all variations and permutations of sexual phantasies
with the mother are available to both sexes alike. The father,
if he enters at all, is a 'troublesome rival', no more. To the
Oedipal boy he continues to be a rival, to the girl he must
become the loved one. She makes the shift from mother-love to
father-love only because she has to, and then with pain and protest. She has to, because she is without the phallus. No phallus,
no power – except those winning ways of getting one. Recognition
of her 'castration' is the female infant's entry to girlhood, just as
acceptance of the threat and deference to the father in exchange
for later possibilities is the boy's debt to his future manhood. The
girl's entry into her feminine 'destiny' is characterized by
hostility to the mother for her failure to make her a boy; it is
an entry marked by penis-envy, that in its turn must be
repressed or transformed. Accepting castration means not only
acknowledging the lack of the phallus, but, out of disappointment, abandoning the inferior clitoris as a source of sexual
satisfaction. Luckily, in response to this predicament, because
she must also repress the desire for incest, at this point the
child's sexuality has to go underground to a greater or lesser
extent, to re-emerge at puberty for a fresh start. After her
recognition of castration, the girl has three courses open to her,
only one of which is 'normal'. With her self-love already shattered by her 'lack', her hostility to the mother (who was supposed
to be phallic but who was discovered to be likewise castrated) can
make her turn away from women and womanhood altogether; in
which case, debasing and despising women, as men do, she is
liable to become inhibited and neurotic. Or she can refuse to
abandon the pleasures of her clitoris; if so, she remains at the
pre-Oedipal 'masculine' phase. Finally, if by exploiting 'her

passive instinctual impulses' – that is, the passive aims of her sexual drive – she can transfer her sexual attentions from her mother to her father, she can want first his phallus, and then by the all-important analogy, his baby, then the man again, to give her this baby. Thus she becomes a little woman. This transference from mother to father is the girl's 'positive' Oedipus complex and, as it is the first correct step on her path to womanhood, there is no need for her to leave it. She can with impunity continue to love her father and hate her mother as a rival, especially as these emotions are 'desexualized' with the latency period. That her mother as rival is stronger than the little girl does not seem to matter much, because she has no absolute strength and the girl has nothing to lose. But the little boy fears the father who is his rival for his mother's love, because the father is truly powerful and potent and the boy has just that potency to lose. So while the girl can linger secure in this phase for life, the boy must leave it quickly, before, like Oedipus, he is blinded (castrated) for killing his father and copulating with his mother. Such is his power that he must lose it in order to keep it, for the future and for his sons' sons.

Freud's suggestion of the girl's supposed envy for the penis pre-dated its being brought into line with the Oedipus complex, just as did the whole notion of castration. Even in 1916 Freud talks of the 'Richard III' in all of us, our resentment for wounds to self-love, for not being born with a golden spoon, for being without super-brains or beauty or some other aspects of Nature's or man's bounty and, he concludes, there is one general instance of people being born with the crippled, deformed King Richard's winter of discontent:

... we may point out that the claim of women to privileges and to exemption from so many of the importunities of life rests upon the same foundation. As we learn from psycho-analytic work, women regard themselves as having been damaged in infancy, as having been undeservedly cut short of something and unfairly treated; and the embitterment of so many daughters against their mother derives, ultimately, from the reproach against her of having brought them into the world as women instead of as men.[1]

1. Freud, 'Some Character-Types Met with in Psycho-Analytic Work', 1916, S.E., Vol. XIV, p. 315.

But so far this notion of penis-envy is contained within the concept of narcissism, and though this perspective was not to change, its implications were to become more far-reaching as Freud's work developed.

The drawing of the castration complex into line with the Oedipus complex brought the realization of the psychological differences between the sexes to a head. In a narcissistic moment the girl merely hopes that later she will have a penis, or that her clitoris will grow – she is not content to think her own fate of being sold short is anything other than temporary. If she doesn't abandon this conviction, then she will develop what has popularly become known as a 'masculinity complex' in later years. Or she may see her castration as a specific punishment meted out to her alone, but not, as yet, as in any way a sex characteristic. The castration complex for the girl thus comes to mean the repressed ideas that surround the acceptance, or failure of acceptance, of castration as a sex characteristic – to this situation Freud applied the term 'penis-envy'. However, the girl's *acceptance* (failed or achieved) as opposed to the boy's initial *fear* of castration has important differential consequences:

The fear of castration being thus excluded in the little girl, a powerful motive also drops out for the setting-up of a super-ego and for the breaking-off of the infantile genital organization. In her, far more than in the boy, these changes seem to be the result of upbringing and of intimidation from outside which threatens her with a loss of love. The girl's Oedipus complex is much simpler than that of the small bearer of the penis; in my experience, it seldom goes beyond the taking of her mother's place and the adopting of a feminine attitude towards her father.[2]

Freud was soon to abandon this notion of a hopeful simplicity. After all, it does beg an inordinate number of questions. The only conclusion of 'The Dissolution of the Oedipus Complex' was to establish the high probability (though even here Freud stipulates the need for further discussion) of the role of castration in putting an end to the boy's Oedipal desires. And though he did further develop his concept of penis-envy, what he says about the girl is as yet speculation. However, already here Freud proposed that

2. Freud, 'The Dissolution of the Oedipus Complex', op. cit., p. 178.

because the girl does not have to internalize, to the same degree, a powerful and punitive father, her own superego, with all that implies for authority, conscience, sublimation and so on, will, of necessity be weaker.

The primary clitoral and penile masturbation of the sucking infant seems not to have any specific psychical connotations, but already, *before* the object-relations of the Oedipus complex set in, the relative value of the two 'phalluses' seems to have made its mark – at least for girls.

The psychical consequences of envy for the penis, in so far as it does not become absorbed in the reaction-formation of the masculinity complex, are various and far-reaching. After a woman has become aware of the wound to her narcissism, she develops, like a scar, a sense of inferiority.[3]

There seems no way out of it – either she must go on wanting one, or deny that there is any difference, or accept the situation and its psychical consequences of inferiority. Even if, in all humility, she takes the latter course, the displaced penis-envy has yet more important consequences than this for the development of femininity. The sense of the inferiority of the clitoris inaugurates a wave of repression – masturbation is usually absolutely renounced, as the girl does not want to be reminded of her sense of humiliation. In Freud's account, the distinction between the sexes has thus moved back from puberty to the Oedipus complex and now to the pre-Oedipal situation. Castration in the context of the Oedipal situation takes precedence as its psychical determinant.

Where the castration complex shatters the boy's Oedipus complex, it inaugurates the girl's, as in despair and despite she turns from the mother to the father:

Thus in women the Oedipus complex is the end-result of a fairly lengthy development. It is not destroyed, but created, by the influence of castration; it escapes the strongly hostile influences which, in the male, have a destructive effect on it, and indeed it is all too often not surmounted by the female at all. For this reason, too, the cultural consequences of its break-up are smaller and of less importance in

3. Freud, 'Some Psychical Consequences of the Anatomical Distinction Between the Sexes', op. cit., p. 253.

her. We should probably not be wrong in saying that it is this difference in the reciprocal relation between the Oedipus and the castration complex which gives its special stamp to the character of females as social beings.[4]

In other words, it was only when he had seen castration in the light of the boy's Oedipus complex that Freud was able finally to drop his analogous proposition for the two sexes and at last propose the groundwork of the distinction.

4. Freud, 'Female Sexuality', op. cit., p. 230.

9 Faeces–Penis–Baby

The girl's entry into her Oedipal attachment to the father and away from her pre-Oedipal mother, which is the result of her castration complex, takes place along the line of what Freud calls the equation 'faeces – penis – baby'. It is often this notion, of all others, that gives most offence (*vide* Kate Millett). In the repudiation of the suggestion we have evidence that the strongest opposition to Freud's theories of femininity are made no more solely on the grounds of his male-chauvinist stance than early objections to his work were made solely on the grounds of his scandalous imputation of infantile sexuality: both oppositions have buried within them a strong protest against the fact of an unconscious mind. Here we have an example of how nearly all cases of relentlessly hostile criticism, though paying nominal tribute to Freud's 'discovery', deny it in their subsequent analyses. For, as I said earlier, here as elsewhere it is with the manner of the working of the unconscious that we are concerned in this equation.

It is perhaps easiest to get at the matter in further detail by the way that Freud got at it, through dreams – though obviously only his conclusions can be indicated. Behind the manifest dream-content there lies the latent content composed of largely preconscious thoughts to which the dreamer can reach through his associations. But there is always an absolutely unconscious element – an aspect of the drive's representation, thirsting for satisfaction; it is the unconscious drive that produces the psychical energy for the dream's construction. The strength of the person's resistance may make this for ever inaccessible, but most often, by a breakdown of the structure and composition of the dream, part of it can eventually be reached. But because the representation of the drive, for instance, a person's wishes, can only find satisfaction within the state of sleep, certain conditions determine the nature of its expression. The dream thoughts are transformed into visual and sensory images and in the course of this process, the linguistic habits of consciousness are abandoned, 'just as in a primitive language without any grammar, only the raw material of thought is expressed and abstract terms are taken back to the concrete ones that are at their basis'.[1] Instead of all the devices of conscious language, symbols play an immense part in the language of the unconscious. Everything appears compressed and condensed: 'Such of those elements as allow any point of contact to be found between them are *condensed* into new unities'[2] – one element may thus stand for many, or vice versa. Another important feature that Freud describes he labels 'displacement': here the affect or emotions, from one idea can be displaced on to another and altered out of all immediate recognition:

> Thus something that played only a minor part in the dream-thoughts seems to be pushed into the foreground in the dream as the main thing, while, on the contrary, what was the essence of the dream-thoughts finds only passing and indistinct representation in the dream.[3]

It is this process that is chiefly responsible for the strangeness of the dream.

The structure of dreams, the royal road to the unconscious, was soon confirmed by studies of parapraxis, slips of tongue and pen, jokes and wit. The language of the primary process is symbolic, it makes use of condensation, displacement and symbolization and all may occur concurrently, as they do in the instance we are now considering. Children believe that babies are born anally, like faeces: the straining, the release, the production of something new out of oneself is a prototype of birth. The faeces produced for the mother, or whoever cares

---

1. Freud, *New Introductory Lectures on Psychoanalysis*, 1933 (1932), 'Revision of the Theory of Dreams', S.E., Vol. XXII, p. 20. What Freud is describing here are the workings of unconscious thought-processes, not of a systematic mental region 'The Unconscious' – for after *The Ego and the Id* Freud always stated that large parts of the ego and superego could also be unconscious.

2. ibid., p. 20.   3. ibid., p. 21.

for the child, are offered as a gift, from here one train of 'thought' leads to an equation with money, but another to a reconfirmation of the production of a baby which is also always 'given', a gift ('he's *given* her a child', 'she's *given* him a son'). At the same time the faeces, a column that stimulates the membranes of the bowel, is – in psychic terms – a forerunner of the penis – and, unfortunately, like the faeces, the penis is also thought to be a part of the body that can be lost, given up, renounced (castration). (The penis also inherits the feelings the infant had for the mother's nipple.) Elsewhere, Freud mentions a common return to this infantile thesis in the case of a manic woman who will lead a visiting doctor to her excrement and claim it as the baby she has produced that day. On this whole area of symbolization Freud comments:

> If one is not aware of these profound connections, it is impossible to find one's way about in the phantasies of human beings, in their associations, influenced as they are by the unconscious, and in their symptomatic language. Faeces – money – gift – baby – penis are treated there as though they meant the same thing, and they are represented too by the same symbols.[4]

Such symbolization is not peculiar to girls – the mechanisms of the unconscious processes are not sex-determined; it is that such symbolization is *made use of* by girls in their progress towards femininity. (It was no less useful to Senatspräsident Schreber.)

On the other hand, another example of it can show how necessary is its exploitation for the achievement of womanhood. In *The Interpretation of Dreams*, Freud records the interpretation a patient gives of her own dream:

> She recollected having once seen her father naked in the bathroom from behind; she went on to talk of the distinctions between the sexes, and laid stress on the fact that a man's genitals can be seen even from behind but a woman's cannot. In this connection she herself interpreted 'the little one' as meaning the genitals and 'her little one' – she had a four-year-old daughter – as her own genitals.[5]

The equivalence and interchangeability in unconscious thought

4. Freud, Lecture XXXII, 'Anxiety and Instinctual Life', *New Introductory Lectures on Psychoanalysis*, p. 101.
5. Freud, *The Interpretation of Dreams*, 1900, S.E., Vol. V, p. 363.

of faeces – penis – baby can then be seen in the linguistic utterances of everyday life and of dreams: a penis and a baby are both spoken of as 'a little one'. (Would this perhaps explain the extra tinge of indecency that seems to be attached to the sexual innuendo of the marital well-wishing, 'May all your worries be little ones'?) Freud makes a further comment to account for such instances as the meaning of the woman's dream, just mentioned:

> It is a well-known fact that symbolic speech often ignores difference of sex. The 'little one', which originally meant the male genital organ, may thus have acquired a secondary application to the female genitals.[6]

The little girl, having at least tried to give up her wish for a penis, will nevertheless continue to want it as a gift of a 'little one' first from her father, then later from her husband. It is at this point that another of Freud's contentions enters in: only the birth of a male child really gives the woman the penis she is longing for, and, less importantly, a woman will probably only be content with her marriage (as distinct from her maternity) when she can come to mother her husband and turn him into her 'little one' too.

6. Freud, 'On Transformations of Instinct as Exemplified in Anal Erotism', 1917, S.E., Vol. XVII, pp. 128–9.

10 The Clitoris and the Vagina

Despite the controversy that was rife in psychoanalytic circles in the twenties and thirties, Freud held to his belief that the vagina was only, in the majority of cases, discovered for what it was at puberty. In 1924 Karl Abraham wrote to Freud:

I have for a long time questioned whether the displacement from the clitoris to the vagina could have occurred in an earlier version though in an inverse direction . . . This assumed sexual stage would have to have as a sexual aim the reception of the penis . . . Two neurotic symptoms have forced me to assume something which we could call an early vaginal-anal stage: frigidity and *vaginismus*. In the light of all my psycho-analytic experience, I cannot believe that frigidity is merely based on the failure of the libido to pass from the clitoris to the vagina. There must be a prohibition which has an immediate and local basis; this is even more valid for *vaginismus*.[1]

Freud had the greatest respect for Abraham's work, and on this issue (with which Abraham was much concerned) acknowledged his own greater ignorance. But when he came to write on the matter (Abraham had meanwhile died), Freud was still unconvinced.

There is an obvious reason for Freud's assertion of general infantile ignorance of the vagina – other than the absence of its presence in the repressed memories of his patients. If every evidence goes to prove that the child at one stage believes in the universal presence of the phallus, the hypothesis of the vagina is neither called for nor compatible. One of Freud's last words on the subject was not really his – it comes in a paper by Ruth Mack Brunswick, the development of which was aided and approved by Freud although in fact it was not published until shortly after his death:

1. 26 December 1924. *A Psychoanalytic Dialogue*, The Hogarth Press, London, 1965, pp. 377–8.

The vagina, as we know, derives its sensitivity primarily from the clitoris and secondarily from the anus. It has become a question whether, as heretofore stated, the vagina is always, or even usually, a 'silent organ' until adolescence. It now seems probable that an early vaginal sensitivity of anal origin frequently exists ... Needless to say even when such vaginal sensitivity exists, its role is decidedly minor and secondary to that of the clitoris as the organ of the infantile sexuality.[2]

But the correction of earlier suppositions here referred to is only partial, for there are two questions at stake: the physical sensitivity of the vagina and the psychological acknowledgement of it. Of course, the two are connected – if the little girl engages in vaginal masturbation she must in some sense be aware of the vagina's existence. But it is worth separating out the issue because the two are frequently so confused in repudiations of the inverted Freudian assertion. By 'inverted', I mean that what concerned Freud and early analytical writers on the subject was: does the infant know of the vagina? Whereas what concerns present-day opposition is: why on earth should a girl ever give up her clitoris for her vagina? In this reversal, the erotogeneous sensitivity of the vagina and its psychological consequences have got inextricably mingled.

Freud never thought that the clitoris became automatically physiologically desensitized. Its stimulation could play a preparatory role in sexual intercourse, but if all sexual interest remained focused on it, then the vagina was likely to remain anaesthetic and the 'clitoridal' woman would have no wish for penile penetration. So the 'normal' woman must transfer the sensitivity of her clitoris to her vagina. In a way there is really little difference in the basic position of Freud and his opposition – the distinction lies more in the imputed values and the refusal to realize that Freud is talking about a psychological process. Freud confessed to ignorance of the full cause of frigidity. But the characteristic feature of frigidity is the absence of vaginal orgasm – the achievement of this orgasm may require stimulation of the clitoris, but can, according to Masters and Johnson,

2. Ruth Mack Brunswick, 'The Pre-Oedipal Phase of the Libido Development', 1940, reprinted in *The Psycho-analytic Reader*, ed. R. Fliess, The Hogarth Press, London, 1950, p. 247.

be seen to be pelvic contractions that affect the whole body. Orgasm can also occur under the influence of phantasies. A clitoridal woman is one who gets an orgasm solely from the stimulation of the clitoris and wants nothing else. Freud thought the later importance of the clitoris infinitely variable but that clitoridal sex alone indicated an arrestation of the development of femininity; to some feminists it indicates an independence of men. You can put it whichever way you like, the opposition only lies within the value judgement. Now, Freud may, for all we know, have favoured receptive 'feminine' women in his private life, but in his writings all he is indicating is the path prescribed for 'normal' womanhood. Like it or not, vaginal receptivity is still regarded as indicative of this feminine normality. We are back once more with the danger of reading Freud's descriptions as prescriptions; it is often the fault of his method of presentation that makes us do so. It is far more the fault of the social status of women.

There are, of course, more questions buried within the issue than this one. In Freud's theory, the development of femininity *depends* on the early suppression of the clitoris, and his theory of the psychical consequences of bisexuality *depends* on clitoral activity in the phallic phase and on ignorance of the vagina. That does not, of course, mean that he wouldn't have abandoned these notions if evidence had proved them untenable or if the logic of ideas had failed to confirm them.

The pre-Oedipal girl abandons her mother as love-object under the influence of her sense of the ultimate inferiority of her clitoris. At the same time, she is likely to give up her clitoris too – that is to say her manual masturbation of it. She wants nothing to remind her of the wound to her narcissism – neither her all-responsible, 'castrated' mother, nor her own 'little penis'. The two go together. The girl realizes that she cannot possess her mother, hence the clitoris loses its active connotations, and when its sensitivity re-emerges at puberty it is likely to be in a masturbatory role with passive aims, no longer expressing the thrusting urge that the pre-Oedipal girl shared with the boy, but now either auto-erotic or as a preliminary to vaginal penetration. When the very young girl renounces the masturbation of her clitoris, she therefore also gives up a part of her active *aims*. If the repression is not too great the new dominance of passive aims will help a transition from the active wanting of her mother to the passive aim of wanting to be wanted by her father. The progress of a lady then involves a transition from the pre-Oedipal dominance of the active clitoris to the pubescent and adult dominance of the vagina to which the re-awakened clitoris conveys its sensitivity. There is nothing chemical or biological in this transition – at least not that Freud knew or cared about – the question is one of a psychological shift to the 'destiny' of wifehood and maternity.

The transference from the clitoris to the vagina which aids and abets the coming to dominance of the passive aims for the furtherance of femininity is a tricky process, as Freud never tired of stressing. It is tightly bound up with the second change demanded of the one-day-to-be woman: the shift from mother-love to father-love.

11 The Pre-Oedipal Mother and the Oedipal Father

To revert to Freud's archaeological metaphor, Greek culture, or the making of a man, stood in the way of analytical discovery of an earlier layer of civilization – the Minoan-Mycenean pre-Oedipal phase so crucial for femininity. Of course boys and girls share this early period, but the implications of it are different for each sex – altered by the Greek superstructure which obscured it for analysis as it did for history. The Oedipus complex which can almost be said to stand for the structure of patriarchal culture, hid the pre-Oedipal phase, as Freud, a male analyst, echoing in his way the ways of the culture, obscured the role of the mother for his women patients. Greek civilization dominates in this analytical set-up, so that the mother-attachment, that most decisive of factors, was late in being discovered by Freud. He explained thus the difficulty he had in unearthing the 'Minoan-Mycenaean' relics:

> Everything in the sphere of this first attachment to the mother seemed to me so difficult to grasp in analysis – so grey with age and shadowy and almost impossible to revivify – that it was as if it had succumbed to an especially inexorable repression. But perhaps I gained this impression because the women who were in analysis with me were able to cling to the very attachment to the father in which they had taken refuge from the early phase that was in question.[1]

Women analysts, Freud contended, should have better luck as their patients are liable to transfer some of this mother-attachment to them. Freud's own observations are therefore only of a generalizing nature.

The girl's share in Greek culture is represented by her Oedipus complex – her devotion to her father – but it is only a secondary formation. The region behind it Freud refers to as 'prehistory',

1. Freud, 'Female Sexuality', op. cit., p. 226.

and with good reason, even if Minoan-Mycenaean civilization is a culture entirely in its own right. History starts with the Oedipus complex, or rather with its overcoming and the inauguration of structured language that accompanies it; that is to say it starts with patriarchal civilization, the 'Greeks', within which the girl is supposed to learn the meaning of her femininity, as the boy of his masculinity. The prehistoric or pre-Oedipal period nevertheless permeates and influences the Oedipal phase in a way that must make us resist any temptation to see these as clearly demarcated, temporarily distinct phases; it is rather, as in its archaeological analogy, a rough-and-ready overlaying of the one by the other. But in the case of the boy, the two are far more compatible. The distinction between them could avoid perception because here the 'Greeks' just took over and built on the strength of their Minoan-Mycenaean predecessors. But for women Greek history represented a massive defeat, and it will be at their peril that their prehistory, though it will be always in evidence, will continue to dominate in their lives. All its values must be abandoned or thoroughly displaced on to the new Oedipal possibilities, the overcoming of which thus constitutes the girl's heritage of her feminine place in the world. Concretely, this means that the boy's Oedipal situation is nothing more than an intensification of his pre-Oedipal mother-love. In the Oedipus situation he finds that the place he always imagined himself to occupy is instead his to succeed to – one day. What is important is that he should *overcome* the Oedipal position with his acceptance of symbolic castration and enter into the promise of his patriarchal heritage. The girl's Oedipal situation is a complete displacement of her mother-attachment on to her father. And as with all displacements, what has been displaced remains highly vocal. The distinction between the girl's pre-Oedipal and Oedipal periods is thus what counts, and the strength of the former, though denied by the latter, is visible at every turn – either because the girl has hung on to it and remained a 'masculine' woman or because she has denied it and the supremacy of her 'excessive' femininity is witness to the effort it cost.

From the time of his awareness of the importance of the pre-Oedipal mother onwards, Freud realized how this all-powerful

figure underlay most of the girl's phantasies in relation both to
the father and to his later substitutes, such as the husband. Both
sexes concentrate all their earliest attention on the mother:
whether in identifying with her activities in repetitious play,
such as acting out the mother's behaviour towards themselves,
with dolls, or in actively taking her as the object of their desires.
The boy gives up the latter only to the father's superior powers,
the girl gives it up because of her absolutely, not relatively,
inferior condition. The realization that she is like her mother,
'castrated', makes her turn often violently against her. But at
the 'best' her hostility can only repress the attachment, and
what is repressed is always liable to return, or find itself merely
disguised in the new attachment. Thus behind every girl's love
for the father, there lurks her love for the mother; for every
'normal' woman who chooses her husband on the acceptable
model of her father, the difficulties that ensue are just as likely
to echo those that arose with the love and hate for the mother.
The father, so crucial for the development of femininity, and
the men that follow him, so essential for the preservation of
'normal' womanhood, are only secondary figures, for pride of
place as love-object is taken by the mother – for both sexes.

In both sexes, castration is the signal to give up the mother –
but for the boy only so that he should wait for his turn and in
good time get his own woman; for the girl acceptance of 'castration' indicates that she should become *like* her mother. The
overcoming of the Oedipus complex of both is a sign to start
identifying finally with the parent of the same sex – so that
society can go on accordingly. The *confirmation* of his first love-
object for the boy *which is his Oedipus complex* is renounced till
he grows up like his father whom he meanwhile internalizes
as his superego by identification. The *contradiction* of her first
love-object for the girl, *which is her Oedipus complex*, never
really need be renounced, for that is her feminine destiny. She
may feel some rivalry with the mother for the father, but its
strength will not be commensurate with the boy's rivalry with
the father for the mother because, in a sense, the father is only
second-best anyway, and furthermore, how much point is there
in competing with another one of the same 'castrated' sex?
Identifying with and thus to some degree internalizing the

mother does not provide for the formation of a strong superego, for it is not she who, in a patriarchal culture, ever has the final word.

In the pre-Oedipal period, identification and attachment jostle one another for pride of place in the relationship with the mother – the girl must build on her identifications, the boy on his attachment. In order to displace her active desire for her mother on to her father, the little girl must identify with her mother and stress her passive aims. She is helped to do this by the fact that she has had to put into operation an act of massive repression – the burial of the Minoan-Mycenaean civilization. But the truth will out. The *combined* force of the pre-Oedipal desires and of their repression, in differing proportions, make their mark on the woman's future. The strength of the pre-Oedipal period in girls, which is so loud in its protests only because it is so fiercely denied, and within which occurs her recognition of her 'castration', predisposes the woman to a particularly feminine type of neurosis (hysteria); as the Oedipus and castration complexes predispose men to their brand of neurosis (obsessionality). At least in Western society, obsessionality is closely linked to excessive rationality, a quality that is valued – the description 'hysterical' is invariably derogatory. Of course, there is *no* absolute dividing line: men, too, have a pre-Oedipal period which can make itself felt, they can go through the Oedipus complex, or come out of it, in a way more typically feminine and vice versa. We are talking here of the production of typicality, of 'ideality'.

12 The Marks of Womanhood

(i) Masochism

A recurrent dream or phantasy found in both men and women proved to have different meanings for the two sexes. The content of this was the pleasurable phantasy that a child was being beaten; the climax of the phantasy is usually accompanied by masturbation. This phantasy can be traced back to its occurrence in early childhood. Freud's analysis revealed that at one particular moment one particular type of sexual desire has been separated off from others and is receiving satisfaction on its own – it is hence an important source of the understanding of perversions. The phantasies assume many and changing forms. To start with, in *girls* the child being beaten is another child, usually a brother or sister – this is expressed as 'my father is beating the child'; then a second and crucial phase takes over – 'I am being beaten by my father.' The sadism of the first phase gratifies the girl's jealousy, that of the second her sense of guilt (it is thus an important index of masochism). In this phase the phantasy is both the punishment for the forbidden gratification and, by repression, the satisfaction of it. The last phase is once more sadistic and the object another child, usually a boy. This phase, in fact, blocks out all memories of the second phase. (In boys the process is different and what emerges is a wish to be put in a feminine, passive relationship to a punishing father.) In girls, the phantasy is a neat expression of the transition from active, clitoral sexuality to a desire for incest with the father:

The peculiar rigidity which struck me so much in the monotonous formula 'a child is being beaten' can probably be interpreted in a special way. The child which is being beaten (or caressed) may ultimately be nothing more nor less than the clitoris itself, so that at its very lowest level the statement will contain a confession of masturbation, which has remained attached to the content of the formula from its beginning in the phallic phase till later life.[1]

The second phase, which is never conscious and is only reconstructed in analysis, refers to a satisfactory consummation of the Oedipal attachment to the father with all the pleasure and guilt that that implies. The whole phantasy expresses the pains, forbidden pleasures and difficulties of the positive Oedipus complex for girls, which, being unresolved along the path of 'normal' femininity, thus burst through: 'People who harbour phantasies of this kind develop a special sensitiveness and irritability towards anyone whom they can include in the class of fathers.'[2] The dreams also proved to be for Freud a valuable source of a new theory of masochism and of its particular relevance, along with jealousy, for the mental life of women.

The beating phantasy shows the presence of clitoral masturbation, the nature of the desire for the father and the violent repression which the girl's infantile sexuality has undergone. Implicit within the second phase is the masochism to which the child's original sadism is likely to be converted as a concomitant aspect of the shift from mother-attachment to father-attachment. 'Masochism' – pleasure in pain – which is the turning against the self of the wish for the satisfaction of a drive, typifies the feminine predicament. It expresses the wish to submit to castration, copulation or childbirth and to get erotic pleasure out of painful experiences. But feminine masochism is of course inherent within both sexes.

In his fullest discussion of masochism, Freud divided it into three types: erotogenic, feminine and moral – the first underlies the second two. The third is the most complex and is largely unconscious; the second is the easiest to perceive and it is consequently with this 'feminine' masochism that Freud starts his discussion. His references all pertain to men. The masochist, in the extreme versions that explain the underlying content, wants to be in a female situation. Behind 'moral' masochism, too, is the wish to be punished by the father which is close to the wish to

1. Freud, 'Some Psychical Consequences of the Anatomical Distinction between the Sexes', op. cit., p. 254.

2. Freud, '"A Child is Being Beaten." A Contribution to the Study of the Origin of Sexual Perversions', 1919, S.E., Vol. XVII, p. 195.

have a passive (feminine) sexual relation with him. In this case the masochism has only apparently lost its erotogenic content, for it has formed an alliance with the internalized father's sadistic representative – the superego. Sadism is turned back against the self when aggression is allowed no outlet. The conscience and morality that the superego brings into play show, in masochism, all too clearly their origin in the sexual Oedipus complex. The subject is complicated, but for our purposes here, we need to note one thing: in the phantasy life of men and women, the female situation of 'castration', passive intercourse with an aggressive father (or his replacements) and childbirth all suggest pleasure-in-pain. Masochism is 'feminine' in whichever sex it occurs.

(ii) Passivity

The proverbial passivity of women is really quite a simple issue. At first both sexes are identical in the sense that their drives have both active and passive aims. Of this period, Freud clearly said that though it was possible to give descriptions of sex-typed characteristics, these 'sexual differences are not, however, of great consequence: they can be outweighed by individual variations'.[3] With the end of the pre-Oedipal attachment to the mother for the girl and the end of the Oedipus complex for the boy, the psychological recognition of the sexual differences consists of, on the one hand, being 'castrated' and on the other of fearing castration. In order to enter into her Oedipal desire for her father the girl has to salvage what is left of her sexual drive and devote it, most actively, to this passive aim of being loved. The boy and the girl could now be said to be distinguished by the preponderance in the one of active aims and in the other of passive aims. Throughout the greater part of his working life, Freud found the vocabulary of active/passive inadequate and the distinction of masculine/feminine merely conventional.[4] Though this, of course, is not at all the same thing as saying that there

3. Freud, *New Introductory Lectures*, op. cit., Lecture XXXIII, 'Femininity', p. 117.
4. It seems worth quoting now in full the passage that expresses most clearly Freud's dissatisfaction with these terms. 'We are accustomed to employ "masculine" and "feminine" as mental

are not important differences in the psychological formation of the sexes.

(iii) *Vanity, Jealousy and a Limited Sense of Justice*

Attendant on the transition from an active mother-attachment to a mother identification and the passive aim of father-attachment is the narcissistic wish to be loved rather than to love. Caught out, too, at the height of the narcissistic phase in the enforced recognition of her inferior clitoris, a woman compensates for the great hurt by making her whole body into a proud substitute. She has to develop her threatened narcissism in order to make herself loved and adored. Vanity thy name is woman.

We have already seen how a greater sense of jealousy seems to result from the woman's envy of the penis, and this envy has a

---

qualities as well [as biological ones], and have in the same way transferred the notion of bisexuality to mental life. Thus we speak of a person, whether male or female, as behaving in a masculine way in one connection and in a feminine way in another. But you will soon perceive that this is only giving way to anatomy or to convention. You cannot give the concepts of "masculine" and "feminine" *any* new connotations. The distinction is not a psychological one; when you say "masculine", you usually mean "active", and when you say "feminine", you usually mean "passive". Now it is true that a relation of the kind exists. The male sex-cell is actively mobile and searches out the female one, and the latter, the ovum, is immobile and waits passively. This behaviour of the elementary sexual organisms is indeed a model for the conduct of sexual individuals during intercourse. The male pursues the female for the purpose of sexual union, seizes hold of her and penetrates into her. But by this you have precisely reduced the characteristic of masculinity to the factor of aggressiveness so far as psychology is concerned. You may well doubt whether you have gained any real advantage from this when you reflect that in some classes of animals the females are the stronger and more aggressive and the male is active only in the single act of sexual union. This is so, for instance, with the spiders. Even the functions of rearing and caring for the young, which strike us as feminine *par excellence*, are not invariably attached to the female sex in animals. In quite high species we find that the sexes share the task of caring for the young between them or even that the male alone devotes himself to it. Even in the sphere of human sexual life you soon see how inadequate it is to make masculine behaviour coincide with activity and feminine with passivity. A mother is active in every sense towards her child; the act of lactation itself may equally be described as the further consequence. The demand for justice, for things to be 'fair', is a modification of envy and one, therefore, that women are less able to make. More importantly, the fact that there is no pressing need for them to put an end to their Oedipal relationship with their father means that women do not have to shatter this complex by a massive act of identification with a powerful figure, thus they do not have so powerful a superego. Less of a superego, less of a capacity for sublimation, less social sense; though this is clearly the fate of psychological femininity, it should also be noticed how frequently Freud refers all these qualities to the influence of 'social custom', 'social conditions', 'matters of convention' and so on. The demands of human culture as such (which to Freud is patriarchal) and the particular patriarchal society interlock.

The situation adds up to the fact that the shock of her lack, her 'castration', and the end of her pre-Oedipal mother-love forces the little girl to *take refuge* in the Oedipus complex. Exactly contrary to the experience of the boy, it is a haven from the castration complex, a love nest in which the girl can gain the love she requires by winsome flirtation and pretty ways.

---

mother suckling the baby or as her being sucked by it. The further you go from the narrow sexual sphere the more obvious will the "error of superimposition" [mistaking two different things for a single one] become. Women can display great activity in various directions, men are not able to live in company with their own kind unless they develop a large amount of passive adaptability. If you now tell me that these facts go to prove precisely that both men and women are bisexual in the psychological sense, I shall conclude that you have decided in your own minds to make "active" coincide with "masculine" and "passive" with "feminine". But I advise you against it. It seems to me to serve no useful purpose and adds nothing to our knowledge.

One might consider characterizing femininity psychologically as giving preference to passive aims. This is not, of course, the same thing as passivity; to achieve a passive aim may call for a large amount of activity. It is perhaps the case that in a woman, on the basis of her share in the sexual function, a preference for passive behaviour and passive aims is carried over into her life to a greater or lesser extent, in proportion to the limits, restricted or far-reaching, within which her sexual life thus serves as a model. But we must beware in this of underestimating the influence of social customs, which similarly force women into passive situations.' (ibid., pp. 114–16).

In this request for love, the little girl partly remains; in general as a woman, this world of the family is the world she will represent. We should note that, despite the conventional saying, love makes the world stand still:

> We also regard women as weaker in their social interests and as having less capacity for sublimating their instincts than men. The former is no doubt derived from the dissocial quality which unquestionably characterizes all sexual relations. Lovers find sufficiency in each other, and families too resist inclusion in more comprehensive associations.[5]

The woman's task is to *reproduce* society, the man's to go on and *produce* new developments. There is an obvious link between the security of Oedipal father-love and the happy hearth and home of later years. But, before and after, much stands in the way.

(iv) The True Woman and the Alternatives

The pre-Oedipal identification and a secondary affectionate attachment to the mother after she has relinquished the full strength of her Oedipal desire for her father and her hostility to her mother, is crucial for the girl's development of her femininity; during this first phase,

> preparations are made for the acquisition of the characteristics with which she will later fulfil her role in the sexual function and perform her invaluable social tasks. It is in this identification too that she acquires her attractiveness to a man, whose Oedipus attachment to his mother it kindles into passion.[6]

This identification with her mother (so pleasing for the man and so useful for the patriarchal status-quo!) can be confirmed by what is allowed to remain of the girl's passive Oedipal love for her father – but even in this ideal stereotype for the development of womanhood there lurk the dangers for the man which are inherent in loving the second sex. Freud goes on to comment how this 'Oedipal' husband, loving his mother reincarnated in his wife, finds that only his son is really granted the love to which he aspires. With the birth of a son, the two strands of the woman's early sexual desires can come together, she can *be* the

5. ibid., p. 134.　　　　6. ibid., p. 134.

mother she loved and identified with, and have the phallus (now the son) that she so envied.

The man, as second comer, may, from the most 'feminine' of women, find he receives his share of both the hostility and attachment to the mother that precedes him. For often the strongest attachment to the father and his heirs is an indication only of denial of an over-strong mother-attachment. Or, alternatively, it can be the glorification of narcissism so that a man is chosen according to the type the woman would like to have been. These are things a man stands in danger of from a truly feminine woman.

Then there are the various alternatives to the tortuous path to womanhood itself. There is the relatively straightforward road of a retention of the original mother-attachment, which will probably emerge as later lesbianism; or an undisguised penis-envy in the emulation of male pursuits.

The ambitious and the 'perverse' women share the same heritage of retaining intact the Minoan-Mycenaean civilization – a love for the pre-Oedipal mother on the one hand, and on the other a wish for the male phallus. But the 'normal' woman, too, conceals behind her femininity the same two factors. In all types of women, the two-tiered structure – the civilization of Minos-Mycenae and that of the superimposed Greeks makes itself felt in one way or another. Behind everyone there is a woman – the mother, both for the boy and the girl, the man and the woman. Or, as Freud preferred to put it, bisexuality is stronger in women than in men – because the little girl always has two love objects, her mother and then her father, the little boy only one. But human culture subjects all, including the primacy of this mother-attachment, to the law of the father in whose name the boy and the girl take up their different destinies.

That is all I had to say to you about femininity. It is certainly incomplete and fragmentary and does not always sound friendly . . . If you want to know more about femininity, inquire from your own experiences of life, or turn to the poets, or wait until science can give you deeper and more coherent information.[7]

7. ibid., p. 135.

Freud, the Freudians and the Psychology of Women

In 1931, in his essay 'Female Sexuality', Freud made reference to eight recent articles written by his colleagues on the question of female psychology. Although Karen Horney and Helene Deutsch went on to write further studies, and Clara Thompson and Marie Bonaparte, who had not participated in the earlier years of the debate, came to join them with their own books on the subject, it is, I think, fair to say, that the inter-war period and in particular the decade from the mid twenties to the mid thirties saw the crystallization of two opposite positions, and that within psychoanalysis little momentous on this question has been added since.

Whether it is further evidence of the 'phallocentrism' that Ernest Jones condemned in Freud or not, most discussions of the debate in subsequent psychoanalytic literature refer to it as the Jones–Freud controversy. In fact Jones's position was, on his admission, really an amalgamated re-statement of the different theories arrived at by Karen Horney and Melanie Klein. Perhaps the reason is that it was Jones who undertook to expound the differences between what he saw as the diverse positions of the English and Viennese schools. Always a good ambassador, he in some ways managed to obscure the significance of the difference. In fact the inter-war conflict over the meaning of femininity never led to any split within the movement such as had been occasioned by the earlier dissensions with Stekel, Adler and Jung. Clearly by this point the psychoanalytic movement was so widespread within various countries that, although centralized control versus national autonomy was a point to be recurringly argued over, in reality diversity was a condition of growth and no disagreements could produce the fruitful intensity of the early days when concepts had to be fought for and defended within a tiny circle of theorists and practitioners. Perhaps, in addition, the nature of the subject was not felt to be so worth fighting over? Be that as it may, the fact is that though real differences were aired, these were left to sag back into comfortable non-resolution: psychoanalysts just begged to differ and femininity went its inadequately analysed way.

Freud first referred to the problem (as he saw it) of women's transference from clitoral to vaginal sensitivity or the pubertal 'awaking' of the vagina in a letter to Fliess in 1897: but this turned out to be one of those numerous occasions in which we find Freud mentioning something in this correspondence which he takes up only years later, and with apparent novelty. The *Three Essays on Sexuality*, published in 1905, made little play with the distinction between the sexes, but the introduction of this theme could be said to be a distinguishing feature of the footnotes and additions Freud made to the text in 1915 and 1920, and by 1920 there seems to have been growing up a general interest in the subject among analysts. The editors of the Standard Edition suggest that the later work was triggered off by Freud's 1925 essay 'Some Psychical Consequences of the Anatomical Distinction Between the Sexes' (his first *directly* on the subject). But even if we leave out the accumulation of female case-histories, this is to ignore the fertile irritant provided by Adler's reduction of all psychic motivation to 'masculine protest', and (relevantly here), the truly reciprocal exchange of ideas between Karl Abraham and Freud. In fact, a great part of the subsequent literature on femininity should be read as an exchange of ideas: one essay provoked another.

As Van Ophuijsens' 1917 essay, 'Contributions to the Masculinity Complex in Women', was only published in 1924, Abraham's 'Manifestations of the Female Castration Complex' (written 1919, published 1922) can be said to inaugurate the debate. From 1909 onwards, letters between Freud and Abraham reveal their common interest in psychological questions of femininity and male attitudes to it: they discuss fetishism, castration, the relationship of the child to the parent of the same sex; Abraham was particularly concerned with what was to become known as the pre-Oedipal period – so essential for femininity – because he was working on the closely related questions of paranoia, megalomania and schizophrenia. Freud had been estranged from Fliess for ten years, but he now recommended Abraham to go and see him in Berlin where both Fliess and Abraham were living. This encounter may have resurrected dormant thoughts of subjects that had interested Freud years before.[1] In itself, Abraham's article on the female castration complex was a response, on the grounds both of theory and of his own clinical practice, to certain ideas put forward by Freud in *The Taboo on Virginity* (1918). In 1931, when Abraham was long dead, Freud singled out this essay of his as 'unsurpassed'.

As are all the male analysts writing on this subject in this period (Freud included), Abraham is implicitly and explicitly concerned with the claims made by the contemporary women's movement: the wish for sexual parity Abraham regards as one (but, note, a non-neurotic one) of the manifestations of the castration complex in women. Starting from the observation that at some time in their lives all women want to be men, and feeling sure that the social advantages that are claimed would accrue from such a shift, are rationalizations, Abraham sets out to seek a psychological explanation. I will give just a brief resumé of this complex and seminal paper.[2] Much of it will be familiar, for some of it builds directly on Freud and some of it Freud incorporated in his later work. The girl's initial high estimation of her body is shattered by her sense of mutilation (castration) when, at a time when a child is jealous of all possessions, she finds she has no penis; this notion of a wound is confirmed by menstruation and defloration (hence female hostility to the latter act). But here Abraham makes what I believe is the first *full* play within this context of the notion of the gift. Love and the gift are inextricably associated: the

1. I am, of course, referring here to the possible resurrection of concepts and topics that were to become associated with Freud's theory of femininity; but the fact that Freud talks to Abraham of the grain of truth in Fliess's theory of periodicity, and that this grain some years later was to be massively developed into his own notion of the 'compulsion to repeat', would seem to support the more general likelihood.

2. This is a simplification of a simplification, for Abraham stressed that he had isolated one theme at the expense of others: ideas and symptoms are overdetermined and he has selected one aspect for clarity's sake.

mother gives the first gift of milk; the child then repays this by giving its mother its faeces ('now give Mummy a lovely big one'); but 'giving' also suggests taking away: the boy thinks he might have to give up his penis as he has his faeces, but, contrarily, the girl thinks that she can make herself a penis as she has made her faeces or that someone might give her one as a gift. Here we have spelled out the metaphorical equation faeces=gift =penis. (The two different translations of Abraham's article both use the word 'motion' but I have substituted the more familiar 'faeces' to indicate the similarity between Freud's and Abraham's idea.) When, however, the girl finds she can neither grow a penis nor be given one, she extends the equation to what she can both grow and be 'given' – a child; she now envies her mother her children and wants her father to give her one. Both the envy of the mother and desire for the father must be sublimated, but the wish for a child retained if 'normal' femininity is to be acquired. The castration complex need have no ultimately disturbing effect; non-neurotic femininity can be assumed by a cultivation of passive trends as a revenge for the absent penis, or the original bisexuality or 'masculinity' can be re-attained in which case the woman will deny that there is any significant meaning to the difference between the sexes (this last choice, Abraham saw reflected in the women's movement). If such conscious solutions are not adopted then the problems of the repressed castration complex will return with all the force of the unconscious – the wish for a penis or for revenge against men and a refusal of a female role will be expressed in diverse symptoms. Abraham cites as instances the desire to urinate (envy of ejaculation and micturition) in intercourse; and the fixed stare in which the eyes stand for the erect penis: the woman tries to terrify by the sight of a phantasized phallus much as does the male exhibitionist by the sight of the actual one. On the other hand, the penis unconsciously can be denied any importance, as in phantasies of immaculate conception – or revenge and counter-castration can be expressed in various types of frigidity or in prick-teasing and a preference for wounded men (who, like women, are also mutilated). Extreme femininity is a further neurotic non-resolution of the castration complex – wanting to be an adored beauty so as to be able to reject men, or exaggerating the female sexual role of receptivity by turning the tables – keeping the man waiting on all possible occasions. The castration complex can be resolved in diverse ways, or repressed and then return in various symptoms; fundamental is the concept of the absent penis and the substitute gift. Crucial, too, is that Abraham, like Freud, stresses the presence of these female passive desires in both men and women. Abraham is discussing the ideas people have and the symptoms they display; he is reconstructing the infantile past from the adult's words and bodily symptoms.

In 1924 Karen Horney in 'On the Genesis of the Castration Complex in Women', took up the cudgels on behalf of women in an explicit response to Abraham's paper whose theses she first summarizes. To Horney male chauvinism ('masculine narcissism') is responsible for the unquestioned assumption that women feel their genitals to be inferior. The supposition that 'one half of the human race is discontented with the sex assigned to it and can overcome this discontent only in favourable circumstances – is decidedly unsatisfying, not only to feminine narcissism but also to biological science'.[3] Her first task is to see whether, if there is dissatisfaction on the part of women, there is good reason for it. As in analytical literature on women the castration complex has come to signify penis-envy, it is this conflation of terms that she will investigate. Karen Horney first turns her attention to what she thinks can strictly be described only as penis-envy, not as castration. Little girls want to urinate like a man because (a) the jet of urine suggests power, omnipotence, (b) it satisfies scopophiliac urges as the man can *see* his genitals, (c) it facilitates masturbation. The woman with her hidden genitals has nothing to display (hence she later displays her whole body) and she is liable to turn inward on herself in greater subjectivity. To Horney, these are *real* circumstances:

... *as an actual fact*, from the point of view of a child at this stage of development, little girls *are* at a disadvantage compared with boys in respect of certain possibilities of gratification. For unless we are quite

3. Karen Horney, 'On the Genesis of the Castration Complex in Women', *International Journal of Psycho-Analysis*, V, 1924. Reprinted in Horney, *Feminine Psychology*, Routledge & Kegan Paul, London, 1967, p. 38.

clear about the *reality* of this disadvantage we shall not understand that penis-envy is an almost inevitable phenomenon in the life of female children, and one that cannot but complicate female development.[4]

This is the first stage: a biological handicap compounded by social reality. But, Karen Horney asks, can we reduce the castration complex to this envy of the penis? In her theory the little girl, rightly fed-up with her bio-social lot, proceeds to identify with her like-fated mother and take her father as love-object. At first the father would seem to reciprocate, respond to and encourage the little girl's seductions, but then he rejects her: this rejection is the second and crucial phase of the castration complex. It has nothing to do with penis-envy, but rather with a little girl's phantasy of a father's rape and his subsequent rejection of her. Forced to renounce her love for her father – and along with it her womanly wish for a baby – the little girl identifies with him instead and regresses to her pregenital phase when realistic penis-envy was dominant. Her feelings about him (and all subsequent men) will retain simultaneously a remnant of love, a vehement wish for revenge and disappointment at having been turned down and a good deal of guilt on account of her incestuous desires. In her very womanhood (her feminine heterosexual love) the girl is castrated – raped and rejected.

The theoretical difference between Abraham and Horney is important, but so, too, is something that has happened to the terminology of the debate. In the Abraham–Freud thesis, penis-envy, which is the feminine equivalent of the castration complex, is an experience through which all must pass; as a concept it is neutral. Horney in taking it up has treated it as a reproach; she is at pains in this paper to show that 'normal' women experience it too, and that it is quite realistic of them to do so. Abraham and Freud's position accords with this: the difference between the disputants has become one of *moral imputation*. This moral distinction has been conveyed to us down the decades, and the theoretical disagreement has been forgotten.

Helene Deutsch's 'The Psychology of Woman in Relation to the Functions of Reproduction', written the same year and published the next (1925) amplified ideas on the psychology of

4. ibid., p. 42.

women in coitus and reproduction and did not add or alter the terms of the theoretical dispute. Deutsch's work fitted roughly into the framework of the Abraham–Freud thesis. But again something has happened to the tone and implications. Deutsch's analysis is a prescription for normal womanhood: femininity has become identified only with the female and masculinity with the male. Based like Horney's opposite theories on notions of biology and reality, Deutsch's account has become redolent with normative morality. Libido has become biological: 'as a zone of active energy the clitoris lacks the abundant energy of the penis; even in the most intense masturbatory activity it cannot arrogate to itself such a measure of libido as does the latter organ.'[5] The presence of the masculine clitoris is 'unfortunate', 'inner secretions' help to divert attention away from it, the clitoris is anyway inferior 'in reality'. I think the distasteful psychologizing to which Deutsch is prone has obscured this underlying biologism; it is this latter which in my opinion produces the former: 'I even assume that the act of parturition contains the acme of sexual pleasure owing to the relief from stimulation by the germ-plasm.'[6]

Later the same year, in their correspondence, Abraham and Freud were again discussing female sexuality. Abraham was making a case for early vaginal sensations in the little girl – Freud was dubious but keenly interested. Six months later he had 'written a few short papers, but they are not meant very seriously'.[7] One of these was 'Some Psychical Consequences of the Anatomical

5. H. Deutsch, 'The Psychology of Woman in Relation to the Functions of Reproduction', 1925, *International Journal of Psychoanalysis*. Reprinted in *The Psycho-analytic Reader*, op. cit., p. 168.
6. ibid., p. 172.
7. *A Psycho-Analytic Dialogue: Letters of Sigmund Freud and Karl Abraham, 1907–1926*, op. cit., letter of 21 July 1925, p. 391. Two months before he wrote these papers, Freud confided to Lou Andreas-Salomé: '. . . Otherwise existence is still bearable. I even think I have discovered something fundamental for our work, which I am going to keep to myself for a while. It is a discovery of which one ought almost to be ashamed, for one should have divined these connections from the beginning and not after 30 years. One more proof of the fallibility of human nature.' 10 May 1925, *Letters of Sigmund Freud, 1873–1939*, op. cit., p. 362. I can discover no knowledge or even speculation as to what Freud was referring; we might merely note that though these

Distinction Between the Sexes'. Both Abraham and Freud were certainly interested in anatomy, but the stress was clearly on the *psychic representation* of this. Freud's paper provoked Ernest Jones to a polite questioning on the origin and structure of the superego, a contribution which really had only an indirect bearing on the subject of sexual-psychological difference, though it interestingly reinforces the preoccupation with questions of responses to external reality. But Karen Horney, responding to both Freud's and Deutsch's contributions, takes her early thesis a stage further by stressing the envy of reproduction evidenced by boys – this notion was to become the main thrust of her further work. In this paper, 'The Flight from Womanhood: the Masculinity Complex in Women as Viewed by Men and Women', 1926, she strengthens her contention that psychoanalytic theories of femininity are male phantasies, by reference to George Simmel's philosophical position that 'our whole civilization is a masculine civilization'. The male analyst, she claims, theorizes about women much as the little boy speculates about the little girl, and women submit to being this receptacle of masculine phantasy – often against their true nature. Worthy as were Horney's intentions, correct as were her assertions that women were not *actually* inferior but subject to a masculine civilization, nothing could have been more disastrous for the future of the psychoanalysis of women than this call to a 'true nature'. Most of Karen Horney's important references to the social subordination of women are rendered pointless by this implicit and explicit search for the essential woman. In this instance, as in others, there is nothing neither true nor false but thinking makes it so, and if patriarchal thought is dominant then femininity will reflect that system: 'nature' is not exempt from its representation in mental life.

---

three papers were by no means the most important he was still to write, subsequent ones (if we except the problematic brief and incomplete 'splitting of the ego') did not contain any radically new ideas.

At the two momentous points in connection with Freud's work on the issues that I have singled out as crucial for the development of his theories on femininity (narcissism and the female Oedipus complex) though Freud rejected a number of Abraham's specific ideas, yet the latter's work clearly acted as a catalyst.

The following year Jeanne Lampl de Groot offered a lucid summary, largely from within the Freudian perspective, though she offered one correction that was to assume considerable importance: she, too, stressed that the castration complex in girls was a secondary formation and that its precursor was what she termed the 'negative Oedipus complex'. This negative Oedipus complex or pre-Oedipal phase, already of course referred to, but not elaborated in Freud's work, was to become the centre point of future work and of future controversy. Melanie Klein[8] was to take the work furthest, but meanwhile the disagreement on the psychological distinction between the sexes had settled into a rut from which it never really freed itself.

Horney and Jones believed that the biological division of the sexes was directly reflected in the mental life of each sex. Quite realistically either sex may envy the other what she or he lacks: the girl envies the penis which suggests power and instant sexual gratification; the boy envies the girl her future ability to reproduce, which suggests instant creativity. Only when in his potential manhood is the boy 'seduced' and then rejected by the mother, and the girl in her potential womanhood 'raped' and then rejected by the father, does the castration complex take place – it is thus a secondary formation though it causes regression to earlier envious ways and days. Freud, roughly speaking, was arguing for a theory in which there is an

8. I have omitted any serious consideration of the work of Melanie Klein, as it would take us far outside the field of femininity. At this stage Jones used Klein's theory of a very early Oedipus complex as evidence on his side of the debate. Klein, as a pupil of Abraham, was concerned with the first months of life and the fixation points there, in the paranoid-schizoid position, as she termed it, of the psychoses. Commensurately, her work made her focus on the mother-child relationship and this has inspired a great many studies on the subject. Interestingly this preoccupation has avoided contributing anything really new or specific to the understanding of feminine psychology. Roughly speaking I would suggest that, for our purposes here, the important distinctions between Klein's theories of an early Oedipus complex and Freud's theories are that Klein's suppose a primary innate, if unorganized, ego, make the Oedipus complex relate to all phases of object-gratification (thus to oral as well as to phallic desire), and place a heavy reliance on constitutional factors. Freud's theories disagree with all these suppositions.

important gap between, on the one hand, biological femaleness and maleness, and on the other psychological femininity and masculinity. He was also arguing against a theory of symmetry between the sexes. Initially, both sexes strive for active masculinity in relation to the attachment to the mother but in women this striving must be massively repressed and transformed into a feminine wish for a baby from the father. In the psychological formation of sexual distinctions the castration complex (and for women this is equivalent to penis-envy) is primary. The necessarily different attitudes to the castration complex of men and women show how – by repressing the qualities of the opposite sex – the social meaning of the biological sex of each can with greater or lesser success (and never totally) be psychically acquired. This repression is certainly not biological (as Fliess, too, had long ago postulated) but psychological.

Helene Deutsch and Karen Horney continued, from their opposite positions, their work on femininity. Horney gave a sociological gloss and Deutsch a psychologistic one to their respective biologisms. But as far as psychoanalysis went, the debate really ended in the thirties – it ended in an impasse because the concepts did not tally.

With Horney and Jones putting one position and Deutsch the other, the debate, as they expressed it, had become one about biology and 'reality'; meanwhile Freud continued to write about ideas, symptoms and representations but his own interest in the biology and the 'reality' thus represented seems to have prevented him for some years from perceiving that the battle of theories that was apparently being fought could, in fact, never take place because it was being waged on two completely different fields. As this courteous and ghostly fencing-match is known often as the Jones–Freud debate, we might as well use these two analysts to show the gulf between the battle sites. In a letter to the psychoanalyst Carl Muller-Braunschweig about female sexuality, Freud wrote:

I object to all of you (Horney, Jones, Rado, etc.) to the extent that you do not distinguish more clearly and cleanly between what is psychic and what is biological, that you try to establish a neat parallelism between the two and that you, motivated by such intent, unthinkingly construe psychic facts which are unprovable and that you, in the process of so doing, must declare as reactive or regressive much that without doubt is primary. Of course, these reproaches must remain obscure. In addition, I would only like to emphasize that we must keep psychoanalysis separate from biology just as we have kept it separate from anatomy and physiology . . .[9]

And on the other side Jones has given his reasons for endorsing Horney's theories of equivalence between the sexes against Freud's phallocentrism thus: the little girl's 'femininity develops progressively from the promptings of an instinctual constitution . . . The ultimate question is whether a woman is born or made.'[10] And 'Lastly I think we should do well to remind ourselves of a piece of wisdom whose source is more ancient than Plato: "In the beginning . . . male and female created He them."'[11] To Jones and Horney there is an innate biological disposition to femininity which expresses itself in females (and is only secondarily disturbed by society): the woman and the man are *created* in nature. To Freud society demands of the psychological bisexuality of both sexes that one sex attain a preponderance of femininity, the other of masculinity: man and woman are *made* in culture.

9. Letter to Carl Muller-Braunschweig, 21 July 1935, published in *Psychiatry*, Vol. 34, August 1971, trans. Donald L. Burnham.

10. E. Jones, 'Early Female Sexuality'. First read to the Vienna Psychoanalytic Society, 24 April 1935, subsequently published as Ch. XXVII of *Papers on Psychoanalysis*, London, 1948, p. 495.

11. E. Jones, 'The Phallic Phase'. First read 1932 and subsequently published as Ch. XXVI of *Papers on Psychoanalysis*, ibid., p. 484.

PART TWO *Section I*

RADICAL PSYCHOTHERAPY AND FREUD
(Wilhelm Reich and R.D. Laing)

Wilhelm Reich:
Sexual Politics, I

Political Psychotherapy and Pre-war Berlin

The recent popularity of Wilhelm Reich, the application of his thought by contemporary anarcho-left-wing movements, makes it hard to realize that some of his most important ideas were developed in the same decades and the same cities as those of the analysts we have been discussing. Indeed many of his ideas were created in an active relationship with their work.

Without making any specific references to the psychoanalytic debate on the nature or meaning of femininity, Reich was acutely attuned to the scientific and philosophical implications of which it was a symptom. Writing in 1929, he condemned the prevalence of ego-psychology within contemporary psychoanalysis, seeing it as a tribute to the ruling orthodoxies of bourgeois society. Concentration on the development of the ego rather than on the sexual drives would, in any case, have been anathema to Reich. But the work of the Freudian analysts on women falls well within many of his strictures. Reich singles out Ernest Jones's stress on the superego and the creation of guilt as an instance of an adaptational psychology that willy-nilly was contributing to a demand for social obedience. Reich's evidence aside, as we have seen, cultural conformity and prescriptions for normality do seem to have been the main order of the day for the later Freudians – whatever the intentions.

I think Reich was correct in singling out the implicit subordination of the role of sexuality to the creation of the ego as an important sign of this psychoanalytic decline. I also believe his failure to perceive that his preoccupation with biology (even where masked by sociology) and his gradual evasion of culturally produced ideational mental structures doomed his attempts at correction: he fell finally for a way-out other side of the same natural-biological coin. But before this decline on his part, Reich, having realized that this tendency within psychoanalysis had political implications of a decidedly reactionary nature, first set about applying his Marxist knowledge in an attempt to claim psychoanalysis for communism and to liberate it from its death-by-adaptation within bourgeois capitalist society.

Freud's efforts to 'keep psychoanalysis out of politics' and his disclaimers of any understanding of Marxism are well known. Ill-read and largely uninterested he may have been, but unaware of the arguments he was not. When Reich and some anthropological psychoanalysts in the twenties and thirties presented him with the notion that the Oedipus complex was culturally specific to capitalism, they were treading old ground. Adler (whose reduction of sexuality to the will-to-power Reich later condemned) had argued such a so-called 'Marxist' position at least as early as 1908 in a debate on the position of women. The editors of the minutes of that particular psychoanalytic meeting, who were both there at the time, point out that Marxist ideas on these questions were very much the vogue at this time in Vienna and that Freud, who numbered among his close friends active leaders of the Social Democratic Party, would have been as familiar as was Adler with them.

The Vienna, however, that Reich went to live in at the end of the First World War was a very different city in a very different country from that of ten years earlier.[1] Certainly Austro-Marxism was really established as a practice and theory distinct from the work-syndicalism and state-oriented policy of the Social Democrats by 1904. In 1905 the only result of a general strike had been a march of a quarter of a million workers and the final granting of universal male suffrage; but by the end of 1918, the city was visibly divided as never before, on the one hand a starving war-shattered population, and on the other, war profiteers making fortunes on inflation. In near-by Bavaria a communist workers' republic had been established and under Béla Kun, Hungary had declared itself Bolshevik (incidentally, to Freud's great pleasure, appointing Ferenczi the first ever university professor of psychoanalysis). But in Vienna, despite an attempted putsch, the massive unemployment and poverty produced no sustained uprising, for the Social Democrats and

1. See Appendix for a fuller description of Vienna at the turn of the century.

Christian Socials formed a coalition government and Austria gradually stabilized itself. Reich came to work in this city of mass misery and revolutionary impotence. It was the former that struck him first when from 1922 to 1930 he worked in the Vienna free psychoanalytic clinic. Later he added some Marxist knowledge to his experience of working-class wretchedness, and in 1927, after witnessing a massacre of the Viennese workers out on general strike, he joined the Austrian Social Democratic Party. In 1929 he set up a number of free therapy clinics in which people were urged to understand that their sexual problems came from social conditions and could only be solved by political change. In 1930, Reich moved to Berlin and joined the German Communist Party.

Julius Braunthal, himself since 1912 a Viennese exile in Berlin, rightly saw the failure of the 1919 socialist revolution in Germany . as fatal for immediate European socialism. The Social Democratic Party, revisionist to the core, had, as in Austria, refused to oppose the 1914 war and as a result in 1917 had split with its left wing; this anti-war section had broken away with 40 per cent of the members. In 1918 a yet more radical section (the Spartacists) left to found the German Communist Party. From now on there was bitter enmity between the Social Democrats and the Communist Party. Reich deplored this hostility, seeing it as one of the factors in preventing effective opposition to Nazism. The failure of 1919 and the murders of Liebknecht and Luxemburg were preludes to the bourgeois revolution of the Weimar Republic, and the Treaty of Versailles sanctioned a fantastic economic, moral and military reduction of Germany. There were a few years of inflation and immiseration, a few years of economic boom brought about by vast American loans and capitalization, and then collapse following the fall of Wall Street and the withdrawal of loans:

In early 1929 [in Germany] there were two million unemployed, by early 1932 the number jobless was 6 million, and by the end of that year just under half of the working population was unemployed.[2]

2. Unsigned (and very good) introduction to Wilhelm Reich's 'What is Class Consciousness?' (1934), published by Socialist Reproduction – I, London, 1971, p. 6.

The Social Democrats worked with trade union bureaucracy. The Communist Party recruited mainly from the unemployed – largely accepting the comintern line on 'social fascism' in which social democracy and fascism were classed as equal threats; it tended to be unduly optimistic about the imminent fall of Nazism. It was once more this situation of mass misery and relative left-wing political ineffectiveness that Reich moved into in Berlin in 1930; again he grasped the simplicities of the former more fully than the complexities of the latter. It was to mass misery that he hoped to apply the revolutionary therapy of psychoanalysis or, more particularly, its emphasis on the importance of sexuality for liberating the imprisoned personality structure.

The post-war sexual mores against which Reich's work can be set were very different from those that confronted Freud in *fin de siècle* Vienna. Stefan Zweig, who describes the latter, also gives his personal reactions to the social appearance of Vienna in the early twenties. It was the reign of youth and iconoclasm, exoticism and extravagance in the face of economic and social misery:

[The youth] revolted against every legitimated form for the mere pleasure of revolting, even against the order of nature, against the eternal polarity of the sexes. The girls adopted 'boyish bobs' so they were indistinguishable from boys; the young men for their part shaved in an effort to seem girlish; homosexuality and lesbianism became the fashion, not from an inner instinct but by way of a protest against the traditional and normal expressions of love.[3]

But Vienna was tame stuff compared with inflationary Berlin, the Babylon of the world where amusement parks, bars, red-light districts, sprang up like mushrooms.

Along the entire Kurfürstendamm powdered and rouged young men sauntered ... every high-school boy wanted to earn some money, and in the dimly lit bars one might see government officials and men of the world of finance tenderly courting drunken sailors without any shame. Even the Rome of Suetonius had never known such orgies as the pervert halls of Berlin, where hundreds of men costumed as women and hundreds of women as men danced under the benevolent eyes of the police.[4]

3. Zweig, op. cit., p. 228.   4. ibid., pp. 238–9.

With chronic unemployment the mass of the people had little left to sell but their bodies. It is against this bourgeois decadence and working-class wretchedness that the moral tone of Reich's sexual theses must be set – his predilection for hetero- and 'healthy' sexuality, his wish for men to be men and women, women.

Reich was by no means the only psychoanalyst of this period to try to effect a politicization of psychoanalysis and in turn, an acceptance of the latter by Marxists, but as the analyst Otto Fenichel points out in his essay titled like Reich's, 'Psychoanalysis and Dialectical Materialism', Reich did the most to put both the family and sexual suppression on the agenda as the ideological institutions most important for study by both Marxism and psychoanalysis.

Reich was concerned with sexuality and the oppression of women and he also directed his thoughts explicitly to the women's movement.

The 'women's rights' activities of various bourgeois organizations are founded on strong revolutionary impulses – some conscious (toward economic independence), some usually unconscious (toward sexual independence), but all directed toward changing the existing order of things. Only socialism can provide a practical answer to their questions. Yet the socialists do nothing to bring clarity into the ideological confusion of women. They do not explain to them that the things they want are mutually contradictory, that their aims are really socialist, though they cannot formulate them and so they have resorted to a form of sentimental revolt of the Pankhurst type.[5]

Writing fervently in the same decade in which many of the non-political Freudians were considering the psychology of femininity, Wilhelm Reich, though interested in all psychological controversies, did not take up this issue. He thus never got stuck in that particular rut. The question is whether or not his re-analysis of the significance of sexuality, his stress on the family

5. Reich, 'What is Class Consciousness?', 1934, republished in *Sex-Pol*, Vintage Books, 1972, p. 304. All future references are to this edition, though the translations of separate pamphlets currently being brought out by Socialist Reproduction, op. cit., are on the whole also to be highly recommended as critical editions.

and his political awareness of the oppression of women, offer feminism a way out from the impasse of orthodox post-Freudianism? Do we have here a new way to an understanding of the psychology of femininity in a patriarchal, capitalist society?

1 A Brief Biographical Background

There is a good deal both of confusion and of curiosity about Reich's bizarre biography. Reich's life has no more bearing on our final appreciation of his work than does that of any of the other thinkers being considered. But in his case the dramatic changes in his life affected his writings – they were subject to constant alteration. As the confusion of the texts reflects to a degree the changes of his life, it seems pertinent to try and sort out both here.

Reich, a psychoanalyst and Marxist in Europe in the twenties and thirties, became an anti-communist and founder of his own 'science of orgonomy' in America in the forties and fifties. The Trust to which he left his work and property allowed only the publication of the late writings, but recently the banned books of the earlier period have begun to see the light of day. However, critics and followers of Reich still stress only the period with which they are in sympathy. Even the most detailed studies of Reich to date are either baldly chronologically arranged or concentrate on the period of his work to which the critic is committed: the early Reich (Sinelnikoff, Robinson) or the late Reich (negatively Rycroft; positively Ola Raknes).[1] Either method presents problems. Rycroft argues that if one rejects Reich's later works one risks 'falling into a methodological trap, that of using Reich's personality as an argument against his ideas'.[2] There certainly *was* a continuity in his thinking, and yet for anyone other than a naturalist-mystic or Reichean orgonomist the rain-making, desert-fertilizing, evil forces and sun-powered life-energies visible through a wooden tube or with

1. See Constantin Sinelnikoff, *L'Oeuvre de Wilhelm Reich*, Maspero, Paris, 1970, for a full bibliography of Reich's works and most important commentators.
2. Charles Rycroft, *Reich*, London, 1970, p. 13.

the naked eye (when it is closed) of Reich's last experiments put a strain on tolerance. Yet clearly, despite rumours to the effect, there is neither any evidence or likelihood that – notwithstanding chronic bursts of paranoia – he was ever really or incapacitatingly insane, and even if this were so, it would not constitute an argument against the validity or otherwise of his projects.

However, the cultural and political milieu in which Reich worked are, I would contend, important for the direction of his thoughts. And there seems to me to be a world of difference between Vienna and Berlin in the twenties and thirties with the rise of fascism and left-wing opposition thereto, and the post-war and McCarthyite America of the forties and fifties. Though inadequate, opposition to Nazism was never as stupid as was American anti-communism with its terrifying banality. Whatever one's political standpoint, left-wing analysis of political reaction (partly because in the West it has so far always been a minority position) has had to analyse and oppose with a degree of complexity; whereas right-wing opposition to the Left has taken the form of reducing revolutionary phenomena to monolithic simplicities to which one can then react with comparably straightforward passion. Reich, as an active member of the Psycho-Analytical societies of Vienna and Berlin, and as a member of a cultural wing of the Austrian and then German communist parties, could not afford the luxury in which he later indulged of imagining that the Russians were trying to steal the secrets of his orgone research and that the United States President was protecting him with regular air-force flights over his scientific centre. He could not afford such paranoic delusions because in the Europe of the twenties and thirties, such propositions belonged to the racist scare-mongering of fascism as later they belonged to the McCarthy witch-hunts. But where Reich was in strident and argued opposition to one, he was in tacit accord (never more) with the other. What seems fantastic in Reich's later years was, in fact, in harmony with aspects of the cultural climate of that period of American history. So what we are witnessing is that Reich in radical opposition to the capitalist (and specifically fascist) status quo was a more interesting thinker than Reich in agreement with it.

For this reason we cannot, as Rycroft does, entirely discount the importance of Reich's personality, presuming we mean by that not his personal qualities, but his personal history.

Reich was of small country-gentry stock; his family were non-practising half-Jews from Galicia. The death of his parents and the military takeover of his home farmland in the Ukraine left him, after a spell in the cavalry, a relatively impoverished medical student at the end of the First World War. It was from his particular study of sexology that he became interested in psychoanalysis. One of his first publications was on the concept of the libido and of the 'instinct' from Forel to Jung.[3] It was delivered to a student sexology seminar in 1919 and published in 1922. In 1920 he paid a personal visit to Freud, read a paper on Peer Gynt to the Viennese Psycho-Analytical society, and therewith became a member of the organization. His medical studies finished in 1922, his psychoanalytical ones in 1924. His interest throughout this period was in combining the clinical observations of sexology with those of psychoanalysis. In 1922, with the foundation of the Viennese free psychoanalytic clinic, Reich became first an assistant there and then, until 1930, its vice-director. His work in the clinic, where the patients were not the privileged fee-paying people of the consulting-room, led him to stress the necessity of the prophylaxis of neurosis, and to make many reformulations of analytical work. It convinced him likewise of the strictly social causation of neurotic illness and of its prevalence, for different reasons, throughout all classes of capitalist society. This recognition coincided with his knowledge of the sexual disturbance manifest in the overwhelming majority of the population – the coincidence confirmed for him the likelihood of their causal relationship: the social suppression of sexuality was the cause of mass neurosis. His writings during the twenties were concentrated around social-sexual questions and around techniques of therapeutic treatment. It was during this period that he

3. I shall not list all his writings here. All these autobiographical details can be found in Reich: *People in Trouble*, New York, 1953; *The Discovery of the Orgone*, Vol. I, New York, 1942; *Reich Speaks of Freud*, New York, 1967; and in Ilse Ollendorf, *Wilhelm Reich*, London, 1969 and reassembled in Constantin Sinelnikoff, op. cit.

developed his systematic method of analysing a patient's manifest resistances as a means to the revelation of the unconscious, and this in turn led to his study of 'character' which was finally formulated as the technique of character-analysis and the recognition of what he called each individual's 'character armour'. We will discuss these concepts and techniques in detail later.

It is hard to come to an objective assessment of the success of Reich's practical work at this date, as references to it by his contemporaries are brief and infrequent. (It is equally possible that few exist or that they have not yet been published.) Hence most accounts fall back on Reich's own word for his history and achievement. It does, however, seem that Reich was a successful medical student, and that during the first five years of his association with psychoanalysis he was held in high regard. Conflicts started to occur around 1925 and 1926. In 1927 his one-time supervisor-analyst, Paul Federn, complained that Reich was presenting his ideas for approval before the technical seminar instead of the Psycho-Analytical Association. And certainly, despite his personal admiration for Freud, Reich was devoting himself increasingly to social and anthropological studies rather than to questions of psychoanalytic theory. (He was, in any case, always more interested in therapy.)

Given Reich's dedication to social problems, his intellectual milieu and the political situation in Central Europe at that date, his increasing politicization was virtually inevitable. His sociological and anthropological readings took him to Kautsky and Engels. Events in and around Vienna in 1927 led him into the Austrian Social Democratic Party. The judicial acquittal of the monarchist troops who had fired into the crowd attending a Social Democratic meeting, leaving two dead and many wounded had led to a series of incidents – a token strike, the police killing of a number of strikers, the burning of the Law Courts, the indiscriminate firing by the police into the demonstrators and at the end of the day over a hundred dead and a thousand wounded. The Social Democratic municipal council had proved utterly ineffective; the communists intervened the day after it happened.

Disillusioned with the possibilities of the Social Democrats,

Reich turned to the Communist Party, joining an associate organization, 'Workers Help' (*Arbeiter Hilfe*). In his autobiographical retrospection, *People in Trouble*, Reich records that these were years of great intellectual turmoil for him – reading Marx and Engels and trying to estimate the full social function of sexual repression and working more and more on the prevention rather than the analysis of neuroses. According to Reich, Freud initially encouraged him both here and in his sexual researches but as soon as he started to criticize the institution of the family Freud grew cold in his appreciation. Yet it was in this field rather than in his more orthodox psychoanalytical discussions that Reich was, at least at first, most interesting and most original.

It was really at this point, at a practical political, if not at a theoretical level, that Reich was at his most successful. He tried to get the communist groups he addressed not to dismiss psychoanalysis as a bourgeois science, but instead to see that the family was a key institution within capitalist society, not only for its economic repression, but for its sexual perversion and its function as an ideological factory. He explained that the Oedipus complex must be placed firmly within the patriarchal family where incest is tabooed simultaneously with its encouragement – children are urged into forbidden lust for their parents. Ultimately, the Communist Party would have none of it, no more than would the Psycho-Analytical Association.

More and more, his contact with the working class led Reich to reject specific theses of psychoanalysis (whilst confirming and reinterpreting others), but above all, he deplored the separation of an academic science such as this from the practical social and political problems that surround it. Increasingly, he dedicated himself to medical and educational work with workers and adolescents. To implement his ideas, he established in 1929 six socialist centres for sexual counselling and sexology. Their popularity was immense, and the observations Reich made from his work in these were amongst his most crucial.

Politically, Reich was also increasingly critical of the inadequacy of the Left to deal with the mounting brutalities of the reactionaries in Austria. If Marxism was not likewise itself 'an academic science', the parties managed to make it sound so.

Slogans were abstract and appealed to theoretical concepts instead of to the concrete needs of the workers and the unemployed. Fascism was all too successful in precisely this field. In the autumn of 1929 Reich visited Russia and wrote sensitively about his impressions on his return.

While he was criticizing both the Psycho-Analytical Association and the Communist Party for their inattention to people's everyday needs and to the concrete realities of rising fascism, he was offending each by his support for the other. The details of his growing estrangement from both will be discussed, in part, later. In any case, in 1930, Reich left Vienna for Berlin, where the atmosphere was far more congenial to his work in sexual politics. The psychoanalysts there were open to his theory of the liberating significance of complete orgasm and themselves had Marxist leanings – Fromm, Bernfeld, Fenichel all in different ways and degrees were concerned with political questions. With Fenichel, Reich formed a group of young analysts keen on social work; Fenichel directed this group of 'Marxist psychoanalysts'.

In Berlin, Reich worked with the communists to set up a Communist Youth group, and with their backing he established his famous Sexpol Clinics. But his criticism of the communists' out-of-touch tactics was reinforced by this work that he now undertook with adolescents, and his attack on the communist incomprehension of the nature and power of fascism (as he saw it) became more strenuous. He predicted that in the ensuing years many communists would turn fascist simply because the nature of the latter had never been really understood. Whilst Nazism grew from strength to strength on its popular base, the Communist Party dismissed it as Hitler's 'demagogic' powers, his ability to 'dupe' the populace. Reich argued that the popularity of racism would not be overcome by calling it 'nonsense'. He complained that few revolutionaries had even taken the trouble to read *Mein Kampf*. Out of his concern for this grotesquely inadequate opposition grew his book *The Mass Psychology of Fascism*, in which he tried to combine a Marxist concept of ideology with the insights into character-formation offered by psychoanalysis. His link was his interpretation of 'ideology' which he defined not as consciously expressed ideas, but as the underlying, virtually unconscious aspirations of a people.

Reich was also encountering problems with his work in Sexpol. The movement's astounding success received a check in 1932 when the Communist Party prohibited the distribution of some immensely popular pamphlets in the Youth Organizations. The works in question were Reich's *The Invasion of Sexual Morality*, and two papers: one for parents, 'When your child questions you' (by Reich's first wife Annie Reich), and one for children, 'Grown-up secrets revealed to children'. After various decisions and counter-decisions, a Sexpol congress in January of 1933 reaffirmed their opposition to Reich's particular work here.

A month later, on the burning of the Reichstag, 1,500 communists were arrested and Reich, for safety's sake, returned to Vienna. Back in the homeland of psychoanalysis, his problems with the Institute arose anew. A series of incidents led to the cancellation by the Psycho-Analytical publishing house of the contract for his book *Character Analysis*. There were also constant attacks on his political affiliations. In this atmosphere, Reich decided to move to Copenhagen in the late spring of 1933. There his attempts to establish contact with the Danish Communist Party were foiled by bureaucratic obstacles, and after various attacks on his sexual theories the Danish Party expelled him, though they had as yet not admitted him to membership! The organs of various Communist Parties now attacked *The Mass Psychology of Fascism*. Meanwhile Freud refused to support Reich's application for a post as a teacher of psychoanalysis, and finally the Danish Government decided not to renew his residence permit.

Reich visited London where he had a mutually enthusiastic meeting with the social anthropologist Malinowski, who recommended that he move to America. Instead Reich settled in Malmö (Sweden) to enable him to continue seeing the young analysts whom he had been training and the friends that he had made in close-by Copenhagen. On moving to Sweden he had revisited Berlin – to find his prediction that many communists would turn fascist too fully realized. He had stayed in Malmö only a few months when an extension of his residence permit was once more refused.

Illegally Reich revisited Denmark and then made for the Psycho-Analytical Congress in Lucerne, only to find that the executive committee had voted for his exclusion from the Austrian Institute. He moved house once more, this time to Oslo. It is here in Norway, I think, that there emerged what was not so much a marked change in his work as a drastic confirmation of his earlier predilections but with remarkable results. He turned his attention away from sociology and anthropology to biology and physics. His aim was to discover the *visible material* nature of the libido. His old friend and colleague, Otto Fenichel, who was also in exile in Oslo, quarrelled bitterly with him over the direction his work was taking. According to Reich, when Fenichel left for the United States he initiated there the hostile rumours of Reich's schizophrenia. Opposition from both sides (psychoanalytical and political) may indeed have made Reich paranoid – it certainly made him more persistent. In 1936 the 'Institute for the Study of Life', which he had established in Oslo, was harshly criticized by psychiatrists and biologists in a massive press campaign against him. It was at this stage that Reich made his first claim to have discovered the 'bion' – the particle of energy that was to determine his future research.

From 1936 until he left for the United States in 1939, slanderous rumours were rife, about his personal life, his therapeutic malpractices, his running of a 'sex-racket'. He was isolated in a tiny country, practising a new and unacknowledged science (psychoanalysis), an immigrant with a communist past. In this predicament, Reich continued to work and publish (the Sexpol Publishers still produced his work) but his criticism of any form of organization grew stronger. In his work on what he first called 'vegetotherapy' and then 'sex economy', Reich wished to avoid all the bureaucratic structures of organization as he felt he had already succeeded in doing in the non-hierarchical groups of Sexpol. On these organizational grounds, he likewise criticized Trotsky's concept of a Fourth International and the growing bourgeoisification, as he saw it, of pre-war Russia.

Sinelnikoff contends that in his denunciation of the very notion of organization, Reich leant, at this stage, towards anarchism, but I would suggest that by 1939 he was more importantly antipolitical than positively anarchist in his inclinations. At this point, Reich emigrated to America to teach at the New School for Social Research in New York. The bizarre forms of suspicion accompanied him – the F.B.I. raided his home and seized *Mein Kampf*, Trotsky's *My Life* and a Russian Dictionary. Later, after he had established his research centre, 'Orgonon', in rural Maine State, a journalist, Mildred Brady, wrote a defamatory article in *Harper's* which led to inquiry and then prosecution by the Food and Drug Administration. They burnt his books, on the grounds that they were misleading the public into buying 'orgone boxes' – the restorative energy accumulators Reich had devised. But these peculiar petty persecutions were outstripped by the strangeness of Reich's own work at the Orgonon Institute. Here, Reich's science of 'orgonomy' – the study and harnessing of the energy of life – branched out in various directions. Reich kept the Institute of Atomic Energy informed of his many observations. He continued to develop his analysis of cancer (started in Oslo) and to propose that treatment with accumulated life-energy would eventually lead to a method of curing this disease, which he analysed as the death-disintegration process, made visibly manifest. Sexual energy, which now became synonymous with life-energy itself, was therefore likewise deficient in cancer patients. He also, with his cloud-bursting device, brought rain to the parched fields of Maine and watched the blue sparks of energy dance in the sky above the near-by lake; through his microscope he found this energy concentrated in sand particles. Believing in the priority of his science, Reich refused to answer the philistine summons of the Food and Drug Department and was hauled up for contempt of court and condemned to two years' imprisonment in May 1956. His appeal was dismissed and, having witnessed the State's destruction of all his work, he started his prison sentence in March 1957; eight months later he died of a heart attack. Robinson comments: 'Such was the sad but (one can't help feeling) appropriate end to a career so utterly serious and hopelessly grandiose that it faded imperceptibly into farce.'[4] To me, there is something more crucial about the homology between Reich's

4. Paul A. Robinson, *The Sexual Radicals*, Temple Smith, London, 1969 (originally *The Freudian Left*, New York, 1969), p. 73.

individual work and the cultural environment in which it was set. Not only was the prosecution quite as 'mad' as the offender, but more important, both Reich's serious early work and his fanatical and bizarre later researches developed in contexts that matched them perfectly.

2 Reich and Psychoanalysis

It is Reich's notion of a sexual revolution, and its contribution then and now to the possible liberation of women, that concerns us specifically. But it is important that his theories of the nature of sexuality and the evidence of its repression that he saw in the rigid character structures and reactionary societies, were developed in a double intellectual context, that of Marxism and of psychoanalysis. Although Reich's purpose was their integration, in the first instance, it has been necessary here to separate them out.

As we have seen, during the second half of the twenties and the early thirties a great deal of Reich's work on sexology engaged directly with controversial arguments rampant within the psychoanalytical movement. For instance Otto Rank, in his theories of the birth trauma, had defined the psychic action involved in sexual intercourse as a return to the maternal womb. Reich objected to this on two scores: it postulated that the phantasy that the neurotic patient experienced was the same thing as the actual impulse itself which would therefore be expressed in the same way in all circumstances, and it made of what is merely an analogy a complete identity. The orgastically impotent man may dream of his mother's womb when he copulates, but such a dream is precisely an index of his neurotic alienation; in other words the phantasy explains the impotence. The one is the condition of the other. In suggesting this, Reich is in fact denying the validity of transposing the phantasies revealed in pathological cases to 'normal' situations; in this he is undermining the premises of psychoanalytical work. Reich may have been right in saying that Rank in this particular description was wrong; but the grounds on which he chose to dispute the thesis are, as we shall see later, ones that clearly showed, even at this date, his divergence from psychoanalysis as a whole.

Reich similarly engaged in controversy with Alexander and Theodor Reik. He opposed not only the development of ego-psychology but also what he saw as the increasing tendency to 'psychologize' psychoanalysis. Reich explicitly and incautiously (unlike Jones's and Horney's more discreet intentions) wanted to return psychoanalysis to a biological base. Reich's writings on psychoanalysis were produced in a period of great controversial debate within the movement: they were written in the decade after Freud's publication of *Beyond the Pleasure Principle* and *The Ego and the Id* and after the introduction of his postulation of a death-drive, still contentious today. Reich's pre-existing stress on the libido and his pansexual inclinations received new fire from his hostility to this proposition. Increasingly he saw himself as the defender of true psychoanalysis embattled against timid conformists bent on obliterating the socially explosive concept of sexuality in favour of a highly conservative ego-psychology. He remained admiring of Freud, but increasingly derogatory of lesser colleagues and disciples. His criticisms of the 'betrayers' of Freudian theory sometimes contained a general truth at the expense of any accurate analysis. This is an interesting characteristic of Reich's work which we will have to account for later – that he often had a perceptive 'hunch' about the drift of an intellectual or political development while he could rarely adequately back it up. So Reich's denunciations of ego-psychology and the cultural adaptation of psychoanalysis had a pertinence that outstripped his understanding of the details, and his conception of the post-Freudian shift away from the implications of Freud's theory (even in Freud's lifetime) often displayed his insight at its best.

There was no doubt in Reich's mind that personal sexual inhibitions drove Freud and the majority of analysts in the twenties and early thirties away from the revolutionary discovery of the libido. For Reich the pleasure principle was all. There was sexual energy and its frustration – nothing more. Anxiety arose from the latter, aggression was a rechannelling of libido (aggression is a going out towards something, as is love); the formulation of other principles or instincts was redundant. Yet this period of psychoanalytic theory was replete with the multiplication of previously unified notions, the diversification of previously simplified concepts. Two such developments Reich deplored above all: the death-drive and what he saw as the necessary result of it: the demotion of the libido theory. He also condemned all developments that tried to interpret sexuality in psychological terms (to him the sexual urge was nothing other than its physiological self) and all theories that differentiated various aspects of sexuality. He disliked any notion of a distinction between pregenitality and genitality. Sexuality was all and genitality was the only true sexuality.

Freud's proposal of a death-drive arose from and gave rise to changes in the interpretation of anxiety and aggression. Reich initially attacked these head-on whilst he merely kept his fingers crossed that Freud, finding no clinical confirmation of the death-drive itself, would sooner or later withdraw his hypothesis. An early article illustrates this approach most lucidly. 'The Sources of Neurotic Anxiety: A Contribution to the Theory of Psycho-analytic Therapy', published in the *International Journal of Psycho-Analysis* in 1926, shows Reich twisting and turning with a rather desperate open-mindedness within the framework of psychoanalytical debate. His language is already biological in its imagery and his analytical vocabulary limited to substantive concepts and a constant, almost nervous, reference and deference to Freud, a nervousness which inhibits his text and consequently prevents him presenting his best arguments with adequate force or eloquence. Against Freud's theory of primary masochism and Otto Rank's notions of an initial, all-influential birth trauma, Reich re-stressed the primacy of the libido. Birth was a secondary shock:

Even although birth anxiety is ontogenetically earlier and although anxiety possibly derives its normal content (choking, darkness, narrow space, etc.) in consequence from the process of birth, nevertheless from the dynamic point of view birth is a secondary source of anxiety, becoming operative as a result of pathogenic repression. It could only operate as a primary source of anxiety when post-natal development has come up against crude external obstacles, as, for example, serious difficulties at the oral phase.[1]

1. 'The Sources of Neurotic Anxiety', *International Journal of Psycho-Analysis*, 1926, p. 384.

In other words, the phantasies that a man can have in sexual intercourse of a 'return to the mother's womb' are pathological ones. Later, criticizing Helene Deutsch's theories on much the same grounds, Reich stresses his opposition to them in such a way that any phantasies incurred during coitus are abnormalities and evidence of a person's inability to experience natural and therefore phantasy-free orgasmic potency. Phantasy itself has become pathological and despicable. The wish to retreat to the intra-uterine state is a form of defence against the prohibited demands of the libido. We are born with sexual urges alone; these seek their immediate fulfilment with the first possible love objects they encounter: our parents. But incest is taboo and in our society the impulse is repressed by means of the threat of castration. Repressed sexuality turns into aggression or anxiety. The process can be extrapolated as follows: born with genital love we grow to fear castration (passive); we defend ourselves against this by aggression (active castration) which in turn only makes the dread of castration stronger and hence induces anxiety and a sense of conscience; against this we renew our defences and repress as hard as we can our aggression; as a result of this stifling of aggression we become depressed. The primacy of sexuality also affects the end product: frustration of sexuality in the present brings to the foreground aggressive impulses which, in the past, were activated by incest repression, the aggression itself assumes some of the overtones of the sexuality it replaces, and hence we have sadism.

It is typical of Reich's method of arguing that he draws confirmatory examples from different spheres of action. He applies, or finds, his theory on many levels. Thus he will point out that the relationship between the analyst and his patient demonstrates his thesis: here the patient's 'transferred' love for his analyst is prevented from arising as soon as it otherwise might, because it is held up by memories of the incest barrier and consequent castration anxiety. The patient is often aggressive because his love must be repressed. But at least aggression is one stage nearer the source of love than depression, and Reich always urged analysts to welcome and cope with the patient's hostility as it was far less serious than apathy. Or Reich will illustrate his thesis from everyday life, so, for example, he 'proves' that aggression is caused by sexual deprivation by referring to the common assumption that, because they gratify aggressive instincts, professional athletes should not have sexual intercourse before competing, as it diminishes athletic powers.

In Reich's schema it doesn't matter if you thus put the cart before the horse. Alternatively, he will comment from within the sexual field itself. Thus he points out that menstrual depression is of psychic not somatic origin, it is merely the end product of the chain set in motion by sexual frustration. Everything bad is psychological, everything good, uninhibited biology. For during menstruation libido is in fact somatically slightly increased; it is the impossibility of satisfaction that gives rise to the depression. Interestingly, here, Reich maintains the taboo against intercourse at this time, merely commenting that if the menstruating woman is enabled (by an analyst) to realize the cause of her feelings and thus to look forward to future sexual satisfaction, the depression will lift and the sexual excitability be free to be felt even though the consummation is anticipated, not actual. Unfortunately this suggestion did not lead Reich to reassess the significance of sexual phantasy.

Repressed libido passing through permutations of anxiety and aggression finally ends up as depression or as a destructive impulse. Reich argues that it is this latter *secondary* formation which is the only possible (because only clinically verifiable) meaning of the death-drive. The death-drive arises when there is an acute sense of guilt; which is itself a sign of defused aggression and which, therefore, prompts self-destruction and hence a form of death.

Conscious death-anxiety may represent an endo-psychic perception of this tendency. During analysis, however, death-anxiety, no matter how intense it had been, is invariably unveiled as castration-anxiety and a longing for (or anxiety concerning) the intra-uterine position.[2]

Although this sounds similar to Freud's stress on the relationship between castration and death, Reich pertinaciously retained a monistic model: a sexual one.

It was not only the death-drive that Reich saw as causing the destruction of the libido theory, it was also the whole notion of

2. ibid., p. 388.

sublimation. As freely expressed, 'natural' sexuality to Reich was always a positive good, it followed that even its re-expression in another form was bad. He found obnoxious Freud's theory that the rechannelling of sexual energies into other creative fields had enabled the advance of culture, for it proposed, as he saw it, a necessary opposition between nature and culture, where there should be only harmony. Ever more stridently, as his work grew away from psychoanalysis, Reich emphasized the compatibility and coincidence of the ability for intellectual and creative work and sexuality. By the time of the American writings, only the sexually potent man was capable of meaningful work performance. Certainly, throughout, Reich seems to have made a familiar mistake and forgotten that sublimation signified the use of the sexual drives for other creative purposes – not the repression of sexuality altogether. In an interview given late in his life, Reich claimed that Freud's work *Civilization and its Discontents* (in which Freud spells out the theory Reich here objects to) was written in reply to his own paper on 'The Prophylaxis of Neuroses'. This is unconfirmed, but certainly the whole notion of Reich's thesis of the achievement of sexual satisfaction as an absolute means of prophylaxis was against the tenor of Freud's work long before the twenties.

On the issue of sexuality as the be-all and end-all cure and prophylaxis, Reich is quite explicit –

My contention is that every individual who has managed to preserve a bit of naturalness knows that there is only one thing wrong with neurotic patients: the *lack of full and repeated sexual satisfaction.*[3]

Of course, such an argument slapped him firmly into a causal dilemma: how does the neurosis arise and why in one person and not another? One of Reich's earliest published case-histories of a patient gives us insight into how he repeated Freud's

3. Reich, *The Discovery of the Orgone, I*, New York, 1966, p. 73. This book is more usually known as *The Function of the Orgasm*, which is the title of a study that Reich published in Vienna in 1927. So far this book has not been translated into English. The later book is, in fact, more correctly known as *The Discovery of the Orgone, Part I: The Function of the Orgasm*. It was published in America in 1942. For clarity's sake I refer to it as *The Discovery of the Orgone*, Part I. Part II is subtitled *The Cancer Biopathy*.

process and stopped short at a particular point: the point of an actual sexual trauma. It is as though Freud had rested content with his seduction theories of the nineties. The possibility of phantasy was banned from Reich's account in a more thorough way than it was absent in the early Freud. Yet Reich's analysis, for all that, is interesting, at least for its sociological value. Sexual crises did and do, after all, *actually* occur and Reich was laying a very correct emphasis on them; it is, I feel, only his transmutation of his observations of the social implications of sexuality into psychoanalysis that is astray. Reich wrote up a number of case-histories: the best known is that on the masochistic character which will be referred to later. Here I want to pay some attention to a lesser-known account of a hysterical patient because it shows us the precise links with the work from which Freud and Breuer were in the process of departing thirty years earlier.

In 1925[4] Reich reported on a nineteen-year-old woman who had moved to him from another analyst. Reich treated her for four months (not an unusually short time, although the length of analysis was in general increasing at that date). She suffered from autistic states, hysterical abdominal pains and insomnia. She was highly intelligent but her depressive personality expressed itself in her dull dress and totally 'unpushing' manner and behaviour. Reich never rid himself of the impression, suggested by the nature of her autism, that this was also a case of schizophrenia. In fact, however, he conformed to the earlier diagnosis and entitled his report 'An Hysterical Psychosis in Statu Nascendi'. An interesting feature of the account is Reich's method of presentation. In reconstructing his report here I have stressed how Reich made his discoveries of the crucial event, but in fact Reich pays little attention to this, zooming in on the incidents themselves and then reintegrating the symptoms in the light of the 'facts'. This contrasts forcefully with Freud's usually prolonged and detailed recounting of the unfolding of the analysis (through contradictions, transference and many dead ends) to a reconstruction of the events which by then are in no need of a different interpretation.

4. I am in fact using the English version, published a year later in the *International Journal of Psycho-Analysis*, 1926.

On emerging from her periods of autism, Reich's patient would call out to her mother 'give it back'. She was terrified by the thought of pregnancy and used to dream recurrently that there was a child in her bed. The autism with its specific feature of mutism had commenced with the death of an older sister. The patient also suffered from severe dissociation, and periods in which she was unable to speak her native German.

Suddenly and spontaneously the woman revealed that the event the autism masked was her rape (somewhere between the ages of five and seven) by a young Hebrew teacher. The question Reich set himself to answer was: why had she hitherto so thoroughly repressed this all-significant *fact*? Through the patient's recollections Reich found that between the ages of three and four she had believed that a child was produced by eating or kissing (a suspiciously archetypal psychoanalytic theory of a child's phantasy of intercourse). She was four when her brother was born and from that point on for some time she would only eat if held in her father's lap. At barely two, she had been prohibited from playing with her genitals and had developed the theory that there were two types of boys: those who were allowed to keep their penises and those who were not. Her mother had been the repressive agent and hence it was to her that the young woman called in her later life: 'give it back'. Because this role was allotted to the mother, not the father, and, because it happened so early on, the patient had remained fixed at the oral stage. This oral fixation was revealed in the present-day characteristic of orality – mutism. Then – apparently – had come the rape of which all memory was repressed. In adolescence she had developed a strong attachment to a previously hated elder sister and they used mutually to caress each other's breasts. It was from the occasion of this sister's death that the patient's mutism dated. Reich comments that being dumb is nearly always associated with being dead, and further adds: 'I should like merely to hazard the suggestion that autism might stand for regression to the oral stage of the inarticulate infant at the breast.'[5] Given the terms of his own analysis, Reich need not have been quite so tentative: if the girl's adolescent sexuality

5. Reich, 'An Hysterical Psychosis in Statu Nascendi', *International Journal of Psycho-Analysis*, 1926, p. 170.

with her sister had presented the first step beyond the oral stage at which her mother's threats had previously left her, then this sister's death would be likely to throw her back to this position, and mutism, at least in this case, would clearly be a reference to this predicament.

Reich's case-history of a 'Hysterical Psychosis' is a model of his better methodology; it also demonstrates how, while still at the heart of the psychoanalytical movement, Reich was moving off its terrain. Tribute is paid to many of the classic concepts, but something has happened to them. They have become concrete, actual social events. Freud, as mentioned, had long since shifted from the theory of actual parental seduction to that of infantile phantasy desire, he had also stressed that the castration threat was not necessarily, as he had once thought, the real threats of nursemaids or parents, but a more tenuous amalgam of this and of the child's phantasy fears (got from, among other things, mental inquiry about a woman's absent penis and necessitated by the law of patriarchal culture). Yet here was Reich discovering that these seductions and these threats actually happened. Quite likely they did, as Freud acknowledged; Reich, however, never thinks to inquire whether the patient had desired her Hebrew teacher (had not, in fact, been raped by him), had hated her mother (not been threatened by her); the unconscious mental processes of the girl are totally absent from his discovery; they are absent likewise from his method. Freud had long since claimed that we can rarely remember our infancy, and that such amnesia called for an explanation. Indeed its explanation was one of the clues that led him to the theories of infantile sexuality: the sexuality of this period is dangerous and must be forgotten.

Reich's nineteen-year-old autistic hysteric burst into a sudden and explosive memory of times past. Reich barely recounts her manner of recollection, how she got there, or her emotions on arrival at 'the source'. Apart from a recurrent dream, easily explained by Reich, we get no problems of interpretation, no reconstructions through associations, verbal slips or the disguises of dreams. It is remarkably clear and quick, more like a sudden revelation than a process of analysis, indeed Reich himself recognized this. Too much came too quickly here. Is this, as

Reich half-postulates, because of the relative weakness of the
ego in a psychosis as opposed to a neurosis? If so, such an
observation could be the beginning of an important theoretical
point – one Reich nowhere goes on to make.[6] Or did Reich
provoke the revelation and never get to the bottom of it?

In any case, phantasy has been banished from the picture. It is
somewhat hard to credit that the mother's refusal of her child's
sexuality alone caused such total suppression and, in turn, the
patient's chronic hysteria and autism. One must at least ask
whether what was breaking through here was not the actual
events, but the onset of desire? If so, then the analysis had only
just begun by the time Reich 'solved' it.

In fact, it is where Reich is most tentative that he is most
interesting. The patient revealed a classic instance of infantile
sexual experience and, for that matter, a classic trauma case of
rape – both almost too perfect to be true; but the case led Reich
to ponder on another factor that was also preoccupying Freud:
the importance of the pre-Oedipal sexual relationship with the
mother. Reich discovered in this patient, what Abraham had
already proposed for melancholics, that disillusionment (the
result of the castration threat) could set in *before* the Oedipal
phase. Freud had likewise earlier commented on this possibility,
but without the clear implications that Reich drew. Reich
implicitly pushed back the Oedipal phase by explicitly stating
that genitality arose much earlier than previously believed. It
was a step on the road to his later, much more confident, belief
in perpetually omnipresent genitality: '... we cannot help
noticing how very early her genital libido came into action, for
we must assume that that occurrence represented the close of a
period which had already been going on some time.'[7] Two years
later, in *Die Funktion des Orgasmus*, he is already more com-
batively disputing the division and diversification of sexuality – as
though it were a retreat into Victorian prudery not to allow full

6. The account reads more like an interview that Tony Parker
recently held with a woman prisoner than like a Freudian analysis.
Suddenly, after a thirty-year silence, the woman broke down and told
him of her childhood intercourse with a man she later found to be her
father. The story is tragic in its later implications of tortured silence.
See Tony Parker, *Five Women*, Hutchinson, London, 1965.

7. 'An Hysterical Psychosis in Statu Nascendi', op. cit., p. 169.

genitality to the neonate (or indeed, as later, the foetus). Commenting on this period of his research nearly twenty years later, Reich demonstrated how his own awareness of the connection between mental disturbance, anti-social behaviour and disturbed genitality was already leading him into disputatious ground precisely in these terms – the diversification of sexuality. He points out how all his work was going against psychoanalytic distinctions between genitality and pre-genitality and against the very notion of partial impulses. Reich was to discover that, as with phantasies, pregenital sex was a sign of disturbance. His statements are somewhat confusing but they can be elucidated in the light of his general theories: genital sexuality is always present, in infancy it coexists with wrongly called 'pre-genital' sexuality (oral and anal desires and gratification), and any adult return to anything other than genital sexuality was a probable indication of neurosis. Genitality is profoundly different from other sexual impulses, *it* alone cannot and should not be sublimated or rejected except at great hazard, it is only its orgastic release that fully discharges the instinctual energy of the body and thus allows for release and relaxation.

It was not until his 1915 edition of the *Three Essays on Sexuality* that Freud had formulated the three sexual phases: oral, anal and phallic. Until that point he had enumerated erotogenous zones but had not specified that sexuality was organized around these with a different area predominant at different times. As we have seen, after his reformulation in 1915 he still stressed that the stages overlapped and that no clear demarcation line could be drawn as one element persisted into the next. Though his model at this time was still one of progressive evolution in his descriptions, Freud was aware that as these are re-expressed in adulthood the various 'stages' will be experienced simultaneously or in a new temporal sequence, a different structural arrangement. Reich's alteration of Freud's thesis amounts to what could be described as a moral assertion: genitality is unique and best. Given this supposition, all that detracted from genitality was perverse or disturbed. Freud's careful diversification of sexuality into component parts, and various erotogenous zones and different sexual objects, was rejected in favour of a value judgement. In doing this Reich fell headlong for the proposition Freud had been so anxious to avoid: if genitality was the only instinct, what could distinguish between abnormal and normal psychology? Reich embraced the dilemma: there was none. All neurotics were sexually disturbed; all sexually disturbed people were neurotic. Seventy to ninety per cent of the advanced world was orgastically impotent: the world was neurotic – mass neurosis or, as he later called it, 'the emotional plague'. From here we move into Reich's analysis of a society that drove its subjects neurotic; first it was capitalism, then all 'authoritarian' structures, then all social forms that detracted from 'natural', biological man.

3 Reich's 'Character Analysis'

If his interpretation of the all-importance of genital sexuality was, as Reich claimed, anathema to the timid spirits of his contemporary psychoanalysts and, as I would claim, was contrary to all the insights that Freud had had since his early pre-analytic days, then, just as certainly, it is his theory and therapy of 'character analysis' that is widely praised. It is this theory that has kept his name within the Pantheon. Republished in present-day readers for students of psychoanalysis, it is seen as one of the most important contributions to the analysis of 'resistances'. Rycroft hails Reich's theory of the resistances, which forms a crucial part of his 'character analysis' method, as his major contribution to psychoanalysis; Robert Fliess, republishing the work in its earliest versions, writes: '*The significance of the three papers on psycho-analytic characterology . . . can hardly be over-rated.*'[1]

Much of Reich's book *Character Analysis* appeared first as articles in psychoanalytical journals. The publishing house of the Psycho-Analytic Association and later the Association itself rejected the work, though they had accepted the articles. The reasons were never given and certainly it seems that no one took the trouble to debate with Reich what they regarded as the key error of his ways. Certainly, from Reich's point of view, the work was an orthodox extension (and a much needed one) of analytic practice in the therapeutic field. If either Reich or his readers had realized that Reich's novelties were based on a number of confusions, it might have been more productive for both. I want here only to single out what seem to me the confusions that are most significant for the development of Reich's work. In the first place Reich confuses the unconscious with the instincts, and in the second he is unsure of the difference

1. *The Psycho-analytic Reader*, op. cit., p. 104.

between a symptom and a resistance – it is only this latter uncertainty that enables him to make his original definition of a character trait.[2]

It is hard to pinpoint Reich's confusion of instincts and the unconscious, for when he has to define one or the other, the descriptions are quite distinct. It is rather that he uses the terms interchangeably and applies the characteristics of one to the other without any hesitation – thus he talks, for example, of the task of therapy being to make the *instincts* conscious (a transposition of the well-known formula of making the unconscious conscious). For Reich, the unconscious is the pool of the instincts, a reservoir of repressed vegetative excitations. The healthy person recognizes these excitations as sexual urges, the neurotic as the anxiety and aggression into which he has converted them. The task of the therapist is to free the genitality which this anxiety and aggression mask. Reich's system for restoring genitality he called the 'analysis of resistances', meaning something rather different from that implied by other analysts who were, at the same time, interested in this field. In the analytic situation the patient puts up resistances to recognizing the unconscious wishes, etc. that are clamouring to be heard in the dreams, slips, symptoms and so on. Freud, too, analysed the resistances that stood in the way of an approach to the unconscious; that approach was then made through dreams, slips of the tongue, free-associating thoughts and many other instances that give access to unconscious language. Analysing resistances did not on its own make aspects of the unconscious conscious in Freud's work: in Reich's it constitutes the entire procedure. And yet this is only a half-mistake, because another confusion saves it from absurdity. Reich conflates 'resistances' and symptoms. Thus he will comment that the distinction between chronic (childhood-developed) and acute (adult- or adolescent-formed) *resistances* is unimportant:

For the important thing is not whether the *symptoms* have made their appearance early or late. The important thing is that the neurotic character, the reaction basis for the *symptom neurosis*, was,

2. I am not going to discuss Reich's therapeutic practice as it seems to me that any problems it might have arise out of his theoretical mistakes.

in its essential traits, already formed at the period of the Oedipus phase [my italics].[3]

The resistance is not then, for Reich, the specific defence that the patient puts up to block interpretation, but the defence that the symptom represents. Of course, a symptom *is* a resistance – it is both the expression and the refusal of the expression of danger-ous unconscious desires and fears, but it is *not* synonymous with the ego-resistances which become so vocal (in the mind and the body) as a means of preventing cooperation in the consulting-room. Freud was concerned to make as specific as possible the different types of defence: Reich, as usual, to return them to a generality.

Reich then makes a further transition from the assimilation of resistance to symptom, to its equation with the entire character. If a person's behaviour patterns are resistances (which they quite probably are), resistances are symptoms, then so are character traits. It follows as night follows day because *it is the same pro-position*. What Reich calls 'character armour' – the expression of the resistance-symptom – is, he claims, formed in infancy, just as the later resistance-symptom is developed as a defence by the adult on the analytical couch. But: 'While the symptom corres-ponds essentially to a single experience or striving; the character represents the specific way of being an individual, an expression of his total past.'[4] Yet symptoms can become such an important part of the person's character that they resemble character traits. So the task of character analysis is to isolate these character traits and make their owner feel towards them as though they were symptoms. (Though doesn't Reich's previous hypothesis make them just that?) Again Reich describes the *character* in a reduced version of Freud's definition of a symptom. The simple, speci-fically Reichian gist is that the character is formed as a result of the refusal of genital longings: so the character contains the long-ings and the prohibitions.

Then by a further spiral back into the whirlpool of the argu-ment, the neurotic character must be altered to the extent that it forms the basis of the symptoms and thus prevents either gratify-

3. Reich, *Character Analysis*, Berlin, 1933. Enlarged edition, New York, 1945. Reprinted London, 1969, p. 42.
4. ibid., p. 44.

ing work or gratifying sexual relations. By this point the egg and chicken are changing places in such a rapid tumbling fashion that further elucidation of the process is hardly necessary. There are so many minor contradictions and confusions in Reich's theory of character analysis that it would take a book to document them. I think it is fair to say that almost every other sentence begs a question as to how we are to understand it.

The position stands thus: if the resistance is the symptom is the character, then that is the 'ego' and, as Reich says, one has to deal with the 'ego' before the 'id'. (Later he says they are both the same.) That means getting rid of narcissistic defences, of sadism, anal and oral fixations, anxiety and numerous other characteristics, before one gets down to what it is all about – the 'id' which is the unconscious, which is instinctual life, which is sexuality. The character, which is more or less the ego, and is more or less just an undesirable structure of 'character armour', must be dissolved in order for the true, that is the genital, person to emerge.

It is not surprising that Reich's great breakthrough in later years was the discovery that the id and the ego are one or, to repeat the process of his equation: as the id equals the unconscious, the unconscious equals the instincts, the instincts equal the sexual drives (genitality), then as the id equals the ego, the ego is the true person, the person *is* his or her genital sexuality.

Genitality, unlike all perverse pre-genital sexual fixations, cannot be dissolved; once it is there, it is there to stay. So the patient who has attained this point can only transfer it on to a suitable object of love, he cannot repress or ignore his achievement. Reich does not comment on the social problems that might arise here in a society with narrow aesthetic and social models; the ugly or old person might not find the realization of this easy. He does, however, comment on the strains put on the analyst: the analyst is working in a milieu hostile to his theories, so he has to be very sure of them; also he cannot, himself, have less health than that which he sets his patient as a goal. This thesis of the personal suitability of the analyst (he must have resolved his own repressed aggression and have attained genital potency) was to become of increasing importance in Reich's later orgonomic work.

If the end of Reich's proposition of character analysis is a long way from Freudian practice, the initial premise is really no nearer. It is simply that it is clothed in more orthodox and psychoanalytic terminology. Although in itself there is nothing wrong with this if the new theory holds up, yet it is clear that the task Reich originally set himself would lead him away from psychoanalysis. In the first chapter of *Character Analysis*, Reich refers to a classical division of methods of approaching neurosis: the dynamic/topical which deals with the qualitative aspect and the economic standpoint that relates to the quantitative dimension: that which gives the neurosis its energy. Of course, Reich was again referring to his reiteration of Freud's early notion that this sexual drive transfers its energy on to neurotic manifestations, and in his customary way, making this as concrete as he could. Thus he claimed that clinical observation showed that patients who, in early infancy or puberty, had attached libido to genitality were more likely to be cured by therapy than those who had not. He also stated that erective potency was unimportant, the importance of orgasm was all. With this awareness:

> ... it became suddenly clear where the problem of quantity lay: it could be nothing else but the somatic basis, the 'somatic core of the neurosis', the actual neurosis (stasis neurosis) which develops from the dammed-up libido. That is, the economic problem of the neurosis as well as the therapy of the neurosis was largely in the somatic realm and not accessible except over the somatic contents of the libido concept.[5]

This realization enabled Reich to turn his attention to the quantitative, somatic base, arguing that if one eliminated this (i.e. achieved orgastic powers) the superstructure of the psychoneurosis would automatically fall down too. Cure the body and the mind will follow suit. Exit psychoanalysis.

5. ibid., p. 14.

4 Psychoanalysis and Sexuality

Reich started where Freud started. Thirty years into the development of psychoanalysis, he took it back to its beginnings. Initially this seems to have been due to a preoccupation with the topics that interested the early Freud, later it became a forceful critique of the progress of psychoanalysis: what to him were its deviations from its true beginnings. At every level Reich had a veritable obsession with origins. I do not want to argue that there is no justification, then or now, for a return to where Freud started; certainly those beginnings could lead in different and productive ways from those which Freud took. The question is, did they do so in Reich's work? I would suggest that the greater part of Reich's contribution was based not on a genuine new departure, but on misunderstandings.

Reich concretized all concepts, took phantasy for fact or made it into a neurotic irrelevance and believed in the acting out of all natural impulses. His underlying motivation for this was his preoccupation with man's instinctual nature. I think it is safe to say that in latching on to this aspect of psychoanalytical theory, Reich grasped at its weakest part. As we have seen, Freud repeatedly said that the biological instinct was the inadequate and generalized assumption on which the psychoanalytic notion of the drive had to rest. Maybe, one day, it was not that important, biology would come to the aid of psychoanalysis with a more precise concept. Instead Reichian orgonomy came to its assistance.

Reich, always more interested in therapy than theory, the concrete situation rather than the abstract concept, acts rather than ideas, redeveloped every one of Freud's early social concerns about sexuality. Indeed he made experience of sexual strains in present-day life the nub of his major contribution to psychoanalytic theory.

Freud had early divided neuroses into 'actual neuroses' and

psychoneuroses. The former were neurotic outbursts provoked by some contemporary crisis in the patient's life, the latter determined by infantile events. Freud had also claimed that the 'energy' that drove the psychoneurotic symptoms and behaviour was produced by some current crisis, or, in other words, that at the core of every psychoneurosis was an actual neurosis. Though the actual crisis might be the death or the marriage of someone else, or a hundred other seemingly asexual events, these invariably provoked a sexual crisis, for two reasons: they always concealed a sexual problem and conversely all neurotic-inducing problems were sexual. Freud found this last proposition contained within the lesser radicalism of the first. As we have seen, initially Freud thought that either everything happened in the present or that everything happened in fact (his trauma theory). So when he first stressed the sexual etiology of hysteria it was because of the scandalous stories of seduction his patients confessed to him. In amazement, Freud began to picture the respectable bourgeois fathers as a gang of rapists or Lolita-obsessed perverts, whose paternal affection was mere predatory sensuality. With his discovery of the Oedipus complex and the role of sexual phantasy in the child's life, Freud was well on the way to formulating his notion of infantile sexuality and non-actual reality. The child is born with a sexual impulse and the demands made on this by human culture provide the channels into which it must or must not flow.

Reich did two things with this material. He brought back into major predominance the actual neurosis both for itself and as the centre of the psychoneurosis. Indeed gradually he reduced all neuroses to 'actual' ones which he renamed 'stasis' neuroses. Finally he found Freud's distinction totally false and opted for the concrete occurrence of actual crises rather than the intermingling of a crisis with its psychic representation as recollected trauma. This so-called psychoanalytic contention drove him back on to (and was reinforced by) his preoccupation with the social conditions in which sexual needs had to be expressed. The second consequence was his reinterpretation of the importance of infantile sexuality. Though Freud was very careful to avoid pansexualism, Reich was not. Free sexual expression became the highest good; and naturally it followed from this

that the child's sexual impulses were not only not to be discouraged but, on the contrary, fostered and satisfied – the
meaning of 'infantile sexuality' becomes entirely and simply
social. A libertarian education in a libertarian society can
provide the answer. The larger question of the acquisition of
the human order, the transmission of the most residual demands
of general culture is excluded.

The task to which Reich first addressed himself was the problem of the relationship between quantity and quality. Psychic
life was clearly a question of quality, but it was just as clearly impelled by a quantitative excitation. Reich found his answer in the
universal significance of sexuality – but, of course, typically, he
had his answer before he asked his question: sexuality was all-
important, the dilemmas that then arose within a theory were
automatically all soluble within its terms. Reich's reasoning ran
somewhat as follows (though one could reverse the direction):
sexuality is the only true instinct, instincts are the biological
basis of man, psychoanalysis claims to be a science not a philosophy, hence it must be, like the natural sciences, empirically
verifiable and about measured facts, therefore the biological
energy source of man is *the* scientific object of psychoanalytic
research and the actual neuroses are 'much more in keeping with
natural science than the "interpretation" of the "meaning" of
symptoms in the "psychoneuroses"',[1] we must therefore reduce
psychoneuroses to their actual neurotic core; we will call them all
'stasis neuroses' and we will find that the blocking of sexual
energy is their quantitative impulsion and the sexual feelings
their qualitative expression: quantity and quality will become
one and psychology and biology will likewise be unified in one
tremendous whole.

Neurotic conflicts then are clearly of a psychic nature, but
their energy, which is provided by inhibited sexual excitation, is
physical; a disturbance of the one creates an immediate response
in the other, for the psychic idea and somatic base are in complete harmony and mutual interdependence. This is a simple
solution to the problem that psychoanalysis certainly never completely solved, so simple that it denies the problem and along
with it the importance of psychoanalysis:

1. Reich, *The Discovery of the Orgone*, op. cit., p. 66.

But the main issue in this as in all other similar tasks of medicine and psychiatry will be the world of homo normalis, so long as he cherishes age-old ideas and laws which do untold harm to the biological core in every child of each new generation.[2]

Typical of the transformations that Reich made of psycho-analytic theory are his valorization of the child, his belief in the instant expression of infantile sexuality and his pursuit of pure and healthy normality.

Reich shifted his ground (or rationalized away an earlier contradictory idea) as to what he considered to be the most crucial of Freud's discoveries. In the twenties and thirties, the importance of sexuality and the unconscious together held pride of place in his tributes to Freud. Later he dropped the unconscious in favour of sexuality or amalgamated the two: the unconscious became the perception of orgonotic streamings.

In his treatment of infantile sexuality Reich moves from condemning the negative inhibiting effects of the patriarchal family to glorifying the child as the living spirit of Nature, pure in its animal impulses before it finds what man has made of man. Reich's last Will and Testament bequeathed everything to the Wilhelm Reich Infant Trust Fund, for Mankind's future, his infant heirs.

... there is a *sharp conflict between natural demands* and certain *social institutions*. Caught as he is in this conflict, man gives in more or less to one side or the other: he makes compromises which are bound to fail; he escapes into illness or death; or he rebels – senselessly and fruitlessly – against the existing order. In this struggle, human structure is molded.[3]

In pessimistic moods of hopelessness one is prone to ask what use there is in saving people from death by cancer if babies are being killed emotionally before and soon after birth by the million in nearly every single home all over the planet with the consent and help of their parents, their nurses, their doctors ...[4]

2. Reich, *Character Analysis*, op. cit., p. 507.
3. Reich, 'The Breakthrough into the Vegetative Realm', reprinted in *Selected Writings*, New York, 1970, p. 103.
4. Reich, 'The Rooting of Reason in Nature', *Selected Writings*, ibid., p. 518.

5 The Oedipus Complex and Family Politics

The Oedipus complex – or rather, his own version of it – is the terrain on which Reich can be seen most clearly to effect the union that he desired between psychoanalysis and Marxism. Freud's original notion of a child's love for its mother and jealousy of the father had grown more complex when he had turned his attention to female sexuality, and, even earlier than that, to homosexuality and a 'negative' Oedipus complex – the passive desire for the father and the simultaneous fear of him. On this issue Reich systematically ignored the problems that vexed his contemporary analysts in the twenties and thirties. The Oedipus complex was, for him, the psychic representation of the patriarchal nuclear family. Unfortunately, it is too simple. Freud had, as early as 1899, called it a 'universal event of childhood'; Reich, along with many others, restricted it to patriarchal capitalist childhood, thereby clearing the way for offering a solution in Utopian socialism, or primitive matriarchy. Characteristic of Reich's use of the concept of the Oedipus complex, and all such uses, is the absence of· the many modifications Freud made to his original simple plan of incestuous desire and murderous rivalry. Again Reich returns us to Freud's beginnings, concretizes the extrapolations about how an individual experiences his society, and thereby, somewhat obviously, gives us that society. The Oedipus complex is how the infant finds his place in a world of taboos and laws (expressed in our society by his relationship to his immediate parents); such a search cannot be reduced to the situation itself, without loss of the meaning of the concept, yet this is really what Reich effects.

One of the fullest presentations of his thesis is to be found in *The Imposition of Sexual Morality*, published in 1932. Reich had recently read Malinowski's account of the Trobriand Islanders, a matrilineal people apparently without an Oedipus complex.

His book is a unification of sociology and psychoanalysis through the anthropologies of Morgan, Engels and Malinowski. The Trobrianders were a godsend – providing a critique of capitalism and a legitimation of the use of psychoanalysis for Marxists. The Preface waves the banner:

A direct road was opened leading toward Marx just as soon as the sexual environment of a person's existence was recognized as the determinant of neuroses in childhood ... Freud glimpsed the key aspect of the etiology of neuroses in the conflict of the child with its parents, crucially in the sexual domain and most sharply around the Oedipus complex. Why should life in the family have this result? The neurosis is produced in the conflict of sexuality with a surrounding world that wants to suppress it. Sexual repression stems, then, from the society. The family and entire system of education operate together to impose sexual repression by all means. Yet why should this ever happen? *What is the social function that is gained by a family upbringing and the sexual repression that it instils?*[1]

The last questions were the important ones. Reich's strictures always had a pertinence that his solutions lacked.

The taboo on incest is usually accepted as universal; so too, after Freud, is infantile sexuality. How then does any society avoid the Oedipus complex? Reich answers this by pointing out that for the Trobrianders the incest wish is not suppressed; though incest is forbidden the wish is quite conscious, hence it is not dominant because it is not made unconscious; it is not problematic.

According to Reich the pathological dominance of the incest wish in our society is due to the refusal of all the other outlets for children's sexual impulses, and also to the parents' frustrations, which encourage them to compensate by sexual provocation and over-adoration of their children. In fact the fixing on incestuous love-objects is only one of many possibilities, and, as Reich was soon to imply, the choice of object is secondary to the sexual aim and as such can be 'perverse' without affecting the naturalness of the original desire. The sexuality of the Trobriand children is not simply allowed, but is actively encouraged; it is thus much more than the sort of non-punishment that liberal families in the West think of as sexual

1. *The Imposition of Sexual Morality, Sex-Pol*, op. cit., p. 94.

tolerance. Presumably, the incest wish can be consciously repudiated (much as Reich had claimed that the urge for intercourse during menstruation could be consciously postponed) through the prospect of other forms of sexual gratification. Incest defused of paramount desire, the Oedipus complex becomes likewise unproblematic. Or is it even there? Reich's account leaves us uncertain. Indeed Reich's avoidance here, as elsewhere, of any discussion of sexual objects makes for many gaps in his theories. Given that the baby is born to its mother and breast-feeds from her, some sensual attachment is to be expected. Is Reich's implication that the making conscious of this urge is the solution – much as 'making conscious the unconscious' is a crucial stage of the 'cure' in the psychoanalytic situation? If that is the suggestion it provides an interesting contradiction to Reich's own objections to the psychoanalytic aim, formulated repeatedly elsewhere. Furthermore, exactly what is envisaged by alternative sexual satisfaction and sexual affirmation of children is not set out here. The Trobriand children play genitally with each other but notably not with their elders. If inter-generational sexuality is tabooed and sibling sexuality allowed (as it is likewise somewhat more tolerated in our culture),[2] could we not legitimately call this an 'extended Oedipus complex' much on a par with the extended family? Though, of course, this is answering Reich in his own terms. For again, nothing in Reich's recounting of Malinowski's work indicates the psychic life of the Trobrianders.

There is a dilemma at the heart of Reich's works. Even in some of what he describes as the sex-affirmative 'matriarchies' at least one act of sexual suppression has been found to take place. Reich discusses the problem of these repressive procedures. In the 'matriarchy', he says,

The procedures endured by young people are not pre-emptive punishments for sexual activity, nor are they 'acts of revenge' committed by adults; they are rationally validated measures taken by the dominant group for the purpose of violently suppressing pubertal sexuality detrimental to this stage of economic development.[3]

2. See particularly Philippe Ariès, *Centuries of Childhood*, Jonathan Cape, London, 1962, for an account of sibling sexual games in the seventeenth century.

3. *The Imposition of Sexual Morality*, Sex-Pol, op. cit., p. 170.

If this is rational, then why isn't the more violent repression of infantile sexuality by the patriarchate also 'rational' from the viewpoint of its economy?

In the future when the patriarchate is more mature it becomes more sophisticated and more successful: it initiates a battle against childhood sexuality and harms sexual structure from the very beginning in the sense of orgastic impotence, not without coincidentally bringing down on themselves neurosis, perversion and sexual criminality. The fear of castration, which Freud discovered in bourgeois man, is historically rooted in the economic interests of the budding patriarchate. And the same motives which originally created the basis for the castration complex maintain this complex in capitalism today: the patriarchal private enterprise system's interest in monogamous permanent marriage – an interest in which parents, totally on an unconscious level, function as the executive organs.[4]

Clearly if one is 'rational', so is the other; all we are left with saying is that one is 'worse' or we dislike it more: the inevitable moral value judgement which Reich again implied, and with which we may agree, does not really help us.

Although he makes constant reference to Freud, Reich's treatment of the Oedipus complex rapidly comes to have little to do with psychoanalysis. It is perhaps more interesting for the development of his Marxist ideas. Reich gradually decides that sexual repression is the primary social force. The social suppression of general sexuality precedes what he calls 'the class conflict between male and female'. Primitive communism is somehow 'intruded' upon and its free sexuality put down – it is this process which then leads to class antagonism.

But for the Marxist Reich further contradictions arose in this analysis. Reich had only one acknowledged disagreement with Engels – Engels had claimed that the introduction of father-right led to the first accumulation of wealth, whereas Reich demonstrates that among the Trobrianders the compulsory delivery of tribute from the tribal brothers to their chief, before patriarchy, led to the accumulation of wealth and hence from there to patriarchy; the method for rendering such tribute was the marriage dowry. But the degree to which he coincided with Engels led him to an unacknowledged contradiction. 'It is already apparent that

4. ibid., p. 170.

Engels had correctly surmised the nature of the relationships: he wrote that the origin of class division was to be found in the antithesis between man and woman.'[5] The cause of Reich's confusion is really quite simple: the Trobrianders were his model for a society illustrating the harmony of sexuality and productivity, and yet even here, all was not as well as it might be. When Reich is describing the customs of the Trobrianders his praise flows freely: when he analyses the economic organization and kinship structures, the problems present themselves forcefully.

The practice of exogamy, and the marriage dowry (from the brother of the bride to her husband), mean that Trobriand society is in a transitional phase by Reich's own account. The seeds of devilish patriarchy are already well sown by these economic arrangements. Where then is the primary sexual repression? Whether primary or not, it is there, in the fact of the incest taboo – conscious or not. We are left then with a number of problems. The perfect sex- and work-harmonious society of primitive communism is invaded by genital repression to form the first organized social group, then follows male/female opposition, thence patriarchy and classes. Which is the matriarchal stage? Not primitive communism because in that state there is neither lineage nor property, so somewhere in between? But the Trobriand peoples are, according to Reich, 'matriarchal' and they display residual economic organization and sexual repression. Where finally can our Utopia discover itself? Material conditions bring about sexual restrictions, sexual restrictions change material conditions. In this tautologous chicken and egg situation, Marx (or rather Engels) and Freud have not been married.

The results of this abortive wedding are, nevertheless, quite interesting. In trying to bring about their union, Reich has in fact forced them further apart. His description of customs and of the psychic structures actually overtly contradicts his portrayal of economic conditions, although both are unified in his ideological rhetoric against capitalist conditions of existence:

Inasmuch as we were able to discover the sociological meaning of sexual repression and its capitalist function, it should not be difficult

5. ibid., p. 182.

to find the contradictions which created it and will lead to its destruction. If on the one hand, sexual repression fortifies the institutions of marriage and family, it undermines them on the other hand through the sexual misery of marriage and family developing on this foundation. Sexual repression has the effect of making young people submissive to adults in a characterological sense, but at the same time, it brings about their sexual rebellion. This rebellion becomes a powerful force in the social movement when it becomes conscious and finds a nexus with the proletarian movement undermining capitalism. That the contradictions of sexual repression are seeking a resolution is apparent in the sexual crisis which has enveloped the capitalist countries with a steadily increasing strength since approximately the turn of the century. It fluctuates in its intensity according to the economic crises on which it is directly dependent.[6]

It is Reich's attacks on the capitalist family and so-called monogamous marriage that have had enduring value. How can this be so, when the analysis underlying them is so patently inadequate?

Reich, from his survey of 'primitive man' via Engels and Malinowski, concluded, as he had often concluded before and was to do so again, that the family is the major ideological factory of capitalism because it is the agent of sexual repression. The ruling group first produces morality as its quite explicit cultural demand, but this morality is then reproduced in the internalized psychic structures of each individual and it is here that sexual repression features so forcefully. Man's needs (food, sex, shelter), to which the changing mode of production adds newly created needs, are crucial factors of history – Reich calls them 'subjective factors' (he also, in complete contradiction to his thesis of primal sexual repression, calls both basic and created needs 'secondary' elements). The demand for the satisfaction of these needs thus challenges the political superstructure and ultimately the basic economic mode of production. Reich castigates all communist parties and criticizes the Soviet Union for ignoring these needs. The 'subjective' factor, that is the average psychic structure of any people of any given society, must become a central part of all revolutionary calculations. As, to Reich, the subjective factor is determined by the libidinous forces which cause its existence and

6. ibid., pp. 246–7.

as the only science of sexuality is psychoanalysis (until the time when he broke with the psychoanalytic movement), Marxists ignore psychoanalysis at their peril:

... when psychoanalysis is rejected, the only satisfactory theory of sexuality is abandoned. The changing sexual life in the Soviet Union develops in consequence in a more unconscious fashion, guided to a far lesser degree by the will of its subjects than is true of other aspects of Soviet life. For instance, the steps to eradicate religion are lucid and purposeful by comparison, based as they are on scientific enlightenment of the masses combined with a flourishing technology turned directly over to the laboring operatives.[7]

The 'subjective factor' is Reich's means of politicizing psychoanalysis. Whatever their political implications (and many of Reich's observations, such as that above, were accurate), from the psychoanalytical viewpoint Reich's reductions are disastrous; he is forced to reduce a crucial and complex concept to the simple and concrete elements from which it was originally drawn. The Oedipus complex should indeed be renamed the 'Oedipus simplex' in Reich's work.

As we have seen, Reich denied the presence of the Oedipus complex in matriarchal society, and made its discovery the basis of his assault on the patriarchal family. But as sexual restriction *precedes* the advent of the nuclear family, that family only later becomes its agent. We have here another contradiction. For Reich the nuclear family is the walking, talking Oedipus situation; the Oedipal scene itself becomes unimportant, an entirely neutral assemblage, no longer the 'nucleus' of the neuroses, but merely a skeletal structure around another force: sexual energy. (This is a sharp contradiction to his other use of it: being identical with the patriarchal family, it is, in itself 'bad'.) Twice, in different contexts, Reich reiterated that the pathogenicity of the Oedipus complex depends on whether or not there is an adequate discharge of sexual energy.[8] Presumably, if the child is sexually affirmed in other ways (sibling sex-play or masturbation,

7. ibid., pp. 100–101.
8. One time is in *The Discovery of the Orgone, I*, and the other time in *An Introduction to Orgonomy* where, interestingly, he uses this argument to prove that there is no important distinction to be drawn between the actual neuroses and the psychoneuroses.

although Reich is against the latter?) its incestuous longings for its parents are rendered insignificant? The Oedipus complex is no longer, as in Freudian theory, the difficult entry of the infant into human society, but a more or less superfluous outcome of an original repression of sexuality. The Oedipus conflict of the psychoanalyst Reich and the class antagonistic society of the Marxist Reich are both then the result of sexual repression. A footnote in *The Mass Psychology of Fascism* reveals how far Reich has moved:

> Hence, the 'Oedipus complex', which Freud discovered, is not so much a cause as it is a result of the sexual restrictions imposed upon the child by society. Yet, wholly unconscious of what they are doing, the parents carry out the intentions of authoritarian society.[9]

And elsewhere in the same work, he writes:

> Freud discovered the Oedipus complex. Revolutionary family politics would be impossible without this discovery. But Freud is just as far from such an assessment and sociological interpretation of the family formation as the mechanistic economist is from a comprehension of sexuality as a social factor.[10]

Actually Freud would only have had to discover the patriarchal family for this revolutionary family politics to have come into existence.

9. *The Mass Psychology of Fascism*, New York, 1970, p. 56 n.
10. ibid., p. 58 n.

6 Psychoanalysis and Marxism

Reich's transposition of the Oedipus complex back into the patriarchal family spelt death for the psychoanalytic concept within his works. But the case Reich argues within a psychoanalytical framework ultimately can be just as disastrous for his political theories as it is for his analytical ones. I think we can see how *the same* misconceptions affected both.

In his work on character analysis, the fundamental confusion of the unconscious with the instincts finally undermined his entire work in this field. I would suggest that the same confusion mars his understanding of the nature of dialectics, and that although this is revealed in the area of his thought that deals with psychoanalysis, it also extends, naturally enough, to his Marxist theories.

Reich's fullest attempt to give a theoretical account of an amalgamation of Marxism and psychoanalysis is an early text, written when he was affiliated to the Communist Party and a member of the Institute of Psychoanalysis. This essay, 'Dialectical Materialism and Psychoanalysis' (1929), has the merit, absent in those books where he applies the combination, of having no diversions from its central theoretical preoccupation.

Obviously, in this article, written for a Party paper, Reich was out to convince communists of the dialectical materialist nature of psychoanalysis, while elsewhere he was often more anxious to convince psychoanalysts. Later he reduces both Marxism and psychoanalysis to their sociological content. He abandons both except for whatever empirical social observations he can glean from them. He, then, condemns psychoanalysis for being undialectical by a criterion that itself denies dialectics, and insists that Marxism is not materialist enough because it cannot touch the physical source of life. But in 1929, the task was different.

Reich first defined psychoanalysis as a science with its own specific field: inner life. He then distinguished what he saw as the two aspects of Marxism: a world philosophy (i.e. a revolutionary politics) and a 'sociological science':

> As a science, psychoanalysis is equal to Marxian sociological doctrine: the former treats of psychological phenomena and the latter of social phenomena. And only insofar as social facts are to be examined in psychological life or, conversely, psychological facts in the life of society, can the two act mutually as auxiliary sciences to one another.[1]

But the important question is whether psychoanalysis can prove itself to have a dialectical materialist method. If it can, then Marxists must recognize it as a science, even if, as he states in another article of the same year, contemporary communists are correct to point out that any science propagated in bourgeois societies must have idealist deviations. Did psychoanalysis use a dialectical method or else could it be proved that psychoanalysis 'if only unconsciously, like so many natural sciences – has actually stumbled upon a materialist dialectic in its own sphere and developed certain theories accordingly'.[2]

Already in 1929 Reich's battles with his fellow psychoanalysts were such as to prevent him claiming for the science a dialectical method; therefore he has to prove his second proposition: psychoanalysis has, albeit unawares, discovered the materialist dialectic within its scientific object. So Reich sets out to demonstrate the dialectical tendency of psychical life as it has been revealed by psychoanalysis:

> True, psychoanalysis does speak of predisposition, of developmental tendencies and so forth, but the facts which have so far been discovered by experience concerning psychological development in early childhood suggest only the dialectical development . . . progressive movement by means of contradictions from step to step.[3]

Reich's suggestion here is that the libido of the infant passes through stages, oral, anal, phallic (a theory he is at pains to deny in some psychoanalytic controversies he wages), but that no new stage is reached until satisfaction has been refused in the

1. Reich, *Dialectical Materialism and Psychoanalysis*, *Sex-Pol*, op. cit., p. 8.
2. ibid., p. 8.   3. ibid., p. 38.

previous one. The ego, fearing punishment, represses the forbidden urge, and the symptom that results from this contains both the rejected urge and the rejection itself. The urge or instinct is thus converted into its opposite – for it is a property of all instincts to contain ambivalence and to say 'yes' and 'no' simultaneously. 'In such reversal the original instinct is not destroyed but is fully maintained in its opposite.'[4] Such is the dialectical nature of psychic life. But Reich is guilty here of that error that we have seen to underlie the confusions of his work on character analysis. Here the error is to prejudice his whole concept of dialectics. In this essay, no sooner has he proposed the dialectical flexibility of the instincts (instead, as it should be, of unconscious ideas) than he drops it. Naturally this dialectics within the nature of the material on this misconceived basis of the instincts, gets very short shrift indeed. And before the essay is half-way done, Reich is already offering up completely different psychoanalytic theories on the altar of Marxism. Most notably, he returns to the Oedipus complex and his contention that the Engelian thesis of the family is to be equated with the Freudian Oedipal scene. The basis of his unification of psychoanalysis and Marxism is the dialectical movement of the instinct, the repression of the instinct, the combination of the instinct and the repression appearing as symptom or, later, as 'character'; but this thesis is never elaborated.

Reich does not, for all that, drop his appeal to dialectics. Indeed it is to be one of his main charges against Freud that the latter's 'invention' of the death-drive was an abandonment of the dialectics of sexual instinct for a dualism of the instincts (life versus death) and of the complex contradiction for simple antithesis. Reich also maintains, until the end, that his own science is dialectical; by which, even in the early days, he means that the conflict of biology (which he calls the unconscious) and society and their possible unity (under socialism, later under a sex-economic society) is the reconciliation of opposites: his dialectical principle. But not Marx's. The notion of a complex structure, in which many elements may contradict each other or may become resolved, only to enter into a new contradiction with a new element, is utterly alien from Reich's wish to reduce all

4. ibid., p. 36.

to the simplest terms and simplest laws of existence. His Marxist notion of ideological formation suffered the same fate at his hands as psychoanalysis: it ceased to be anything, and instead was compensated for by sociological observation which was often pertinent but could never be constructed into a theory with these intellectual tools. But something worse has happened, for psychoanalysis has to be proved to be a *materialist* science as well.

In this essay of 1929 Reich reproved vulgar materialist and mechanist Marxists with words that, had he remembered them, he must have eaten later as he sat measuring bions, the good orgone energy OR and the evil DOR. 'The mechanistic error consists in the fact that measurable, ponderable and palpable matter is identified with matter as such'.[5] In Marx, Reich goes on, there is no question of the material reality of psychological activity being denied – if there was we would not speak of 'consciousness' or 'ideology' but wait until their chemical composition is discovered. This is a joke that does not sit well on the lips of the man who claimed to have discovered the chemical formula of the unconscious in his later years. On the other hand, how far away from this vulgar notion of materialism is he here? We have seen that Reich starts by saying that the terrain of psychoanalysis is 'inner life'; a few pages later he states categorically that the basic theory of psychoanalysis is that of the instincts, and we find him saying that psychoanalytic understanding can be confirmed by organic research. At best, this must leave us highly suspicious even though Reich was some way away from claiming that the unconscious was actually palpable. 'Inner life', then, is instinctual life and can be confirmed by organic observation. Indeed when later he comments on the work that he had been carrying out around this period, we find Reich making a similarly confusing statement. He is commenting on Freud's crucial proposition that we can only experience derivatives of instincts:

My interpretation of Freud's statement was as follows: It is altogether logical that the instinct itself cannot be conscious, because it is what governs us. We are its object. Take electricity: we do not

5. ibid., p. 12.

know what it is; we only recognize its manifestations, such as light and shock. Though we are able to measure the electric current, it is nothing but a manifestation of what we call electricity and do not really know. As electricity becomes measurable through the manifestations of its energy, so are instincts recognizable only through their emotional manifestations.[6]

This is like a poor man's guide to the structure of the unconscious impersonating as instincts. Or, the other way round:

If Freud's theory of the unconscious was correct – which I did not doubt – then one could apprehend the inner, psychic infinity. One became a little worm in the stream of one's own feelings. All this I felt very vaguely, not at all 'scientifically'. Scientific theory, seen from the standpoint of life as it is lived, offers something artificial to hold on to in the chaos of empirical phenomena.[7]

The wedding of the theories of Marxism and psychoanalysis, for Reich, took place in the sphere of ideology. There is much that is interesting and almost certainly correct in this supposition, but it is marred by his reading of the unconscious and the reductionism that, as a result, the notion of 'ideology' itself undergoes. Reich's thesis really amounts to saying that man has animal instincts (his 'unconscious') which are outgoing ('towards the world') but which then hit the conflicting social pressures moving against them. In the ensuing conflict man builds himself like an armour-plated monster, suppressing his instincts and using the hostile attitudes of the world as the main component of his armour-plating. The internalization of social mores and restrictions (which is what Reich calls 'ideology') is thus the same as the character structure which is, for the vast majority of the population, the equivalent of character armour. A repressive society thus automatically produces repressive people; the only way of breaking through this and settling the conflict the other way is by loosening the character armour and releasing and satisfying the sexual instincts. We always get back there in the end.

Reich's crucial misconception of the unconscious as merely the pool of the instincts affects his political writings no less, if

6. *The Discovery of the Orgone*, op. cit., p. 12.
7. ibid., pp. 21–2.

more elusively, than his psychological ones. For all further examination of the apparent contradictions within Reich's propositions on psychoanalysis reveal this to be the cardinal error from which all initial confusion and all his future work stems. This is where Reich went wrong; it is the nuclear misunderstanding around which all his work revolves. It is a tragic mistake, for it was this misunderstanding that motivated first his interest in psychoanalysis and later, his own orgonomy. Without such an error, he would never have achieved so much.

7 Sex-Economy, Vegetotherapy and Orgonomy

Sex-economic sociology dissolves the contradiction that caused psychoanalysis to forget the social factor and Marxism to forget the animal origin of man . . . Psychoanalysis is the mother, sociology the father, of sex-economy. *But a child is more than the sum total of his parents.* He is a new, independent living creature; he is the seed of the future.[1]

Reich's sex-economic child thrived on the murder of its mother (psychoanalysis) and on the deathly transformation of its Marxist father into sociology.

There is a prevalent fashion for favouring Reich's early works and rejecting his later ones. Mary Higgins, his trustee, denounces this, claiming that Reich's work is a whole, and that acceptance of any of his theses means acceptance of orgonomy. This is carrying things too far, but there is an unfortunate truth about her contention. Reich's earliest propositions about the importance of man's biological needs, his notion that sexuality=the unconscious=the person, all lead directly into his orgonomic searchings for the tangible source of life. His initial description of the nature of the orgasm as a process of tension-charge-discharge-relaxation is unexceptional (and uninteresting) and can lead so easily into his formulation that this is the basic life pattern itself (after all it is basic enough in any sense). Politically there does seem to be a shift between the communist revolutionary of the twenties and thirties and the Pentagon-Eisenhower fan of the last two decades, but even here (where the change is important, but not unfamiliar) a common element can be detected. The communist Reich's attacks on his fellow revolutionaries for their rigid, ascetic, authoritarian personalities and propaganda is not so far removed from his later labelling of communism as Red

1. *The Mass Psychology of Fascism*, op. cit., preface to the third edition, 1942, p. xxiii.

Fascism. Of course, with such a vulgar simplification, we do get a qualitative change, but it is not an absolute one. There are many telling inconsistencies in Reich's work; an obvious example is in his rejection in the thirties of those who laid the phenomenon of Nazism at the door of Hitler's personality, and then his own later rabid denunciation of all communism in terms of Stalin, whose personality he saw as so all-important that he named him 'Modju' and made him a modern-day devil. Such shifts and inconsistencies should not mislead us into thinking that Reich's work falls into two separate halves – the political, psychoanalytical European days and the days of American orgonomy. The American culture of the forties and fifties merely helped Reich to clear his mind and banalize his confused work.

I do not intend to outline the content of Reich's later work, beyond saying that in his therapy he aimed at dissolving the muscular armature (the character armour of the resistance-symptom-character-trait) in a planned manner. He claimed to have found the somatic location of psychic sensations and would loosen that point in the person's body (thus, for instance, anxiety was rooted in the cardiac region).[2] To Reich the body is divided into segments like those of a worm, and the therapist's task is to release each section in turn so that the harmonious streamings of life energy can be restored to a body that should have free-flowing plasmatic capacity but has instead sclerosed itself into an armadillo.[3] Certainly psychic problems have a somatic equivalent (it was from this point in reverse that Breuer and Freud started),

2. Reich had also decided that many physical illnesses such as cancer, angina, etc. (he called them biopathies) shared with psychological illnesses a fundamental damming up of sexual energy which burst out in malignant growths, sexual perversions, acts of cruelty and aggression where and when it could; he hoped these could all be treated in the same way. But it would be wrong to suggest from this that Reich simply reduced psychic illness to physical illness or psychoanalysis to biology, for he welded the two together, as was his wont, making them, like the actual neurosis and the psychoneurosis, and, like quality and quantity, indistinguishable.

3. 'It took many million years to develop you from a jelly-fish to a terrestrial biped. Your biological aberration, in the form of rigidity, has lasted only six thousand years.' *Listen, Little Man*, New York, 1969, p. 41.

but Reich's notion both that the soma determines all and that there is a constantly flowing energy that should be remobilized (orgastically) has yet to be established. The further thesis that this life-energy unites man and the cosmos, where it is also to be perceived dancing in the blue spots of sunlight and elsewhere, led Reich to his work on cosmic superimposition and to his efforts at weather-control and the rest.

Of greater interest is the intellectual apparatus which Reich utilized for his new 'science'. These general theories establish the continuity with his earlier work, which the content of orgonomy would seem to deny. Here, in his approach, those early errors as to the nature of dialectics, the unconscious, sexuality and the subjective factor in history, find their apotheosis.

Reich's principal scientific method was one he labelled 'functional identity'. So we learn that cell lumination (the blue glow), physiological excitation and psychic sexual emotion are functionally identical, or, for instance, from the standpoint of energy, the vagina taking the penis is functionally identical to the baby sucking the nipple. (Reich proposed this as early as 1934 and repeated it in 1948.) As Reich's work progresses it becomes increasingly clear that 'functional identity' is his application of the dialectical principle: all opposites, all aspects are the same at the base, all are merely diverse applications of the same source – this is his unity of diversity:

Freud ... was mainly a dialectician, a functionally thinking human being. He always wanted two forces to counteract each other. What he did not do, and I don't know why, was to see that *these two opposite forces were actually one in the depth because everything opposed in nature is ultimately a unit*.[4]

To Reich, a dialectician is a functionally thinking human being – he thought Freud failed to carry his ability through for he rejected (as Reich had long ago complained) all 'oceanic' feelings, or the oneness of the universe.

Earlier, Reich (in a one-sided fencing match with Freud) had set up an opposition between Nature and Culture more thorough than anything Freud ever suggested. Of course, he explicitly refuted the very opposition he had created by pointing out their

4. *Reich Speaks of Freud*, New York, 1968, p. 92.

underlying harmony – but this unification of extremes *in profundis* is not, as he claims, dialectics, but religion. Reich's simple proposition was that Nature and Culture are today at loggerheads, but were not so in the primitive past, nor need be so in the primitive future. If Nature and Culture would be one again, so would all lesser conflicts. Thus, Reich conducted his argument against Freud's theory of the death-drive in his usual manner: first he claimed that as it could not be materially measured, it could not be said to exist, then he decided that it was, in fact, a possibility but only if it was united as a concept with its opposite, love:

> *The striving for non-existence, for the Nirvana, for death, then, is identical with the striving for orgastic release,* that is, the most important manifestation of life. There can be no idea of death which derives from the actual dying of the organism, for an idea can only render what has already been experienced, and nobody has experienced his own death.[5]

If death itself is to be orgastic release, surely love can go no further? Finally, in his experiments he 'discovered' the palpable essence of death and destruction (he called it DOR), and with this he returned to a Manichaean world of opposition: there is good and evil, but they emanate from one source.

If 'functional identity' was Reich's dialectical method, functionalism was, from the start, his scientific theory. Living matter simply functions, it does not have 'meaning' or aim. Man has lost touch with this simple function, to him it must be restored. There is a 'functional' connection between living and non-living nature. Orgonomy was the triumphant resolution of the dialectical unity of all dualities in their original one-ness:

> *The discovery of the cosmic orgone functions within the human animal may well represent a major evolutionary step forward in the direction of a FUNCTIONAL UNITY of the cosmic and the intellectual flow of developments, free of contradiction.*[6]

Functionalists are interested in the common and they discover that experiences such as sex or religion are really only the sensa-

5. *Character Analysis*, op. cit., p. 340.
6. 'The Rooting of Reason in Nature', *Selected Writings*, New York, 1970, p. 526.

tion of nature in one's own body; dying of grief is functionally identical with the shrinking of the autonomic nervous system.

The ultimate of Reich's search for the material, quantitative source was his discovery that the 'orgonotic' bodily energy streamings were the actual unconscious – though even this is only the logic of his initial concept of the unconscious as the instincts and of the instincts as palpable. And the ultimate of his union of the Many in the One was his merging of the subjective and the objective. After this point there are no distinctions, or rather, those that are there, are evidence of man's neurotic, armoured condition.

Man cannot feel or phantasy anything which does not actually exist in one form or another. For human perceptions are nothing but a function of objective natural processes within the organism. Could there not be a reality behind our 'subjective' visual impressions after all?[7]

And Reich found that there could: the perceiving subject and the observed object form a functional unity, it is only mechanistic science that splits them into a false duality. The seer and the seen are one. The subjective method, personal hunches, accidents and so on become the foundation of his 'science'. The character of the researcher was all-important, so that the perceiver could be in harmony with the perceived:

Every important discovery originates from the subjective experiencing of an objective fact, that is, from vegetative harmony. It is only a matter of making the subjective sensation objective, of separating it from the stimulus and of comprehending the source of the stimulus.[8]

From the outset, Reich's concept of a science leads to this end. In his early efforts to prove to its opponents (e.g. Jaspers on this issue) that psychoanalysis was a science and not a philosophy, he had set up the distinction that a philosophy dealt with qualities and a science with quantities. Failing finally to make psychoanalysis accept his discovery of its scientific object – the quantitatively measurable sexual energy of the instinct – he branched out

7. *The Discovery of the Orgone*, Vol. II, *The Cancer Biopathy*, New York, 1948. p. 85.
8. 'The Discovery of the Orgone', a chapter in *Selected Writings*, op. cit., p. 219.

on his own, to set up what he claimed as the only scientific psychology – sex-economy and orgonomy.

Throughout his writings, Reich's concept of sexuality was imbued with functional thinking. Rejecting the hoary idea that the function of copulation was procreation, Reich went in search of new purposes. In his psychoanalytical days, one function of sexuality was the pursuit of pleasure (the pleasure principle), but, though this remained a function, it gave way in the middle period to the greater importance of providing an outlet for the body's electrical discharge, only in the last works to become reconciled in panegyrics to nature's cosmic magic:

The orgasm is an event which *happens* in two living organisms, and not something 'to be achieved'. It is like the sudden protrusion of protoplasm in a moving amoeba. An orgasm cannot be 'had' with everyone. Fucking is possible with everyone since all it requires is enough friction of the genital organ to produce discharge of seminal fluid or a feeling of strong itching. An orgasm is more than and basically different from a strong itching. One cannot 'obtain' an orgasm by scratching or biting. The scratching and biting male and female is struggling to obtain bio-energetic contact by all means. Orgastic contact *happens* to the organism. One does not have to 'make' it. It is there only with certain other organisms and is absent in most other instances. Thus it is the foundation of true sexual morality.[9]

9. *The Murder of Christ*, New York, 1966, p. 30.

Wilhelm Reich:
Sexual Politics, II

8 Today and Yesterday

The new political movements of the sixties and seventies have brought about a renaissance of the work of Wilhelm Reich. The majority of his books have only recently become available and reference is most often made more to an acknowledged general gist of his work than to detailed comprehension of it.

Reich was a pioneer of sexual politics (the term is his). As such his thinking in this area is crucial for current libertarian socialist politics, for anarchism, for student cultural revolutionaries[1] and for women's liberation. This is not to underestimate its importance in its own day. When Reich opened his first Sexpol clinic in Berlin in 1931 it was immediately attended by 20,000 people – within the first year the number had risen to 50,000 and there were twelve similar institutions in the rest of Germany.

But a stunning contemporaneity is, however, present throughout Reich's work. Or should we say that the achievement of his suggestions has been so inadequate that we are, today, merely rediscovering them and redemanding their implementation? Often, reading many of his contentions about the political implications of the suppression of sexuality resembles finding the source of a dream – 'So *that* is where the idea came from.' Few present-day militants can have read Reich's work when they first formulated the same demands in much the same terms thirty and forty years later. Accounting for this 'unconscious' heritage of thought offers us simultaneously a way into assessing our own political notions and those of Wilhelm Reich.

A brief mention of some of his ideas most closely echoed today will give an illustration of this sense of inverted '*déja-vu*'. Read-

1. For an important example of the use made of his writings, see Reimut Reiche, *Sexuality and the Class Struggle*, New Left Books, London, 1970, a book originally written at the height of the German student movement (1968), by one of its leaders.

ing him, we've heard it all before, in our own mouths yesterday, today.

I want to concentrate here on those ideas that concern women's status and female sexuality. Sometimes his notions were contained in his psychoanalytic and sometimes in his political writings. As we have seen, the distinction is, in a sense, a dubious one for Reich's concern in his early days was to politicize psychoanalysis and add the insights of psychoanalytical thought to Marxist politics.

As a sexologist in the early twenties Reich criticized contemporary sex reform associations, making the crucial distinction which he maintained throughout his life between liberal sexual reform and revolutionary sexual politics. He pointed out that loosening of the divorce laws was meaningless (or worse) in a society that made the woman and children economically dependent on a man;

[More liberal divorce laws] in themselves mean little. Either the economic position of the woman and the children is such that a divorce is economically impossible. In this case a 'liberalization of divorce laws' does no good. Or the conditions of production change in such a manner that economic independence of the woman and social care of the children becomes possible. In that case, the termination of a sexual companionship will no longer meet any external difficulties, anyhow.[2]

Legal abortion was similarly a demand of limited value – in most instances it was 'above the heads' of the vast majority of working people, whose sexual problems started long before the frequent visits to back-street abortionists or the employment of virtually 'witchcraft' techniques of enforced miscarriage. Adolescent sexuality was inhibited not only, as with the bourgeoisie, by parental prohibition, but by housing facilities and lack of privacy. The family was an incestuous unit in which the

2. Reich, *The Sexual Revolution*, New York, 1969. Revised from an edition published in Berlin in 1936 and reprinted from a New York edition of 1945, p. 57. And: 'any alleviation of the divorce laws is practically meaningless as far as the masses are concerned. The divorce law means nothing but that society, in principle, allows divorce. But is it ready to create those economic conditions which make it possible for the woman actually to effect it?' (ibid., p. 146.)

compulsive morality of the parents (in particular of the mother) made them compensate for their own lack of sensuality by inducing it in their children; the mother alternatively cuddles and reprimands in a sad mimicry of the emotional relationship she no longer has with her husband. The child's sexuality is thus perverted into a mother-fixation – from which it is hard for the adolescent to break away and which later re-expresses itself in the son's choice of a wife, or the daughter's manner of relating in her turn to *her* children. This incestuous sexuality is simultaneously induced and forbidden, leaving the young child with a conflict of encouraged urges and forbidden desires – the (Reichian) Oedipus complex.

Reich perpetually stressed the importance of female sexuality. He saw the passive nature of woman as a pathological product of a society committed to her suppression. Though critical of the limitations of the slogan, he advocated 'control of one's own body' as a primary right of the woman, setting it on a par with economic independence. For women and children were not only economically but also sexually dependent on men: the internalized compulsive fidelity of monogamy for the wife, and the paternal prohibition on sexual exploration for the child. His theories of the means of female sexual fulfilment are interesting in the light of today's debates. Then, as today, in the debates on woman's sexual response, a strong case was being made for clitoral orgasm. Reich, the sexual revolutionary, regarded this suggestion as a *conservative* argument used to *limit* the scope of woman's sexuality, to reduce it to a pale imitation of man's. On the other hand, he rejected the Freudian notion of a two-tiered sexuality for women as reactionary (for Freud the little girl's clitoral sexuality is repressed to enable the development, at puberty, of a vaginal sensitivity); but he criticized yet more strongly those who contended that the clitoral response was the all, and that the vagina was a relatively insensitive area. Such an argument, to Reich, was antagonistic to the liberation of women because it short-measured their potential sexual pleasure. The great majority of men (70–80 per cent) and an overwhelming percentage of women (90 per cent), he was convinced, rarely attained sexual satisfaction, and to suggest that clitoral release was a substitute for vaginal convulsions was to make women rest content with this miserable state of affairs. This is in sharp contradiction to the present trend in American feminism (though not to that in the French women's group – *Psychanalyse et Politique* – which also stresses the repressed primacy of the vagina). Reich's manner of attacking Freud was not to eliminate vaginal sexuality, but to take it right back into infancy as Abraham, Horney and others had done. Reich was, however, interested not, like other analysts, in the psychological implications of this, but only in the simple sexual significance. He was able thus to avoid making the sort of value judgement that Horney offered. To Reich the infant girl has fully awakened vaginal sexual sensations; these are not a secondary development at puberty, nor are they a myth propagated by male chauvinists who have never learnt to stimulate the clitoris.

These battles do seem to be fought on old grounds, although the reversal of the 'conservative'/'progressive' argument is interesting. One can see how Reich could claim his account as the revolutionary position: it not only stressed the strength of the woman's orgasm but it gave the little girl a female potency denied her in the Freudian schema.

There seems to exist a great deal of confusion over Reich's attitude to woman's sexuality. But Reich's position was really quite simple: he felt there was basically no difference in the sexual patterns of men and women. Each experiences tension, then a charge and release (his model is a highly simplified version of the laws of energy), sometimes more, sometimes less according to time, place and partner but never according to an imbalance between the sexes of desire or possible achievement. Yet, though he forcefully condemned the conqueror–Don Juan syndrome in men and the excessive passivity of women he did, despite what Rycroft claims, make a distinction: men feel an urge to thrust and penetrate, women to receive. The orgasm of both is the muscular movement of the *whole* body.

Despite the opposite claims of the majority of present-day feminists and Reich over the relative merits of clitoris and vagina, both can end up in the same position: valuing a natural feminized culture over and against the technocratic male civilization as we have known it (a familiar artistic theme too, in *fin de siècle* Vienna). For Reich, vaginal receptivity came possibly to represent a meeting of the self and the world in universal love; he postulated that it was a new and higher stage on the evolutionary road from beasthood to godhead. In woman's sexuality perhaps mankind would at last rejoin the natural universe.

Reich and present-day radical feminists, such as Shulamith Firestone, share other convictions. Both started their analyses within a broadly Marxist context; then the example of Engels's historical sociology and Malinowski's psychological anthropology encouraged them to break the bounds of Marxism and postulate that a sexist society precedes a class one: patriarchy incorporates all forms of exploitation – it is its vast domains that must be analysed and overthrown.

9 Sex and Society

What I did was to put my eagle's egg in the nest of chickens' eggs. Then I took it out and gave it its own nest.[1]

It is really quite a relief when Reich's eagle's egg finally hatches; for neither Reich's contemporary critics, nor his later ones, seem to know quite what to make of the early works, or the re-editions of them in the forties. No one corrects him; they accept, abuse or merely assess the general gist, but never come to grips with the problem posed. He is a very confusing writer: his transposition of the language of one science on to another, or merely his redeployment of it within the same territory, means that we are often caught napping – the phrase is familiar, acceptable, and we fail to observe a change of object. Reich is not trying to deceive or delude, the lapses in attention are his as well as ours. But there is a further problem. Reich gives excellent, rhetorical expression to radical sentiments which many of us espouse: his denunciation of the sexual and economic dependence of women and children, of compulsive monogamy, of the private-property family, of child-rearing, the methods by which the baby is dragged howling into the world, the physical deprivations of the working class, the housing shortage and so on. If we echo them today, it is because they are still highly relevant. But if what we do is to echo them, that, too is relevant.

It seems to me that our reiteration of Reich's propositions points to both the strength and the weakness of his work (leaving aside, that is, our shared heritage of radical 'common sense'). As a theoretician – Marxist or psychoanalyst – Reich has little to contribute; as an empirical sociologist with more than a fair share of perceptive hunches or 'intuitive' insight he is

1. Quoted as a footnote in *Reich Speaks of Freud*, op. cit., p. 40. From the Archives of the Orgone Institute, 1951.

powerful. We cannot make use of his work for further analysis because its theoretical propositions are inadequate or non-sensical. We can, however, repeat his very pertinent observations. Reich's psychoanalytic and Marxist concerns were not destroyed by his amalgamation of them, for they were each, both independently and together, destroyed by his theoretical muddle-headedness. However, in the reduction of both of them to a rhetorical political sociology lies Reich's triumph. Is it a triumph that we can still use?

We can see in the writings of the twenties and early thirties that it is almost as impossible to separate Reich's social, as it is his sexual, concern from his psychoanalytic pursuits. His first official work was in the Viennese clinic and this convinced him of the crucial effect of social conditions on the etiology of neuroses. Sexuality is the answer, society the mistake.

Reich rightly saw that different classes experienced social restrictions in different ways and consequently produced different types of neurotic behaviour. Actually Reich maintained that they produced different types of neuroses, but this is more debatable. In *Der Triebhafte Charakter*, published in 1925, he described the 'impulsive' characters whom he encountered in the clinic but who were never to be met with among the bourgeois patients of private practice. At this point, he argues wholly within psychoanalytic language. The working-class impulsive person was to be distinguished from his class equivalent – the bourgeois obsessional man – by the inadequacy of the repression of his initial sexuality. The ego-ideal, in both cases, opposes the sexual instincts, but, as a result of inade-quate repression, the superego of the impulsive man does not; it is therefore isolated and acts itself like a repressed impulse to form a symptom, usually a masochistic demand for punishment.[2] The symptom then of the impulsive character has two elements – the inadequately repressed instinct and the inadequate represser itself. But gradually Reich moved away from debating his pro-position of class-determined neuroses within psychoanalytic terminology, and tended instead increasingly to document the

2. Reich was still arguing this position four years later, but then in a theoretical debate with Abraham and Rank. See *International Journal of Psycho-Analysis*, London, 1928.

social conditions that would make this likely. Thus, two years later in *Die Funktion des Orgasmus* (subtitled 'A contribution to the psychopathology and sociology of sexual life'), he merely comments that although the working class adapts to bourgeois morality and tries hard to identify its life-style with that of the petty-bourgeoisie, the sexual inhibitions are less because external restrictions are so great that in this situation there is less need for internal morality. It is this that makes the impulsive character-type more frequent than the obsessional amongst the working class. The point is the same as that elaborated in *Der Triebhafte Charakter*, the range of reference already completely different[3] – it is now almost exclusively sociological.

Reich's next essay explicitly on the sociology of sex was on notions of sexual maturity, fidelity and marital morality. It was a critique of bourgeois sexual reform. It brought together most clearly the social and psychoanalytical theses that in the earlier two works had run on parallel lines, and the point of this convergence was the family. For the very reason that Reich's interpretation of the family detracted from his psychoanalytic work (his abuse of the concept of the Oedipus complex), it augmented his social and political awareness. His was a political sociology of an institution from which psychoanalysis took its beginnings; it is no accident that it was later this sociology that he used as a stick with which to beat psychoanalysis. When he turned against politics he had to find other weapons – so he revealed the mysteries of God and the beasts.

Reich's condemnation of compulsive marriage and the bourgeois family took two forms. The family suppressed the sexuality of individuals; capitalist society used it to produce an authori-

3. This class awareness Reich never abandoned while working in Europe. And even in his American retrospection he confirms it, though by this point a romantic primitivism of the poor had tended to take over his work and this had to lie side by side with etiolated remnants of his earlier political awareness. Incidentally, Rycroft is wrong to state that Reich shared with D.H. Lawrence a faith in the sexual potency of the working class. This is not to say the comparison between Reich and Lawrence is invalid – indeed an entire study by a Reichian, David Boadella, has been devoted to the subject. (This study is his M.A. thesis available from the British Museum Library, not his recent book on Reich.)

tarian or submissive personality. The two are linked, as the one is the means to the other. From his sexological studies, Reich was convinced that monogamy destroyed sexual happiness. He favoured faithful long-term relationships lasting as long as the sexual attraction remained, but the unequal treatment of the sexes (male polygamy and female abstinence) meant that within marriage, sexual happiness was virtually impossible: 'Sexual partnership and human companionship in marriage then become replaced by a child-parent relationship and mutual slavery, in brief, by masked incest.'[4] Reich never fell into the trap of crudely demanding the abolition of the family; indeed he explicitly opposed such a notion.

> What we want to destroy is not the family, but the *hatred* which the family creates, the coercion, though it may take on the outward appearance of 'love'. If familial love is that great human possession it is made out to be, it will have to prove itself. If a dog which is chained to the house does not run away, nobody will, for this reason, call him a faithful companion. No sensible person will talk of love when a man cohabits with a woman who is bound hand and foot. No half-way decent man will be proud of the love of a woman whom he buys by supporting her or by power. No decent man will take love which is not given freely.[5]

Even as late in the day as 1945 (when the above was written), Reich, though by no means any longer a Marxist, did not believe that sexual liberation could occur within the present structure of society. In this respect he finds conservatives more aware than sexual reformers of the implications of sexual changes: such changes would quite simply mean a revolutionary change in the whole social structure, indeed they are meaningless without it.[6]

4. *The Discovery of the Orgone, I*, op. cit., p. 175.
5. *The Sexual Revolution*, op. cit., p. 29.
6. Just to give one example of Reich's powerful arguing here, I will select his opposition to the reformist slogan 'Fighting the causes of prostitution'. 'The causes are unemployment and the ideology of chastity for the "well-brought-up" girls. To fight this, it takes more than sanitary measures. Who is going to take these measures? The same reactionary society which is incapable of managing unemployment and depends for its existence on the ideology of chastity?

Sexual misery cannot be overcome by such measures. It is an essential part of the existing social structure.' (ibid., p. 57.)

This crucial awareness from his Marxist days means that Reich's denunciations, located firmly in the social structure, do not on the whole contain even the utopian illusions of his anthropological days, those days of the matriarchal dream. That side of his Engelian heritage he is able more or less to shed when his biological religion is there to replace it. Ironically, it leaves his social and political analysis of the family much the better for its absence.

10 Politics and the Family

We have seen how Reich waged relentless war with the Communist Parties to which he was affiliated over their interpretation both of the family and of sexuality. Standard contemporary Marxist practice was to see the family as mainly economically oppressive; Reich countered this with tactical and theoretical arguments. The Communist Parties were critically to blame for their failure to appeal to youth, women and workers and they failed for one reason: their refusal to address themselves to the everyday problems and human needs of which sexual satisfaction was paramount. Whether or not we agree with his conclusions, Reich was certainly perceptive on this point; the fascists were quite simply better populists than the communists. Reich was correct also to pay the attention that he did to the methods of Nazi ideological warfare. His conclusion that no revolutionary party should leave human needs and ideological questions to the right wing was forcefully expressed. Yet in the European period, he never, as his opponents then and since have claimed, maintained that sexual liberation was a present-day goal to be sought for on its own. Indeed he reiterated that one thing only was possible under capitalism: *the politicization of sexuality*. The manifesto of Sex-Pol stated:

One must realize that one's demands are not attainable under capitalism – otherwise one sustains illusions and treads the path, whether or not one wishes it, of liberal reformism. One must ruthlessly criticize all sex reform institutions that make it a non-political issue. Class struggle is essential for its resolution. On the sex question, the workers will have to strike a blow against capitalism and cultural reaction – the end is not Utopian and we have before us the way of the Soviet Union – the way of revolution.[1]

1. Sinelnikoff, op. cit., Vol. II, p. 29. Sinelnikoff is right to point out how this statement and all it implies is contradicted by Reich's

In the 1932 German elections, the Nazis made massive gains. In particular they won over large numbers of workers. In Reich's analysis their achievements were based on two factors: their material corruption of the lumpen proletariat and their ideological corruption of the labour aristocracy. Reich set himself the task of urging the Communist Party to compete with this clever political understanding. In his theory of the nature of class consciousness, Reich concluded that there were currently two types: that of the leaders and that of the masses, and that it was high time the former understood the latter. The party leadership must understand the diverse needs of the masses: the need for pleasure, for better housing, for privacy, for food. The concrete conditions of a man's existence, he argued, are reflected in the psychic structure; the current concept of socialism was quite simply too ascetic. Reich argued that everything under capitalism that we consider moral or ethical is in fact used to further oppress 'working humanity'. That which serves the revolution is truly moral. Revolutionaries must encourage all that is hostile to the bourgeois order. For instance, the adolescent tendency to rebel for sexual freedom always makes youth more politically left-wing and it should, therefore, be encouraged. Collective or communal living (Reich had his reservations) is good for young people in the sense that it removes them from the family. Antagonism towards marriage is likewise a very important means of freeing women for revolution, but it must be clearly distinguished from crude legislative devices and feeble slogans such as 'entry into the production process', 'independence from men', 'right to one's own body', for though these indicate a correct insistence on economic and sexual autonomy for women they are phrased in such a way that they ignore the positive side and instead produce anxiety for the losses that will accompany any such emancipation. (Reich was not always consistent here, thus sometimes, as we have seen, he made use of the last two slogans.) But, in short, the socialist revolution must be able to answer the petty-bourgeois needs of the masses, while trans-

---

repudiation of the Soviet Union in the second edition of *The Sexual Revolution* (in German only) in 1936 and is reduced still further by the absence of a Marxist vocabulary altogether in the third (the American) edition of 1946.

forming them. To transform them, only the favourable aspects of such needs and preoccupations must be stressed for of course liberation can, if isolated, bring its obverse: delinquent youths and fearful adults.[2]

All these propositions had a relevance to the political practice of the European Communist Parties, then as now. But as Sinelnikoff points out, Reich never really had a theory of a sexual revolution but what he did have was a clear conception of anti-authoritarian struggle. For this reason, once again, his strictures on the family are most pertinent.

In *The Sexual Revolution* (all editions) Reich commented on the change that had been wrought in the function of the family within capitalism. He reiterates the familiar idea that its economic basis as the pre-capitalist unit of production became less and less significant the more men and women became involved in the productive processes of capitalist industry. The economic function had been replaced by a political function: the family is the factory for authoritarian ideologies and conservative character structures. In *The Mass Psychology of Fascism* Reich turns to look at how Nazi ideologues exploit the family, and to stress how profound the effects of such a programme are:

... inasmuch *as a social ideology changes man's psychic structure, it has not only reproduced itself in man but, what is more significant, has become an active force, a material power in man, who in turn has become concretely changed, and, as a consequence thereof, acts in a different and contradictory fashion.*[3]

2. As it is not strictly relevant to my purpose here, I shall not document Reich's growing disillusionment with Russia. He retained to the end a great admiration for Lenin (though it became an admiration not for a political theorist, but for a charismatic personality), but from the mid thirties onwards he really adopted positions analogous to the criticisms made earlier by Kollontai and the Workers' Opposition: Russia was becoming a State power, the workers' needs were being ignored, the party was cut off from the masses. (This position never led Reich to Trotskyism, though he had a sympathetic meeting with some Trotskyists in Paris in 1933.) See also Reich's roneographed pamphlet, 'The Masses and the State' (1935), in which he asks why the Russian State is not withering away and what is happening to the all-important Soviets? The important details of Reich's political history can be read in Sinelnikoff, op. cit.

3. *The Mass Psychology of Fascism*, op. cit., p. 18.

and:

> *The interlacing of the socio-economic structure with the sexual structure of society and the structural reproduction of society take place in the first four or five years and in the authoritarian family.*[4]

The family, the agent of sexual repression, is the authoritarian state in miniature.

Reich contends that vulgar Marxists are mistaken in supposing that deprivation *per se* produces rebelliousness (by this yardstick, Reich jokes, women would be the most militant!): on the contrary sexual repression and anti-sexual attitudes are a feature of conservative character structures. Nazism appeals to and diverts sexuality: the erotic goose-stepping and the exhibitionism of parades show that militarism is based on libidinous mechanisms: 'Travel to foreign countries – join the Navy' with the foreign country represented by a sensual woman. (Reich's account of the sexual language of Nazi propaganda is fascinating.)

Although fascism arose as a middle-class movement, its success was to exploit all the contradictions of the petty-bourgeoisie and to appeal with one hand to the workers while denying the appeal by promises made with the other hand to big capital. Hitler was only successful in so far as his ideological propaganda related to the character structure of the mass of the population. The family situation of the middle class dominates that of other classes – its utilization is crucial:

> The middle class got caught up in the movement and made its appearance as a social force in the form of fascism. Therefore, it is not a question of Hitler's or Göring's reactionary purpose, but a question of the social interests of the middle-class strata. Owing to its character structure, the middle class has a social power far in excess of its economic importance. It is the class that preserves nothing less than several thousand years of patriarchy and keeps it alive with all its contradictions.[5]

and:

> The social position of the middle class is determined by (1) *its position in the capitalist production process,* (2) *its position in the authoritarian state apparatus,* (3) *its special family situation,* which is

directly determined by its position in the production process and is the key to an understanding of its ideology. There are indeed differences in the economic situation of the small farmers, the bureaucrats, and the middle-class businessmen, but the basic nature of their family situation is the *same*.[6]

The lower middle classes are the key to this: above all they fear a fall to the status of worker, above all they strive for a middle-class appearance: this is best expressed in the gentlemanly pretensions of their family.

Nazi propaganda appeals to the 'honour' and 'duty' of a small-minded, dishonest and competitive class. But the ecstasy these words provoke is not simply because they mask the social reality – rather they call to unconscious emotional life. The patriarchal petty-bourgeois family repeats the social structure in precisely these terms: the father like the *Führer* makes his children subservient and his sons grow in his image, his wife is also resigned and suppressed. (Reich acknowledges that the process is more complex than this.)

In all classes the sibling rivalry for the parents produces competitiveness and the sexual repression of children can be translated directly into self-control, duty and honour in the outside world. Reich outlines one of his familiar sequences: patriarchy, and hence capitalism, inaugurates the necessity of compulsive marriage, which involves sexual suppression which, in turn, becomes a personal struggle against one's own sexuality. This leads to personal compensation with such notions as 'honour'; 'honour' becomes family honour which can then be transposed to racial honour and national honour:

> In their *subjective emotional core* the notions of *homeland and nation are notions of mother and family*. Among the middle classes the mother is the homeland of the child, just as the family is the 'nation in miniature'.[7]

The tie to the mother is claimed by reactionary propaganda as biological whereas its intensity indicates that it is clearly social. In brief, fascism involves the supreme exploitation of all that patriarchal capitalism has brought into being. Patriarchy deprives women and children and adolescents of sexual freedom,

6. ibid., p. 44.   7. ibid., p. 57.

makes sexuality into a commodity and subordinates sexual interests to economic ones –

> From now on, sexuality is indeed distorted; it becomes diabolical and demonic and has to be curbed ... As time goes on, this sexuality, which is so distorted, disturbed, brutalized and prostituted, advocates the very ideology to which it owes its origin. Those who negate sexuality can now justifiably point to it as something brutal and dirty. That this dirty sexuality is not natural sexuality but merely patriarchal sexuality is simply overlooked.[8]

And fascism plays on this situation, encouraging its practice while proposing to emulate a Platonic homosexual state; women are needed for reproduction for the militaristic build-up, hence the concept of 'pure' motherhood and a further refusal of female sexual expression. Hitler offered men the full dependence of women: he returned the wife to the home. Reich commented:

> Hitler promised the subjugation of woman to man, the abolition of her economic independence, her exclusion from the process of determining social life, and her relegation to the home and hearth. The women, whose individual freedom had been suppressed for centuries and who had developed the fear of an independent way of living in a particularly high degree, were the first to hail him.[9]

And with youth, the Nazis likewise exploited a contradiction:

> By advocating the 'preservation of the family' and *at the same time* taking youth out of the family and putting them in its own youth groups, Fascism took into account *the fixation to the family as well as the rebellion against the family*. Because Fascism emphatically impressed on the people the emotional identity of 'family', 'state', and 'nation', the familial structure of the people could easily be continued in the Fascist, national one.[10]

Then Hitler made full use of the 'dirty sexuality' of patriarchy; Nazi mysticism was a creed of purity and asexuality in opposition to so-called Jewish 'materialism' and sexual sin. Over and over again Hitler's pronouncements laid stress on the dangers of syphilis and referred to the perils of inter-racial breeding as 'incest' (thereby completely reversing the meaning

8. ibid., pp. 88–9.
9. *The Discovery of the Orgone, I*, op. cit., p. 209.
10. ibid., p. 214.

of the term but utilizing deep unconscious fears). The whole race theory was based on such rationally incomprehensible arguments, indeed irrationality was its key:

> [The Teuton] feels himself to be 'superior', and that's the end of it. The race theory can be refuted only by exposing its irrational functions, of which there are essentially two: that of giving expression to certain *unconscious* and *emotional* currents prevalent in the nationalistically disposed man and of concealing certain psychic tendencies.[11]

Reich finally saw that the battle against fascism should be fought out between rational sex-economy and irrational mysticism. Mystical daydreaming and sentimentality essential for the success of the Nazi mystique were induced early through the psychophysical tensions which the small child developed in the claustrophobic, sex-repressive family. It was therefore a battle over the basic character structure.

Reich laid out the task of his own theory of sex-economy. Unlike his private therapeutic practice of 'vegetotherapy', which was designed to eliminate repression and restore 'biologic health', sex-economy was to be a sociology whose aim was to make conscious the suffering and the contradictions endured by subjugated man:

> Thus, it is not a question of helping, but of *making suppression conscious, of dragging the fight between sexuality and mysticism into the light of consciousness, of bringing it to a head under the pressure of a mass ideology and translating it into social action.*[12]

Such a task clearly cannot be carried out by a revolutionary party that in a straight fight beats fascism at its own moralistic game. The rejection of the importance of sexuality as 'bourgeois individualism', the stressing of woman's reproductive powers as against her sexual needs, the notion that the family is economically and not sexually and ideologically repressive, doom the revolutionary party to failure in the struggle against fascist

11. *The Mass Psychology of Fascism*, op. cit., p. 78.
12. ibid., p. 187. Echoes of psychoanalytic concepts remain in Reich's phraseology until the end. Here, as so often elsewhere, it is the psychoanalytic task of making conscious the unconscious that is the underlying motif.

mysticism which makes use of much the same theses to greater effect.

The Mass Psychology of Fascism is an attempt to explain the way in which the economic and social situation relates to ideology and how ideology in turn becomes embedded in the character structure of the population (if in somewhat different ways in different classes). Reich is quite aware of his selective presentation of the multifarious aspects of the nature of fascism and of the battle against it; originally, the book was a substantial work of propaganda.[13] It was the last of Reich's major works to try to make the Communist Party take note of psychoanalysis and psychoanalysts of communism (in the later editions this aspect is largely obscured). Again, this time in analysing contemporary political phenomena, the terrain he chose for their conflation was the family – but this time with much more success, because what he offers is a political sociology.

13. Naturally my account of Reich's account is still more selective.

11 Politics within the Family

Reich never presented a family case-history. In his psycho-analytical days, his reference to the patient's family was largely formal, revealing no particular concern with intricacies or particularities. With his literalizing mind, Reich tended to take the patient's word for it and thus showed no interest in family drama or in the details of interpersonal relations or perceptions. Hence the comments on the internal dynamics of nuclear family life came from his political interests and were rarely reinforced with any direct observations. They were, however, confirmed by generalizations and extrapolations from an orthodox body of psychoanalytic theory, and as such reveal fairly clearly what Reich took from psychoanalysis for political purposes, originally ostensibly Marxist, later decisively his own:

> Such unconscious desires as that of eating feces can be found in a great many individuals, regardless of their social class. Such psycho-analytic discoveries as that the over-solicitude of a mother for her child or of a woman for her husband corresponds to the intensity of her unconscious phantasies of murder were highly inconvenient for the ideological champions of 'sacred mother love' or of the 'sacrament of marriage' ... These contents of the unconscious were shown to be remnants of infantile attitudes toward parents, siblings, etc. In order to exist and to fit into our culture, the children have to suppress these impulses ...[1]

It is easy to see how Reich came to use the insights of psycho-analysis against it, as he came to use his Marxist knowledge against communism. Both psychoanalysis and Marxism are reduced to the sociology of the family and as the family as a social institution is found to be at fault, natural biology can be made to triumph against social evils. Nevertheless, however dubious his latterday conclusions, Reich's rhetorical descriptions

1. *The Sexual Revolution*, op. cit., p. 11.

of intra-family relationships have a force that it still relevant and a pertinence that redeems their repetitious quality.

Reich maintains that all contemporary jealousy is pathological because the economic dependence of women makes each partner in a monogamous marriage treat the other as a possession. On the other hand, brief relationships suggest a desire for promiscuity which is itself a fear of attachment and a flight from the fear of incest which is always reawakened by prolonged love of another person. Promiscuity generally suggests an unsurpassed homosexual attachment or tendency to idealize which makes all actual people seem worthless. Furthermore, all Reich's work completely undermined any notions of woman's 'naturally' monogamous constitution. Thus both promiscuity and compulsive marriage are to be condemned, though he realized that one cannot want to get rid of marriage within the terms of a society in which marriage is an economic necessity. One can only introduce minor 'reforms' such as various ameliorative aspects to divorce legislation. Marriage remains a protective institution for women as long as they play no independent role in production, and this protective aspect obscures the degree to which women are exploited within it, providing the free services of housekeeper and child-rearer that enable capitalists to get workers to labour longer hours for lower pay. If the wife works, she does two jobs; if she fails to cope with both, the home and marriage disintegrate.

Both parents compensate for their own deprivation by their 'love' and ambition for their children. This love, particularly that of the sexually starved mother, makes the family an oppressive, incestuous unit:

A further characteristic of family education is that parents, especially the mother, unless she is forced to work outside the home, see in their children the only content of their lives, to the great disadvantage of the children. Facts such as that the children then play the role of household pets whom one can love but also torture according to one's whims, that the emotional attitude of the parents makes them altogether unsuited for the task of education, are platitudes which need no further mention.[2]

2. *The Sexual Revolution*, op. cit., p. 77.

These are sentiments we have heard many times since. Indeed, maybe their most striking feature is that their truth can only be reiterated. Certainly Reich even in his American days never relinquished their vituperative powers:

> You want a marital partner to sue the other, to accuse him or her of immorality or brutality when they no longer can live together. Divorce on the basis of mutual agreement you do not recognize, you little descendant of great rebels. For you are frightened by your own lascivity. You want the truth in a mirror, where you can't grasp it. Your chauvinism derives from your bodily rigidity, your psychic constipation, Little Man.[3]

> The sticky love of the mother toward her child is true hatred; the rigid faithfulness of the wife is true hatred; she is full of longing for other men. The dependent caretaking of men for their families is true hatred. The admiration of the crowd for their beloved führers is true hatred, potential murder.[4]

3. Reich, *Listen, Little Man*, op. cit., p. 53.
4. Reich, *The Murder of Christ*, op. cit., pp. 68–9.

12 A Woman's World

In 1922, Reich, a young sexologist working within the confines of psychoanalysis, wrote an article entitled *Coitus and the Sexes*, in opposition to a statement by Karl Urbach that the female orgasm came later than the male one. Reich, in his refutation of this and in his advocacy of simultaneity, took the opportunity to emphasize a theme that he had already stressed in many debates: the importance of social attitudes in determining the nature of sexual relationships. He argued that social customs produced the significant differences between male and female sexuality (although he thought a combination of biological and social factors responsible for what he saw as the lesser excitability of women). He commented on the fact that middle- and upper-class young men split their sexual urges into sensuality (satisfied by prostitution) and sentimentality (their fiancées, wives and mothers) and consequently had no interest in the sexual satisfaction of women in love-making. On the other hand, the forced abstinence of women until marriage, and this sexual devaluation and artificial, sentimental hypervaluation of them within it, led to their real frigidity. It was not a new theme, but its trenchant reiteration in bourgeois Vienna was salutary.

Reich, as he moved closer to the Communist Party, retained and broadened his belief in the supreme importance of the social factor. He stressed, on many occasions, that the economic dependence of woman and her abuse as a 'sexual object' determined her need for that self-perpetuating evil but nevertheless protective institution of marriage as it also determined her fundamentally conservative character. Sexual deprivation, unlike economic hardship, never produced a revolutionary character structure:

The vulgar Marxist who thinks in mechanistic terms assumes that the discernment of the social situation would have to be especially keen when sexual distress is added to economic distress. If this assumption were true, the majority of adolescents and the majority of women would have to be far more rebellious than the majority of men.[1]

And indeed, Reich pointed out how the increasing sexual emancipation of women and their massive war-time participation in industry did lead to an immense increase in stress and to numerous contradictions which would ultimately lead to their greater refusal of conservative, oppressive customs. The contradiction could often be between a historically accumulated character structure and new social conditions. Thus he wrote of the woman of 1925: 'Her character requires, for example, a strictly monogamous sexual life while in the meantime compulsive monogamy has become undermined socially and ideologically,'[2] hence her rearguard action in clinging to stifling traditions. But Reich was optimistic:

A frigid woman of 1900, who stayed at home doing her housework, did not have a job and no outside contacts with men, was much less endangered than she is today, where she takes an increasing part in social life. She does so as a result of industrial development as well as a result of the present war. No doubt we will have to expect even far more revolutionary changes in the life of the woman. Nobody – except Fascists – will demand her return 'to the hearth'. And even fascism becomes impotent here.[3]

Reich carried his contention of the social conditioning of sexuality and character formation right into the heart of psychoanalytic doctrine. The nature of the nuclear family and social attitudes to women produced those characteristics thought of as immutably feminine. Freud had proposed penis-envy as a source of woman's striving for masculinity and the lesser need for sublimation at the time of the Oedipus complex as one, among many, reasons for her intellectual inferiority. Reich sallied forth against the implication that such characteristics were inherent. He agreed that some such 'unconscious sexual attitude' makes

1. *The Mass Psychology of Fascism*, op. cit., p. 31.
2. *Character Analysis*, op. cit., Introduction to 3rd edition, 1948, p. xxv.
3. *The Discovery of the Orgone*, Pt II, *The Cancer Biopathy*, op. cit., pp. 357–8.

each parent prefer the child of the opposite sex, but this does not have to be ruthlessly suppressed. Thus, for example, if the father is mild and loving, his daughter can retain him as her love-object and does not have to repress this by identifying with him as she would have to if he were domineering and punitive:

True, she also is likely to have acquired penis envy; but, as there were no serious frustrations of heterosexual tendencies, it remained harmless as far as character-formation is concerned. We see, then, that to say that this or that woman has penis envy does not mean anything. What matters is its influence on character or symptom formation. The decisive factor in this type is that a mother-identification in the ego took place; it expresses itself in those character traits which are called 'feminine'.[4]

Reich maintained until the end that any inferiority or passivity in women was imposed on them *in sexuabiles* by a culturally specific morality which thus defined them. As we have seen, it is not that this argument in itself is wrong, it is rather that a partial explanation is made to stand for the whole answer. Reich's way of solving the problem is to eliminate it.

Reich, however, was not averse to using the culturally determined sexual modes as part of his own methods of character analysis. Thus, in 'A Case History of an Inferiority Complex', his entire analysis of the male patient is conducted in terms of the man's femininity complex. This makes the whole proposition tautologous, at best, although it does give us some insight into how femininity is experienced (not Reich's intention). The same objection is valid for his central theory of masochism; here he takes the cultural conditioning as crucial, finds it present and concludes it is there: 'Masochism flourishes like a weed in the form of the diverse patriarchal religions, as ideology and practice, smothering every natural claim of life.'[5] It is not 'biological' but pathogenic. Reich's explanation of it is nevertheless physical: it is the bladder-like urge to burst, repressed by social institutions and turned back on itself: '*What it could not bring about spontaneously from the inside, it would passively, helplessly, expect from*

4. *Character Analysis*, op. cit., p. 154.
5. 'The Breakthrough into the Vegetative Realm', *Selected Writings*, op. cit., p. 111.

the outside.'⁶ Again Reich's description of the sensation of masochism, like his descriptions of the male patient's experience of femininity and fear of masculine aggression, are good reflections of the sensation of femininity. But they are reflections.

Reich's emphasis on the cultural production of sexual traits is accurate only because he omits cultural influence from the formation of his 'unconscious'. If the unconscious is biological then, of course, it is essential to point out the crucial meeting point of biology and society. But Freud's 'unconscious' was precisely a structure that, in a complex and uneven manner, had already done this. Reich never understood this and so his work ignores the entire purpose of psychoanalysis, and his theses on women, despite their sympathetic appeal, suffer the same fate. Reich's stress on how needless is femininity ignores the reasons as to why it is there. His equation of man and woman, their unity and affinity, is biological wishful thinking. Are they, too, functionally identical? But this is also indicative of another dimension of his work.

If at first it is a great relief to read Reich's notion that there is no important difference between the sexes, it gradually comes to seem an evasion. Social attitudes and conditions may well specify masculinity and femininity – but they are there and cannot just voluntaristically be castigated for existing, they cannot be waved away by magic. Except that this is what Reich's whole 'science' of orgonomy would do; it would get us back to some invented entity of 'pre-social' man:

I love the birds and deer and chipmunks who are close to the Negroes. I mean the Negroes from the jungle, not the ones from Harlem, in stiff collars and zoot suits. I don't mean the fat Negro women with ear-rings whose inhibited pleasure turned into the fat of their hips. I mean the svelte, soft bodies of the girls of the South Sea whom you, the sexual swine of this or that Army, 'lay'; girls who do not know that you take their pure love as you would in a Denver brothel.

No, daughter, you long for the living which as yet has not understood that it is exploited and despised. But your time has come. You have ceased to function as the German racial virgin. You continue to live as the Russian class virgin or as the Universal daughter of the

6. ibid., p. 112.

Revolution. In 500 or 1000 years, when healthy boys and girls will enjoy and protect love, nothing will be left of you but a ridiculous memory.[7]

The unity of all antitheses and all diversities in an original 'one' posed a problem: why two sexes? Could Plato's Aristophanes have been right, are we a divided androgyne? Or is it, maybe, that one sex is only a stage on the way to the other sex?

Already in the twenties, Reich's insistence upon the superiority of the vagina at all stages had an urgency to it that was missing from the Freudian notion of the two aspects of feminine sexuality. He claimed that the penis was particularly well adapted to the build-up and release of electrical discharge, and in 1934 he thought that the concept of *mechanical tension* was really only an accurate description of male sexuality, it did not properly explain a woman's response. However, this did not then lead him to demote the female orgasm, but to search for its meaning anew. The later premise of orgonomy provided a partial answer: a clitoral orgasm is a neurotic substitute, for the true orgasm is the meeting point of the internal energy streamings of the individual and the outer world. In this interpretation the vaginal orgasm, in its miraculous loss of self and flowing towards the world, may yet be the pinnacle:

... from a biogenetic standpoint we may consider whether a developed vaginal excitability exists throughout the animal kingdom, including the female of the human species, or whether we are moving in the female of man toward a *universal vaginal orgonotic functioning* as a further step in phylogenesis.[8]

It is the logic of Reich's dualistic concepts that would resolve themselves into one. This, and this alone, can be the meaning of the dialectics of sex. The duality of sex should finally be submerged in the feminine principle. Flattery is no compensation for illusion. For the same reason that his sexual revolution appeals, it also ultimately fails. The contemporary fashion for separating his early from his later works arises from our real need to go on repeating the same sort of sociological insight and

7. *Listen, Little Man*, op. cit., p. 98.
8. *Reich Speaks of Freud*, op. cit., pp. 284–5.

the same sort of political rhetoric. Reich's work, at all points, faithfully reflects and denounces crucial ideological attitudes; but his conquest of them is his obliteration of them: nature and culture, man and beast, man and cosmos, man and woman will all discover their so-called 'dialectical' unity. Reich's dualistic ideology, and its simple-minded overthrow, is one that – without considering it – we all share; hence its attraction, hence also its fatality. Reich reflects the way we live, the way we object to the way we live, and our religious hopes for a future that lies in a mythical past. And if we do think about such dialectics what does it add up to? An ecological revolution,[9] a satyr, an angel and a feminized androgyne?

9. See Shulamith Firestone, *The Dialectic of Sex*, New York, 1970.

R.D. Laing:
The Family of Man, I

Social Psychotherapy and Post-war London

In 1947 the left-wing sociologist Richard Titmuss joined hands with the Moderator of the Church of Scotland (and others) to write a pamphlet on rebuilding the family in Britain. Left and right united in this effort because the war, which, as all wars do, had altered the political nature of the countries involved without affecting their basic economic modes of production, had changed as much as anything the face of family life. In fact the wartime de-structuring and post-war re-structuring of the family is a perfect instance of the vulnerability of this type of political change (in this case alteration of a primary ideological institution) when it is not a part of a fundamental overthrow of the state and of an economic system. The absence of men, the recruitment of women into productive industries, the social care of children in crèches and nurseries, the erosion of the family dinner with cost-price meals available to all (including children on their own) in communal restaurants ('the British restaurants'), evacuation with the break-up of class lines and of exclusive family responsibility for its own children and no others, cross-class, cross-sex and cross-age camaraderie in the face of a national crisis, were all factors that, even if unintentionally, were powerfully antithetical to the characteristics of the family under advanced capitalism. Defence of the nation's home superseded protection of the private home and possessions. Predictably, there was an increase in divorce and in the emancipation and independence of children and women.

But whether one argues from the perspective of so-called 'social reality' or of ideological indoctrination, the fact was that after the war political stabilization and economic reconstruction brought about a restoration of conservative social forms. Nurseries and communal restaurants were closed down. Where women had been recruited to industry they were now encouraged to marry and, if married, barred from most professions and many jobs: instead of national workers they were to be private wives. But the decade and more following the war was above all the decade of the child. It is doubtful whether praise of the patriarchal family has ever, since its hey-day in the mid nineteenth century, been as rampant as in the years of the cold war. Britain didn't want to go the way of 'matriarchal' America with its horror-comics and rude and violent kids, nor on the other hand did we fancy those tales of children disciplined by the State to inform even on parents in Stalinist Russia. The family, not as an iron disciplined off-shoot of a totalitarian state, nor as ruled over by a castrating Mom, but cosy and comfortable, an area of protection and place of leisure, was the vogue. Child-and-mother was the theme song. Children often left to their own resources during the war had developed peer group gangs and an alternative play and work world to that offered by the adult society. After the war this alternative play was dubbed antisocial and the term 'delinquent' came into its own on everybody's lips. Joyce Cary in his novel *Charley is My Darling* gives an excellent portrait of the joys and pains of such delinquency from the child's point of view. But in the effort to rebuild the family the equation went: delinquent = latch-key child = having been abandoned by its mother in infancy to crèche or evacuation. From now onwards appeals to maternal guilt vied with the political exploitation of the economic situation to keep women at home. At least, at home in mind even if the mass of working-class mothers still in body had to go out to a job at half-pay.

By the end of the fifties sociology had established itself as a major academic discipline and there was an efflorescence of sociological studies on various aspects of family life and society-family interaction. Within psychology the stress was all on mother-care; from the psychoanalyst John Bowlby, whose work was popularized on radio and in women's magazines, we learnt that a person sucked his emotional stability literally with his mother's milk. A popular analysis of this relationship was entitled *The Nursing Couple* – the couple were no longer the parents but the mother and baby. Evacuee children were 'maternally deprived' – bombs and poverty and absent fathers didn't come into it. Psychoanalysis, persecuted out of existence on the continent, emigrated to America or resurrected itself in England. The debates of the thirties bequeathed, instead of an interest in the psychology of femininity, a heritage of a mother-child obsession. It does not amount to an estimation of the intrinsic merits or otherwise of the work if one points out that the development of child psychoanalysis contributed very neatly to the political demands of the epoch.

In London Anna Freud and Dorothy Burlington established a developmentally orientated form of child analysis. Anna Freud also undertook her major psychoanalytic study of adolescence. The shift within psychoanalysis is away from explication of psychic structures through the neuroses to developmental theories of the formation of both normal and abnormal character structure.

A different school of child analysis was also set up in London at the Tavistock Clinic. The main influence here was Melanie Klein with D.W. Winnicott and Susan Isaacs carrying out in the same institution somewhat independent studies on children and mother–child relationships. The Tavistock provided (and provides) marriage and family counselling services. Winnicott's very sensitive work nevertheless had an effect somewhat like Bowlby's in its earliest popularizations. Paeans to the family obscured its more interesting content though his later work in the sixties (a somewhat different decade) was, I think, exempt from this. Susan Isaacs's theses, again exploited for ideological purposes, contributed to creating a stultifying status quo. Thus she would write of how the mother, feeling her child as a possession, also therefore saw it as an extension of herself, rather than as a person apart. One can see that when the reaction set in with Laing and others in the vanguard, it was to this sort of formulation perhaps as much as anything else that they were objecting.

At the opening of her book *Envy and Gratitude: a Study of Unconscious Sources*, published in 1957, Klein wrote:

Throughout my work I have attributed fundamental importance to the infant's first object relation – the relation to the mother's breast and to the mother – and have drawn the conclusion that if this primal object, which is introjected, takes root in the ego with relative security, the basis for a satisfactory development is laid. Innate factors contribute to this bond.[1]

Though this was intended as analytical description, naturally in the climate of the time it was also read as ideological prescription. But the work of Klein, Rivière, Winnicott and others serves as a yet more interesting background to Laing's radical theories than simply that offered by its sustenance of the secure family and mother-and-child bond. These child analysts (unlike the school of Anna Freud) were all concerned with studying psychosis and with locating its fixation-points in the first mother-child dual relationship, as Freud had located the fixation-point of neuroses in the triadic relationship of the Oedipus complex. As we have seen, Freud's work demonstrated that both psychosis and femininity involve a deeper understanding of the pre-Oedipal phase. When in 1957, Laing went to work at the Tavistock on the particular psychosis of schizophrenia, and from 1961 to investigate families under the auspices of the Tavistock Institute of Human Relations, this was the psychoanalytical and political background to his study.

By the 1960s the post-war baby, once nurtured by its home-bound mother, had become a teenager. Wages for young people were relatively high; a prosperous generation of teenagers had to face the question of leaving the home that had done so much to nourish them. After the teddy-boys a new catch-phrase came into play: the generation gap and teenage culture. As the cult of mother and child went its relentless way, the child, become adolescent, escaped either in day-dreams of rebels without a cause, or increasingly with a cause – a cause against their parents. The late fifties and early sixties marked the rise of youth politics – the Campaign for Nuclear Disarmament, the New Left, the Committee of One Hundred, were dominated by young people. Schizophrenia was prevalent in adolescents – was it, too, a symptom of the revolt against the claustrophobic family? Laing caught and helped create the moment with this question.[2]

1. M. Klein, *Envy and Gratitude: a Study of Unconscious Sources,* London, 1957, p. 3.

2. Although Laing's first book was published by Tavistock Publications, it is surely significant that the young editorial board of the *New*

The political reconstruction of the family in post-war and cold-war Britain was buttressed by social welfare, which was family oriented, and by sociology, psychology and psycho-analytical theories, massively popularized. In a way, it was a logical turn of the screw when the family, having been made – by conservatives – to bear the brunt of personality reconstruction, was suddenly – by radicals – made responsible for personality destruction. Either way, trapped at the centre of it were the mother and the child.

British psychoanalysis, in particular, having thus forgotten the questions of the thirties on feminine psychology, explored with great complexity the primary mother-child relationship. Whatever else was achieved by this, and I think a great deal was, nothing really new about the psychology of women was revealed. Much important work was done, however, on the formation of psychoses. Laing's work was forcefully oppositional to this on two fronts: he attacked the family on political and social grounds and he attempted to discredit the location of psychosis in the child's *infantile* relationship with the mother. Orthodox child psychoanalysis has taught us little about the woman who as infant-girl and adult-mother is so central to its theses. Laing's primary attack and alternative explanation, like Reich's earlier case for the sexual opposition, has been of great importance for radical politics of the sixties and seventies. Does it show us a way forward in understanding the oppression of women as it takes place within the family that is supposed to give them both their definition and their rationale?

Left Review were the first to print his work outside analytical circles. 'Series and Nexus in the Family' was published in *NLR* in 1962.

13 A 'Science of Persons'

We believe that the shift of point of view that these descriptions both embody and demand has an historical significance no less radical than the shift from a demonological to a clinical viewpoint three hundred years ago.[1]

R.D. Laing, though a psychoanalyst and a political radical, was never interested in an amalgamation of the two sciences that Freud and Marx began to develop. From the outset he has wanted to do something new. His main project has been to render intelligible patterns of behaviour that are labelled 'schizophrenic'. Intelligibility is, naturally, the aim of anyone offering an analysis of any situation, but for Laing the source of intelligibility is quite specifically the set of social interrelationships in which a person is situated.

The 'signs and symptoms' of psychosis are thus rendered intelligible when the patient is considered not, as is usually the case, in a depersonalized way, as *the object* of study, seen in isolation, but as a person created in and by his relationships with other people. No man is an island ... and the manifestations of schizophrenia illustrate how false it is to treat him thus.

Laing would seem then to be further claiming that there is a strict homology between the way schizophrenia is *caused* and the way it is *treated*. Both the family that drives one of its members mad, by reifying and isolating him, and the doctor who diagnoses schizophrenia, make use of the same method: '... why do we not regard a theory that seeks to transmute persons into automata or animals as equally crazy?'[2]

1. R.D. Laing and A. Esterson, *Sanity, Madness and the Family*, Vol. I, *Families of Schizophrenics*, Tavistock Publications, London, 1964, p. 13. Although the study was written jointly by Laing and Esterson, here, as in the case of other joint works, for convenience, I have referred to it as though Laing were the sole author.

2. *The Divided Self*, Tavistock Publications 1960; Penguin Books, 1965, p. 23.

Laing's scientific method thus aims at re-establishing the original social cause of the illness. And as it would seem that the parents related to their child with possessiveness, with hate masked as love, anger as gentleness, collusion as compliance, intolerance as acceptance, now, in his cure the physician will relate to the patient with true love:

> The main agent in uniting the patient, in allowing the pieces to come together and cohere, is the physician's love, a love that recognizes the patient's total being, and accepts it, with no strings attached.[3]

The good physician is thus not the parent surrogate, on to whom, in the classical analytical situation, the patient can transfer the passions (hostile and friendly), but a new, accepting parent, an *actual* new other person, who by seeing the patient as he *really* is, gives him back himself.

The patient and doctor thus become the 'self and other', the original social situation out of which the 'disease' grew is re-established, only because this time there is love and tolerance instead of condemnation of the illness, there will come forth a cure.

The model is neat – if we don't treat people as people, we drive them crazy: if we don't analyse our crazy people as people we keep them crazy. On the other hand, if we *do* treat people as people, then, even if they do the odd crazy thing, we accept this, because we accept them as people. If we analyse those who have been de-personalized and made crazy, once more as though they were people, then they become people again, and they are 'cured' of an illness that wasn't 'in' them in the first place.

Throughout his work then, Laing makes clear statements about what he thus designates 'a science of persons', and he situates this new science in relation to other sciences: negatively to the natural sciences and to psychoanalysis, and positively to the disciplines and philosophies of sociology and phenomenology. Laing's wish for a new science seems to have sprung from his *dissatisfaction* with psychoanalysis and the *inspiration* he received from certain philosophies. It did not arise, as did Reich's sex-economy, from a progressive frustration with other ways of analysis, but from an

3. ibid., p. 165.

original project. From the beginning, Laing, taking his bearing in dissatisfaction, has aimed at instituting a new system of knowledge.

Laing's basic premise (and the point from which his radicalism takes off) is his contention that the 'estrangement of *our own theory* from *our own actions* goes deep into our historical situation'.[4] Laing declares that Freud, the greatest psychopathologist of all time, dared the final abyss, raked around in the horrors of the subterranean psyche, but nevertheless managed to come up with a theory that was to some extent defensive.

Freud was a hero. He descended to the 'Underworld' and met there stark terrors. He carried with him his theory as a Medusa's head which turned these terrors to stone. We who follow Freud have the benefit of the knowledge he brought back with him and conveyed to us. He survived. *We must see if we now can survive without using a theory that is in some measure an instrument of defence* [my italics].[5]

This was written in *The Divided Self* – at that stage Laing's wish to break down the defence-barrier between the scientist and the object of his research (the psyche of the psychotic patient) extended only to empathizing and treating as authentic experience all that the psychotic claimed to feel; the psychotic is the person with misunderstood problems, but problems nonetheless. In his later works Laing is claiming the necessity of undertaking the pilgrimage into the void of loss of self on one's own behalf. Describing the 'Ten Day Voyage' of a schizophrenic breakdown, Laing writes:

Can we not see that *this voyage is not what we need to be cured of, but that it is itself a natural way of healing our own appalling state of alienation called normality.*[6]

Again this extension of Laing's position can be foreseen in the early statements of the original project:

4. R.D. Laing, *Self and Others*, Tavistock Publications, 1961 and 1969, and Pantheon Books, New York, 1969 ed., p. 110. The first edition was called *The Self and Others*. I have used the second New York edition, which is considerably revised, except where stated.

5. *The Divided Self*, op. cit., p. 25.

6. *The Politics of Experience and The Bird of Paradise*, Penguin Books, 1967, p. 136.

How, even, can one say what it means to hide something from oneself or to deceive oneself in terms of barriers between one part of a mental apparatus and another? This difficulty faces not only classical Freudian metapsychology but equally any theory that begins with man or a part of man *abstracted from his relation with the other in his world* [my italics].[7]

It seems extraordinary that whereas the physical and biological sciences of it-processes have generally won the day against the tendencies to personalize the world of things or to read human intentions into the animal world, an authentic science of persons has hardly got started by reason of the inveterate tendency to depersonalize or reify persons.[8]

In this, his first book, *The Divided Self*, Laing is situating his objections clearly in terms of his opposition to classical psychoanalysis. Later he will generalize his position, but it is from this basic disagreement that Laing builds his theories of what *should* be done. Before investigating his disagreements with psychoanalysis, I want to look at what constitutes his 'science of persons' and at the positive influences which help him to mould it – existential philosophy and some aspects of American sociology.

Laing defines his 'science of persons' as a 'study of human beings that begins from a relationship with the other as person and proceeds to an account of the other still as person'.[9] He is proposing two related projects: the analysis of a person as a person, and an analysis of interpersonal relationships. A primary question that poses itself is: what does a 'person' signify to Laing? One answer that he gives is clearly the second half of his project – a person *is* his relationship with others. But then in contemplating that answer as a question – what *are* interrelationships? – we get back to the original problem: they are about how we perceive each other as a person, so what is a person? This dilemma underlies the entire Laingian preoccupation. It can be seen sometimes as a pursuit of complexity and sometimes as an obsession with the circularity of tautology (*Knots?*). The analyst must see the analysed as a person; that person is a person in his relationship to other persons; one of his relationships is with the analyst

7. *The Divided Self*, op. cit., p. 19.
8. ibid., p. 23.   9. ibid., p. 21.

as a person; the language the analyst uses, and the methods he chooses to describe this person (who is only a person because *he* is a person) must be personal. No wonder the end is silence:

One cannot talk about a rule about which one cannot talk. We have reached a limit to what we can talk about . . . I have thought about the problem of how not to think a thought one is not supposed to think. I cannot think of any way to do so except, in some peculiar way, to 'think' what one must not think in order to ensure that one does not think it.[10]

But in the beginning, Laing defines the area in which a person finds himself as a person, so to speak. One term sums up the terrain on which we are to search for the meaning of the self and of all interpersonal relationships. This term is Laing's far reaching conception of 'experience'. It finds its apotheosis in his *Politics of Experience*, but it is deployed right from the start as the beginning, the end, and the essence of the 'science of persons'. The 'science' is the charting of 'experience' because what he or she 'experiences' is the person. *Self and Others* is 'an attempt to weave *experience and behaviour* into a consistent theory, since they are so woven in real life'[11] and in the *Politics of Experience*:

Experience is man's invisibility to man. Experience used to be called The Soul. Experience as invisibility of man to man is at the same time more evident than anything. *Only* experience is evident. Experience is the *only* evidence. Psychology is the logos of experience . . . Natural science knows nothing of the relation between *behaviour and experience*. The nature of this relation is mysterious – in Marcel's sense. That is to say, it is not an objective problem. There is no traditional logic to express it. There is no developed method of understanding its nature. But this relation is the copula of our science – if science means *a form of knowledge adequate to its subject*. The relation between *experience and behaviour* is the stone that the builders will reject at their peril. Without it the whole structure of our theory and practice must collapse.[12] [Italicization of 'behaviour and experience' is mine.]

10. *The Politics of the Family* (The Massey Lectures, 1968), Toronto, 1969, p. 41. Reprinted with some alterations as *The Politics of the Family and Other Essays*, Tavistock Publications and Pantheon Books, 1971.
11. *Self and Others*, Preface to 2nd edition, 1969, op. cit., p. ix.
12. *The Politics of Experience*, op. cit., pp. 16–17.

A 'science of persons' is, then, further specified as to be sought in the nature of the relation between 'behaviour and experience'. Although possibly it comes from one source, Laing's use of the term 'experience' goes in two directions: into the philosophy of existentialism and the practice of empirical research.

Before Laing ever made direct application of Sartre's work, the preoccupation with existential thought was explicit.[13] It seems to be the case that when he uses the term 'experience' he is referring to something that makes a human being 'a person'. Much as Kierkegaard excluded the inanimate and animal world from his use of the word 'existence', Laing excludes them from his use of 'experience'; which likewise is the state of being that is lived by a person either with authenticity or insincerity. Of course, it is relevant that Laing substitutes the term 'experience' for the earlier notion of 'existence' as, in his usage, this implies the action of perception and relationship as well as of 'being'. The person as *existential self* would still be a discrete, isolated entity, but Laing's *experiential self* proposes to exist in himself and in terms of others – his *experience* of others and theirs of him. (Though Laing is not always quite sure: for sometimes nothing, not even complete love, bridges the inexorable separateness between man and man.)

In fact, despite Laing's use of the term 'experience', it is, in many contexts, overtly overlaid with many of the values given to 'existence' in 'existential' philosophy. For instance, his notion that a person has a true or a false self, though it may be pragmatically proposed in partially sociological terms of how others can force one to play a role that goes against the grain of one's original character, really amounts to a re-statement of the phenomenological notion of the true-self-in-its-existence.

At this stage (*The Divided Self*) the person needs to ally both his subjective self and his objective, being-for-others self: 'experience' is the mode in which the two 'dimensions', objective and subjective, are united. The 'inner' self of *The Divided Self* or the 'unconscious' (in a sense different from Freud) of *Self and Others* are terms used for the self-in-its-being-for-itself.

13. The first chapter of his first book (*The Divided Self*) is entitled: 'The existential-phenomenological foundations for a science of persons'.

At this point in Laing's work, a psychotic-schizophrenic is someone trying to preserve his 'self' (inner or unconscious) separate from his experience in the objective world – how others perceive him. On the other hand, the person whose life has *not* gone thus astray unites inner and outer, subjective and objective, by forming his subjectivity in relation to his experience of objectivity, self to others. The schizophrenic has split himself into a divided self, in which his authentic being is unauthenticated because it is separated from his being-in-the-world and is lived not in terms of 'experience', but of phantasy. The living of the self solely in phantasy is the subject of a chapter entitled 'The Counterpoint of Experience' in *Self and Others*, a book in which the unity of the subjective self and the objective experience is implicitly suggested as an index of health.

Laing makes three quite clear objections to previous scientific procedure: the language of science dissects the whole man – in his total selfhood; all sciences treat the individual as isolated from other individuals; human sciences mimic natural sciences in treating people as 'mechanical things', simply because they are the *objects* of study:

Instead of the original bond of *I* and *You*, we take a single man in isolation and conceptualize his various aspects into 'the ego', 'the superego', and 'the id'.[14]

But by the time of *The Politics of Experience* and its celebration of the schizophrenic Voyage, Laing is endorsing all those religions and existential philosophies that contend that the original egoic experience of an objective self is a preliminary illusion, a veil that must be ripped off, a womb from which one must be born. This time the chapter is entitled 'Transcendental Experience' and the subjectivity of the person is all. As usual, we find that the definition of the 'science' he is pursuing follows the same path as that of the 'person' who is its object.

So many people feel they have to translate 'subjective' events into 'objective' terms in order to be scientific. To be genuinely scientific means having valid knowledge of a chosen domain of reality. So in

14. *The Divided Self*, op. cit., p. 19.

the following I shall use the language of experience to describe the events of experience.[15]

Laing proceeds to use the language of experience (his experience) to describe our present-day alienation in terms of how we feel ourselves split into inner and outer with the inner bereft of substance and the outer of meaning. It seems to be that now we are all 'divided selves' (schizoids) who can regain health not by the previously posited unity of subjective and objective but by an exploration into the depths of subjectivity – the self before it was even a self, when it was one with the cosmos. So from 'experience' being that which relates us to others and then to ourselves, it has become a supramundane search for the before-all-that. The early Laing prunes his existential heritage of any mystical-religious overtones, the later Laing restores them in full force.

Laing gives the title 'Politics' to his credo of *transcendental experience*, and to understand this rather perverse but now popular label it is perhaps useful to recall his reference, in the same book, to Gabriel Marcel: 'Natural science knows nothing of the relation between behaviour and experience. The nature of this relation is mysterious – in Marcel's sense.'[16] Marcel, the Catholic existentialist who contends, as a result of his attacks on scientific tendencies to generalize and abstract, that if we could substitute for such abstractions as 'fascists' or 'communists' the particular human beings involved, wars would be less likely, is clearly a kindred spirit, or perhaps a direct influence on Laing, who claims:

As long as we cannot up-level our 'thinking' beyond Us and Them, the goodies and baddies, it will go on and on . . .
Millions of people have died this century and millions more are going to . . . because we cannot break this knot.
It seems a comparatively simple knot, but it is tied *very, very* tight – round the throat, as it were, of the whole human species.[17]

The 'politics of experience' then, may mean returning all occurrences – macrosocial as well as microsocial – to the test of personal and interpersonal experience, to trying them on your

15. *The Politics of Experience*, op. cit., p. 102.
16. ibid., p. 17.
17. *The Politics of the Family*, Toronto, op. cit., p. 49.

pulse; at other times, it may mean jumping back into the void that was before all distinctions, the point when experience is 'soul'.

Laing, then, is preoccupied with experience in three ways: he wants to develop a *science* of experience, to institute a *politics* of experience, and advocate a *mystico-religious* pursuit of transcendental experience. But along with all his more abstract philosophical interests, at a very concrete level, Laing *does* want to know how people relate in particular families and he wants to know whether psychosis, specifically schizophrenia, is induced by definable types of social interaction. In this he is working in a field where philosophical presupposition is not enough. It is here in 'proving' his case that the more grandiose empiricism of his philosophical tradition meets a narrower empiricism adopted mainly from the behavioural sciences.

Laing asks, first, *what* schizophrenia is, and second, whether it is in fact 'there' at all. Is it simply a particular type (or particular types) of human communication? Hence what is communication, the means by which discrete people bridge the gap, the space between the self and others?

It is in examining the other element that composes the range of his 'science of persons' – behaviour – that we get a clue to the second important influence on his work. Laing describes his central concern as 'the relation between behaviour and experience'. We have seen that in many instances 'experience' is generalized out, into 'existence'. It is also frequently specified down to 'perception' and 'conception'; and it is as such that it is counterposed to 'behaviour', itself sometimes generalized to mean 'interaction' or 'action', sometimes narrowed down to mean 'how one acts, responds to stimuli', etc. At this level of 'behaviour and experience' Laing is explicitly indebted to certain American social scientists.

Peter Sedgwick, an interesting critic of Laing, comments:

The pathology of family communication has become one of the great research enterprises of American science. Hundreds of families have trooped into the laboratories of academic institutes and hospitals, there to have their entire verbal output tape-recorded over many sessions, their gestures and eye-movements filmed and their biographies unearthed in depth ... The families inhabit this select theatre for a period of hours or more, enacting a kind of real-life T.V. serial based on their usual domestic interchange, and then depart ...[18]

And in the introduction to his book of case-histories Laing both laments and rejoices:

Within the terms of phenomenology itself, this study is limited methodologically and heuristically.

Most of our data is in the form of interviews ... the majority of these interviews were conducted in our own consulting-rooms, and not in the family homes, and second, and more serious, an interview is itself not a naturally occurring family situation.

We are also dissatisfied with our method of recording. Its main limitation is that all our permanent records are restricted to the auditory transactions of the family members in our presence. Although such a permanent library of magnetic recordings is an advance on clinical notes made during or after interviews, it can be regarded only as a stepping-stone to permanent audio-visual records.[19]

In his case-studies, Laing collects the 'factual' data of behaviour, records the immediate exchange of words and gestures and devises a method of collating his information in the straightest of all modes of psychology and sociology.

Of course, Laing is trying to fit the assumed 'neutral' methods of American researchers into his overall philosophical system to prove a point: that schizophrenia is a method of communication or refused communication.

The Divided Self does not seem to be influenced by American social psychology. It is much more a purely existential-phenomenological project: an attempt to *humanize* a 'science of persons'. And although schizophrenia is already pronounced intelligible in terms of the person's praxis, this praxis is the contradiction between his being-for-self and being-for-others. The distinction between behaviour and experience has not yet been formulated. In *The Divided Self*, the patient is still at the centre of his own case-history; his problem originates in early infancy when some interaction caused him never to gain full secur-

18. Peter Sedgwick, 'R.D. Laing: Self, Symptom and Society', *Salmagundi*, Spring 1971, reprinted in *R.D. Laing and Anti-Psychiatry*, Harper & Row, New York, 1971, pp. 16–17.

19. *Sanity, Madness and the Family*, op. cit., p. 11.

ity of his own identity; it is this 'ontological insecurity', re-evoked at the time of the crisis (usually adolescence), that is the basis of schizophrenia. At this stage in Laing's thought schizophrenic symptoms may certainly be intelligible, but the schizophrenia is still *there*, and that minority of people who thus regard themselves as automata 'are rightly regarded as crazy'. Their symptoms express a *way* of interacting; but by the next book *The Self and Others* (1961), the *way of interacting* is the 'disease'. This shifting emphasis – indeed, changing conception – is marked by a new definition of the field: the relationship between how we behave and how others experience our behaviour and we experience theirs. Interacting people are now seen to *infer* from behaviour what is meant by an action, and the psychoanalyst infers from these inferences. The 'self' is composed of inferences from experience – even the specifically Laingian 'unconscious', apparently something outside such immediate experience, is, in fact, likewise formed by inferences from experience. And yet at all levels our inferences can be hideously wrong. We may so infer something from someone's behaviour that we drive them mad by our false inference. We put them (or we put ourselves) into a false position. The 'false self' in *The Divided Self* was a false projection of the self – here it is produced by *dishonest* interaction between people. Again the whole orientation has shifted to the *area* of communication – the place *in between* people:

> The loss of one's own perceptions and evaluations, which comes with occupying a *false position* (doubly false in that one does not see that it is false), is only 'realized' retrospectively. A false position is not necessarily totally 'untenable' . . . The person in a doubly false position feels 'real'; without '*feeling*' numb, he is numbed by this very feeling of 'reality'. To shake one's self out of the *false sense of reality* entails a *derealization* of what one falsely takes to be reality, and a *rerealization* of what one falsely takes to be unreality. Only then is one able to apperceive the social phantasy system in which one is. The *normal* state of affairs is to be so immersed in one's immersion in social phantasy systems that one takes them to be real . . .[20]

From now onwards the 'true' self that experiences the real 'real' constantly has to behave/act as a false self which fits the

20. *Self and Others*, op. cit., p. 23.

false social reality in which he is incarcerated. The child learns to *pretend* to be a little boy, his face becomes a 'mask'. But Laing's language gets a bit confused – experience as well as behaviour can be false, thus we can have 'pseudo-real experience', and even *within* our 'experience' we can make what are ultimately *false* distinctions: inner/outer; real/unreal; full/empty, etc. The fact that Laing himself must use these distinctions compounds, of course, the confusion. To help himself sort out this problem, Laing seems to say that there *is* a true experience – though we don't know what it is. Paradoxically, as a result of this, his urge to move away from the discrete self into the *area* of intercommunication has landed him right back in an even more essentialist position than that from which he started.

If we examine carefully Laing's use of the term 'experience' we can see that he uses it in two ways which often have a tendency to be either contradictory or mutually exclusive. 'Experience' as a noun, is thus Laing's existential, essentialist 'existence' – always 'true' – and 'experience' as a verb is to perceive or conceive of something and these conceptions can play us true or false.

What we have then is a background of 'experience' (noun) as 'true existence' (easily merging into 'transcendental experience') and a foreground of 'experience' (verb) of how one perceives (conceives one's own and the other's behaviour). All Laing's case-histories – actual, or imaginatively reconstructed as in *Knots* – fit into this background schema. (The essentialist description of the self as true experience is, of course, beyond description.) So really Laing's achieved 'science of persons' amounts to his *demonstrating* the difference between behaviour and perception of behaviour – the project he set himself to analyse. Given his premises, it is ultimately only possible to show, at the most, the degrees of disjuncture that occur, and to document the infinity of the 'dyadic spiral'.

> Jack can see that he sees
> what Jill can't see
> but Jack can't see
> that Jill can't see
> that Jill can't see it.[21]

21. *Knots*, Tavistock Publications and Pantheon Books, New York, 1970, p. 57.

14 The Various Scientific Methods

The Divided Self and *The Self and Others* both simply pose the problem of founding a science: they postulate it in opposition to the depersonalizing methods of natural sciences and psychoanalysis. Neither book advances its own 'scientific' formulations. However Laing's next publication, an article entitled 'Series and Nexus in the Family', does do so. It uses a modified version of Sartre's terminology in his *Critique de la Raison Dialectique*. (Although Laing makes footnote references to Sartre's earlier works in his first two books, he never made direct use of them – simply shared elements of their philosophy.) What he takes from Sartre's *Critique* was formulated as a method for making behaviour intelligible: what you have to do is to find out who did what and why; you have to 'personalize' the apparently impersonal, restore 'the process' to 'the praxis'. Here was a neat methodological formulation for the theory at the centre of existentialist belief (Laing's version of Sartre is, as Laing would wish it to be, Laing not Sartre):

If an idea, for instance, has become a social fact (my neighbours object to 'coloured' people), if it appears to be a thing, its intelligibility is in the retracing of the steps from thing → social fact → idea → the men who thought it up: its apparently uncontrolled power, its anonymity, its unavowed authorship, are intelligible to the extent that one can discover the way it is a deed estranged by doers from themselves.[1]

Here, in finding the relationship of behaviour (the deed) to the experience (at both ends: how it was 'experienced' as process – the thing – and the experience it came out of in the original praxis 'the man who thought it up'), Laing re-finds the subject matter

1. R.D. Laing, 'Series and Nexus in the Family', *New Left Review*, No. 15, May/June, 1962, p. 8.

of his science and a vocabulary for defining its purpose – the pursuit of intelligibility. What Laing wanted was a way of understanding individuals in themselves and in their groups, a way of seeing the part in the whole. His use of Sartre finds him his method. In his essay on the *Critique* and in his joint introduction with David Cooper to their book on Sartre, *Reason and Violence*, Laing specifies for us the dimensions of the Sartre with whose project he is in accord:

> It is necessary to emphasize that we are concerned here with decisive developments in man's understanding of himself – as important for demystification of the present as Freud's and Marx's formulations, for instance, were in their day. Here we have a more ambitious theoretical venture than either Freud or Marx attempted – no less than a *totalization*, as Sartre would put it, of the whole of existing socio-historical knowledge.[2]

This notion of 'totalization' coincides with what Laing is trying to assert at every level. Thus in the same introduction, the authors comment on how Sartre's totalizations of the perceptions and conceptions of collectivities enable one to see the conceptual and perceptual violence done to people by abstractions and reifications . . . and so on to *The Politics of Experience* and the tribute to Marcel. And in Laing's earlier article:

> [A group] is not, and cannot be, an object, a totality. The group can never be finally and conclusively grasped as a whole; any group is in continual *totalisation*, a perpetual series of actions that maintain its existence, but can never complete it once and for all.[3]

The group being studied is comparable to the way that it is studied. We are once more back with the perfect homology of the object studied with the method of studying it. Of course, such an echoic relationship between the object and its science is, as we have seen, Laing's aim: a 'science of persons' uses a language of persons. Except, of course, in thus becoming 'technical' it doesn't: process, praxis, series, nexus, totalization . . . The next book – *Sanity, Madness and the Family* – originated as the first in

2. R.D. Laing and D.G. Cooper, *Reason and Violence*, Tavistock Publications, 1964, p. 10.
3. 'Series and Nexus in the Family', op. cit., p. 11.

a series of comparative studies on 'schizophrenic' versus 'normal' families. It was with this work that the compilation of tape-recordings commenced. The second volume (normal families) failed to appear.

After the Sartrean influence, Laing's 'scientific method' displays a surprising episode. *Interpersonal Perception* is an effort by three psychotherapists, of whom Laing is one, to devise a series of questions that can be put to married couples and whose answers will show the concordance/discordance between the partners. Yet the basic preoccupations from which such a project emerged are the same as in Laing's previous work. The first chapter is entitled 'Self and Other', and we learn:

> Over a hundred years ago Feuerbach effected a pivotal step in philosophy. He discovered that philosophy had been exclusively orientated around 'I'. No one had realized that the 'you' is as primary as the I. It is curious how we continue to theorize from an egoistic standpoint. In Freud's theory, for instance, one has the 'I' (ego), the 'over-me' (super-ego) and 'it' (id), but no *you*.[4]

These instances of marital therapy are to be another example of inserting the 'you' into a new 'science of persons'. Yet, most significantly, the book reveals a search to establish a new sort of scientificity.

Although the authors of *Interpersonal Perception* assert that the method they have devised for assessing dyadic relationships could be elaborated to test triads – the basic unit of the family –

4. R.D. Laing, H. Phillipson, A.R. Lee, *Interpersonal Perception: A Theory and a Method of Research*, Tavistock Publications, London, 1966, p. 3. Sedgwick comments on this work: 'The assumptions of the book are by and large those of orthodox marital counselling: we do not have here a radical-nihilist critique of the lie at the heart of human relationships, but a liberal-reformist statement that some relationships are discernibly better than others' (Sedgwick, op. cit., p. 30). This is true, particularly in so far that the tests reveal the somewhat unsurprising result that disturbed relationships reveal a higher degree of disjuncture of perception between the couple than do 'non-disturbed' ones. A neat conclusion – or another tautology? But then the aim of the research is to discover a system of rapid testing which can be used therapeutically in marital and family therapy; in other words, we are no longer concerned with analysis, or even with rendering intelligible, but with human adjustment.

none of Laing's later work makes use of this methodology. When Laing next comes to study the family, it is tentatively to explore a new system. The model now is the *topological* one of 'mapping'.[5]

We have passed from the project of *a systematic* use of Sartre's suggestions as he develops them in the *Critique* ('Series and Nexus in the Family') through the empirical case-study collection of a library of magnetic tapes (*Sanity, Madness and the Family*) to the question-and-answer control-studies of the 'Interpersonal Perception Method' and finally, to the topological vocabulary of *The Politics of the Family*. It is interesting that each book introduces a new system of inquiry and promises that it is only a beginning: there will be another volume to *Sanity, Madness and the Family*, the charts devised for dyads can now be applied to triads, with the mapping system of *The Politics of the Family*, Laing wants to be counted as one 'who has made a start'. In a way, this diversity is very exciting, but one has at some point to ask: are these real beginnings, or so many false starts?

A preoccupation has remained common to all tried systems: a wish to find a way of moving from the individual to the microsocial to the macrosocial – even *Interpersonal Perception* concluded:

... it seems that our schema of the *dyadic spiral* for the interplay of two perspectives has relevance in the international sphere.

Unless we can break the spiral of mistrust in East–West relations the likelihood is that we are all going to die. The first step is to be

5. 'If ϕ is a mapping of A into B, set A is called the domain of ϕ, and set B the range of ϕ.

Projection can then be regarded as a mapping of inside onto outside, and introjection a mapping of outside into inside. Families are of peculiar significance and interest because, more than any other social set, they are both domain and range, for projections *to* outside, introjections *from* outside into them ...

One's body is of unique significance because it is *the* range for "introjective" mappings ...

... The infant is the *final common range*, as it were, – where all introjections converge and permutate, are pooled and stored to become a sort of ϕ *bank*, the subsequent *domain, from* which subsequent projections will be released ... to find *their range*, anywhere from a marital relation, a nuclear family, a social network to the *total social world system*, or even the total cosmos.' (*The Politics of the Family*, op. cit., pp. 44–5.)

able to see and think about what is going on. The outcome is life or death.

The West reasons: We do not want to make the first move, but we are not sure whether East does or not. However, even if East does not want to make the first move, East may think that we do, so in order to forestall us . . .[6]

The wish to totalize and make intelligible is present in all the 'scientific' methods Laing deploys. However, in the last – the topological scheme – we have set clearly before us the flaw at the heart of the project. The mathematical formulations of *The Politics of the Family* must seem to most people to be further removed from an ordinary 'language of persons' than the 'defensive' and depersonalizing way of expressing things that Laing originally objected to in Freud.

6. *Interpersonal Perception*, op. cit., p. 138.

15 Dialectics and Totalizations

Laing, no less than Reich, is interested in finding a dialectical method of *totalization*. This latter concept runs through his work like a theme-song. In first trying to attain 'totalization', that is to say a view that looks at the whole in its entirety without destroying the parts, Laing deploys Sartre's 'dialectical' method. From his comments on Sartre we learn that the dialectic is a method of experiencing (*per*ceiving) the concrete, of developing a conceptual schema for describing this experience (*con*ceiving it) and 'knowing' the object that is thus perceived and conceived – the relation between the knower and the known and the nature of the known. It is this tripartite project that aims at a totalization; to Laing, psychoanalysis (like theories of sociology and other disciplines) helps us only with a part; Laing, like Sartre would thus *incorporate* psychoanalysis in a larger 'science of persons'. All other sciences, not being 'of persons', murder to dissect.

I think that, given the preoccupations of the body of Laing's work, we can quite legitimately apply his explanation of what interests him in Sartre's thought to his own position. Thus Laing writes of the Sartrean dialectic:

> In Sartre's view, there is one realm of being where dialectical principles are constitutive of the nature of the known itself. This is the realm of human history. As for the processes of the non-human world, the realm of natural science, the dialectic can furnish regulative but not constitutive principles. Thus, in the realm of the human, Sartre uses dialectic to characterize both the relation between the knower and the known, and the nature of the known.[1]

In other words, in this field the relation between knower and known *is* the known; or in a Laingian concretization, 'Jack's

1. *Reason and Violence*, op. cit., pp. 10–11.

experience of Jill's experience of Jack ...' The dialectic is a *method* in natural sciences – 'an experimental conceptual strategy' – here, in human history, the subject itself is dialectical as the two elements always compose a third. Hence the 'science of persons' incorporates all the other sciences that have tried to account for a partial aspect of human history. For instance, the limit of such a science as Marxism is that 'a whole theory of society will be elaborated starting from the conflict between classes, without any adequate grasp of the classes themselves being constituted by a prior dialectic beginning with praxis'.[2]

From this we can now see why Laing proposes what I would characterize as a romantic concept of truth for his 'science of persons'. In natural sciences he claims truth is correspondence between what is *in intellectu* and *in re*, but for *his* science, Laing would deploy the other Greek notion of truth as an unveiling. Logically if the dialectic resides *within* the subject matter of human history, all your dialectical method has to do is 'unveil', reveal it – much as Michelangelo said he found his statue waiting in his block of marble. Through thus 'unveiling' truth, Laing gets rid of a problem that bothers him (along with many social scientists, anthropologists, etc.), of the role of the interviewer, analyst, etc. – the interviewer (the 'knower') is simply his relationship to the would-be-known, he vanishes into his action. Phenomenological truth thus gets rid of 'artificial' structures, it gets rid of the doctor and rid of the patient. It gets rid of the sane and of the mad. All is communication – good or bad, true or false. The 'science' is to unveil the communication, in the fullest sense of the word; the communication between people, from which all human society originates. The 'science' is as large as its object. In this view, ultimately, if it is any good it is in fact indistinguishable from it. It follows that the

2. ibid., p. 16. This is not so far away from Reich's efforts to find dialectics within the very subject matter of psychoanalysis. In both cases dialectics, are, of course, there – but can we, as both Reich and Laing would have us do, either assume transparency, or be satisfied with such a result? The notion of the revelation of dialectics within the object is one of the most persistent hangovers from the Third International. Dialectic, as used in these instances, without the concept of contradiction, is meaningless.

'science of persons' is – from a human point of view – the largest science of all.

Leaving aside the question of what constitutes a science, it seems relevant here to bring together the various elements in Laing's project. As has been seen, the most dominant idea is 'experience'. Sometimes this goes in one direction to merge in a more or less metaphysical or essentialist notion of 'existence' or 'transcendental experience'; at other times it is a straightforwardly empiricist notion. Knowledge cannot go beyond the range of possible experience (though we in our essentialist existence can go thither, transcendentally). But, of course, empiricism is usually counterposed to metaphysics. Not so with Laing. 'Experience' is widened by him to include all ways of perceiving, apperceiving, feeling, conscious or unconscious, it thus seems to approach a Berkeleian notion that everything is how we perceive it. At least *people* are how we perceive them – in their mutual and constant perception of us. So where Berkeley's material 'thing' disappeared behind the ideas of it – Laing's 'person' never does, because the person himself is always there as a conglomeration of other-directed and self-directed perceptions. People *are* interacting experience. And hence to the embrace of phenomenology: matter, thoughts, values are apprehended in a psychical 'act of experience'. We can then reflect on this act and see how the objects of it appear within it. These 'appearances' are the phenomena which are thus 'conscious of' the object they contain. The 'objects' are not necessarily material – they may be real or unreal – they are anything and everything we think, or that exists. And so in such a study of appearances we reach the ultimate in empiricism – and virtually come out the other side.

As a breaking of boundaries was his original project, it should come as no surprise that any categories of 'normal' and 'abnormal', health/psychosis, ultimately all but disappear for Laing (his retention of them usually seems a mere gesture). But it seems to me that it is Laing's *basic philosophical position* that eradicates the locatable 'disease' schizophrenia; not, as is usually contended (and counter-contended) his empirical demonstration of its absence – his elucidation of its intelligibility. The phenomenological concept of 'being', the study of the appearance in which one presents oneself, presupposes the intelligibility of *all* actions. On its premises *any* action is comprehensible, because it is *about the comprehending of experiences*. Thus for a committed existential phenomenologist the signs and symptoms of schizophrenia are, as Laing admitted in his first book, difficult to discover. They are, after all, just so many other appearances. The action of schizophrenia is a *choice* not to be oneself in untenable circumstances.

The demand for intelligibility is as such a merely truistic one. What is needed is not a reiteration of this premise that underlies the action of *all* human thought and efforts at understanding, but some explanation that accounts for why one thing leads to another, why a certain response to a certain situation produces this and not that particular result.

With Laing we have then, on the one hand, a two-pronged empiricism, one side of which rests on belief and assumption, the other on demonstration. The one is naturally called constantly to the aid of the other. This can sometimes result in confusion. Thus intelligibility of action is all. But on the other hand, behind this there rests the essentialist notion of the 'true' self, of 'having a mind of one's own'; the isolated discrete individual is posited as an existence prior to action, an unknowable being-in-the world who mysteriously becomes a being-for-the world. The very existential philosophy that Laing espouses seems to me to land his 'science' back in the notion of the separate individual for which he condemned classical psychoanalysis. At least this seems so in the early work; in the later work it is as though this contradiction has been resolved in a religio-mystical prior-existence in which each is all but also one. The false divisions by which we live in the world are reflected in the false divisions of psychoanalysis, therefore we must create a 'science of persons' that bridges them with its stress on interaction. But interaction constantly seems to come from two (or more) points and therefore to acknowledge division; so we must posit an original unity which can be reattained by transcendental experience – holy or psychotic. The dialectics of totalization once more have discovered an undifferentiated monism which is simply *preferred* to the dualities which are said to emanate therefrom.

16 Laing and Psychoanalysis

(*i*) *The Unconscious*

Laing makes many references to psychoanalysis, a number of specific comments on Freud, and is concerned with certain psychoanalytic concepts: the unconscious, defence mechanisms, psychoses, neuroses, narcissism, phantasy – to name those he most frequently refers to or takes issue with. They occur most frequently in *The Divided Self*, and to some extent in *The Self and Others* (1961); thereafter, their presence declines sharply. Laing's thesis of the complete *social* intelligibility of schizophrenia really forces him to set himself up in opposition to most generally accepted tenets of psychoanalysis. Already in *The Divided Self*, he makes it quite clear that reference to the psychoanalytic concept of the 'unconscious' can distract us, and has done so, from seeing the obvious meaning (and cause) of the symptoms. It has stopped us seeing what is going on *before our eyes* in the interpersonal relations confronting us:

... the central or pivotal issue in this patient's life is not to be discovered in her 'unconscious'; it is lying quite open for her to see, as well as for us ...[1]

In *The Divided Self* the visibility is all-important, for here Laing *does* date the foundation of the patient's crucial 'ontological insecurity', or loss of sense of being, from early childhood; but by *Sanity, Madness and the Family*, the *actual* social nexus of the family seems to cause the schizophrenia *in the present*, though the ongoing interpersonal relationships in the past (that is, usually, *before* the patient's birth) to some extent predetermine it. Schizophrenia is, as he says later, a 'social event'.

The Self and Others is transitional from Laing's use of psychoanalytic terms in *The Divided Self* to his abandonment of them in

1. *The Divided Self*, op. cit., p. 56.

later works. It is the book in which he discusses them most explicitly. In the first essay in *The Self and Others*, Laing engages in a surprisingly academic discussion of the meaning of 'unconscious'.

In a sense, Freud discovered the unconscious by default. It had to be there – nothing else could account for what he found. The concept of the unconscious is essential 'because the data of consciousness have a very large number of gaps in them; both in healthy and in sick people psychical acts often occur which can be explained only by presupposing other acts, of which, nevertheless, consciousness affords no evidence'.[2] But it is not directly with Freud but rather with a seminal psychoanalytic paper by Susan Isaacs, 'The Nature and Function of Phantasy' (1952), that Laing engages here. Isaacs contends, among other things, that unconscious phantasy is a way of *experiencing* our desires. It is clear that the question that attracted Laing was whether the unconscious could be said to 'experience':

> Is it a contradiction in terms to speak of 'unconscious experience'? A person's experience comprises anything that 'he' or 'any part of him' is aware of, whether 'he' or every part of him is aware of every level of his awareness or not.[3]

Laing uses what he sees as this 'contradiction' in Isaacs to take issue with the presentation of the problem in psychoanalytic theory in general. He suggests that the psychoanalytical notion of the unconscious as distinct from consciousness has set up the false theoretical dualities of inner life and outer experience and their various correlates. These, he claims, land one up in a welter of contradictions such as the notion that 'mind' is a reality outside experience – yet is the 'place' from which experience comes. This problem is peculiar to psychoanalysis and not to any of the natural sciences because the 'object' of the science (a person as opposed to *anima mundi*) *experiences* the investigation of the scientists:

> Things are going to be difficult if you tell me that I am *experiencing*

2. Freud, *Papers on Metapsychology*, op. cit., 'The Unconscious', 1915, p. 166.

3. *Self and Others*, op. cit., p. 8.

something which I am not experiencing. If that is what I think you mean by unconscious experience.[4]

The analyst, to Laing, is investigating the *experience* of the analysand, as such he can in fact only be directly aware of his own experience of him; he cannot see through the patient's eyes, etc. Yet it seems to him the whole science of psychoanalysis rests on these wild inferences:

> Beyond the mere attribution of agency, motive, intention, experiences that the patient disclaims, there is an extraordinary exfoliation of forces, energies, dynamics, economics, processes, structures to explain the 'unconscious'. Psychoanalytic concepts of this doubly chimerical order include concepts of mental structures, economics, dynamisms, death and life instincts, internal objects, etc. They are postulated as principles of regularity, governing or underlying forces, governing or underlying experience that Jack thinks Jill has, but does not know she has, as inferred by Jack from Jack's experience of Jill's behaviour. In the meantime, what *is* Jack's experience of Jill, Jill's experience of herself, or Jill's experience of Jack?[5]

Here Laing is conflating some Freudian concepts with more generally debased and popular notions deriving from these. But rather than use what is to him the contradictory term 'unconscious experience', Laing prefers to state that there are different *modes* of experience – imagination, memory, perception, dreaming, etc. When one is *not aware* of what one is imagining (for instance) one is not in good communication with either oneself or the other. This gives us one important sense of Laing's notion of the 'unconscious'. '*The "unconscious" is what we do not communicate, to ourselves or to one another*',[6] that is, to Laing, it is untransformed by the action of what in psychoanalysis is called the primary process. In other words, the unconscious can be understood (rendered intelligible) in *exactly* the same way as consciousness. It has no different laws – it is quite straightforward, if only we will look at it.

Laing thus wants to change the whole meaning of the psychoanalytic concept of the unconscious, making sure there is nothing distinctive about it. For although he says that all he is doing is shifting it from its assumption that it is about a person and transferring it to being an aspect of communication *between* persons – a way of experiencing/not experiencing others' experience/behaviour – what he is in fact doing destroys the entire concept. To Laing the unconscious means merely the *untransformed* mode of experience that we are simply unaware we are experiencing. Its importance as a concept and as the object of scientific investigation has vanished. Not surprisingly, after this point, Laing does not see much point in making use of it. It has no specific laws of language – what we then make of dreams, slips, jokes, is anyone's guess. But then Laing doesn't refer to them. Such a relegation of the unconscious to an aspect of unseen experience (the non-communication that must accompany communication) is, of course, inevitable within the aims of phenomenology and, for that matter, of existentialism as Laing and Cooper reformulate it in their discussion of Sartre's relation to psychoanalysis in *Reason and Violence*.

In up-dating schizophrenia to its present (rather than discovering its past origin in its present as a psychoanalytic method would aim to do), Laing *has* been successful in his project of removing the 'disease' from a person to his family nexus. He takes the interrelationships of this nexus back in time (indeed to their grandparental prehistory) but not to show what has happened to them in the immediate prehistory of the person concerned. This achievement, however, is really the dilemma of his 'science of persons'. In being, in the main, not about the 'person' but about the interrelationships, it separates the two in a way utterly alien to Freudian thought. So, for example, though its terrain is 'transition' or 'communication', yet the proposition on which this choice of territory is established assumes the existence of an 'essential self', i.e. a discrete, pre-communication person. So he will claim that the 'person' is the *object* of the science, but in the way he analyses psychoses he removes the person (here the patient) from the terrain of communication that his science is exploring. So the 'object' of the 'science' is separate from its place and space – quite clearly an impossibility. The stress on communication defeats its own end. I will try to illustrate this unresolvable contradiction. Laing has been protesting about a tendency, within 'sciences' that involve people, to depersonalize them and treat them as objects:

It may be maintained that one cannot be scientific without retaining one's 'objectivity'. A genuine science of personal existence must attempt to be as unbiased as possible. Physics and the other sciences of things must accord the science of persons the right to be unbiased in a way that is true to its own field of study. If it is held that to be unbiased one should be 'objective' in the sense of depersonalizing the *person who is the 'object'* of our study, any temptation to do this under the impression that one is thereby being scientific must be rigorously resisted [my italics].[7]

Now here we have clearly stated that the person-in-himself is the *object* of study. Yet Laing's investigation of that person in a schizophrenic condition shows that that person *is* his relationship to others (except for the essential self he has left behind). How is Laing's 'science of persons' to reconcile this apparent transposing of the field? Influenced, I suspect, by sociologists such as Talcot Parsons,[8] Laing attempts to conflate his area of communication with his object of 'the person' by talking about perpetual 'internalization'. Thus he writes of Lucie Blair:

We must recognize of course that this situation as internalized by her undergoes further refraction in the process of internalization and re-projection: she sees the world at large in terms of her original family experience. That is, her experience of the world continues to resemble the social realities that were mediated to her by her family.[9]

Or, put theoretically, in 'Family and Individual Structure', internalization entails the transference of a pattern of relations from one modality of experience to others: namely from perception to imagination, memory, dreams, phantasies, etc. What are internalized are *patterns of relationships between human presences*; thus the *area* of communications overlaps with the person as 'object' of the science. This Laing sees as distinct from Freud's notion of, say, the formation of the superego as the internalization of parental attitudes. One could make two objections to Laing here. In the first place, I cannot see that it is meaningfully different from Freud's notion – it extends the

7. *The Divided Self*, op. cit., p. 24.
8. See, for an outline of this 'Freudian' aspect of Talcot Parsons, Urie Brofenbrenner in 'Freudian Theories of Identification and Their Derivatives', *Child Development*, No. 31 (March 1960), pp. 15–40.
9. *Sanity, Madness and the Family*, op. cit., p. 59.

range of what is internalized but at a loss to specificity and at little gain other than 'looseness'. Secondly, Laing offers no suggestions as to how this happens and with what effect. Thus in bringing together the *field* of his science with its postulated object, 'the person', he has *not created a newly defined object which would be the object, and the only object, of scientific study.* An *a priori* existent object, in this case a person, is not an 'object' of science until it is transformed by the knowledge that is brought to bear on it. Thus, by way of illustration, capitalism does not in itself provide the object of the scientific study; only when its defining feature has been isolated does the essential aspect of its political economy (in this case the nature of its particular class relations) become the *object* of scientific study; it is then that these areas can be charted and their laws outlined – and a science established.

The nature of the 'object' is the primary confusion in Laing's 'science of persons'. It is precisely what makes it *not* a science, or even the beginnings of one. Looking at a person and saying 'that's our object' is like looking at the sky. Laing has got caught up in his protest against treating a person as 'an object' (i.e. as an automaton or what have you) and merely transposed his 'cleansed' object into the object of science. But science has a different sort of object than the 'object' of such ideological ways of talking about the world. It is this *transformed* 'object' with its distinctive, particular characteristics, that Freud defined in his concept of the unconscious. Laing wanted to create a 'science of persons' that did not treat them as objects. Instead all he has managed to do is to get rid of the *object* of a science.

(ii) Psychoses and Neuroses

Laing's frequent assertion of the continuum between madness and sanity was, as we know, one of Freud's fundamental propositions. Over and over again he claimed that using the terminology of 'disease' was a purely practical one – borrowed, for the time being, perforce from elsewhere. No sharp line could be drawn between normal and neurotic; all the features of neuroses and psychoses were to be found in everyday life. And Freud, like Laing, had a consistent humanitarian aim. There is no question in his work of treating the patient as an object to be assaulted either intellectually or physically (electro-shock, etc.):

> We refused most emphatically to turn a patient who puts himself into our hands in search of help into our private property, to decide his fate for him, to force our own ideals upon him, and with the pride of a Creator to form him in our own image and see that it is good. I still adhere to this refusal, and I think that this is the proper place for the medical discretion which we have had to ignore in other connections.[10]

It is not, in fact, Laing's radicalism that is antithetical to the spirit of Freud's work; it is its 'scientific' claims that go counter to psychoanalysis as to other sciences. As Freud said: 'The true beginning of scientific activity consists ... in describing phenomena and then in proceeding *to group, classify and correlate them* [my italics].'[11] But Laing, like Reich, does everything he can to restore things to their pristine, unanalysed condition. Such an ideological quest for unity masquerading as a search for a new system of totalization only ends by achieving the state *prior* to the time when the first analysis was made.

One of the important psychoanalytical positions that falls victim on one level to Laing's wish to abandon all differences, and on another to his rejection of the concept of the unconscious, is the distinction between psychosis and neurosis.

Although there is not a rigorous dividing line between the formation of a psychosis and of a neurosis, different areas *are* dominant, and this difference *is* important. Thus some features of neurosis can clearly come from pre-Oedipal days (aspects of hysteria, for instance, which Freud connected with the mother-attachment) and psychotic ones which have to do with the pre-Oedipal period can also in their reiterated form in adolescence or early adulthood – a time of sexual initiation – take on some of the sexual characteristics associated with the Oedipus complex (which, after all, the person has 'experienced' by then) and hence merge with neuroses or, more frequently, be covered by a neurosis. But the fact that there is no hard and fast

10. Freud, 'Lines of Advance in Psycho-Analytic Theory', S.E., Vol. XVII, 1919 (1918), p. 164.

11. *Papers on Metapsychology*, op. cit., 'Instincts and their Vicissitudes', 1915, p. 117.

distinction between the two syndromes is not at all the same as allowing them to dissolve into each other in an undifferentiated analysis.

It is, of course, possible that Laing, in company with some other analysts, implicitly regards psychosis merely as a more severe form of neurosis. Such a position seems to me not to recognize that the later event of the Oedipus complex – the nucleus of the neurosis – is an ever-in-waiting 'overlay'. The acquisition of the human order by the individual, in the process of dissolving the Oedipus complex, can go astray and thus produce neurosis. The neurotic person has made a mal-entry into society; in the analytic 'cure' he has the chance to try and make it again. The psychotic person has never, so to speak, reached the point of entry, though his failure to get there recognizes that the unreached entry does exist and thus colours all that has preceded. The psychotic has not, as far as his psychosis goes, entered into patriarchal culture, he is 'out of his mind' because he has been untouched by the law of the father which, for better or worse, would assign him his place in society.

The details of the distinction between psychosis and neurosis are complex and outside the scope of this book.

To insist on the distinction is not, however, merely an academic point. We shall see later how Laing's accounts of schizophrenia omit to set this dyadic syndrome in the context of the absence of a third term, the 'Oedipal' father. The fusion of neurosis and psychosis has the same effect – indeed it is part of the same issue – both instances ignore the importance of patriarchal culture. All I want to do here is select certain features of this difference between psychosis and neurosis and show how ignoring these has affected Laing's interpretation. However, as I do not regard this as an exercise in controversy, but rather as an issue with political implications for feminism consequent upon it, I have chosen three topics that I think have bearing on our construction of an analysis of feminine psychology. They are: words, hate and the pre-Oedipal mother-attachment.

Laing is dealing with psychosis, while by far the greater part of Freud's work concerns neurosis. Indeed, though he made a

number of crucial observations, Freud never did more than hint
at a theory of psychosis, and Laing, just as did Klein, may well
have the very necessary intention of stepping into the breach.
There is, of course, no *a priori* reason why Laing, or anyone else,
should follow Freud's suggestions about psychosis. It is to some
extent a different matter when we are discussing Freud's *achievements* in a theory of neurosis. But this is, perhaps, the wrong way
of stating the problem. What Freud contended was that, as yet,
for very good reasons, psychoanalysis could not handle the problem of psychosis within the therapeutic situation – this is a very
different thing from suggesting he did not have at least an emergent theory thereof. Some recognition of a point of departure
from the tentative tenets of psychoanalysis could then be expected and yet Laing offers no such recognition. He does not try
to make any distinction between psychosis and neurosis. If his
argument is that we can analyse psychoses and neuroses in much
the same way, then some explicit refutation of Freud's discoveries
would be in order. In fact it is not clear if Laing thinks they are
identical syndromes or not. We have one explicit comment on
them, and that is in *The Divided Self*. Laing is describing a patient
who, as a schoolboy, hated literature but wrote a prize essay
enthusing about a performance of *Twelfth Night*:

> This, however, was a neurotic and not a schizoid incident. This
> patient continued in other ways to do what he secretly wanted, while
> persuading himself he was only doing what other people wanted. In
> this way he succeeded in carrying through his desires, although he
> always had difficulty at the time in admitting this to himself. The
> neurotic may, therefore, pretend that he has a false-self system
> superficially resembling the schizoid's, but on closer inspection we
> see that the circumstances are, in fact, widely different.[12]

To Laing the neurotic may thus *play* the game and be dutifully
compliant but:

> In the schizoid person . . . the whole of his being does not conform
> and comply in this way. The basic split in his being is along the line
> of cleavage between his outward compliance and his inner with-
> holding of compliance.[13]

12. *The Divided Self*, op. cit., p. 97.
13. ibid., p. 99.

For the schizoid, compliance is achieved with fear and hatred which are revealed clearly in psychotic breakdown:

> Indeed, what is called psychosis is sometimes simply the sudden removal of the veil of the false self, which had been serving to maintain an outer behavioural normality that may, long ago, have failed to be any reflection of the state of affairs in the secret self. Then the self will pour out accusations of persecution at the hands of that person with whom the false self has been complying for years.[14]

Although here in this *one* instance they have these distinctive features in their behavioural patterns, Laing's 'neurotic' and 'psychotic' states usually seem to blend. Thus, after an analysis of a schizophrenic patient, he will cite with approval Paul Tillich's 'Neurosis is the way of avoiding not-being by avoiding being'.[15]

The Oedipus complex – the sexed entry of the child into his or her place in the world – is the nucleus of the neurosis. When, through the analytical 'cure', as far as possible, the unconscious return of the repressed desires and ideas connected with this entry have been made conscious and consciously accepted or rejected, the task of the analysis of neurosis is, in a sense, done. (It is neither, of course, as simple as that in Freud's theory, nor in the analytic practice nor in the patient's experience. I am simplifying here in order to try to establish a distinction.) Often, when the neurotic symptoms and difficulties have been thus analysed, psychotic ones reveal themselves – Freud's 'Wolf Man' was a case in point. On the other hand psychoses tend to express themselves, among other ways, in delusions and hallucinations which are fully believed in. (This difference from neurosis is to be perceived behind Laing's phenomenological account in *The Divided Self*, quoted above.) The symptoms do not seem so closely connected with sexuality as they do with a crisis in the assertion of the ego. (Laing's observation, again, in *The Divided Self* that any reference to sexual incestuous longings masks the problems of a patient's 'ontological insecurity' is again an accurate observation, but an inadequate analysis.) The psychotic is rejecting present reality and

14. ibid., pp. 99–100.   15. ibid., p. 111.

replacing it with a delusion that contains a grain of truth from some reaction to a past historical 'event'. As, from its expressions, it is clear that this has to do with some primary ego-assertion, the 'time' of the 'event' must be very early in the person's life.

Perhaps it may be a general characteristic of hallucinations to which sufficient attention has not hitherto been paid that in them something that has been experienced in infancy, and then forgotten returns – something that the child has seen or heard at a time *when he could still hardly speak* and that now forces its way into consciousness, probably distorted and displaced owing to the operation of forces that are opposed to this return [my italics].[16]

An untenable situation in the present makes the psychotic turn away from the real world and replace it by some distorted, fragmented terror or wish-fulfilment from the past. That past is the earliest of all pasts, and it involves a good deal of violence in order to preserve the ego from destruction, it involves the first use of words, and it is characterized by a pre-Oedipal attachment to the mother. The phenomenology of all Laing's case-histories reveals one or more of these aspects, *but* because he takes them to exist only in the present, they are simple, for untransformed by any primary process – they are just what they say they are. We can see this most clearly in considering the question of the language of schizophrenia. One of the characteristics of schizophrenia is its language, its 'schizophrenese'. Laing gives one beautiful instance of it, again in *The Divided Self*. He is describing the utterances of the chronic schizophrenic girl, Julie:

Since she was anyone she cared to mention, she was no *one*. 'I'm thousands. I'm an in divide you all. I'm a no un' (i.e. a nun: a noun: no one single person) . . .
'She was born under a black sun.
She's the occidental sun.'
The ancient and very sinister image of the black sun arose quite independently of any reading . . .
She always insisted that her mother had never wanted her, and had crushed her out in some monstrous way rather than give birth to her normally. Her mother had 'wanted and not wanted' a son.

16. Freud, *Constructions in Analysis*, 1937, S.E., Vol. XXIII, p. 267.

She was 'an occidental sun', i.e. an accidental son whom her mother
out of hate had turned into a girl. The rays of the black sun scorched
and shrivelled her. Under the black sun she existed as a dead thing.
Thus,
   'I'm the prairie.
   She's a ruined city.'[17]

When the past returns in the present in psychoses, it comes
through in language that is transformed by the laws of the
system to which it has been repressed – the unconscious. Freud
describes the mechanisms of hallucination and comments: 'This
is after all the familiar mechanism of dreams, which intuition has
equated with madness from time immemorial.'[18] The same kind
of distortion that turns a dream-thought into an image, here
occurs with words. This is why schizophrenic language often
sounds like dream-poetry: one word can stand for many:

In schizophrenia *words* are subjected to the same process as that
which makes the dream-images out of latent dream-thoughts – to
what we have called primary psychical process. They undergo condensation, and by means of displacement transfer their cathexes to
one another in their entirety. The process may go so far that a single
word, if it is specially suitable on account of its numerous connections, takes over the representation of a whole train of thought.[19]

Laing's paraphrasing of Julie's condensed thought processes
bears eloquent witness to the mechanisms that Freud is here
analysing. But as, after *The Divided Self*, the present family praxis
is all, and as, again after this book, the unconscious as a distinctive
system is discounted, words too must vanish. With his denial of
the unconscious, Laing must deny that anything particular
happens to the schizophrenic words – they are intelligible by
the processes of consciousness. It cannot be accident that after
Julie, not one of Laing's case-history schizophrenics utters a
single 'psychotic' phrase. Indeed, the next time Laing refers
to 'schizophrenese' at all, and that is in the 1969 essay, 'Intervention in Social Situations', he means by it not the language

17. *The Divided Self*, op. cit., pp. 203–4.
18. Freud, 'Constructions in Analysis', op. cit., p. 267.
19. Freud, *Papers on Metapsychology*, 'The Unconscious', op. cit.,
p. 199.

of the 'patient', but the terminology employed by the psychiatrist – 'hypomanic', 'mutism', 'negativism', etc.

This transformation of words that characterizes schizophrenia points to an early pre-verbal (or scarcely verbal) state, although the relationship is by no means as simple as that makes it sound. However, the emotional effect that Laing constantly comments on, and that does distinguish the outbreak, offers a further confirmation. Hate and anger are characteristic features of this 'schizophrenic' asserting self; the recurring pattern is for the psychotic patient to go through a long period of childhood as 'good' (too good), then suddenly, in or around adolescence, a 'bad' phase takes over:

> Julie's diatribes against her mother were endless and were always on the same theme: she would accuse her mother of not having wanted her, of not letting her be a person, of never having let her breathe, of having smothered her. She swore like a trooper. Yet to other people she could be charming, when she wanted.[20]

Freud observes that hate seems to arise not from a person's sexual life, as is commonly supposed ('love to hate is near-allied'), not from the frustration of libido, but in response to a sense of unpleasure caused by the frustration of all needs. Hate, he discovered, arises from the ego's original struggle to preserve and maintain itself, it does not arise, as love does, with sexuality.

> So we see that love and hate, which present themselves to us as complete opposites in their content, do not after all stand in any simple relation to each other. They did not arise from the cleavage of any originally common entity, but sprang from different sources, and had each its own development before the influence of the pleasure–unpleasure relation made them into opposites . . .
>
> Hate, as a relation to objects, is older than love. It derives from the narcissistic ego's primordial repudiation of the external world with its outpouring of stimuli. As an expression of the reaction of unpleasure evoked by objects, it always remains in an intimate relation with the self-preservative instincts . . .[21]

Hate arises both from the narcissistic ego's repudiation of the external world, and as a response to the fears of destruction

20. *The Divided Self*, op. cit., p. 189.
21. Freud, *Papers on Metapsychology*, 'Instincts and Their Vicissitudes', op. cit., pp. 138–9.

brought about by separation from the mother. These features of hate point to the pre-phallic, ego-formation period of the pre-Oedipal phase.

The expression of schizophrenia may be overlaid with remnants of other events; a neurosis may conceal a psychosis. When Laing finds that the patient is expressing a crisis of being, he is either getting at the psychotic problem behind the neurotic one or rightly correcting interpretations that have confused the two. But just because the nucleus of the psychosis lies somewhere in the narcissistic pre-Oedipal moment, it does not mean that it is exempt from the later experiences of the Oedipus complex. Laing discounts the Oedipus complex, and in this he is both right and wrong. Unwittingly, Laing's case-studies concern almost exclusively a mother-child relationship. As a phenomenological description of the pre-Oedipal period this is correct. But no 'period' is pure, the pre-Oedipal child is also subject to the Oedipus complex, and *the mother-child relationship is likewise subject to the presence of the father*. The crisis of ego that occurs, pre-Oedipally, as the child can or cannot endure the necessary separation from its mother, will in later years also be expressed as other forms of separation, such as that revealed in castration-anxiety, which in its turn casts its light back on the early instances. Laing's descriptive rendering perfectly illustrates the pre-Oedipal moment, but because he refuses to find the person's infantile history important, he believes that what he has stripped from the case (the sexual Oedipal cover-up) means that he has arrived at the naked truth. So his descriptions of the mother-child relationship may be very accurate but, because they are happening here and now, they are given *no* context: it is as though the pre-Oedipal period were being repeated in an 'ideal' purity in the present, unsubjected to any later developments.

'Schizophrenese', chronic problems of identity and ego-assertion, anger and hate are all characteristic expressions of schizophrenia's onset – Julie's struggle against her mother reads like an illustration of Freud's contention that 'hate' is to do with the ego's fight for self-preservation. Indeed, Laing also claims that the schizophrenic is fighting for the right to exist – but he makes this fight take place *in the present* and it is a fight on behalf of a hidden 'true self' against a compliant 'false self'. Whereas if we follow Freud's insights, what is breaking through at puberty, or whenever, is an unresolved battle *from the past* – the language of which bears all the marks of 'the return'. The struggling ego gives up, as it gave up before in infancy, when it lapsed into total mental compliance.[22] This time, as it is giving up on the threshold of adulthood, the situation is more chronic, and the 'ego' retreats right back to where it started – the pre-Oedipal world of 'before-distinctions', the holy one-ness of foetus and suckling babe. After the violent shout for self-preservation, of the search for self against the threat of separation, comes withdrawal, mutism, autism – the pre-verbal infant. His Majesty the Baby; the self includes the world. Religious mystics may have the capacity to temporarily abandon their ego-boundaries; the chronic schizophrenic has none properly developed to give up. The ecstasy of the mystic, the choice of the drug-taker, is the predicament of the psychotic.

22. Schizophrenia can, of course, occur in the very young child; in this case the original incidents are too strong for the infant even to fight temporarily against – hence we find autistic three- or four-year-olds, children who have *never learnt to speak*, or have instantly forgotten, because they have never battled through to make distinctions.

17 The Schizophrenic World

... I shall try to show that there is a comprehensible transition from the sane schizoid way of being-in-the world to a psychotic way of being-in-the world.[1]

The project of showing such a transition from sanity to madness that Laing set himself in *The Divided Self* would come as no surprise to Freudians. *Of course*, a universal schizoid infantile situation underlies a later psychotic episode – where else would it come from? The question is rather: how does Laing, setting himself such a task, manage to reverse its implications in his later works? I think that if we examine a central analysis made in *The Divided Self* we can discover the moment that enables this reversal and thus see predicted for us the drift of his later apparently more way-out theses.

Laing's preoccupation with communication revolves a good deal around perception – seeing and being seen. It is in these terms that he comments on the famous and extremely important observation that Freud made on a small child (see pp. 382ff.). The child, temporarily left by his mother, plays a very usual game in front of the mirror whereby he goes and comes back – the child also throws away and reclaims a cotton-reel, exclaiming with each appearance '*da!*' ('there!') and with each disappearance '*fort!*' ('gone!'). (I shall quote Laing's explanation at some length.) Laing sees it as a game against anxiety, as, indeed, among other things, it is.

If this is so, the fear of being invisible, of disappearing, is closely associated with the fear of his mother disappearing. It seems that loss of the mother, at a certain stage, threatens the individual with loss of his self. The mother, however, is not simply a *thing* which the child can see, but a *person* who sees the child. Therefore, we suggest

1. *The Divided Self*, op. cit., p. 17.

that a necessary component in the development of the self is the experience of oneself as a person under the loving eye of the mother. The ordinary infant lives almost continually under the eyes of adults. But being seen is simply one of innumerable ways in which the infant's total being is given attention. He is attended to, by being noticed, petted, rocked, cuddled, thrown in the air, bathed: his body is handled to an extent that it never will be again.[2]

The child makes himself disappear (from the mirror):

That is to say, if he could not see himself *there*, he himself would be 'gone'; thus he was employing a schizoid presupposition by the help of the mirror, whereby there were two 'hims', one *there* and the other *here*.[3]

The self then identifies with the phantasy of the person by whom one is seen; it thus becomes the observing-self, observing it-self. The observing-self frequently kills anything under its scrutiny:

In the game of this little boy, he, in the position of the person who was perceiving him, that is, his mother, was in a sense killing himself in a magical way: he was killing the mirror-image of himself. We shall have occasion to return later to this peculiar state of affairs when studying schizophrenia . . .[4]

This *normal* game of the child is described by Laing as a 'peculiar state of affairs'; it is seen by him as an original schizoid act – a creating of a split self, one half murdered – and is to be compared to schizophrenia.

On one level, Laing's analysis fits perfectly with orthodox psychoanalysis. Melanie Klein proposed an original schizoid self, but as this has constitutional elements, Freud's own conception of the incident is more pertinent to what Laing 'discovered'. Freud, too, in analysing the earliest construction of the ego saw it as created in alienation, it must 'take' itself from other ways of seeing it and its ways of seeing others see it. (Only later in the Oedipus complex does it have to discover its place in terms of the larger laws of human culture.) The first ego-formation is, to Freud, and must be if it is not to come ready-made into the world, an 'alienated' ego – it finds itself 'inverted'

2. *The Divided Self*, op. cit., p. 116.
3. ibid., p. 117.   4. ibid., p. 118.

in the eyes of mothers and surfaces of mirrors. What Laing has added is not a fresh insight, but a value judgement. Freud's little boy was also mastering the meaning of absence and its attendant anxieties and threats of destruction. As Laing will have nothing to do with Freud's notion of a death-drive, he finds, to his amazement, the little boy 'killing' himself. It would seem here that a rose by any other name is not a rose.

In *The Divided Self* Laing sensitively re-creates the condition of the schizoid 'normality' by which we live and from which *in extremis* schizophrenia arises. But his reformulation of this essentially psychoanalytic thesis in the terminology of a transposed existential philosophy leads him to substitute value judgements for analyses. These value judgements become the source of his radicalism: a 'false' self, a 'depersonalized' world, a schizoid normality, become conditions to be condemned and battled against.

It is a predictable, indeed automatic, step from this analysis in *The Divided Self* to the introduction to *The Politics of Experience*: 'There is little conjunction of truth and social "reality" . . . No one can begin to think, feel or act now except from the starting-point of his or her own alienation.'[5] Truth is the pre-egoic world of oneness and life, like a dome of many-coloured glass, shatters its white radiance, fragmenting us into our separate selves (self and others) and splitting us even within ourself into true and false, real and unreal. We are all schizoid and are pushed into schizophrenia when we are forced by our relationships with others to live more according to our false than to our true selves. In such an emergency we bury our true selves out of harm's way and try to live out our false selves coherently; but we can't, so the line that divides them breaks down and in the extremities of psychosis our 'selves' meet up in what seems to be – but never, of course, actually is – the original unity of pre-'human' life.

This, of course, is once more a re-statement of Laing's philosophy but we can see the circular 'normality is schizoid', 'schizophrenia is normal', quite concretely, if we trace through some of the characteristics of his schizophrenic patients into their natural resting place in Laing's injunctions to all of us. What Laing

5. *The Politics of Experience*, op. cit., p. 11.

advocates in *The Politics of Experience* was once what Julie suffered from in *The Divided Self*:

Together with the tendency to perceive aspects of her own being as not-her, was the failure to discriminate between what 'objectively' was not-her and what was her. This is simply the other aspect of the lack of an overall ontological boundary. She might for instance feel that rain on her cheek was her tears.

William Blake in his description of split states of being in his Prophetic Books describes a tendency to *become what one perceives*. In Julie all perception seemed to threaten confusion with the object. She spent much of her time exercising herself with this difficulty. 'That's the rain. I could be the rain.' 'That chair . . . that wall. I could be that wall. It's a terrible thing for a girl to be a wall.'

All perception seemed to threaten mergence and all sense of being perceived by the other threatened her similarly.[6]

The truth I am trying to grasp is the grasp that is trying to grasp it.[7]

Having made sure that it is the best sort of sanity, Laing becomes his own schizophrenic. In *The Divided Self* he comments on how, in an acute schizophrenic state, the person seems to fragment into several different parts. Each one has an I-sense and feels the other parts as in some way not-me. One such chronic patient told Laing of herself, '*She's* an *I* looking for a *me*', and Laing later reflects on himself: 'The I that I am is not the me that I know, but the wherewith and whereby the *me* is known.'[8] He, himself, will try the psychotic voyage and his scientific project will be to describe it.

A scientific, existential hero, Laing will dare the unknowable as he claims Freud once dared the abyss. His many different methods are so many various ventures into a realm that, as he often states, is ultimately unchartable in this way. I would suggest that it is unchartable because it has defined itself as outside human experience. And so we move onwards to a quite logical, simultaneous assertion of the transcendental: we will try to explore what can *never* finally be mapped and the fact that our experience shows us that all our methods are thus of limited use

6. *The Divided Self*, op. cit., p. 198.
7. *The Politics of Experience*, op. cit., p. 156.
8. ibid., p. 147.

proves that there is something beyond. The 'scientific' project itself reveals the transcendental unknown: the two can thus alternate, overlap, become one and the same assertion.

The patterns delineated here have not yet been classified by a Linnaeus of human bondage. They are all, perhaps, strangely familiar.

... Words that come to mind to name them are: knots, tangles, fankels, *impasses*, disjunctions, whirligogs, binds. I could have remained closer to the 'raw' data in which these patterns appeared. I could have distilled them further towards an abstract logico-mathematical calculus. I hope they are not so schematized that one may not refer back to the very specific experiences from which they derive; yet that they are sufficiently independent of 'content', for one to divine the final formal elegance in these webs of *maya*.[9]

Laing's work approximates more and more to art:

The dreadful has already happened.
>   Debris
>   The old style
>   All those endearing ...

I want you to taste and smell me, want to be palpable, to get under your skin, to be an itch in your brain and in your guts that you can't scratch out and that you can't allay, that will corrupt and destroy you and drive you mad. Who can write entirely with unadulterated compassion? All prose, all poetry, to the extent that it is not compassion, is failure.[10]

A great number of existentialist philosophers have expressed themselves in creative literature of one form or another. Laing is seeking a 'science' but seems more and more inclined to put his thoughts in verse. To the contrary, Freud very firmly rejected Havelock Ellis's flattering attempt to show that psychoanalysis was not a science but a creative art. Art and Science have to be considered differently; what are we to do with Laing's work? In fact, I think the scientific pursuit and the incipient artistic intention are unified in that they are merely diverse expressions of one ideology.

Laing's 'science of persons' would, he hoped, be a perfectly homologous structure. That is, the 'science' would reflect its

9. *Knots*, op. cit., preliminary pages.
10. *The Politics of Experience*, op. cit., p. 153.

object. Its 'object' is the 'person' and the science must thus be personal (possibly subjective). Such a *reflection* is not *science* – as Laing himself confirms when he writes in *Self and Others*, 'There is no final assurance that one can attribute correctly the other's relation to his actions'[11] (one of the tasks of his 'science'). A science must, from within its own domain, offer the possibility of consistency and of some form of proof. But if we acknowledge that it is not a science, we can see how in fact Laing, despite this, *does* achieve his aim. His work precisely does *reflect* how the person lives. Reflection is ideology, not science. Laing's intention is thus an ideological and not a scientific one. Given this as our starting point for estimating his work, we can see that his achievement is significant. He lucidly exposes for us how most of us in Western capitalist culture live, the terms of our lives, what constitutes our illusions, our reality, our hopes and despairs. Laing offers them to us from within, for he is himself bound firmly therein. Freud, on the contrary, was attempting to found a science which would analyse how the way-we-live operates.

Laing repeats the same phenomenological ground that Freud trod and partially analysed; but Laing's project is total reflection, where Freud's is specific and limited comprehension:

> The charge of one-sidedness made against psycho-analysis, which, as *the science of the unconscious mind*, has its own definite and restricted field of work, is as inapplicable as it would be if it were made against chemistry.[12]

Freud was out to analyse, Laing is here to present. But Laing's work has the merit of lucidly giving us new (and forgotten old) aspects of the phenomenological terrain for future analysis. Laing places our assumed ideology before our eyes. As the field he is working in directed him consciously to the family and unintentionally to women he gives us some very useful food for thought.

11. *Self and Others*, op. cit., p. 111.
12. Freud, 'Two Encyclopaedia Articles', (a) 'Psycho-Analysis', S.E., Vol. XVIII, 1923, p. 252.

R.D. Laing:
The Family of Man, II

18 Rebels with a Cause

Laing's work demands attention both because of his popularity and influence in the last decade and because he claims a lot for his discoveries. Though he may have written no more on either the family (and considerably less on women) than many other psychologists or analysts in recent years, the fact that he has a coherent attitude and a battle to fight make him (for our purposes) stand out. Like Wilhelm Reich he is a dominant psychopolitical ideologist.

The progress of Laing's work has been from an analysis of the split individual, through a study of the individual divided from, and against, others, to others against the individual within the small unit of the family, to each against each in microsocial personal relationships (i.e. marriage) and to the two sides of the macrosocial political world of Them and Us, East and West, Black and White, etc. This movement is the logic of his preoccupation with division and distinction; from *The Divided Self* to

All distinctions are mind, by mind, in mind, of mind
No distinctions no mind to distinguish.[1]

Man's separateness, his alienation from his own 'true' self and from 'real' others, is encapsulated for Laing in the predicament of the schizophrenic who is scapegoated – i.e. made more alienated, therefore incarcerated in incomprehension: private autism and public mental hospital.

In the early work, the schizophrenic's 'madness' is found to be an intelligible response to certain mad-making social pressures; in the middle work the mad-making social pressures come to seem the real madness; by default, the schizophrenic's response has moved from being intelligible to being 'normal';

1. *Knots*, op. cit., p. 82.

in the late works the schizophrenic's 'madness' has become the true sanity from which the vast majority of people are divorced. Many critics have decried Laing's descent/ascent into mysticism, but it is clearly the completely logical progress of his preoccupations.

It is precisely because Laing is such a perfect ideologist and one who assumes a radical, oppositionist stance that his psychological vocabulary has entered so freely into the arena of left-wing political life. Terms like 'mystification' and 'honesty' have gained political currency; his revelations about the horrors of the nuclear family have endorsed commune-seeking; women liberationists protest in Laingian terms that they are 'reified', treated like 'things', 'sexual objects'. Laing's work has co-incided with the youth movement, student politics, women's and gay people's liberation; it has given them some of its language and they have given it its popularity. All these radical movements assert humanitarian values in what is claimed to be an inhuman and depersonalized capitalist world. I am not concerned here with the political argument, but I am concerned to point out the implications of using the Laingian ideology in this way. Laing has isolated for us features of the family which instead of being taken up as slogans for protest should be analysed. If the predicament of women, children, gay people is just used as a battle-cry and its origin and function in society not comprehended, it will never be overcome. I think it is crucial to see what Laing presents us with in this field and then move on to an analysis of it.

Laing reflects the current political dichotomies of East and West. He virtually parodies them with his TV imitations of 'goodies and baddies'. He believes that divisions plague us all. His remedy, he tells us, is to cease to have divisions. It is quite logical, for after all, the only thing you can do if you are trapped in a reflection is to invert the image. But nothing, of course, is calculated to appeal more to the humanitarian politics of the sixties and seventies. Class politics having given way to what, in their debased versions, have been presented as 'opposites' politics (Black/White, Young/Old, Women/Men), what is more likely to sound like a resolution (and revolution) than a refutation of the basis of the problem? Philosophers of reconciled dualities (their so-called dialectical synthesis in unity), such as Reich and Laing, are bound to appeal to the 'politics of opposites'; but Laing's theses are attractive for more concrete reasons still.

In the early sixties, era of the problem of the teenage revolt, Laing, intentionally or not, took up the battle on behalf of the rebels. His works speak to the heart of the adolescent predicament. *They are about the crisis of leaving home.* This was not just a radical gesture of support on Laing's part – *the whole project and achievement of his 'science of persons' is dedicated to this end.* By up-dating schizophrenia into the present predicament of the adolescents in whom this psychotic breakdown occurred, Laing provided a myth for the teenage crisis. His driven-mad-by-the-family-nexus schizophrenic is every adolescent writ large. It is no wonder that his writings attract youth, as they attract social workers but not psychoanalysts. For young people they explain their problematic situation and justify their response to it; for social workers, whose task it is to deal with this present-day reality, they provide a most useful elucidation. For understanding psychosis *except* (and it is an important exception) *in its symptomatic phenomenology*, they get us nowhere.

As Laing's theory reverses the sane-mad situation, so, too, do his more concrete illustrations. It is these that, perhaps unwittingly, give support to teenage protest and that seem, if in an elusive fashion, to blame parents, or more particularly the mother. Surveying, in *The Politics of Experience*, the history of his type of work, Laing writes:

It is only in the last ten years that the immediate interpersonal environment of 'schizophrenics' has come to be studied in its interstices. This work was prompted, in the first place, by psychotherapists who formed the impression that, if their patients were *disturbed*, their families were often very *disturbing*. Psychotherapists, however, remained committed by their technique not to study the families directly. At first the focus was mainly on the mothers (who are always the first to get the blame for everything), and a 'schizophrenogenic' mother was postulated, who was supposed to generate disturbance in her child.

Next, attention was paid to the husbands of these undoubtedly unhappy women, then to the parental and parent-child interactions ... then to the nuclear family group of parents and children, and finally to the whole relevant network of people in and around the family ... By the time our own researches started, this methodological breakthrough had been made ...[2]

But though he has relegated such notions as a 'schizophrenogenic' mother to the past history of his type of theory, Laing's whole system *does* depend on a reversal of 'values' that makes comparable conclusions inevitable, if implicit. His notion that 'madness' is an intelligible response runs parallel to his ascription that people drive each other mad in an insane effort to establish their own normality and to confirm the distinction between 'them' and 'us' – here the 'sane' and the 'mad', which is often synonymous with the 'good' and the 'bad':

> I suggest, therefore, that *sanity or psychosis is tested by the degree of conjunction or disjunction between two persons where the one is sane by common consent* ...
> The 'psychotic' is the name we have for the other person in a disjunctive relationship of a particular kind.[3]

With madness and sanity on this sort of continuum and only falsely posed as polarities by those whose sanity depends on such distinctions, it is inevitable that Laing should, to some degree, right the balance. And this he does. In his case-studies of schizophrenics and their families, we find him constantly making such remarks as, of the Blair family, 'But the whole family seems to have been very odd', or of the relationships of one patient's mother and grandmother, 'we shall see ... how extraordinary this bond is'.[4] The point is that in establishing the patient's 'normality' Laing is forced, despite his intentions, *by his own methodology* to say someone else is abnormal. As he is not searching for any other 'cause' of psychosis than that of the present-day social interaction in which the patient is engaged, it is necessary for him to remove the onus of categorization from the classified patient and place it on someone else. Despite his original plea to stop categorizing, ultimately all he can ask for is either more, or differently directed, classifications:

2. *The Politics of Experience*, op. cit., pp. 93–4.
3. *The Divided Self*, op. cit., p. 36.
4. Both quotations are from *Sanity, Madness and the Family*, op. cit., pp. 37 and 211.

It is a curious feature of psychiatric theory that a person who holds such a view in such a manner about his own person would be regarded as hypomanic, but if the person holds it about another person and attempts to fit the other into that mould Procrustean-fashion, there is no term in general currency to describe him or her. We have clinical terms for disturbed, but not for *disturbing* persons.[5]

And for want of new terminology, Laing has in fact had to redeploy the old, so he will conclude of the hospitalized schizophrenic girl, Lucie Blair's, *parents*: that *if* what Mrs Blair says of Mr Blair is true, then the father is probably psychotic; if it is not, then the mother is; or, more likely, both of them. By now one must ask: if the parents are mad, who drove them that way? (Their parents?) Or, alternatively, if 'madness' is, as Laing claims, a false description in the malign pursuit of differentiation, it is no 'truer' to label a parent 'psychotic' than it is to do this to its child. The family becomes 'extraordinary' to make the patient's response 'ordinary'; so too do 'normal' people live in a phantasy-world usually reserved for psychotics. From their comments on the Irwin family it would seem that Laing and Esterson are telling us that the family completely invented their daughter's condition, and that they were disturbingly successful at it too.

We shall here present a radically different gestalt, in which the *attribution* of illness becomes socially intelligible. We shall see how this attributed illness comes to be taken as a fact, and how she is treated accordingly. Such is the *spell cast by the make-believe* of every one treating her as if she were ill, that one has constantly to pinch oneself to remind oneself that there is no evidence to substantiate this assumption, except the actions of the others, who by acting in terms of this assumption conjure up a feeling of conviction that the experience and actions in question are the unintelligible outcome of process, rather than the entirely intelligible expression of Mary's praxis, in a social field where her position is untenable and where her 'moves' (her praxis) are explained on the presumption that they are generated by a mysterious, indubitable, yet indefinable pathological process [second italics mine].[6]

Just as are the Blair parents, the Irwins are on the royal road to their own psychosis, unrecognized only because their full-

5. ibid., p. 136 n.   6. ibid., p. 190.

fledged phantasy existence takes the socially acceptable form of categorizing another. This may well be the case, but Laing, to remove the denigratory value judgement from the classified schizophrenic, has to transfer it to the others. Wishing not to fall into the trap of making distinctions, he can in fact not avoid them, only transpose them. It is this dilemma, I believe, that eventually leads him out of social analysis into mystic celebration.

However, in showing how normal 'abnormality' is and how 'peculiar', 'extraordinary', etc. 'normal' social interaction is, Laing, as his concept of a 'science of persons' demands, has inevitably himself fallen into the trap (or release) of producing studies of people in which one cannot distinguish types of problems or behaviour. This is the concrete dimension to his theoretical project of showing psychosis vanish into its social intelligibility. I will just give a couple of illustrations. In *Sanity, Madness and the Family* he displays the peculiarities of these schizophrenic-producing families, in order to demonstrate the 'correctness' of the patient's response; but by drawing into the same strange bag *all* the members of the nexus, Laing often fails to point out what is really 'odd' – at least from the standpoint of our society. Thus the Edens are a family anxious to hide the illegitimate birth of the daughter's daughter, Ruby, who is the 'schizophrenic patient':

In order to spare the reader the initial confusion of the investigators, not to say of this girl, we shall tabulate her family nexus.

Biological status	*Titles Ruby was taught to use*
Father	Uncle
Mother	Mummy
Aunt (mother's sister)	Mother
Uncle (mother's sister's husband)	Daddy – later Uncle
Cousin	Brother

Her mother and she lived with her mother's married sister, this sister's husband (*daddy* or uncle) and their son (her cousin). Her father (*uncle*) who was married, with another family elsewhere, visited them occasionally.

Her family violently disagreed about whether Ruby had grown up knowing who she was. Her mother (*mummy*) and her aunt (*mother*), strongly maintained that she had no inkling of the real state of affairs, but her cousin (*brother*) insisted that she must have known for years.[7]

Certainly a generally confused situation, but the factor that seems to me to have been a constant problem, and which, to say the least, must have made Ruby suspicious, is not even commented on by Laing and Esterson: this child has simultaneously a 'mummy' and a 'mother' – surely an obtrusively abnormal state of affairs in our society? Likewise, in *The Divided Self*, Laing reports the monologues of a chronic schizophrenic, Joan; Joan in her 'separated' persona always refers to herself as 'he'; later, almost by accident, in the general analysis we learn her parents had wanted a boy – but surely the persistently transposed gender was worth a specific comment? It seems that in a wish to make all intelligible Laing sometimes either merely see-saws the structure so that normal-abnormal change places, or all, in an undifferentiated way, becomes either normal or abnormal, and crucial extraordinary details are overlooked.

It would seem to be a correct criticism of Laing's work that he resists classifying the patient 'schizophrenic' only to classify those that drove him thus (and by classifying we tend to mean blame): the families become 'extraordinary' to account for the 'ordinariness' of the patient. And just as the justification for Laing's 'science' is conceived in the same terms as the original cause of the illness – in reverse (the physician who 'accepts' will replace the parent who 'rejects'), so too, a 'bad' science is seen in the same terms as a 'bad' family. If the Blairs, the Edens, the Kings, etc. are extraordinary, so are many psychiatrists. Dr Kraepelin, the nineteenth-century psychiatrist, who provoked a catatonic patient by arresting her walk, trying to get a response out of her by poking her, etc., comes out a truly ridiculous, sadistic figure whose behaviour is at least as 'extraordinary' as that of his 'victim'. A good parent-doctor must replace him. I am not here concerned with questioning the correctness of Laing's ascriptions – but with suggesting that *as such* they point to a central flaw in Laing's 'scientific' purpose.

Freud's theory of the significance of transference-love in the therapeutic situation has been reversed by Laing. In any case

7. ibid., p. 120.

analysis suggested that only a neurotic, not a psychotic, could become involved in such a transference. Freud's patient co-operates in the cure because he transfers the good feelings that he once had for his parents on to the analyst – and wants to please him as he once wanted to please his parents by working hard at his own self-understanding. The patient repeats anew – as a memory – his infantile predicament, but this time works through it consciously. Laing on the contrary is not concerned about the patient's love for the therapist, it is the therapist who must be able to empathize with and show compassion for the patient. This therapist thus *really* replaces the kindly parent and pre-sumably the patient is comforted. Despite appearances, the behaviour and character of the doctor has gained in importance and that of the psychotic has diminished. Exit analyst, enter guru.

19 Leaving Home and Letting Go: The Feminine Predicament

Laing's denial of the importance both of infancy and of the unconscious naturally gets rid of the problem of psychosis. But his presentation of schizophrenia as a response to a predicament in the present *does* have the merit of eloquently and lucidly describing that situation. As Reich's returning of the Oedipus complex to the nuclear patriarchal family from whence Freud deduced it had the value of enabling him to offer a vivid political sociological portrait of that family, so Laing's returning of schizophrenia to the place and relationships in which it finds expression has meant that he too can give an excellent psychosocial picture of internal family dynamics. Laing's descriptions of family communication-systems, of the mystifications, evasions and ascriptions that *do* go on, have the same pertinence for us as do Reich's accounts of the political manipulation of sex and the family by capitalist society. The advantage of a phenomenological method is not that it gives us a new analysis, but that it offers perfect phenomenology: after reading Laing's studies we understand much better the internal characteristics of the nuclear family.

Laing's case-histories are models of readability, fascinating in their revelations of how we operate in our most intimate relationships. They are of particular interest to women for two reasons. In the first place, by chance, all Laing's detailed accounts are of 'schizophrenic' women. Secondly (because of the nature of the formation of schizophrenia that Laing has discounted – its pre-Oedipal references) all his portraits of the family centre around the mother-child relationship. What we have, then, is the problems encountered by the girl leaving home and by the mother letting her child go.

Freud's theory of the psychology of femininity claimed that the pre-Oedipal period (the phase so crucial for psychosis) was central for the formation of the woman. It is no coincidence that psychoanalytical theory is both less adequate on femininity and psychosis than it is on masculinity and neurosis. The Oedipus complex is familiar territory compared with the shadowy realms of pre-Oedipality which psychosis and femininity 'inhabit'. Freud considered that after the trials and tribulations of self-discovery in the pre-Oedipal period (recognition of 'castration', for instance), the girl *took rest* in the Oedipus complex. Her love for her father, so difficult to achieve, did not have to be so thoroughly abandoned as did the little boy's more culture-disruptive love for his mother. Although it must never be seen as reducible to this, on the level of present-day social reality, the psychic resting in the Oedipus complex would be expressed as remaining in the family – something in our culture that women are certainly supposed to do. Laing's descriptions show us force-fully the difficulty the girl will encounter when she must leave this family. Likewise, because she did not have to shatter the Oedipus complex so completely, Freud believed that the girl's internalization of the authority-figure (at whose threatening behest the boy abandoned *his* incestuous desires) is much less effective. The girl having thus a weaker superego remains more subject to the reprimands and the love offered by external people – her parents, in particular.

The fear of castration being thus excluded in the little girl, a powerful motive also drops out for the setting-up of a super-ego and for the breaking-off of the infantile genital organization. In her, far more than in the boy, these changes seem to be the result of up-bringing and of intimidation from outside which threatens her with a loss of love.[1]

What happens to the little boy is that the 'authority of the father or the parents is introjected into the ego, and there it forms the nucleus of the super-ego, which takes over the severity of the father and perpetuates his prohibition against incest'.[2] This happens only partially in the girl, to whom, in any case, the father is usually something less of an authority figure as he

1. Freud, 'The Dissolution of the Oedipus Complex', 1924, S.E., Vol. XIX, p. 178.
2. ibid., pp. 176–7.

has always been more interested in 'seducing' her affections ('daddy's little girl'), and so she remains in a state of hostile attachment to her mother – relying on *external* injunctions for her mode of behaviour. This very pattern is evidenced in all the case-histories Laing presents to us.

The girl with her greater reliance on *outside* authority-figures, throughout her childhood, has had to be more compliant, less 'naughty' – there is no equivalent of 'boys will be boys'. The boy has, so-to-speak, already made a break – at the time of his resolution of the Oedipus complex – and his whole training has conformed with this original formation of himself as 'independent'. Not so the girl. She has, in adolescence, to make a radical break, where the boy only has to repeat his first efforts. Many women, though nominally they leave home, understandably, never make it. Freud comments – if rather casually – on the effort that the girl has to make in adolescence:

> When a mother hinders or arrests a daughter's sexual activity, she is fulfilling a normal function whose lines are laid down by events in childhood, which has powerful, unconscious motives, and has received the sanction of society. It is the daughter's business to emancipate herself from this influence and to decide for herself on broad and rational grounds what her share of enjoyment or denial of sexual pleasure shall be.[3]

This typical feature of mother-daughter conflict over the daughter's sexual emancipation is a recurrent theme of the Laingian case-histories; his families cannot tolerate either their child's sexual inclinations or her anger, so to the Church family: 'Spontaneity, especially sexual spontaneity, is the very heart of subversion to institutional mores, to pre-set role taking and assigning. Spontaneous affection, sexuality, anger, would have shattered Mr. and Mrs. Church's shell to bits.'[4] The time of the breakdown, whether it is when the patient is fifteen or thirty years old, coincides with the time for emancipation from the family; the re-assertion of the ego.

However, because Laing's schizophrenic women are merely

3. Freud, 'A Case of Paranoia Running Counter to the Psychoanalytic Theory of the Disease', 1915, S.E., Vol. XIV, p. 267.
4. *Sanity, Madness and the Family*, op. cit., p. 85.

responding to abnormal family pressures, something of significance gets lost: the particularity of the mother-child relationship. In psychosis there is evidence that the girl never really entered into her Oedipal relationship with her father, the father is in an important sense 'absent' from her world. We are not talking here of an actual father but of a symbolic father which an actual father can only represent – hence the father's absence is not literal, but symbolic – it does not matter that much whether he is there in the flesh or not as a real father can fail to carry out the patriarchal law with regard to his daughter – though he probably has more chance of being effective than an absent father. It must also be remembered that not even an orphan or a posthumous child lives in a context of *no* parents, he lives either their absence or their very present absence – there is never *nothing*, he is always reminded of what should be.

Where the non-psychotic woman can rest in her family, as in her Oedipus complex, or in other words can leave her childhood home to make another family, the psychotic woman can neither leave nor stay. 'Normal' femininity enables the transference of Oedipal father-love to husband-love; for this woman, the 'family of origin' neatly gives way to the 'family of orientation' and as the daughter becomes a mother her ties with her own mother, whose image she confirms, are usually strengthened.[5]

As we have said, the pre-Oedipal nature of schizophrenia is, of course, also expressed in terms of some aspects of the Oedipus scene which, though never properly entered into, must nevertheless have some effect on the later expression of the psychosis in adolescence-adulthood. But Laing's case-histories bear witness

5. Laing comments on the Head family: 'David disapproved of his wife's failure to separate herself from her parents, on the significant ground that she was now "*a part of me, and not so much part of them*". This we regard as one of the key findings in this case' (ibid., p. 169). Laing is healthily shocked by this revelation. In fact any churchman would agree with David. What is exceptional in this case is not that the woman is expected to become a part of her new family just as she was of her old, but simply the degree of absorption. David's remark suggests that his wife should become a part of him as she was a part of her mother – in other words, not that she should love him as she loved her father but that she should be bound to him as she was to her mother.

to the symbolic absence of the Oedipal father, even though this is certainly *not* their intention. They thus, against their own judgement, demonstrate a crucial feature of psychosis that distinguishes it both from neurosis and from normality.

The father disappears from Laing's stories. Thus, in the case of Sarah Danzig, Sarah 'was angry with her father and was afraid of him. She saw him as the prime agent in her detention in hospital. She said that he was a liar, and would tell lies about her.' We learn that this type of accusation by Sarah in the past had 'involved [her father], *unwittingly*, in order to preserve her trust in him, in destroying her trust in herself, and as far as he could he enlisted his secretary, wife, and son to this end [my italics]'.[6] Doubtless, unless they were murderers all, both parents in such a family act 'unwittingly' but only the father (this is the only time the father is thus criticized) is given this gracious help off the hook. And in Julie's case Laing comments: 'The father, indeed, as he said, had not much to tell me, because he had "withdrawn himself emotionally" from the family before Julie was born.'[7] So Laing lets him withdraw once more, though surely this very statement by the father should have told him a lot that was worth pursuing? But Laing's prejudice is, in itself, very interesting. In *The Divided Self*, Laing commented:

It is out of the earliest loving bonds with the mother that the infant develops the beginnings of a being-for-itself. It is in and through these bonds that the mother 'mediates' the world to the infant in the first place. The world he is given may be one he can manage to *be* in; it is possible, on the contrary, that what he is given is just not feasible for him at the time. Yet, despite the importance of the first year of life, the nature of the milieu in which the child has to exist throughout its infancy, childhood, and adolescence may still have great effect one way or the other. It is at these subsequent stages that the father or other significant adults may play a decisive role in the child's life, either in direct relation with the child or, indirectly, through effects on the mother.[8]

Laing here explicitly gives a different role to the two parents, and he comments in the same section that the mother-child syndrome

6. ibid., pp. 97 and 104.
7. *The Divided Self*, op. cit., p. 191.
8. ibid., p. 190.

is a recurrent theme of schizophrenia. But by the time of *Sanity, Madness and the Family* he seems to have so absorbed this feature as to echo it in his researches without either comment or conclusion therefrom, and by the time of *The Politics of Experience* he implies that he has outgrown such notions. Thus in *Sanity, Madness and the Family* we have the following presentation of information, offered without so much as a murmur about it: the number of interviews with the patient's mother far exceeds those with the father, who receives in almost all cases two interviews, whilst the mother may be given as many as twenty-nine.[9]

What is really important is not that Laing becomes more prejudiced as he appears to become less so (which he does) but that his awareness and apparent rejection of prejudice (the quotation from *The Politics of Experience*) means that he has failed to see the significance of the prejudice, even though his insight into it in *The Divided Self* should have led him there. Quite simply, of course, if psychosis is of pre-Oedipal formation, it is *bound to* have a great deal to do with the pre-Oedipal mother and with the absence of the Oedipal father. Such an observation has *no* moral connotations – though an unwarranted refusal of it does.

Laing's own social preoccupations and the unacknowledged logic of the subject (the pre-Oedipal structure of psychosis) have led him to an interest in the nature of the nuclear family and in particular, to a concentration on the mother-child relationship – from the child's point of view. The mother fares rather badly in these portraits because she is 'guilty' of not letting go. The intelligibility of the patient's response obscures the fact that in psychosis there are important problems of ego-identity and that the mother may find it as hard to cope with these in her child as the child finds it difficult to accept her mother's claustrophobic behaviour; psychosis, in a sense, is about the problematic interaction between mother and child that, *in the absence of the sym-*

9. And in *Intervention in Social Situations* (Association of Family Caseworkers and the Philadelphia Association, London, 1968, p. 10) his final advice on a so-called schizophrenic boy is 'that no one should see the boy if he did not wish to see anyone, but that someone have sessions with Mrs Clark [his mother] and her mother'!

bolic father, such mother-child relationships signify. Laing, by not realizing that his own accounts reveal the lack of intervention by a third term (the father), has failed to set his mother-child dyad in a context which explains them. In psychosis the mother and child remain a dyad, only the triadic structure of the Oedipus complex can break up this 'symbiotic' predicament.[10]

The absence of the 'absent' father from Laing's portrayal of schizophrenia is of particular importance to feminism. Many women who join the women's liberation movement are young and are trying to leave one or other of their family homes. Laing's work, with its forceful descriptions of the problems involved, has an obvious appeal, and from the perspective of a phenomenology of the mother-child situation it is excellent. But in leaving out the father, Laing is omitting to give any significance to the patriarchal law and order in which all our families are placed. The importance of patriarchal law is as absent from his accounts as it is from the pre-Oedipal phase within which the psychosis develops – his 'science' is thus, like ideology, purely reflective, a mirror-image of the predicament.

Laing's therapist will be a good *mother* (compassionate and empathetic) and confirm the patient in a safer dyadic relationship. The dyad of the psychotic and his mother and of the patient-doctor situation finds its apotheosis in a transcendental theory of duality unified. The division-separation which the psychotic could never make will be healed by the unified patient-doctor and the split world will become one again.

Laing's ideological presentation of schizophrenia has led us to be re-aware of its pre-Oedipal source, and his descriptive phenomenology displays some important aspects of 'femininity' for us; the analysis still has to take place. Laing has, willy-nilly, led us back to our territory and this is a far greater service than the totally diversionary and naïve aims of his 'biochemical' or 'geneticist' competitors. Long ago, Freud wrote:

... it seems plausible at first to expect that biochemistry will one day disclose a substance to us whose presence produces a male sexual excitation and another substance which produces a female one. But this hope seems no less naïve than the other one – happily

10. Two important books that present psychosis firmly in these terms are by Maud Mannoni, *The Child, His 'Illness' and the Others,*

obsolete today – that it may be possible under the microscope to isolate the different exciting factors of hysteria, obsessional neuroses, melancholia, and so on.[11]

Thanks to Laing, we can now re-add 'schizophrenia' to his list, only lamenting that it takes so long to repeat a discovery and that we are still having to fight the naïve biochemists of male and female biological determinism.

Tavistock Publications, London, and Pantheon Books, New York, 1970, and *The Backward Child and His Mother*, Pantheon Books, New York, 1972.

11. Freud, 'Female Sexuality', op cit., p. 240.

PART TWO *Section II*
FEMINISM AND FREUD

Transatlantic Psychoanalysis

In 1929 Reich, from Vienna and from the heart of his Marxist attempts to restore the revolutionary possibilities of psychoanalysis, wrote:

Special societies and discussion clubs for psychoanalysis are being formed in America; the market is good and must be exploited; the public indulges its unsatisfied sexuality; and at the same time this craze which they dare to call psychoanalysis is an excellent source of income. So-called psychoanalysis has become good business. That is how things stand outside the psychoanalytical world.[1]

In 1934, less concerned than Reich, Karl Kraus, still busy as a satirist in Vienna, wrote:

Psychoanalysis ... is supposed to be making an undiminished impression on Americans who are interested in everything that they don't have, such as antiques and an inner life ...[2]

Obviously, one does not want to suggest any simple equation between the decline of psychoanalysis and its absorption in America, and a serious discussion of this interrelationship is outside the scope of this book. One or two observations are, however, pertinent to any discussion of feminist reactions to Freud and Freudianism. Ostracized into extreme isolation for the first ten years of his work, Freud had an ambivalent attitude to public interest in his theories. On the one hand he regarded repudiation of his ideas as an important indication of their validity (as he was revealing the repressed unconscious – the revelation must by definition be unwelcome) and easy acceptance made him nervous. He wrote to Jung about a hostile reception that the latter had received in 1907:

1. Reich, 'Dialectical Materialism and Psychoanalysis', *Sex-Pol*, op. cit., pp. 54–5.
2. Karl Kraus, *Endes*, Vienna, 1934, p. 37.

For you, I think this experience will have good results, or at least those I like best. As for me, it has increased my respect for psychoanalysis. I was on the point of saying to myself: 'What? Already on the way to recognition after barely ten years? That can't be sound?' Now I can believe again that it is. But you will see that the conditions for the tactics you have been using up to now do not exist. People just don't want to be enlightened. That is why for the present they can't understand the simplest thing. Once they are ready for it, you will see they are capable of understanding the most complicated ideas. Until then there is nothing to be done but to go on working and to argue as little as possible.[3]

Yet, on the other hand, Freud was most anxious to win adherents, particularly from outside Vienna. When Stanley Hall asked him to come and lecture at Clark University, Massachusetts, this was the first official university recognition psychoanalysis had received and Freud never forgot his large and responsive audience – though, again, it cannot be said that he felt himself personally entirely at home within American culture. Ernest Jones had frequently to nag at Freud to take seriously a number of factors that disturbed him in the American importation of psychoanalysis, such as the poor translations and inaccurate editions of his work. Furthermore, a barely explicit motif runs through the correspondence of the early psychoanalysts: they regarded as an indication of dissidence a wish constantly to return to lecture in America – both Jung and Rank first proclaimed their alternative theories as the true psychoanalysis in New York. Whatever the implication of the coincidence may be, it is true that the popularization of psychoanalysis in America had many sources that were certainly *not* Freudian. It is certainly true also that America got more than its fair share of early popularizing.

Reich was, I think, quite correct in his estimation of the seriousness of the tendency that set in from the end of the twenties onwards: 'Those analysts who are optimistic about the popular propagation of psychoanalytical ideas are making a big mistake. It is precisely this popularization which is a symptom of the decline of psychoanalysis.'[4] Psychoanalytic terms or perversions of them became catch-phrases, every man his neighbour's

3. Freud, letter to Jung, 19 September 1907, *Letters of Sigmund Freud*, op. cit., pp. 266–7.

analyst became a – largely middle-class – vogue. Jacques Lacan in his quarrel with the orthodox French Institute of Psychoanalysis also contends that there is a dangerous popularizing trick within Freud's own work – Freud was anxious to make it all too readily understandable (Lacan's own work rights the balance!). The language and terminology of psychoanalysis was certainly a question of importance to Freud (though Lacan may well be correct in his suggestion), and the misappropriation of psychoanalysis by non-analysts annoyed him, but apart from turning down a lucrative offer from Hollywood for a film of his work, there was little that he did to stem the tide of mass trivialization and ideological perversion of his theories. Particularly in America the cult of pseudo-psychoanalysis became another way of maintaining the repression of those aspects of mental life which it was its real task to uncover. Fascism on the European continent killed psychoanalysis (reasonable editions of Freud's work have only recently become available in France and Germany). In England, perhaps, we just remained more repressed, but in America (quite probably, as Reich claims, because it dealt with sex) the popularization of psychoanalysis was used as a substitute satisfaction.

But in both England and America and wherever it still got a hearing on the continent, psychoanalysis was increasingly used to preserve the status quo. However, its different fates in various countries do, I think, suggest some reasons why there is a descending scale of opposition by feminists to Freud. From my own experience in America I cannot say I have heard a word said even in favour of an interest in Freud's writings: with varying degrees of subtlety, he is portrayed as one of the greatest misogynists of all time.[5] In England there is general prejudice against psychoanalysis but now some interest in studying Freud's work. Among Scandinavians I have found surprise at the thought of feminists utilizing his work but a keen responsiveness to the suggestion. In France there is the large and

4. Reich, 'Dialectical Materialism and Psychoanalysis', *Sex-Pol*, op. cit., p. 56.

5. An actual description in an American Women's Liberation Diary for 1971 depicts Freud with a dartboard superimposed on his head and a bulls-eye dart just beneath his left eye, and labels him 'Misogynist (Male) III'.

important women's liberation group calling itself *Psychanalyse et Politique*. There are, of course, a number of other factors at least as, if not more, important than the specific national history of Freudianism, but the particular negative experience of America does, I think, have a bearing.

America, too, received the main influx of psychoanalysts escaping from the persecutions of Nazism, and these analysts emigrated to America precisely at that time, from the early thirties onwards, when the debate on feminine psychology had, to my mind, got most stuck in the impasse of biological determinism. Although they brought with them an enlightenment and egalitarianism for which feminists have given them scant credit, theorists such as Horney and Deutsch imported to America the sterility of that moment. Although Deutsch, in a recent interview on the question of women's liberation has said, interestingly enough, in arguing *against* the claims of Masters and Johnson for clitoral orgasm: ' . . . that makes me very angry. There is a difference between animals and human beings. In man, the biological is interwoven with psychological factors ',[6] her own further answers reveal that still in 1972 the 'psychological' indicates for her that 'interpenetration of moral, anatomical and sociological' factors which, as I suggested earlier, had already spelt death to a psychoanalytic interpretation of femininity:

There can be no measurements that have any meaning unless they include tenderness and love . . . The little girl sees the penis and starts to look for her own organ. She points to the belly button, what she has that is the same as the boy. But the meaning of penis envy is also sociological. The girl learns from her environment what is the meaning of her sex, and all these delicate matters are sociobiological, as well as psychobiological.[7]

These observations may be valid in themselves, they may indeed be couched in language similar to, if not the same as, that used by Freud, but they are notions formulated *outside mankind's preoccupation with the ideas and thoughts that determine his humanity and which express themselves in language and bodily symptoms –*

6. Anne Roiphe, 'What Women Psychoanalysts Say About Women's Liberation', *New York Times Magazine*, 13 February 1972.
7. ibid.

they are notions that are thus, I contend, outside Freud's psychoanalytic framework.

As psychoanalysis had had from the outset many versions in lay minds, a further familiar confusion was inevitable in America as elsewhere. Understandably, it is rare for most people to make any distinction between psychology, psychiatry, psychoanalysis and psychotherapy. Originally American psychoanalysts fought against Freud for the necessity for all psychoanalysts to have a medical qualification. (Freud was strongly against this restriction, but in America doctors had only recently won the right to debar charlatans and quacks from medical practice and were anxious to defend any future work from a similar invasion by non-experts. Each country was left to decide the matter for itself.) This stipulated medical qualification may have assisted the ana-tomical-biological bias so strong in Anglo-Saxon psychoanalysis and thus, I believe, contributed to the reduction of its theory. It certainly did nothing to distinguish psychoanalysis from a myr-iad other psychotherapeutic practices in the public mind. It is not that I am necessarily attacking these practices in themselves, it is just that much gets accredited to Freud for which neither he nor his science has any responsibility. It is for this reason that I have selected for discussion feminist writers who have written directly on Freud, hoping in this to show how the general popular misunderstandings reflect themselves in these works to the detri-ment of any progress in the feminist understanding of women's psychology.

I think there seems overwhelming justification for the charge that the many different psychotherapeutic practices, including those that by the formal definition are within psychoanalysis, have done much to re-adapt discontented women to a conserva-tive feminine status quo, to an inferiorized psychology and to a contentment with serving and servicing men and children. Furthermore, the tendency to judge men and women in terms of conventionalized psychologies and punish them accordingly is on the increase: imprisonment for aggressive criminal men and mental hospital incarceration for passive 'disturbed' women. With the greater popularity of mental treatment – lobotomy, leucotomy, electric shock, drugs, adaptive therapy – women are the main victims. Though obviously it cannot be entirely dissociated, on the whole this has nothing to do with Freud or psycho-analysis, only with its grotesque perversion for punitive or ideological purposes.[8]

I have considered only those feminist writers whose books on the position of women contain a full discussion of Freud's work. I have not dealt with critiques in underground literature as these are so hard for people either outside the women's movement or outside America to get hold of, nor, for different reasons, have I related my disagreements solely to American feminists. Germaine Greer, an Australian, was when she wrote her book, *The Female Eunuch*, probably as deeply influenced by her experience of American culture as she was by living and working in England. Certainly her book relates in politics and tenor more to the diversity of the American movement than it does to the relatively homogeneous and organized British movement. Eva Figes's was the first of the English books to be published within the present feminist movement and the only one still to offer a full and specific attack on Freud. I have offered a discussion of this as I myself am concerned with making the debate on psychoanalysis an active part of the English movement.[9]

The inclusion of Simone de Beauvoir is, of course, of more seminal importance. Published in 1949, *The Second Sex* remains the most important of the 'totalizing' studies on the oppression of

8. It is another question whether or not there is something within Freud's work that leads to this ideological abuse. In a sense it is obvious that there must be, but exactly why or what is a complex and interesting subject and whatever it is it would not, of course, invalidate what surrounds it, though it should be extracted from it and rejected.

9. I have excluded Viola Klein's earlier and interesting discussion of Freud in her book *The Feminine Character* (Kegan Paul, Trench, Trubner and Co. Ltd, 1946) because it falls outside the period of present feminism. And though it is a more militant book than anything she has said or written since, she would not consider herself to have been a feminist then any more than now. I have also excluded a discussion of Naomi Weisstein's essay: 'Kind, Küche, and Kirche: As Scientific Law: Psychology Constructs the Female', published in *Sisterhood Is Powerful*, New York, 1970, though perhaps I like least of all her experimental-psychological refutation of Freud. The essay is also about psychological practice outside of psychoanalysis and in any case I have referred to my disagreement in a previous chapter on Freud in my book, *Woman's Estate*, Penguin Books, 1972.

women. Its range, depth, and above all the coherent theory that it offers of the inferior status of women, means that it cannot be ignored by any writer on the subject. It represents, so to speak, the base-line from which other works either explicitly (as in Shulamith Firestone's dedication in *The Dialectic of Sex*) or implicitly (in that all feminist writers must have read it) take off, however much at a tangent their specific interest or final analysis may be. Most importantly, the coherent theoretical explanation of women's oppression that she offers is *essentially a psychological one* and it is against this that her refutation of Freud (and this refutation's influence on feminist thought) must be set. Of interest, too, is that de Beauvoir applies to her problem the similar existential-phenomenological psychology that later Laing was to make use of[10] for his counter-Freudian work. But de Beauvoir's critique of Freud is solely on the grounds of his theory and is less impregnated with humanism than Laing's. Laing criticizes Freud from the viewpoint of a clinician who would rather not be one, though like de Beauvoir, he too is a psychological philosopher formulating an alternative theory.

De Beauvoir's analysis of Freud, despite its incommensurably greater sophistication, has compounded certain tendencies within popularized American Freudianism and this combination has had an influence on subsequent feminist reaction to Freud. Thus de Beauvoir, with Sartre, does not believe in the main proposition of psychoanalysis – the unconscious – nor, interested in the person's present existence, does she place much emphasis on his or her infantile past. So, too, does she continue a trend which has been dominant in opponents of Freud, most significantly since Jung: she underplays the importance of sexuality. Many of the factors she criticizes are to be found within later Freudianism, but are counter to Freud. This does not invalidate de Beauvoir's criticism; it *does* mean that the Freud the feminists have inherited is often a long way off-centre. In violently rejecting a Freud who is not Freud, I would argue that the only important possibilities for understanding the psychology of women that we have to date have been lost, and that in misconceiving and repudiating psychoanalysis a crucial science for

10. To call this 'Sartrean' is correct but ignores the creative part played by de Beauvoir's work (among others) in its formation.

understanding ideological and psychological aspects of oppression has been thrown away. Neither Freud's contribution on femininity nor the science of psychoanalysis are anywhere near unflawed or complete – but a return to these would seem to be the way forward.

The Feminists

It is to be anticipated that men analysts with feminist views, as well as our women analysts, will disagree with what I have said here. They will hardly fail to object that such notions spring from the 'masculinity complex' of the male and are designed to justify on theoretical grounds his innate inclination to disparage and suppress women. But this sort of psycho-analytic argumentation reminds us here, as it so often does, of Dostoevsky's famous 'knife that cuts both ways'. The opponents of those who argue in this way will on their side think it quite natural that the female sex should refuse to accept a view which appears to contradict their eagerly coveted equality with men. The use of analysis as a weapon of controversy can clearly lead to no decision.[1]

Freud was inclined to make quips against feminism. One suspects that the intention was to make the militant women feel that they were vainly, and somewhat madly, tilting at windmills. But, although Freud's ironic provocations gave no one the satisfaction of a battle joined, his aloofness has only further infuriated the second wave of feminists who have had the decades of 'the psychological sell'[2] to fan their fury. Freud is target number one as a personal male chauvinist whose so-called 'scientific' propaganda has been responsible for damning a generation of emancipated women to the passivity of the second sex. The outrage is by no means all abuse: much represents an argued rejection of his findings and a more-than-justified denunciation of their application. I shall examine here a number of writings with differing degrees of thoroughness. This in no way reflects the importance of the work criticized. It is simply that as one progresses it is inevitable that one finds the same objections apply to new works. Thus my discussion of each book becomes briefer and briefer, as by the end most theses have already been dealt with. In arguing

1. Freud, 'Female Sexuality', op. cit., p. 230 n.
2. The title of her chapter on Freud in Germaine Greer's *The Female Eunuch*, MacGibbon & Kee, London, 1970.

against the points these writers make, I cannot do so entirely on their terms – their repeated stipulation that they are not dealing with the system of psychoanalysis but only with Freud's specific references to women. As I have already illustrated what I regard as the most pertinent larger theses, I shall obviously not repeat them in any detail here. Only I *would* say that I think it is precisely because they try to discuss Freud's concept of femininity outside the framework of psychoanalysis that their objections (or even their tributes) cannot be made to stand up.

1 Simone de Beauvoir: Freud and the Second Sex

An entire system has been built up in this perspective, which I do not intend to criticize as a whole, merely examining its contribution to the study of woman. It is not an easy matter to discuss psychoanalysis *per se*. Like all religions – Christianity and Marxism, for example – it displays an embarrassing flexibility on a basis of rigid concepts.[1]

Not being a philosopher, Freud has refused to justify his system philosophically; and his disciples maintain that on this account he is exempt from all metaphysical attack. There are metaphysical assumptions behind all his dicta, however, and to use his language is to adopt a philosophy.[2]

Simone de Beauvoir's *The Second Sex*, strictly speaking, is not a part of the second feminist movement. Its publication in 1949 predates by almost twenty years the florescence of the political movement, and its translation into English in 1953 by exactly ten years the next major work to be written on the subject: Betty Friedan's *The Feminine Mystique*. Furthermore, it is explicitly not a feminist statement.[3] But *The Second Sex* undoubtedly had a profound influence on the first generation of new feminists and for this reason an inclusion of de Beauvoir's interpretation of Freud and Freudianism is mandatory.

The most striking feature of de Beauvoir's critique of psychoanalysis is its psychological perspective. What she likes about it is the fact of its psychology; what she dislikes is the nature of this psychology:

1. Simone de Beauvoir, *The Second Sex*, Jonathan Cape, 1960, p. 65.
2. ibid., p. 66.
3. Recently, in an interview in *Nouvel Observateur*, Simone de Beauvoir has announced that she has changed her position, and that now, in contradistinction to her earlier theses, she counts herself politically a feminist.

The tremendous advance accomplished by psychoanalysis over psychophysiology lies in the view that no factor becomes involved in the psychic life without having taken on human significance; it is not the body-object described by biologists that actually exists, but the body as lived in by the subject. Woman is a female to the extent that she feels herself as such ... It is not nature that defines woman; it is she who defines herself by dealing with nature on her own account in her emotional life.[4]

Psychoanalysis purports not to be a philosophy,[5] yet to de Beauvoir, it has philosophical implications. It is with these she takes issue – a task she admits to finding difficult in the face of Freud's repudiation of them. Difficult, but compulsory: for what de Beauvoir is setting up is a counter-psychological philosophy. I shall summarize here what seem to me to be the main elements of her interpretation of Freud, ranged against her alternative propositions. We shall, I think, see that the nature of de Beauvoir's psycho-philosophical intention determines her philosophical reading of Freud.

Put crudely, the core of de Beauvoir's existentialism is the notion that the human being takes on the meaning of his or her existence in the actions and the projects formed. Each consciousness defines itself as subject, by opposing other consciousnesses and defining them as objects. Every consciousness is a transcendence which accomplishes its freedom in a perpetual surmounting of itself towards other freedoms. If any human refuses to exercise this freedom, he falls back into a state of immanence, and his freedom is degraded into facticity. If another person blocks and refuses the freedom of others, that constitutes oppression. Woman is the supreme Other, against which Man defines himself as subject, not in reciprocity, which would mean that he in turn was object for the woman's subjecthood, but in an act of psychic oppression. Woman is the archetype of the oppressed consciousness: the second sex. Her biological characteristics have been exploited so that she has become the receptacle for the

4. *The Second Sex*, op. cit., p. 65.
5. Freud stated: 'Even when I have moved away from observation, I have carefully avoided any contact with philosophy proper. This avoidance has been greatly facilitated by constitutional incapacity.' 'An Autobiographical Study', 1925 (1924), S.E., Vol. XX, p. 59.

alienation all men must feel; she *contains* man's otherness, and in doing so is denied her own humanity. Man, in a definition of his humanity, flings himself towards a freely chosen future. Within the animal species, the female may be superior precisely on account of her reproductive powers; but humanity is distinguished from the animals by the fact that it constantly transcends itself. Animals repeat and maintain; man creates and invents. All that is specific to humanity is concentrated in man, all that is common to mankind and the animals is concentrated in woman.

[Man] aspires in contradictory fashion both to life and to repose, to existence and to merely being; he knows full well that 'trouble of spirit' is the price of development, that his distance from the object is the price of his nearness to himself; but he dreams of quiet in disquiet and of an opaque plenitude that nevertheless would be endowed with consciousness. This dream incarnated is precisely woman; she is the wished-for intermediary between nature, the stranger to man, and the fellow being who is too closely identical.[6]

Woman is the most universal and absolute specification of alterity. She is mystery, essence (the soul). No one is born a woman: a woman is created from man's needs. She is obscure, mysterious, complete, outside the tensions and struggles of existence. For the woman, the man must become all; he is all meaning, the justification and definition of her existence, whereas for him she is a pleasure, an extra, somehow inessential. The language of reciprocity and equality is meaningless in this world divided into subjects and objects. The demand that man abandon his right to alienate himself in another, no longer to root his *natural* being in the woman (an act by which he frees himself to explore his *human* existence), is no light request:

... the evolution now in progress threatens more than feminine charm alone: in beginning to exist for herself, woman will relinquish the function as double and mediator to which she owes her privileged place in the masculine universe; to man, caught between the silence of nature and the demanding presence of other free beings, a creature who is at once his like and a passive thing seems a great treasure.[7]

6. *The Second Sex*, op. cit., p. 160.
7. ibid., p. 685.

Woman's total oppression, in de Beauvoir's scheme of things, is the economic and social exploitation of this *original psychological abuse: the creation of the second sex with its Other Realm.*

The main concepts and the main values that de Beauvoir deploys for her presentation of how it happened, what is going on and what is to be done are manifest even in this brief account. They are 'choice', 'freedom', 'projects' on the one hand, versus 'determinism', 'immanence', 'alienation' and 'alterity' on the other. Confronted with a series of options, man chooses the dangerous future and thus becomes himself: life is the chosen struggle for freedom, death is sitting back content with the given. It is with these values and with this psychological-philosophical explanation that de Beauvoir confronts psychoanalysis. Though appreciative of its insights, she does not like what she finds there.

De Beauvoir summarizes Freud's notions of the girl's development: the polymorphous sexuality of both sexes in infancy as they pass through the oral and anal stages to become differentiated with the onset of genital sexuality. The girl has her two-tier genital development of, first, infantile clitoral sensitivity (this stage is analogous to the boy's concentration on his penis), then she makes a necessary transition at puberty to the vagina as the organ of her womanly sexuality. It is not this notorious latter notion with which de Beauvoir takes issue, but with the in-built masculinity of the model. For Freud, according to de Beauvoir, the norm is the boy, and the girl a deviation from it. This is largely true of Freud's first models, as he later self-critically acknowledged. It became a problem to which Freud made repeated reference, with increasing concern.

De Beauvoir's objection, however, to what may be termed Freud's 'masculine bias' has more to do with the values elicited by this than with the fact that it could constitute a scientific flaw. For what she is contending is that Freud's thesis assumes that there is an original superiority in the male whereas to her this is only socially induced.

> The little girl's covetousness [of the penis], when it exists, results from a previous evaluation of virility. Freud takes this for granted, when it should be accounted for.[8]

8. ibid., p. 68.

The sovereignty of the father is a fact of social origin, which Freud fails to account for . . .[9]

Having dissociated compulsions and prohibitions from the free choice of the existent, Freud fails to give us an explanation of their origin – he takes them for granted. He endeavoured to replace the idea of value with that of authority; but he admits in *Moses and Monotheism* that he has no way of accounting for this authority. Incest, for example, is forbidden because the father has forbidden it – but why did he forbid it? It is a mystery.[10]

The fact is that a true human privilege is based upon the anatomical privilege only in virtue of the total situation. Psychoanalysis can establish its truths only in the historical context.[11]

Finding that Freud fails to account for the high valuation placed on the penis and male sovereignty, de Beauvoir endeavours to make good this failure by placing the insights of psychoanalysis in a historical and philosophical context. She accepts many of the observations Freud makes, but proceeds to ask the question why.

Any account of original motivation must make certain assumptions, and de Beauvoir is no exception: her project for her whole book is, interestingly enough, most succinctly stated in the section where she assesses psychoanalysis:

. . . I shall pose the problem of feminine destiny quite otherwise [than it is proposed by psychoanalysis]: I shall place woman in a world of values and give her behaviour a dimension of liberty. I believe that she has the power to choose between the assertion of her transcendence and her alienation as object; she is not the plaything of contradictory drives; she devises solutions of diverse values in the ethical scale.[12]

Given this presupposition of the existent's free choice in its quest of becoming, it follows that a mixed psychosocial explana-

9. ibid., p. 69.　　　　10. ibid., p. 71.　　　　11. ibid., p. 75.
12. ibid., p. 76. De Beauvoir constantly objects (as do later feminists) to what she sees as the 'determinism' inherent in psychoanalysis. But Freud's science uses the concept of over-determination (indeed it is a term Freud invented). This is a complex notion of 'multiple causation' in which the numerous factors can reinforce, overlap, cancel each other out, or contradict one another – a very different proposition from that suggested by simple determinism.

tion of value must be forthcoming. Quite simply, in the light of this all-prevailing 'choice', what de Beauvoir sees as the Freudian stress on the significance of anatomy and the notion of drives *must* seem crudely deterministic. In de Beauvoir's version, Freud's baby comes into the world with a number of given urges (sexual ones) and a body with a fixed meaning (male or female); all the major events of infantile life follow therefrom. Whereas de Beauvoir's baby comes free of predetermined characteristics into a world of pressures and problems against which it must act or around which it must navigate in a voluntary assertion of its liberty. De Beauvoir's baby looks forward, her version of Freud's looks backwards: in psychoanalysis, she complains, 'the individual is always explained through ties with his past and not in respect to a future towards which he projects his aims'.[13]

The psychoanalyst describes the female child, the young girl, as incited to identification with the mother and the father, torn between 'viriloid' and 'feminine' tendencies; whereas I conceive her as hesitating between the role of *object*, *Other* which is offered to her, and the assertion of her liberty.[14]

De Beauvoir's philosophy (her existentialism) determines her rejection of Freud in two different ways. In one way, as we have seen, she posits an alternative psychology: the human aspiration to be a subject and express one's alienation in another thus making that other the object; in another way, she justifies this premise by explanations of social interaction. So we have a system which presupposes a set of values (and in this it is precisely a morality), which then proceeds to account for them in social terms (this part forms the 'explanation', the 'account' for the absence of which she is always berating Freud). It seems from this that de Beauvoir would have found it easier if Freud had had an explicit philosophy with which her alternative proposition could contend, and in the absence of one she reads it back from the nature of his observations: she gives him a value system which she confesses to have found hard to discover in his work. Thus the terminology of psychoanalysis becomes philosophy-loaded. The child that *identifies* with a parent is *alienating itself* in a foreign image instead of spontaneously manifesting its own existence.

13. ibid., p. 76.   14. ibid., p. 77.

Interiorizing the unconscious and the whole psychic life, the very language of psychoanalysis suggests that the drama of the individual unfolds within him – such words as *complex*, *tendency*, and so on make that implication. But a life is a relation to the world, and the individual defines himself by making his own choices through the world about him.[15]

In other words, concerned to assert a philosophy, de Beauvoir has had to find the source of her rejection of psychoanalysis in its implications alone.

What exactly does she see as these implications? They can, in fact, be summed up quite simply in one overall concept: determinism. I am only concerned here with the distortions of Freud's analysis that I think result from this assumption. Freud and de Beauvoir mean something different by the term, so that by and large, de Beauvoir is correcting something that is really not there; and in doing so she makes a number of quite specific errors.

The errors in interpretation arise, then, out of this charge of philosophical determinism, but they are compounded by de Beauvoir's stress on Freud's masculine model.

Freud never showed much concern with the destiny of woman; it is clear that he simply adapted his account from that of the destiny of man, with slight modifications.[16]

This inaccuracy (Freud was greatly concerned but also greatly unsure on this question) directs de Beauvoir to more serious misreadings:

Freud at first described the little girl's history in a completely corresponding fashion [to the boy's], later calling the feminine form of the process the Electra complex; but it is clear that he defined it less in itself than upon the basis of his masculine pattern.[17]

15. ibid., p. 75. It is interesting to note that though Freud certainly used the term 'complex', its widespread introduction probably owes most to Bleuler, Jung and the Zurich group. The term has become a catchword in popular usage; it was never a major concept of Freud's and was often rather loosely used to mean the totality of ideas relating to a particularly coloured emotional event; Freud's later use of it always included the notion of *repressed* ideas and hence, strictly speaking, it was only applied to the Oedipus and the castration complexes. 'Tendency' quite simply is not a Freudian concept.

16. ibid., p. 66.   17. ibid., p. 67.

Let us hear Freud:

We have already learned, too, that there is yet another difference between the sexes, which relates to the Oedipus complex. We have an impression here that what we have said about the Oedipus complex applies with complete strictness to the male child only and that we are right in rejecting the term 'Electra complex' which seeks to emphasize the analogy between the attitude of the two sexes.[18]

and:

I do not see any advance or gain in the introduction of the term 'Electra complex', and do not advocate its use.[19]

Ironically, what has happened to de Beauvoir's version of Freud's little girl growing up is that the distinctions between the sexes have become *more* rigid and the whole process more rigidly determined than one can ever find it in Freud's original writings. Thus she reiterates Freud's early notions of an oral, an anal and a genital stage as though they were distinct steps on the march of life, whereas Freud was, in his later works, at pains to point out their constant overlap and commingling. So, too, she ignores the permeation throughout Freud's work of the notion of bisexuality: the presence in both sexes of the inclinations of the opposite sex. The dividing line between men and women is absolute in her schema in a way that it never is in Freud's. Some of Freud's musings on problems have become dicta, and what he himself rejected as an inadequate explanation has been taken as his dogmatism. Freud, bothered by the relation between activity and passivity in the two sexes, and by the difference between the aims of sexual drives and their objects, is berated by de Beauvoir for proposing for women a 'passive libido', a notion Freud himself found equally absurd.

Part of the trouble comes from taking all psychoanalysts as Freud. To some extent this is understandable where we are dealing with Freudian analysts; but it is surely illegitimate in cases where there was an explicit break between Freud and these other thinkers? But de Beauvoir accords, without comment, the same status to the theories of Adler and Stekel as she does to

18. Freud, 'Female Sexuality', op. cit., pp. 228–9.
19. Freud, 'The Psychogenesis of a Case of Homosexuality in a Woman', 1920, S.E., Vol. XVIII, p. 155, n. 1.

those of Freud. Both broke with Freud, and neither they nor their followers regard themselves as psychoanalysts. The fact that the break came over precisely such questions as the nature and role of sexuality makes de Beauvoir's elision the more serious. Furthermore her heavy reliance on the findings of Helene Deutsch, who sees herself as working within the Freudian tradition, is more justifiable, but, as we have seen, is bound to present problems. At the very least, even seeing the amalgamation from de Beauvoir's viewpoint, it does make her perspective seem strangely partial. She omits, for instance, analysts such as Karen Horney, whose sociological stress would agree with her own position. Indeed over questions of penis-envy Horney's views coincide to a great degree with de Beauvoir's. Either we are looking at what Freud said, or at what a number of different analysts said, or at what a number of analysts and psychologists contend; if our intention is either of the latter, then surely there must be some rationale for the selection made? But I think the fusion de Beauvoir makes is genuine confusion. For not only does she donate terms that are Jung's or Adler's (the Electra complex, and 'masculine protest') to Freud,[20] but also credits

20. We have seen what Freud had to say about the Electra complex; he was only slightly more tolerant of 'masculine protest'. Denouncing Adler's theories, Freud wrote: 'Adler is so consistent in this that he positively considers that the strongest motive force in the sexual act is the man's intention of showing himself master of the woman – of being "on top". I do not know if he has expressed these monstrous notions in his writings' ('On the History of the Psycho-Analytic Movement', 1914, S.E., Vol. XIV, pp. 52–3); Freud's thesis assumes on the contrary that the little boy, observing sexual intercourse, imagines himself in *both* the position of the man *and* the woman. 'Between them these two impulses exhaust the pleasurable possibilities of the situation. The first alone can come under the head of the masculine protest, if that concept is to retain any meaning at all . . .' (ibid., pp. 54–5). (De Beauvoir does initially attribute 'masculine protest' to Adler.) It seems likely that Freud wrote his extremely important paper 'On Narcissism' in part to combat Jung's notions of non-sexual libido and Adler's 'masculine protest'; here he acknowledges that the 'masculine protest' may, along with many other things, be an aspect of narcissism, but if it is to play a part in neurosis then the concept is simply the same as 'the castration complex'. A few years after the split between Adler and Freud and then Jung and Freud, Adler called his theories 'Individual Psychology' and Jung adopted the term

Freud with the very conception with which Jung took his departure from Freud and from psychoanalysis: the collective unconscious. This attribution would seem to me to be the distinguishing error in her assessment of psychoanalysis. It bears the brunt of the philosophy that she seeks to discover in Freud's works:

It is [the] concept of choice, indeed, that psychoanalysis most vehemently rejects in the name of determinism and the 'collective unconscious'; and it is this unconscious that is supposed to supply man with prefabricated imagery and a universal symbolism. Thus it would explain the observed analogies of dreams, of purposeless actions, of visions of delirium, of allegories, and of human destinies.[21]

But Freud never used the term the 'collective unconscious'; indeed his repudiation of the concept has much in common with de Beauvoir's:

It is not easy for us to carry over the concepts of individual psychology into group psychology; and I do not think we gain anything by introducing the concept of a 'collective' unconscious.[22]

It would seem that de Beauvoir has conflated Jung's notion of a 'collective unconscious' with Freud's rare but very different hypotheses of a 'collective mind'. In fact, Freud's concept here bears a very strong resemblance to the contentions of de Beauvoir and is as far away from the Jungian belief as anyone could wish. His only elaborations of this notion come in his inquiries outside what could strictly be regarded as psychoanalysis, in his speculations on anthropological history and the origins of religions, culture and morality – *Totem and Taboo* and *Moses and Monotheism*. I shall quote at some length, because I believe this to be a key misunderstanding of Freud's work. Freud's first venture into a reconstruction of man's history proposed an original murder of the father by a group of brothers and the subsequent guilt they experienced (see p. 403). *Totem and Taboo* is his first essay in tying up the crucial importance of the individual child's

---

'Analytical Psychology'. Freud retained 'Psychoanalysis' and it is only to his work and that of his followers that the term can be correctly applied.

21. *The Second Sex*, op. cit., p. 72.

22. Freud, *Moses and Monotheism*, Part III, 1939 (1934–8), S.E., Vol. XXIII, p. 132. The term is, at best, a tautology: the unconscious *is* by definition collective, as Octave Mannoni points out in *Freud*, op. cit.

entry into human culture expressed in our society in his relationship with his parents at the moment of the Oedipus complex with a similar event in the generic history of mankind. Freud acknowledges his difficulties.

Before I bring my remarks to a close, however, I must find room to point out that, though my arguments have led to a high degree of convergence upon a single comprehensive nexus of ideas, this fact cannot blind us to the uncertainties of my premises or the difficulties involved in my conclusions. I will only mention two of the latter which may have forced themselves on the notice of a number of my readers.

No one can have failed to observe . . . that I have taken as the basis of my whole position the existence of a collective mind, in which mental processes occur just as they do in the mind of an individual. In particular, I have supposed that the sense of guilt for an action has persisted for many thousands of years and has remained operative in generations which can have had no knowledge of that action. I have supposed that an emotional process, such as might have developed in generations of sons who were ill-treated by their father, has extended to new generations which were exempt from such treatment for the very reason that their father had been eliminated. It must be admitted that these are grave difficulties; and any explanation that could avoid presumptions of such a kind would seem to be preferable.

Further reflection, however, will show that I am not alone in the responsibility for this bold procedure. Without the assumption of a collective mind, which makes it possible to neglect the interruptions of mental acts caused by the extinction of the individual, social psychology in general cannot exist. Unless psychical processes were continued from one generation to another, if each generation were obliged to acquire its attitude to life anew, there would be no progress in this field and next to no development.[23]

The unconscious is everyman's heritage of how mankind lives. As Freud says, each separate individual cannot start the process of human history anew, on his own; he must acquire it. Some common event, which may well be only a psychical event, can be hypothesized and a 'scientific myth' created which would offer the sort of mythological explanation needed

23. Freud, *Totem and Taboo*, 1913 (1912–13), S.E., Vol. XIII, pp. 157–8.

to account for this shared understanding and generic heritage of customs, morals and so on. Referring to the same sort of hypothesis some twenty-five years later, Freud wrote:

We must finally make up our minds to adopt the hypothesis that the psychical precipitates of the primeval period became inherited property which, in each fresh generation, called not for acquisition but only for awakening. In this we have in mind the example of what is certainly the 'innate' symbolism which derives from the period of the development of speech, which is familiar to all children without their being instructed, and which is the same among all peoples despite their different languages ... We find that in a number of important relations our children react, not in a manner corresponding to their own experience, but instinctively, like the animals, in a manner that is only explicable as phylogenetic acquisition.[24]

Freud is certainly not referring here to what de Beauvoir calls 'prefabricated imagery and a universal symbolism'. (Nor is he saying that man has animal instincts – as he remarks elsewhere, this is at best a very inadequate analogy. The 'inheritance' referred to here is that of human culture.) Freud is trying to establish that the individual's psychology cannot be transferred in a complete or simple way to a collective/social situation, nor vice versa, but that the two must share common features, and these can be analysed and the mode of their interrelationship considered. The particularly human idea of the instinct that the person brings with him would seem to come in part from the accumulation of the historical experience of mankind. No more than de Beauvoir, does Freud consider (as she charges) that symbolism comes 'down from heaven or rises up from subterranean depths'. That is Jung. Freud and de Beauvoir agree that it is shared history that makes for shared perceptions and common symbols. Furthermore, de Beauvoir castigates psychoanalysis for positing a 'mysterious unconscious' as the source of explanation; the contrary is true: psychoanalysis undertakes the elucidation of the laws of the unconscious, it precisely exists to repudiate this notional 'mysteriousness'. Jung's hermeneutics claimed to read the revelations of the mysterious unconscious: Freud sought merely to find therein normal thought that had undergone repression and been transformed thereby.

24. Freud, *Moses and Monotheism*, op. cit., pp. 132–3.

I have spent some time on this question, because it is the focal point of de Beauvoir's philosophical attack – after this she challenges only empirical propositions. Her own thesis underlies her criticism and certainly it is a thesis from which – put like that – Freud would have dissented, though the terms of his dissent would have been opposite to those de Beauvoir attributes to him. De Beauvoir believes in 'human unity', so that although her objections to Freud are made on behalf of social reality, this philosophical notion of 'wholeness', is in fact at their base. This preoccupation is manifest as her deeply held faith in her explanations of human behaviour and in her criticism of psycho-analysis as a methodology:

... the concept of a simple association of elements is unacceptable, for the psychic life is not a mosaic, it is a single whole in every one of its aspects and we must respect that unity. This is possible only by our recovering through the disparate facts the original purposiveness of existence. If we do not go back to this source, man appears to be the battleground of compulsions and prohibitions that alike are devoid of meaning and incidental.[25]

It is, however, from this premise of life's unity that, from the point of view of the psychology of women, de Beauvoir's most significant objection to Freud takes place. It is the same objection that all the most important dissidents finally focused on: an objection to the prominence given to sexuality.[26] De Beauvoir believes that the sexual impulse is one among others, and by no means necessarily the most important:

In girls as in boys the body is first of all the radiation of a sub-jectivity, the instrument that makes possible the comprehension of the world: it is through the eyes, the hands, that children apprehend the universe, and not through the sexual parts.[27]

Freud, whose theory never ignores hands or eyes, would have commented sarcastically, as he did of Jung, on how much pleasanter this version makes the whole issue, how much more

25. *The Second Sex*, op. cit., p. 71.
26. Obviously at first glance it seems a bit strange to include Reich in this charge. But we have seen how Reich too first reduced sexuality to genitality and then moved off in another direction and ended up equating it with all-inclusive life-energy.
27. *The Second Sex*, op. cit., p. 273.

acceptable a suggestion it is. De Beauvoir objects to the vagueness of the notion 'sexual', and it is true that Freud's declared intention was to generalize it beyond the genital; it was by means of this extension (as he points out in the *Three Essays on Sexuality*) that he was able to revolutionize sexology by introducing infantile sexuality and seeing that this and 'perverted' sex were on a continuum with so-called normal adult sexuality. His motivation for this was obviously not simply so as to set himself up in opposition to the prevalent concepts of childhood innocence and the public moral outrage at perversions, but to establish a fundamental concept: that the earliest inquiries of children, their drive for knowledge, come with the first sexual questions – which are, roughly speaking, 'Where do babies come from?' and 'What is the difference between the sexes?' Freud does not, as de Beauvoir suggests, generalize the concept of sexuality into vagueness – but into complexity.

De Beauvoir, then, takes issue with Freud for failing to appreciate the fundamental existential situation of alienation, the price the individual pays for separation from the whole; for placing a totally inadequate stress on social factors: it is, to her, the patriarchal culture that endows the girl with an awareness of her real *social* inferiority and the boy with his superiority; and finally Freud is guilty of endorsing the status of the second sex, by always using a masculine model. Many of the specific points she makes about the social influences on sexual differentiation are excellent – Freud would not have disagreed – but in her repudiation of the primacy of complex sexuality and her concept of an all-important original human unity and her implicit denial of the unconscious, there is a substantial difference of opinion. Existentialism is here a philosophic system of belief, whereas psychoanalysis purports to be a scientific method of investigation. They thus claim to exist on different planes, but in order to compare and contrast them and favour one above the other de Beauvoir has had to ensure that they meet on the same terrain; to do this she has infused Freudian psychoanalysis with Jungian metaphysics – this latter is more suitable for confrontation by existentialism, for – unlike Marxism or psychoanalysis – it too is a philosophy or a system of belief.

2 Betty Friedan:
The Freudian Mystique

. . . the very nature of Freudian thought makes it virtually invulnerable to question. How can an educated American woman, who is not herself an analyst, presume to question a Freudian truth? She knows that Freud's discovery of the unconscious workings of the mind was one of the great breakthroughs in man's pursuit of knowledge . . . She has been taught that only after years of analytic training is one capable of understanding the meaning of Freudian truth. She may even know how the human mind unconsciously resists that truth. How can she presume to tread the sacred ground where only analysts are allowed?[1]

One needs only to know what Freud *was* describing, in those Victorian women, to see the fallacy in literally applying his theory of femininity to women today.[2]

In discussing de Beauvoir's objections to psychoanalysis, I paid scant attention to the details she gives of the infant female becoming a woman, because it is this that is stressed by subsequent feminist critics. It is not, however, the emphasis given by the next major work in this tradition to oppose Freud: Betty Friedan's *The Feminine Mystique*. Friedan makes far more effort to separate Freud's theories off from their debased applications by subsequent popularizers and as a result she pays them a fair amount of tribute. Seeing them in their pristine glory in the context of the repressive 'Victorian' society that surrounded them, she credits them for the revolutionary breakthroughs that they truly were. 'Freudian psychology, with its emphasis on freedom from a repressive morality to achieve sexual fulfilment, was part of the ideology of women's emancipation.'[3] But having

1. Betty Friedan, *The Feminine Mystique*, New York, 1963 and Penguin Books, 1965, pp. 91–2.
2. ibid., p. 93.   3. ibid., p. 92.

acknowledged Freud's achievements in discovering the unconscious and in thrusting the importance of sexuality on a highly resistant moralizing environment, she has to account for his pernicious effect on the American way of life. It is not enough that others distorted and abused his works, there is something within them that favours such perversion. In order to preserve her appreciation of Freud's genius and at the same time condemn his theory of femininity, Friedan resorts in the main to a historicist explanation: Freud's discoveries are culture-bound, he cannot escape the mark of his time – and what a time for women that was.

I believe that in any case this is a false argument. Here an immediate way to approach its illegitimacy is to illustrate some of the internal inconsistencies to which it is prone. Historicism of this sort tends to be unviable even in its own terms. Friedan is at pains to show that Freud's theories are obsolete. To do this she sets up, as an excuse for him, the milieu of what she describes as 'Victorian' Vienna from which Freud took his patients, from whom in turn he drew his theoretical observations:

The concept 'penis envy', which Freud coined to describe a phenomenon he observed in women – that is, in the middle-class women who were his patients in Vienna in the Victorian era – was seized in this country in the 1940s as the literal explanation of all that was wrong with American women. Many who preached the doctrine of endangered femininity, reversing the movement of American women towards independence and identity, never knew its Freudian origin . . . One needs only to know what Freud *was* describing, in those Victorian women, to see the fallacy in literally applying his theory of femininity to women today. And one needs only to know *why* he described it in that way to understand that much of it is obsolescent, contradicted by knowledge that is part of every social scientist's thinking today, but was not yet known in Freud's time.

Freud, it is generally agreed, was a most perceptive and accurate observer of important problems of the human personality. But in describing and interpreting those problems, he was a prisoner of his own culture. As he was creating a new framework for our culture, he could not escape the framework of his own. Even his genius could not give him, then, the knowledge of cultural processes which men who are not geniuses grow up with today.[4]

4. ibid., p. 93.

Doomed through no fault of his own, to the limitations of his 'Victorian' epoch, Freud unwittingly was responsible for the main thrust of the sexual counterrevolution that condemned to an early death the budding American emancipated woman.

Yet there is a snag to this thesis. Friedan admits that one cannot doubt that what Freud observed in his patients was there to be observed – but they were *Victorian* hysterics, not emancipated twentieth-century women. However the essay of Freud's on 'Femininity' that she almost exclusively cites and quotes was written in *1932*.[5] Indeed a great deal of the major work by Freud and the Freudians on the psychology of women was carried out in the twenties and thirties. Absolute historical explanations of this sort are inclined to have to overlook the very need for accuracy which is their own original justification. Living in Habsburg Austria, Freud founded psychoanalysis only in the eighteen-nineties and he died a still prolific writer and thinker in 1939, yet Betty Friedan is by no means alone in her stress on the 'Victorianism' of Freud.

The same type of internal objection can be made to the personal explanations Friedan offers. Freud's love letters to his fiancée Martha Bernays have proved a happy hunting ground for those interested in specifying Freud's prudish 'male chauvinist' attitudes. These certainly illustrate a patriarchal attitude in which the woman is to stay gentle and sweet, removed from the toils and corruptions of the world; the husband is to be bread-winner, household-head and, in such circles, to a certain degree, educator. (They are, incidentally, illustrative of much else as well, even in this connection.) Martha, the perfect *hausfrau*, has certainly made up for all the help she gave Freud during their lifetime by the deep disservice she has been to him ever since. A woman's fate – one might remark! But what is more ironic here is the persistent absence of any reference to Anna, Freud's youngest daughter and a world-renowned analyst and author in her own right. In all his references to her, Freud displayed the profoundest respect, both for her personality and her work; there was no question at any time that he wished her

5. Excluding Freud's personal letters and Ernest Jones's biography of Freud, all but two of Friedan's references are to this essay from *The New Introductory Lectures*, published in 1933 (1932).

to fulfil a doll-like, 'feminine' existence. And for all the references to Freud's so-called quasi-homosexual attachments to his male colleagues, what of his encouragement of women analysts? Psychoanalysis must be one of the very few scientific professions that, from its inception, exercised no discrimination against women. Indeed, particularly in the field of research into femininity and pre-Oedipal attachments (on the importance of which he placed very heavy stress in the last decades), Freud, because of the nature of the transference situation, hoped to rely on women analysts to be able to discover more than men analysts could do. He says this explicitly in the essay from which Friedan deduces his position.

Really, however, all this is quite beside the point. I have attempted only to indicate the internal inconsistencies which *ad hominem* arguments such as these are liable to fall into whether they are based on the historical setting or on personal life. The real objection to these arguments is not to their flaws, but to themselves. As Octave Mannoni[6] says, Freud made history, he was not made by it. If psychoanalysis merits the title of a science within a valid definition of the term, then precisely at its inception it makes a break with previous ways of thinking even if it is naturally very dependent on these for its own development. It is not that a science is a once and for all thing (on the contrary it will, of course, be supplemented, altered and corrected) but that in establishing itself it discovers a new object which can be charted by new laws (that are determined by the nature of the object) and which can be tested for consistency and accuracy. Although philosophers and creative writers had for centuries talked of the unconscious, when Freud set about discovering the way it worked he was introducing something completely new. If he is right in the claim which he makes for the workings of the unconscious, what he calls the laws of the primary process, then we can prove it from the consistency of the application of these laws. I think this powerfully affects the position Friedan is asserting.

Friedan claims that it is a truism that all social science is culture bound:

6. Octave Mannoni, *Freud*, op. cit.

... It is not a slogan, but a fundamental statement about truth to say that no social scientist can completely free himself from the prison of his own culture; he can only interpret what he observes in the scientific framework of his own time. This is true even of the great innovators.[7]

I think a number of confusions are operating here. There can be no meaningful distinction made between social and natural or physical sciences. A science is a knowledge. What it can be distinguished from are the disciplines, sociology or what have you. These, though they obviously have a subject matter, an area of study, do not have a scientific object, nor do they pretend to establish the laws thereof. Friedan's reference here is to the uncertain status of an observer in any one of the disciplines. But the setting or personality of a scientist, by definition of his work, is largely irrelevant; if it becomes relevant, then we have to question whether it is a science that he is working in. Freud, himself, was clearly anxious that psychoanalysis should not become confused with the social disciplines; he thus referred to it as a 'natural science', a specification that should have been unnecessary.

There is a sense in which, of course, Freud *was* culture-bound, but it is a sense the diametric opposite of that deduced by Friedan. Freud, in staking out his new territory, had of course to do so in old land – he had to use the terminology, the concepts of his day. I have already pointed out that the term 'unconscious' was not new, nor were many other crucial aspects of his vocabulary – what was new was the meaning he gave them. In other words, the degree to which Freud operated within available thought, *and changed it*, is an index not of his being produced by his culture (that is a self-evident observation when you come to think of it), but of *his distance* from it, of his making something new of that very culture, of his break with it. Such a break did not happen on just one day, nor did it ever happen completely. Freud was as capable as anyone else of being pre-Freudian – but he had less to gain from it. Friedan's efforts make all psychoanalysis pre-Freudian, in precisely this way:

Much of what Freud believed to be biological, instinctual, and changeless has been shown by modern research to be a result of

7. Friedan, *The Feminine Mystique*, op. cit., p. 93.

specific cultural causes. Much of what Freud described as characteristic of universal human nature was merely characteristic of certain middle-class European men and women at the end of the nineteenth century.[8]

Freud precisely did *not* believe things were biological, instinctual and changeless: he thought they were cultural. But here my concern is simply to point out how if we believe Friedan, psychoanalysis is nothing more than a mediocre documentary account invalidated by masquerading as something else.

Such a historicist position is fraught with more assumptions than the worthlessness of psychoanalysis, it also carries its own evolutionary vision of history: it suggests that today, by virtue of the march of progress, we are far advanced from those dim nineteenth-century days. Echoing through every paragraph of Friedan's chapter is 'today', 'nowadays', 'modern progress'. . .

The whole superstructure of Freudian theory rests on the strict determinism that characterized the scientific thinking of the Victorian era. Determinism has been replaced today by a more complex view of cause and effect, in terms of physical processes and phenomena as well as psychological. In the new view, behavioural scientists do not need to borrow language from physiology to explain psychological events, or give them pseudo-reality.[9]

I shall take up the notion of pseudo-reality later. The suggestion that Freud did not have a complex concept of cause and effect is ludicrous – it is precisely that complexity that concerned him. Poor Freud, he was born before we were. But historicism demands evolutionism of this kind. No one (that is, except someone with a religious cast of mind that inverts evolutionary progress to the notion that we are all hell-bent on going *down* hill) would deny that knowledge advances, but so, too, does it regress (as the development of psychoanalysis perfectly illustrates). However, it never advances just because the world gets older: such a notion involves transposing the 'wisdom of old

8. ibid., p. 94.
9. ibid., p. 95. Whence, may one ask, do today's behavioural scientists borrow their terms – how come they, unlike Freud, are not culture-bound? As we have seen, Freud's concept of over-determination was developed to describe *complex* relations of multiple cause and diverse effect.

men' hypothesis to human history, a notion dubious in the first instance, disastrous in the second.

Let us, for the moment, however, revert to accepting Friedan's terms and see what she finds, for this will lead us to her major content-criticism of Freud's work. We have seen how she has rejected his method, now what of his substance?

The outstanding feature of Freud's social environment was that 'cultural hypocrisy forced the repression of sex'. Now comes the curious part: 'Certainly the fact that his culture denied sex focused Freud's interest on it.'[10] But surely, if we are to glean interest from such a conjecture, what is curious is how Freud, and not others (who were likewise forced by their society to deny sex) managed mysteriously to acknowledge it? The mystery only deepens when we learn of the particular aspect of Freud's character that must have singled him out for such a response: 'His chief biographer, Jones, pointed out that [Freud] was, even for those times, exceptionally chaste, puritanical and moralistic. In his own life, he was relatively uninterested in sex.'[11] Though Friedan does not explicitly make the connection, are we to assume that it was this surplus-repression, this bonus of personal sexual inhibition that made Freud see sex everywhere? And if so, what significance are we to draw from her next comment that Freud gave 'more attention to infantile sexuality than to its mature expression'?[12]

All this apparent explanation of the source of Freud's sexual theories is not, of course, an end in itself. On the contrary, it is first a prelude to, and then a justification of, Friedan's rejection of the significance of sexuality. In this she is on well-trod ground. Her substitution for sexuality is couched in different terms and fits with different precepts from those of de Beauvoir, but, despite this, the two bear a striking resemblance. Friedan proposes to replace Freud's sexual drives with the urge for growth:

10. ibid., p. 94.   11. ibid., p. 99.

12. ibid., p. 99. Friedan also writes: 'Since *all* of Freud's theories rested, admittedly, on his own penetrating, unending psychoanalysis of himself, and since sexuality was the focus of all his theories, certain paradoxes about his own sexuality seem pertinent' (p. 99 [my italics]). Although certainly Freud's 'self-analysis' was absolutely crucial at one stage for his discoveries, he did also look elsewhere!

Today biologists, social scientists, and increasing numbers of psychoanalysts see the need or impulse to human growth as a primary human need, as basic as sex. The 'oral' and 'anal' stages which Freud described in terms of sexual development . . . are now seen as stages of human growth, influenced by cultural circumstances and parental attitudes as well as by sex. When the teeth grow, the mouth can bite as well as suck. Muscle and brain also grow; the child becomes capable of control, mastery, understanding; and his need to grow and learn, at five, twenty-five, or fifty, can be satisfied, denied, repressed, atrophied, evoked, or discouraged by his culture as can his sexual needs.[13]

No one for a moment would deny that the human being has a need to grow, but then so too does the amoeba. It is, in fact, a characteristic of living organisms. Freud's stress on the role of sexuality has to do with the special conditions of human society: how the animal man becomes the human being. Friedan would have us replace what she sees as Freud's reductionist stance (whereby all is reduced to sexuality) with the more expansive notion of an urge to growth. Again we have the by now familiar argument: reductionism (were it to exist here) is to be combated by substituting the specific factor that has been isolated as a determinant for the vaguer general concept that may include it.

Given these background assumptions, Friedan's attitude towards Freud's theses on femininity is not hard to guess. Victorian women, sexually repressed, became hysterical. Freud demarcated the causal factor accurately. Victorian women had good cause to envy men their privileged status – it was the social benefits they clamoured for, not a penis. Freud accepted his society's faith that women were inferior and went on to state that any woman who could not adjust to this was neurotic, so must be cured/adjusted accordingly. Freud in his person and hence automatically in his science summed up the patriarchal culture of the Victorians, and of Jewry to boot:

The fact is that to Freud, even more than to the magazine editor on Madison Avenue today, women were a strange, inferior, less-than-

13. ibid., p. 95. Freud, of course, paid at least as much attention to 'cultural circumstances and parental attitudes' as these biologists, social scientists and increasing number of psychoanalysts: indeed from Friedan's summary, all these other scientists would seem to be heavily influenced by biology.

human species. He saw them as childlike dolls, who existed in terms only of man's love, to love man and serve his needs. It was the same kind of unconscious solipsism that made man for many centuries see the sun only as a bright object that revolved around the earth. Freud grew up with this attitude built in by his culture – not only the culture of Victorian Europe, but that Jewish culture in which men said the daily prayer: 'I thank Thee, Lord, that Thou has not created me a woman,' and women prayed in submission 'I thank Thee, Lord, that Thou has created me according to Thy will.'[14]

Freud's Jewish, 'Victorian' notions of women's inferiority were then, according to Friedan, redeployed to suppress the emancipation of women. This would seem to be quite correct and Friedan's account of the influence of *popularized Freudianism* is both the main preoccupation and the greatest success of her thesis here; but Freud cannot be held responsible for this on the evidence offered: at least he can only be held responsible if Friedan's analysis of his work is correct – then indeed he is guilty of many crimes, not the least of them being stupidity.

14. ibid., p. 96. Freud, by the way, though proud to be a Jew, was definitely not religious and protested long and loud against his fiancée's insistence that they would have to have a Jewish wedding to legalize their German marriage in Austria.

3 Eva Figes:
Freud's Patriarchal Attitudes

Of all the factors that have served to perpetuate a male-orientated society, that have hindered the free development of women as human beings in the Western world today, the emergence of Freudian psycho-analysis has been the most serious. The fact that theoreticians have since split into a dozen schisms, that Freudian theory has been adapted and large parts of it rejected by some analysts since it is only important in a strictly clinical situation (and not always then), it is Freud that most people read and know about. Psycho-analysis, whatever individual therapists may say, does tend to encourage conformity which may amount to something like brainwashing. If you are unhappy, the tendency is not to look at your situation and change that, you look within yourself and try to adapt yourself to the situation.[1]

Eva Figes's intention is to fit Freud within a 'history of ideas'. Her criticism naturally thus bears a strong resemblance to that of Betty Friedan's 'historicism'; but as such a perspective is her explicit aim, it cannot be simply dismissed as yet another version of this tendency. Figes makes many of the points made by Friedan (usually with greater stridency and wit):

> The one serious criticism that must be levelled at Freud time and again is his inability to see beyond the immediate social situation, so that he is constantly confusing cause and effect, his obstinate refusal to recognize that his own present day was itself transitional.[2]

> Freud's whole theory of civilization is based on the narrow world he lived in . . .[3]

A Jew himself, Freud was following a long Hebraic tradition

---

1. Eva Figes, *Patriarchal Attitudes*, Faber & Faber, 1970, p. 148. All very short quotations which are not referenced are to Chapter VI, 'Learning to be a Woman'.
2. ibid., p. 136.   3. ibid., p. 137.

already familiar to us from the Old Testament, *Genesis* in particular.
Man came first, then woman.[4]

Freud was a child of his own times.[5]

In one way, these statements are identical to those offered by
Friedan, and can be attacked accordingly, but in another way,
their context renders them different. Figes does not offer us an
evolutionist view in which our own times are the last step in the
march of progress; instead she sees all epochs as relative: this
notion would seem to have far greater validity. As Freud himself
was at pains to point out, ideas *are* shared, there *is* a cultural
heritage, a complex continuity of ideology; and to fit Freud into
this history of ideas is legitimate. However, it is only legitimate
in certain instances. A history of ideas does not deal with the
relationship between the new knowledge and the surrounding
and preceding concepts from which this knowledge takes its
departure, it deals only with shared, common ideas. When
psychoanalysis shares its terminology with earlier formulations,
it is its *different* meanings that are important. But this history of
ideas is interested not in differences but in similarities. A
legitimate historicism, then, as regards Freud, cannot be concerned with the work in which he establishes all that is distinctive
in his theory; it cannot, in other words, deal with psychoanalysis
proper. Whether or not from some unacknowledged sense of
this, the fact is that, by and large, Eva Figes's account of Freud
avoids psychoanalysis. Like Friedan she uses Freud's letters to
Martha Bernays, but, unlike Friedan, she uses them *not* to
determine the implications of his psychoanalytic theory, but to
tell us about Freud as a man of his time (a perfectly plausible
project). The public writings that she makes use of in this
pursuit of shared ideologies are *Civilization and Its Discontents,
The Future of an Illusion* and *Moses and Monotheism* – a fascinating
selection.

All three works, as Freud said, are works of speculation and
fall largely outside the strict province of psychoanalysis. They
all post-date the confirmation of Freud's incurable cancer and
come within the period and scope of what he regarded as his
intellectual self-indulgence. After 1923 and the publication of

4. ibid., p. 140.   5. ibid., p. 136.

The Ego and the Id, Freud felt himself free to pursue another dimension of his intellectual curiosity:

... since I proposed a division of the mental personality into an ego, a super-ego, and an id (1923), I have made no further decisive contributions to psycho-analysis: what I have written on the subject since then has been either unessential or would soon have been supplied by someone else. This circumstance is connected with an alteration in myself, with what might be described as a phase of regressive development. My interest, after making a lifelong *détour* through the natural sciences, medicine and psychotherapy, returned to the cultural problems which had fascinated me long before, when I was a youth scarcely old enough for thinking. At the very climax of my psycho-analytic work, in 1912, I had already attempted in *Totem and Taboo* to make use of the newly discovered findings of analysis in order to investigate the origins of religion and morality. I now carried this work a stage further in two later essays, *The Future of an Illusion* (1927) and *Civilization and its Discontents* (1930).[6]

Moses and Monotheism which was still to be written in 1937 completed these major extra-psychoanalytic studies of culture and social-mythological history. They are, among other things, accounts of patriarchal culture and speculations as to the pre-histories thereof. They are predicated on one major supposition, one all-important concept for equating individual lives with social history:

Our knowledge of the neurotic illnesses of individuals has been of much assistance to our understanding of the great social institutions. For the neuroses themselves have turned out to be attempts to find *individual* solutions for the problems of compensating for unsatisfied wishes, while the institutions seek to provide *social* solutions for these same problems. The recession of the social factor and the predominance of the sexual one turns these neurotic solutions of the psychological problem into caricatures which are of no service except to help us in explaining such important questions.[7]

Freud's later works contain forceful criticisms of some cultural solutions (e.g. religions) which therefore come to be seen as no

6. Freud, 'An Autobiographical Study', op. cit., Postscript, 1935, p. 72.
7. Freud, 'The Claims of Psycho-Analysis to Scientific Interest', 1913, S.E., Vol. XIII, pp. 186–7.

better than neurotic ones. This is a very different conclusion from the one drawn by Figes.

Eva Figes, then, for her history of ideas, uses those works of Freud which strictly speaking are outside psychoanalysis and which are also in part themselves dedicated to speculations on the formation and history of ideas. However, because she does so inexplicitly, an illegitimate elision then takes place between this intention and her second fundamental thesis: the reactionary nature of Freud's concept of femininity. Figes brings the fatal letters to Martha and the cultural histories to bear on Freud's analysis of women. It is in doing this that her statement that Freud is confined to his 'Victorian' epoch leaves the realm of her own work on the history of ideas and joins the historicist preoccupation of Betty Friedan. This means, incidentally, that we always have to read her comments on two levels. On one level, she is very interesting: on the other I think she is simply wrong. On the second level, the historicist framework itself is false.

Where Friedan concentrated on Freud's personal sexual inhibitions and curiosity (do the two add up to prurience?), Figes stresses his reactionary social and political caste of mind. There might be some truth in both contentions – it doesn't matter if there is – but it is, perhaps, worth setting the record straight here as elsewhere, if for no other reason than that these *ad hominem* arguments are the main source of the opposition to Freud by these feminist writers.

Figes states that though Freud is thought of as a revolutionary thinker who shocked the bourgeoisie, this is not nearly so important as the fact that he was himself a thoroughly bourgeois individual. Freud was used to this charge, but as he once remarked on the occasion of a similar criticism from Stefan Zweig:

... I feel inclined to object to the emphasis you put on the element of *petit-bourgeois* correctness in my person.

The fellow is actually somewhat more complicated; your description doesn't tally with the fact that I, too, have had my splitting headaches and attacks of fatigue like anyone else, that I was a passionate smoker (I wish I still were), that I ascribe to the cigar the greatest share of my self-control and tenacity in work, that despite my

much vaunted frugality I have sacrificed a great deal for my collection
of Greek, Roman and Egyptian antiquities, have actually read more
archaeology than psychology, and that before the war and once after
its end I felt compelled to spend every year at least several days or
weeks in Rome, and so on.[8]

'The fellow is actually somewhat more complicated' ... how
often does one wish to reiterate that as one reads accounts of
Freud as the simplest Victorian of them all.[9]

There is a good reason, however, for Figes's efforts to restrict
Freud's character to that of a well-meaning prig, an exemplar
of his era: for her thesis he needs to sum up in his person all
that he proposed in his theory. He enacts what he propagandizes
and propagandizes what he acts:

The middle-class morality of the nineteenth century was highly
hypocritical, but Freud, like so many intellectuals before and since,
made life difficult for himself by taking the ideals seriously and
actually living up to them.[10]

Figes must read his life to fit what she wants to find in his works.

... his theories are based on a total acceptance of the *status quo* as a
norm of civilized behaviour ... In Freud's work the emphasis is on
the superego, on a conscious restraint of libidinous demands in the
interests of civilization, and the values of the civilization he understood were thoroughly middle-class: he did not doubt that marriage
should be faithful and monogamous, that a father should be absolute
head of his family, that industriousness, hard work and a lack of self-
indulgence, particularly sexual, were qualities that should be
cultivated. Neurosis was a regrettable but inevitable by-product of
civilization, the price that had to be paid.[11]

To present Freud's analytical descriptions as mandates is, of

8. Freud, Letter to Stefan Zweig, 7 February 1941, published in
Letters of Sigmund Freud, op. cit., pp. 401–2.
9. If in this account I have defended Freud's character as well as his
theory of psychoanalysis, it is not because I consider it in any way
important. No one is particularly concerned to know whether or not
Einstein was a nice man. But the subject matter of psychoanalysis
makes Freud particularly vulnerable to this critical red herring. My
'defence' should thus be seen as an irrelevance, introduced to counter
an irrelevance – not a very defensible aim!
10. *Patriarchal Attitudes*, op. cit., p. 137.
11. ibid., p. 136.

course, another version of the attempt to personalize his theory. No less than Friedan, Figes has to determine his character in order to interpret his work. If his work is to be prescriptive then it must be based on a system of beliefs and where else can one find such a thing than in his private life? Although at the beginning of her chapter on Freud, Figes disarmingly comments that she has, in an earlier section of the book, dealt with 'Freud's more personal, *ex cathedra* statements', she is, by the nature of her preoccupation, forced to repeat them here. For the second part of her thesis we have to note again that Freud the stern moralist believed a woman's place was as a doll in a dolls' house, and that sexuality was to be rigorously repressed in the interests of a male civilization. 'Neurosis was a regrettable but inevitable by-product of civilization, the price that had to be paid.' 'Civilization is and must be repressive.' '. . . civilization depends on a small, determined *élite* who are ruled by the reality principle rather than the pleasure principle.' Once you have interpreted Freud's theories as recommendations for the Victorian status quo, it is an easy step to reverse the order and, presenting your interpretation of the society, find that, in its turn, in Freud's work. For instance, as it was a patriarchal society, so then must Freud's recommendations be for such; the *élite* he is said to have believed in 'was undoubtedly masculine' and as civilization was male, so must be the psychic agent for that civilization, the superego:

The idea of the male superego is authoritarian, punitive and repressive. It is fallacious if only because no civilization could make any progress through a body of males who had learned to conform to their elders' values through fear of castration – progress depends on adventure, the original mind has to break away from the values of the previous generation. By saying that man gave up his instinctual demands and woman did not, Freud was in fact over-simplifying the nature of those demands.[12]

A number of values are confused here. In that the 'cultural past' is that of a patriarchal society, the values transmitted bear those marks, but the superego itself is not sexualized, even though it derives its nature from the paternal authority-figure,

12. ibid., pp. 146–7.

it is not, in itself, male; Freud considered that women were
likely to have a less strong superego than men, because the
superego is instituted at the point of the dissolution of the
Oedipus complex and this is unlikely to be so thoroughly
dissolved in women as it is in men. As we have seen, it has a
different history in the two sexes: there is no suggestion that
it was because of its maleness that women were excluded from
the values of the superego (though obviously there is a connection of another kind here). Nor is the question to do with
who gives up what 'instinctual demands' – at least not in
Figes's sense in which she defines instinctual demands to
include 'freedom and variety of action', work, money, power,
full sexual gratification and so on, in which case once again any
specific point or truth is buried in a vast and vague generalization.

Overwhelming 'maleness', grotesque Victorian sexual repression, woman as a square peg needing to be knocked into the
round hole of patriarchal culture (a reiterated image), and a let
out for the occasional intelligent women he encountered amongst
his colleagues and audiences – such is Figes's picture of Freud.
There are little mistakes all along the line. Take some of these:

Since [Freud] had never thought to ask [a woman] what she wanted,
since his whole life and work had been devoted to telling her what
she should want, the fact that woman should have remained an
enigma is hardly surprising.[13]

Considering that practically all Freud's first psychoanalytic
discoveries were made when he was listening to hysterical
women patients, this is a remarkable claim.

Neurosis was a regrettable but inevitable by-product of civilization,
the price that had to be paid.[14]

This theme-song of Figes's analysis is too simple. Again, in this
very area where Figes most forcefully castigates him, Freud was
in fact quite liberal. He explicitly considered that civilization
was overdoing its amount of sexual repression and that, although
he had personally not taken advantage of his beliefs, he favoured
far more sexual freedom than that prescribed by notions of

13. ibid., p. 141.   14. ibid., p. 136.

premarital virginity and marital fidelity. Figes further maintains that, in one of his 'relatively rare' moments of doubt, Freud 'hesitantly adopted a theory of bisexuality'. His moments of doubt on questions of femininity, as on other important and complex issues, were remarkably frequent, and bisexuality was a concept he stuck to pertinaciously from the beginning to the end of his psychoanalytic thinking. But the most important of Figes's mistaken imputations is the notion that Freud was *prescribing* not describing womanhood.

Freud's ideas on feminine psychology all spring from the tenet that woman's role in life is to stay at home, be passive in relation to man, bear and raise children.[15]

... Freud certainly did not consider it desirable for a woman's masculine traits to remain unsuppressed. If they did she was liable to become neurotic, frigid, thoroughly dangerous to her husband, and might try to compete with males in intellectual pursuits.[16]

... Freud's basic view was that every woman was a square peg trying to fit into a round hole. It did not occur to him that it might be less destructive to change the shape of the holes rather than to knock all the corners off ... The 'cured' patient is actually brainwashed, a walking automaton, as good as dead. The corners have been knocked off and the woman accepts her own castration, acknowledges herself inferior, ceases to envy the penis and accepts the passive role of femininity. Sadly, man recognizes that the ideal, submissive woman he has created for himself is somehow not quite what he wanted.[17]

A correct theory must indeed be predictive, but this is not to be confused with prescription. But to Figes, Freud is prescribing not just a woman's role, but the whole repressive society as well, hence her statement that Freudian psychoanalysis has been the most serious threat of all to women becoming human beings. The responsibility for this she lays directly at Freud's door: 'it is Freud that most people read and know about'. This last statement is highly dubious; but if we can ignore it and talk instead about Freudianism, then we are on more interesting ground. Figes articulates into a coherent thesis the common notion that psychoanalysis encourages 'conformity which may amount to something like brainwashing':

15. ibid., p. 142.   16. ibid., p. 144.   17. ibid., pp. 147–8.

the psychoanalytic 'cure' to her, as to others, is a process of ruthless adaptation – that is the nature of its success.

Adjustment, one can state again categorically, is a concept entirely alien to Freud's thought. Indeed, if we want to play games, it is a word that cannot be found in the index to any one of the twenty-three volumes of the English Standard Edition of his works (and that is not due to a translator's or compiler's error). Octave Mannoni, in the different context of how American psychoanalysts expect psychoanalysis itself to *adapt* to the American way of life, makes some salutary remarks on the nature of adjustment-theories and on Freud's relation to them:

> The 'modernist' illusion – namely that the changes occurring in the environment force a readaptation of the very principles of psychoanalysis as Freud posited them – itself obviously depends on prejudices tied to the notion of adjustment. Freud never concerned himself with the adaptation of his patients to the society of his time; he enabled them to solve their problems themselves, and their relationship to their milieu was one of them – no more and no less, for example, than their marital relationship, one he did not treat at all on a realistic plane as a counselor would have.[18]

To read psychoanalysis as a prescriptive system and to regard the analytical cure as the success of a treatment of adaptation and conformity is to misjudge the whole. Illustrations and quotations from here and there are pointless in the face of this misconception. The analytic relationship – despite Freud's early models – is not one between a doctor and a sick patient, but between a man whom the other assumes to be knowledgeable and who enables him to speak his unconscious desire. It is within the nature of the transference that the meaning of the analytic relationship lies. In his last full work, Freud tried to explain what happens between analyst and analysand. It takes a whole chapter of the overly concise *Outline of Psychoanalysis* (1938); he describes the nature of the pact of candour and discretion made between the two and the need for the neurotic person to tell what he does not know, in addition to what he knows:

> But it is far from being the case that [the patient's] ego is content to play the part of passively and obediently bringing us the material

18. O. Mannoni, *Freud,* op. cit., pp. 182–3.

we require and of believing and accepting our translation of it. A number of other things happen, a few of which we might have foreseen but others of which are bound to surprise us. The most remarkable thing is this. The patient is not satisfied with regarding the analyst in the light of reality as a helper and adviser who, moreover, is remunerated for the trouble he takes and who would himself be content with some such role as that of a guide on a difficult mountain climb. On the contrary, the patient sees in him the return, the reincarnation, of some important figure out of his childhood or past, and consequently transfers on to him feelings and reactions which undoubtedly applied to this prototype. This fact of transference soon proves to be a factor of undreamt-of importance, on the one hand an instrument of irreplaceable value and on the other hand a source of serious dangers . . .

. . . However much the analyst may be tempted to become a teacher, model and ideal for other people and to create men in his own image, he should not forget that that is not his task in the analytic relationship, and indeed that he will be disloyal to his task if he allows himself to be led on by his inclinations. If he does, he will only be repeating a mistake of the parents who crushed their child's independence by their influence, and he will only be replacing the patient's earlier dependence by a new one.[19]

Within the safety of the analytic situation, the patient can afford to be as abnormal as he need, but this is always, of course, only a remembrance of things past. The task of the analyst and the patient is to give back into his own control the things that the patient has previously repressed into the unconscious. It is likely that what has been repressed are the most forbidden desires; in resurrecting them and in giving them to the patient to *choose* to control, the analyst is hardly prescribing a way of life. All he wants is for the patient to have a little bit more self-

19. Freud, *An Outline of Psycho-Analysis*, op. cit., pp. 174–5 and p. 175. We might note here how far Laingian thought has returned the analyst to his pre-analytic position of being a mountain-guide (only, of course, the mountain is very spiritual). (See particularly R.D. Laing, 'A Ten Days Voyage'.) Furthermore, in this same work, Freud gives a specific warning against what was to become prevalent practice for Reich, and implicit theory for Laing – acting out. 'We think it most undesirable if the patient *acts* outside the transference instead of remembering' (ibid., p. 177). If the patient thinks he hates or loves his analyst *for real*, then he must be torn out of 'this menacing illusion'.

knowledge, and instead of the repressed returning as a neurotic symptom, it should be made conscious, to come and go as the patient (no longer a patient) thinks fit.

Naturally, to understand what had been repressed, Freud had to comprehend the nature of the growth of the individual, the social taboos and accidental dilemmas he would encounter. These are going to be different for boys and girls. What Figes has taken as Freud's mandate on how to be a true woman are merely his observations on how a girl is supposed to become a woman, what repressions she must undertake on that perilous path, what inhibitions, what prohibitions, what possibilities she may hope for.

Psychoanalysis does not describe what a woman is – far less what she should be; it can only try to comprehend how psychological femininity comes about. In revealing to a woman patient the course of her individual history, in enabling her to bring to consciousness the repressed desires, reconstruct the dilemmas, the unconscious choices made, a Freudian analyst is not (or should not be) recommending femininity, although the reconstruction involves, for both men and women, memories of what are conventionally called masculine and feminine aims and desires. The neurosis, involving as it does the unsatisfactory repression of a sexual desire, is not itself genderised, but the content of the repressed must depend in part on the sex of the person – what she or he could not, in infancy, allow to be thought. A knowledge of the different social-sexual history of the boy and girl is therefore relevant from the therapeutic point of view; it is, of course, no less urgent from a theoretical standpoint. Psychoanalysis must try to understand what are the psychological implications of the distinction between the sexes. But all the patient has to understand is why he does what he does – but, of course, this involves a knowledge of what psychoanalysis knows!

To believe that the 'cure' is adaptation, to insist that psychoanalysis is a social programme, is a resistance to its insights that is fostered by much post-Freudian work. It does not come from reading Freud. It is, however, possibly the most common resistance: it is there beneath the charges of determinism made by both de Beauvoir and Friedan. The contrary is the case:

what the psychoanalyst wants is that the individual should know the complex way his reaction to his many and various desires and his encounters has determined him and choose to act on that knowledge or not. In this sense, knowledge is the 'cure'. Know thyself! is the aim, a venerable but never-ending pursuit.

It almost looks as if analysis were the third of those 'impossible' professions in which one can be sure beforehand of achieving unsatisfying results. The other two, which have been known much longer, are education and government.[20]

In trying to understand the psychology of women Freud took into account the specific cultural demands made upon them. It was not his concern whether they were right or wrong, for in this respect, he was neither a politician nor a moralist. We might have preferred it if he were, but neither in his theory nor his practice can we find an excuse for this supposition. His private life is another affair, an irrelevant one.

20. Freud, 'Analysis Terminable and Interminable', op. cit., p. 248.

4 Germaine Greer and Freud's Female Eunuch

Freud is the father of psychoanalysis. It had no mother. He is not its only begetter, and subsequent structures of theory have challenged as well as reinforced his system. Probably the best way to treat it is as a sort of metaphysic but usually it is revered as a science. Freud himself lamented his inability to understand women, and became progressively humbler in his pronouncements about them. The best approach to Freud's assumptions about women is probably the one adopted by Dr Ian Suttie, that of psychoanalysing Freud himself.[1]

Germaine Greer has a disarmingly cavalier attitude to her mistakes. She compounds many errors – with facility and wit. In the opening paragraph to her chapter 'The Psychological Sell' she writes indifferently, twice of psychoanalysis, six times of psychology, twice of psychiatry, and the second paragraph opens with the conclusion: 'So much for the authority of psychoanalysis and the theory of personality.'[2] In common parlance, these confusions are frequently made; but the distinctions are quite important. To paraphrase Freud's own

1. Germaine Greer, *The Female Eunuch*, op. cit. and Paladin, 1971, p. 91. Challenged in a television interview about the meaning of her book's title, Germaine Greer said it was not she, but Freud, who said women were castrated, hence eunuchs. The aim of her work is to restore to women their uncastrated femininity. (Incidentally, a eunuch is someone who is castrated 'afterwards'; Freud's point was precisely that the woman was *already* castrated.)

2. Greer has been led to this conclusion by her reiteration of Naomi Weisstein's reiteration, in 'Kind, Küche and Kirche', op. cit. (Firestone repeats it too), of Eysenck's notorious claim that 44 per cent of psychoanalytic patients improved, 64 per cent of drugged, shock-treated, etc. improved and 72 per cent of those untreated improved. This statement was made in 1952 – it has not improved with age and reiteration. What exactly is being measured – adaptation? We have seen that the psychoanalytic cure is not concerned with this. The absurdity of such a 'control' experiment, except as polemic, does not need comment.

definition of psychoanalysis – it is a procedure for the investigation of mental processes inaccessible in any other way (in other words, unconscious ones), a method of treatment of neurotic disorders based on this, and a collection of psychological information obtained therefrom which is gradually becoming a new science. Germaine Greer repeats a favourite maxim that women go to psychoanalysts for guidance; in fact the vast majority of patients are in the type of psychotherapy which does not deal with the unconscious mental processes except by chance; psychiatry and this sort of psychotherapy relate to conscious mental actions. Indeed psychiatry, which tends to describe and classify, is often still oriented to somatic rather than psychological problems. It doesn't attempt to explain the phenomena it observes. Although Freud stressed that psychoanalysis was not hostile to psychiatry, the same cannot be said the other way round. In any case, there is no doubt that they are not the same thing, as Greer seems to believe them to be – her hypothesized female patient resorts to 'the paternal guidance of the *psychoanalyst*', 'seeks academic guidance from *psychologists*' and then finds 'it takes another *psychiatrist* to explain to her the function of observer bias, and the essential conservatism of *psychology*' (my italics), finally she is doomed by Eysenck's so-called findings that *psychoanalytic* patients do worst of all. With each major defection that took place, Freud fought hard to keep the term psychoanalysis for his school of thought. Though Adler and Jung finally accepted this restriction of psychoanalysis to Freudians, Freud's efforts have been in vain so far as popular knowledge goes.[3] These confusions are no slip of the pen, for Greer goes on to throw

3. 'But outsiders who are unconnected with analysis are evidently as unskilful in appreciating the differences between the views of two psycho-analysts as we Europeans are in detecting the differences between two Chinese faces . . . There is room enough on God's earth, and anyone who can has a perfect right to potter about on it without being prevented; but it is not a desirable thing for people who have ceased to understand one another and have grown incompatible with one another to remain under the same roof. Adler's "Individual Psychology" is now one of the many schools of psychology which are adverse to psychoanalysis . . .' ('On The History of the Psychoanalytical Movement', op. cit., pp. 51–2).

every writer she has come across who touches on psychological questions into her hated Freudian bag. She is not content with the common feminist anti-Freudian habit of amalgamating Freud with Helene Deutsch (I suppose this has some justification, as she is a psychoanalyst, but as I asked earlier, why is Karen Horney with her womb-envy theories, so near and dear to feminist thinking, regularly excluded?).[4] But Greer includes anthropologist Margaret Mead and educational psychologist Bruno Bettelheim, popular psychologist Joseph Rheingold and psychoanalyst Erik Erikson. It is a gallery of psychological 'baddies' – there is no other reason for their sharing the same rostrum.

Greer repeats the erroneous interpretations we have outlined earlier – though she relies on them rather than works at them. Indeed, the very vivacity of her argument seems to be based on a contempt for understanding them. I will select one example. Greer offers the following quotation from Freud's *Three Essays on Sexuality*. The transcription is hers, but I omit the last line she gives of Freud as it raises issues other than those she takes up:

Freud: *As we all know* [sic] it is not until puberty that the sharp distinction is established between the masculine and feminine characters. From that time on, this contrast has a more decisive influence than any other on the shaping of human life. It is true that the masculine and feminine dispositions are already easily recognizable in childhood. The development of the inhibitions of sexuality (shame, disgust, pity, etc.) takes place in little girls earlier and in the face of less resistance than in boys; the tendency to sexual repression seems in general to be greater; and where the component instincts of sexuality appear they prefer the passive form. The auto-erotic activity of the erotogenic zones is, however, the same in both sexes, and owing to its uniformity there is no possibility of a distinction between the two sexes such as arises after puberty . . .

4. In fact Greer does quote from Karen Horney in this chapter, yet, though it is correctly attributed in the footnotes, in the text it is misquoted and accredited to Helene Deutsch – who is seen thereby to be feebly correcting herself!

| Greer comments: | This must be nonsense. The concepts of sameness and difference are without meaning. The description of personality regulating itself in a mysterious way towards repression is likewise not informative.[5] |

(Freud did, as we have seen, very explicitly, in his later essays on femininity, correct his notion that sexual differences only really emerged at puberty.) I am not concerned to explain the concepts 'sameness' and 'difference', as an understanding of their generalized meaning is not specific to psychoanalysis; I am concerned with the concept of repression, which *is* a fundamental tenet. As Freud summed up the matter for an Encyclopaedia article:

The Corner-Stones of Psycho-Analytic Theory – The assumption that there are unconscious mental processes, the recognition of the theory of resistance and repression, the appreciation of the importance of sexuality and of the Oedipus complex – these constitute the principal subject-matter of psycho-analysis and the foundations of its theory. *No one who cannot accept them all should count himself a psycho-analyst* [second italics mine].[6]

The concept of repression, in its broadest outline, is really quite simple;[7] the ego has to push out of consciousness all those associations to the sexual drives which are incompatible with the demands of human culture, which are not acceptable to specific

5. *The Female Eunuch*, op. cit., p. 92. There are other examples that could have served my purpose, such as Greer's castigation of a quote she gives from Freud's 'Some Psychic [*sic*] Consequences of the Anatomical Distinction Between the Sexes' in her next chapter. On this she comments: 'The circularity of this utterance is quite scary. After all, are the sexes equal in position and worth or not? What is position? What is worth? He promises to explain unsubstantiated deficiences in the female character by an unsubstantiated modification in an unsubstantiated entity, the superego: if physiology is destiny Freud is anxious to invent a physiology of the mind' (p. 110). Bland incomprehension is a familiar trick of rhetorical denunciation; the same exhaustion confronts us in thinking how we might explain to Greer what might be meant by 'worth' and 'position' as with 'sameness' and 'difference' – one simply isn't intended to answer.

6. Freud, 'Two Encyclopaedia Articles', op. cit., p. 247.

7. I am not dealing here either with its metapsychological characteristics, nor with primary or secondary repression, nor with its all-important place in the symptom-formation of neuroses.

ethical standards and so on. As Freud's theories developed, repression became only one sub-category of the ego's mechanism of defence, others included 'isolating' what is unwanted, the 'splitting' of the ego, 'undoing' or negation. Freud, fairly late in his work, thought that 'repression' may be the method most favoured in hysterical neuroses and 'isolation' in obsessional cases. At first he had tended to think of repression as the general mode of defence, not just as one instance of it. In any case, in repression the ego withdraws its interest and its energy from the ideas attached to sexual impulses that are unacceptable. The two sexes *may* repress different ideas, but there is no absolute distinction: a boy can repress his feminine aims (viz. the 'Rat Man') and the girl her masculine ones, or vice versa. The 'difference' and the 'sameness' of what is repressed are therefore important, and analysing the nature of the repression must surely be informative?

There is, however, another aspect of Freud's work that Greer finds more congenial: it is her notion that he set up a polarity between creation and destruction, aggressors and victims, eròs and death. With Greer we find once again the political prescription that this polarity must be overcome. Greer both misconceives Freud's meaning and then endows this misconception with her own original contribution. Freud did *not* perceive a polarity in the way Greer suggests; and he did *not* subscribe to the idea also prevalent in turn-of-the-century Vienna that one pole was occupied by men, the other by women. Do we need to ask which? Men are the aggressors, with their destructive impulses run riot as universal violence (Hiroshima and megadeath) and as personal sadism; they take away from women their natural sexuality and love (Eros); women must drag them back from this pursuit of violence. (In Firestone's book we are to meet the same suggestion in the form of the Male Technological World finally joining in harmony with the Female Aesthetic World). Meanwhile:

> If we are to achieve a stable relationship between the forces of creation and destruction, we will have to abandon the polarity. We cannot survive in the environment of male sadism and female masochism, a universe of aggressors and victims. Freud himself admitted this, but he did not link this insight with his own assumptions about

the essential character of women ... [Freud] did not suggest that one way Eros could recruit his forces would be by re-endowing women with their sexuality, their fealty to Eros. Instead, he and his followers elaborated the concept of female masochism as divinely ordained by biology.[8]

and:

The same pressures that bind with briars a woman's joys and desires are the pressures that will destroy the world. If half the world is to remain hostage to Death, then Eros must lose the battle to the total weapon. What is the arms race and the cold war but the continuation of male competitiveness and aggression into the inhuman sphere of computer-run institutions? If women are to cease producing cannon fodder for the final holocaust they must rescue men from the perversities of their own polarization.[9]

Women make love – if only you will let them – and men make war. Though Freud opposed the sexual drive to the death-drive, it was not thus dualistically, but dialectically. As we saw in discussing Laing's work, aggression was not absent from love, nor vice versa. They come from different sources; they can enter into conflict or be joined together. For the moment we can just register the implications of Greer's proposal: if she accepts (and simplifies) Freud's notion of eternal Eros at war with his immortal adversary the death-drive, and then makes Eros (or rather Eros denied) equal women, and death equal men, so that the only way to save the world is for Eros-women to overcome death-men, then surely that accords a very aggressive role to Love? Is it poetic justice that Greer, who most fully ignores what Freud said when she writes of him, should be led back there in the end?

8. *The Female Eunuch*, op. cit., pp. 92–3.
9. ibid., p. 98.

5 Shulamith Firestone:
Freud Feminized

But was there any value in [Freud's] ideas? Let us reexamine some of them once again, this time from a radical feminist view. I believe Freud was talking about something real, though perhaps his ideas, taken literally, lead to absurdity. In this regard, consider that Freud's genius was poetic rather than scientific; his ideas more valuable as metaphors than as literal truths.[1]

In 1917, Havelock Ellis wrote an article in which he maintained that Freud was a great artist but not a scientist; Freud reacted in a letter to his friend and colleague, Eitingon, that this was a highly sublimated form of resistance . . . 'the most refined and amiable form of resistance, calling me a great artist in order to injure the validity of our scientific claims'.[2] Greer with her psychoanalysis as metaphysics, and Firestone with her title of Freud the poet, repeat the 'resistance' of the famous sexologist. But perhaps that is an unfair comment, the sort of action that Betty Friedan criticizes – you can't attack psychoanalysis for one can always psychoanalyse your motives. So let us examine Freud as poet, writing in metaphors, not literal truths.

The task Firestone sets herself is to translate Freud's poetry back into the literal truth from whence it came. Her thesis that Freudianism was a minor and misguided version of feminism presupposes Freud's poetic delinquency. Freud and the feminists started work at the same time and discovered the same crucial problem of modern life: sexuality. From there on Freud diagnoses and poetizes what feminism would cure. Freud ignored the social context and never questioned 'society itself'. We have heard this before. But Firestone's version has a novel consistency.

To purge Freudianism of poetry (and thus to make it political

1. *The Dialectic of Sex*, op. cit., p. 52.
2. Cited in Ernest Jones's *Life of Sigmund Freud*, op. cit., Vol. III, p. 22.

feminism), Firestone returns us to the social context from which Freud deduced his crucial theories of infantile sexuality and the Oedipus complex: the family. She interprets all Freud's 'metaphors' in terms of the literal facts of *power* within the family:

> *I submit that the only way that the Oedipus Complex can make full sense is in terms of power* . . .
> Let us take a look at this patriarchal nuclear family in which the Oedipus Complex appears so markedly. In the prototypical family of this kind the man is the breadwinner; all other members of this family are thus his dependents . . .[3]

The father has all the power, the child shares his oppression and dependency with his mother whom he therefore loves. After all, she cares for him and loves him unconditionally, whereas his father is the agent of punishment and conditional love. He sees his father bully his mother and from this he probably concludes that sexual intercourse is an act of violence perpetrated on the female by the male. Boys will learn to be little men, because not being fools, children do not want to be stuck with . . .

the lousy limited lives of women . . . But it is hard. Because deep down they have a contempt for the father with all his power. They sympathize with their mother. But what can they do? They 'repress' their deep emotional attachment to mother, 'repress' their desire to kill their father, and emerge into the honorable state of manhood.[4]

No wonder the kid has a complex! Firestone then undertakes the same literalization programme for what she, like de Beauvoir, following Jung but attributing to Freud, calls the Electra complex of the little girl.

What Firestone does is to reduce Freud to the social realities from which he deduced his psychological constructs. Freud never denied that the father had the power, but what he was interested in was how this social reality was reflected in mental life. What Firestone has achieved in her efforts to free Freudianism from poetry is to get rid of mental life. It all actually happens . . . and there is no other sort of reality than social

3. *The Dialectic of Sex*, op. cit., p. 53.
4. ibid., p. 58.

reality. In this, of course, her work closely resembles that of Wilhelm Reich.

Freud did not exclude social actuality (the generic experience or the accidental experience of the individual), but he simply assumed it had some psychological effect and it was that effect that he was investigating. Furthermore he didn't have to be Firestone's confidence either that social reality was *all*, or that it 'came first' and hence, once grasped, could be done away with, leaving no trace in mental life.

Let us see the sort of objection Freud might have raised against Firestone's efforts to tell him his efforts were futile – that it was all under his nose, he didn't have to be so fantastical about it. Firestone's system is a total theory of human behaviour, something psychoanalysis never claimed to be. She attempts to make every desire of the individual, and every sexual urge, completely rational,[5] in other words, she too completely denies that there is such a thing as the unconscious: every move the person makes is a sensible, conscious choice. Where she cannot turn Freud to her purpose in this (i.e. cannot show the *real* reason why the child thinks up some crazy idea such as that his father attacks his mother in sexual intercourse, because actually he *is* a bully), then Freud can be dispensed with – this time, somewhat contradictorily, on account of his 'literalism'.

As for [the child] desiring his mother – yes, this too. But it is absurd what Freud's literalism can lead to. The child does not actively dream of penetrating his mother. Chances are he cannot yet even imagine how one would go about such an act . . . [6]

In other words, either an actual occurrence explains why a child quite sensibly believes something, or, if there isn't the possibility of an actual situation – as in the above instance – then we must just drop the suggestion. Literalism would seem to fit the other foot. Let us take another example of this point, as it is very important to our misunderstanding of Freud. Firestone quotes Freud on fetishism, thus:

5. Perhaps it is for this reason that Firestone, in recounting Freud's theory of infantile sexuality, updates everything to around the sixth year of the child's life.

6. ibid., pp. 56–7.

Freud: The object is the substitute for the mother's phallus which the little boy believed in and does not wish to forego.

Firestone   Really, Freud can get embarrassing. Wouldn't it be a
comments: lot more sensible to talk about the mother's power? Chances are the little boy has not even seen his mother undressed, let alone closely observed the difference between the penis and the cunt.[7]

Freud has often been found embarrassing. What he revealed about unconscious phantasies was not 'nice' – it was partly for that very reason that they were unconscious.

For Firestone the only phantasies a child might have come as a result of his conscious choice to avoid or adapt to a nasty social reality: they are either literally what happened or they are not there and Freud is imagining things (goodness knows why, as nobody else does).

A central feature of this retransposition of mental life into social reality, and the consequent stress on power, is that it denies the very truth for which Firestone approved of Freud in the first place – his stress on the importance of sexuality. Firestone's child has no phallic desires, as after all he can't have sexual knowledge, and he wouldn't be so unrealistic as to think his little penis could penetrate his mother! Finally, like de Beauvoir and others before her, Firestone explicitly expands sexuality to mean some sort of generalized life-energy. When Firestone credited Freud with having discovered sexuality, what she really meant was 'sexism', as she acknowledged that Freud understood patriarchal society. Indeed he did, but he was concerned to see how it came into being in each individual and with what effects.

If we want to get rid of the notion of problematic sexual and aggressive drives, can we legislate, from our rational standpoint, as Firestone would have us do, against such perversions as the incest-taboo (much as Greer would have us see that violence should be got rid of by love)? Psychoanalysis finds things more complicated than that. Firestone tells us that the Oedipus complex is really the nuclear family – if so, let us get rid of

7. ibid., p. 62.

psychoanalysis, for it tells us nothing. The Oedipus complex and its dissolution is the mental reaction of the child trying to discover its place in the world; in our society, this is in the context of two parents and its prohibited sexual desires towards them. It is how this primary social conjuncture of birth to two people of the opposite sex is *lived* in the mental life of the off-spring and it is how that mental life and the drives brought by the infant into the world and developed therein also affect that social reality. For Freud was concerned with how social reality (patriarchal culture, at that) came into being, how it was reborn in each individual and how each individual reacted to it in his mental life. Firestone, Greer, Figes and Friedan all assume that social reality is there and that somehow the individual comes afterwards. Psychoanalysis does not subscribe to this logical sequence, but to another sort of relationship altogether.

Given Firestone's perspective, feminism does not, as she claims, make sense of psychoanalysis, it treads on utterly different ground. Psychoanalysis is about man and woman in culture, in other words about man and woman, for so far all human societies have been distinguished precisely by their culture, however minimal that may be.

Firestone, who ostensibly is the only feminist to praise Freud, is in fact furthest of all away from him.

6 Kate Millett:
Freud, Facts and Fantasies

Yet Freud believed that female autoeroticism declines as a result of enlightenment, finding in this 'yet another surprising effect of penis-envy, or of the discovery of the inferiority of the clitoris'. Here, as is so often the case, one cannot separate Freud's account of how a child reasons from how Freud himself reasons, and his own language, invariably pejorative, tends to confuse the issue irremediably. Indeed, since he has no objective proof of any consequence to offer in support of his notion of penis envy or of a female castration complex, one is struck by how thoroughly the subjectivity in which all these events are cast tends to be Freud's own, or that of a strong masculine bias, even of a rather gross male-supremacist bias.[1]

... Again, Freud's own language makes no distinction here between fact and feminine fantasy.[2]

Kate Millett gives the most detailed outline of Freud's work of all the feminist writers considered. It seems perverse, therefore, to give it the most scant attention. However, her work serves as a perfect illustration of my thesis that if you study Freud's writings on femininity outside the context of the main concepts of psychoanalysis they are doomed to sound absurd and/or reactionary. Millett shares with Friedan, Figes and Firestone a wish that Freud had seen the social explanation staring him in the face, and she pursues this with greater intricacy than do the other three.

I do not intend to examine the differences of detail between the sociological injunctions of Millett and the other feminists, but this variation should not be mistaken for substantial differences, for in fact, despite different stresses, different intentions and

1. Kate Millett, *Sexual Politics*, Doubleday, New York, 1970, p. 182.
2. ibid., p. 183. For English analysts, 'phantasy' is unconscious and 'fantasy' conscious; American writers tend not to preserve the distinction.

even different results, all these writers have far more in common than they have in diversity. And by what they have in common, I do *not* mean only their feminism. It is not what Freud says about women and femininity that is the real stake in the battle, but the very objects of psychoanalysis themselves, sexuality and the unconscious, that offend. Of course without them, Freud's theories of sexual differences become far easier to attack – for then, indeed, *robbed of their entire significance*, they are only prejudices. What all these writers share is quite simply a fundamental rejection of the two crucial discoveries of psychoanalysis: the unconscious and with it infantile sexuality. I would just point out how in each case each of these authors, after paying tribute to the discovery of the importance of sexuality in human life, proceeds to deny it by converting it, after all, into something as generalized as 'life-energy' – a generality from which Freud originally rescued it and to which, time and again, he had to forbid it to return. From his first experiences of dissension with Adler and Jung, Freud realized that this would be the recurrent reaction to an unpalatable idea; he is still being proved correct – whatever their intention, every major dissident disputes or denies the specificity and importance of sexuality.

Obviously Freud's discussions of the psychological differences between the sexes concern his theories both of sexuality and the unconscious. My concern here, however, is in the main with the denial of the unconscious. Millett, like Friedan, pays the respects due to its discovery, but I would like to select a few examples of her criticism that illustrate how totally she denies it.

At this stage of her childhood the little girl at first expects her father to prove magnanimous and award her a penis. Later, disappointed in this hope, she learns to content herself with the aspiration of bearing his baby. The baby is given out as a curious item; it is actually a penis, not a baby at all ... Although she will never relinquish some hope of acquiring a penis ... a baby is as close to a penis as the girl shall get. The new penis wish is metamorphosed into a baby, a quaint feminine-coated penis, which has the added merit of being a respectable ambition.[3]

And:

What forces in her experience, her society and socialization have

3. ibid., p. 184.

led [a woman] to see herself as an inferior being? The answer would seem to lie in the conditions of patriarchal society and the inferior position of women within this society. But Freud did not choose to pursue such a line of reasoning, preferring instead an etiology of childhood experience based upon the biological fact of anatomical differences . . .

. . . it is supremely unfortunate that Freud should prefer to bypass the more likely social hypothesis to concentrate upon the distortions of infantile subjectivity . . .[4]

In other words, it is supremely unfortunate that he discovered the unconscious and infantile sexuality, that he did not leave well alone and merely protest about it. But Millett goes further and proposes that Freud invented psychoanalysis precisely so as to avoid acknowledging social reality. In Firestone this proposition is explicit in her statement that Freudianism is merely misguided feminism, in Millett it is implicit in her elaboration of Freud's unfortunate discoveries: the importance given to childhood experience is little short of a conspiracy.

In formulating the theory of penis envy, Freud not only neglected the possibility of a social explanation for feminine dissatisfaction but precluded it by postulating a literal jealousy of the organ whereby the male is distinguished. As it would appear absurd to charge adult women with these values, the child, and a drastic experience situated far back in childhood, are invoked.[5]

Millett, Firestone, Figes, et al. would return Freud whence he came. They want to bar the very notion of psychical reality which was his simple jumping-off point. Firestone would dismantle the Oedipus complex in favour of actual incest (which she would welcome, not ban), Millett would substitute *real* rape for phantasied castration. She points out how it is unlikely that girls would suffer from the terrors of castration as it never *in fact* takes place – on the contrary, what they are really dreading is rape, '*since it happens to them*' [my italics]. Certainly the castration-fear in women/girls could be experienced as the dread of rape, but it would be a fear *in phantasy* – none the less *real* or powerful for that. (That rape does indeed occur is only an indirectly related issue.) This is exactly where Freud started

4. ibid., p. 180.   5. ibid., p. 183.

with his trauma theory in the eighteen-nineties.[6]

Desire, phantasy, the laws of the unconscious or even un-consciousness are absent from the social realism of the feminist critiques. With Millett, as with the other feminist studies, empiricism run riot denies more than the unconscious; it denies any attribute of the mind other than rationality. As a result it must also end up denying the importance of childhood ex-periences. The feminist's children are born directly into the reality principle; not so Freud's. This underlies Millett's mis-understanding in such criticisms as: 'Freud's own language makes no distinction here between fact and feminine fantasy' – or that cited initially: 'one cannot separate Freud's account of how a child reasons from how Freud himself reasons . . .' No indeed not, and for a very good reason. Freud was trying to explain what feminine 'fantasy' did with social facts and cultural demands, and how a child reasoned. Millett claims that:

Confronted with so much concrete evidence of the male's superior status, sensing on all sides the depreciation in which they are held, girls envy not the penis, but only what the penis gives one social pretensions to. Freud appears to have made a major and rather foolish confusion between biology and culture, anatomy and status.[7]

These eminently sensible little girls that Millett, like Firestone, conjures up can only respond to what actually happens. We have seen how time and again these writers remark that Freud accepts the status quo and prescribes within its terms the course of normal womanhood. This insistence on Freud's belief in the desirability of normality is only an aspect of the profounder refusal of unconscious mental life. In one sense, in believing that Freud advocated normality, and in denying anything other than the processes of conscious rationality, these accounts them-selves subscribe to such notions. Consciousness, rationality,

6. Ferenczi, as well as the others we have mentioned, and many besides, made a comparable return to the early Freud in the very late twenties. See Ernest Jones, *Life*, op. cit., Vol. III, pp. 156 ff. I only comment on this here to stress the predictability of the nature of the opposition. An implicit denial of the unconscious and of infantile sexuality is ultimately bound to come up with the same answers.

7. ibid., p. 187.

social actuality are all. Let us take a final quotation which encapsulates this feminist position – an average, not a grotesque, illustration:

So far, Freud has merely pursued a line of reasoning he attributes, rightly or wrongly, to the subjectivity of female youth. Right or wrong, his account purports to be little more than description of what girls *erroneously* believe. But there is prescription as well in the Freudian account [my italics].[8]

This feminist belief in the exclusive presence of the reality-principle is wish-fulfilment indeed. But, speaking seriously, this places everything Freud had to say about women in an entirely false context.

8. ibid., p. 183.

Epilogue

It is no accident that, for all their differences, Reich's, Laing's and the feminists' theories come to resemble one another in so many ways. All these writers deny the unconscious – Reich by finding it to be nothing other than a pool of biological energy, Laing by treating its constructs as though they were identical to those of consciousness, the feminist critics by believing above all in social actuality and conscious choice. Reich by equating the Oedipus complex with the *actual* family, and Laing by treating psychosis as caused by an *actual* present-day predicament, have managed to give us good phenomenological descriptions of these social realities. The feminists have produced a necessary attack on debased Freudianism with its biologically deterministic theory and adaptation therapy. None has helped us to any analytical understanding nor – in the case of Reich, Laing and Firestone – despite all their intentions, have they been able to situate their dualistic worlds in a patriarchal culture which by definition demands at least three elements. So long as we see their dyads and their unified dualities for the reflective ideologies that they are, we can make good use of their descriptions. On the other hand, Freud's psychoanalytical theories of femininity, though, I think, in principle correct, do not go far enough. Among other things, he did not have sufficient material of a certain sort with which to work. Reich and Laing's descriptive accounts of the family and political structures and of internal family dynamics present in much greater detail the actual situations from which Freud developed psychoanalytic understanding. They give us more material for analysis. But the testimony of women will be yet more crucial for this work. Such an analysis could attach to itself the polemical strength and political commitment of feminism, of which it should be an integral part.

CONCLUSION:

THE HOLY FAMILY AND FEMININITY

I The Holy Family

What is originally holy is what we have taken over from the animal kingdom – *the bestial.**

* Engels to Marx, 8 December 1882, *Selected Correspondence*, 1934 edn., p. 406.

The Holy Family

I so rarely feel the need for synthesis. The unity of this world seems to me something self-understood, something unworthy of emphasis. What interests me is the separation and breaking up into its component parts what would otherwise flow into primeval pulp. Even the assurance most clearly expressed in Grabbe's *Hannibal* that: 'We will not fall out of this world' doesn't seem sufficient substitute for the surrender of the boundaries of the Ego, which can be painful enough. In short, I am evidently an analyst and believe that synthesis offers no obstacles once analysis has been achieved.[1]

In brief, the thesis of this book is know the devil you have got . . . We have a culture in which, with infinite complexity, the self is created divisively, the sexes are divided divisively; a patriarchal culture in which the phallus is valorized and women oppressed. Long before a situation is analysed, people wish for its overthrow; such is Utopianism or millennarianism and it requires a creative or mystical turn of mind. Often its perceptions are perceptive, its descriptions accurate: Reich, Laing and Firestone offer us near perfect models of this;[2] Freud, I would contend, starts the analysis. That Reich, Laing and Firestone wrote chronologically after Freud in no way prevents their work

1. Freud, letter to Lou Andreas-Salomé, 30 July 1915, *Letters of Sigmund Freud*, op. cit., pp. 316–17.
2. '. . . the terror which is connected with the deep experience of the Self. To stand aside, entirely logical and drily "intellectual", and observe your own inner functioning amounts to a splitting of the unitary system which only a very few seem to bear without deep upset. And the few who, far from being frightened, enjoy the submerging in their own Selfs are the great artists, poets, scientists and philosophers. Are they, now, exceptions from the rule or the original rule itself?' (Wilhelm Reich, 'The Rooting of Reason in Nature', *Selected Writings*, op. cit., p. 534.)
'True sanity entails in one way or another the dissolution of the normal ego, that false self competently adjusted to our alienated social

being, in this sense, *before* his. That Freud did not more emphatically denounce what he analysed is a pity; certainly aspects of the denunciations made by the other three are valuable. However, I think we can only go further with analysis. That Freud's account of women comes out pessimistic is not so much an index of his reactionary spirit as of the condition of women. The longevity of the oppression of women *must* be based on something more than conspiracy, something more complicated than biological handicap and more durable than economic exploitation (although in differing degrees all these may feature). It is illusory to see women as the pure who are purely put upon: the status of women is held in the heart and the head as well as the home: oppression has not been trivial or historically transitory – to maintain itself so effectively it courses through the mental and emotional bloodstream. To think that this should not be so does not necessitate pretending it is already not so. On the contrary, once again we need pessimism of the intellect, optimism of the will.

---

reality: the emergence of the "inner" archetypal mediators of divine power, and through this death a rebirth, and the eventual re-establishment of a new kind of ego-functioning, the ego now being the servant of the divine, no longer its betrayer.' (Laing, *The Politics of Experience*, op. cit., p. 119.)

'What we shall have in the next cultural revolution is the reintegration of the Male (Technological Mode) with the Female (Aesthetic Mode), to create an androgynous culture surpassing the highs of either cultural stream, or even of the sum of their integrations. More than a marriage, rather an abolition of the cultural categories themselves, a mutual cancelation – a matter-antimatter explosion, ending with a poof! culture itself.

'We shall not miss it. We shall no longer need it: by then humanity will have mastered nature totally, will have realized in *actuality* its dreams. With the full achievement of the conceivable in the actual, the surrogate of culture will no longer be necessary. The sublimation process, a detour to wish fulfilment, will give way to direct satisfaction in experience, as felt now only by children, or adults on drugs . . . Enjoyment will spring directly from being and acting itself, the process of experience, rather than from the quality of achievement. When the male Technological Mode can at last produce in actuality what the female Aesthetic Mode had envisioned, we shall have eliminated the need for either.' (Shulamith Firestone, *The Dialectic of Sex*, op. cit., pp. 214–15.)

A whole number of questions arise at every level in accepting Freud's analysis, even as a beginning. Freud rejected most emphatically any attempt to circumscribe psychoanalysis by making its theories revelations only of the psychic structure of capitalist man. The question still remains as to how generally or specifically applicable are its theses? Certainly it would seem arbitrary to assume that a given mode of production produced its own exactly commensurate group or individual psychology, although of course it must affect it in no small measure. On the other hand, can the universal structures Freud claims to have revealed truly be said to be universal – that is, are they really appropriate to all forms of culture? These questions are frequently raised and here I want only to touch on those issues that directly concern the question of the psychology of women. As a generalization perhaps it is possible to say that the basic structure can be universal, its application varied and specific. Thus, for instance, at one level, the Oedipus complex is the means whereby any infant finds its place within the fixed laws of the human order, at another, in our society, those laws are first expressed within the nuclear family. But the Oedipus complex is *not* about these attitudes, set up within the family, hence the Reich–Firestone thesis that it is only the expression of this type of family, apart from reducing it to a banality, is simply inaccurate. On the other hand, questions are posed by Freud's hypothesis about the very concept of culture. For instance, has civilization – even where matrilineal – been hitherto coincident, despite all its variations, with patriarchal power? Is the phallus always valorized? Is the particularity of the formation of the ego in alienation a characteristic of Western society? The degree of specificity and of universality has, I think, still to be worked out. The presentation of Freud's work here is a minimal precondition of this.

1 When Did It All Start?

All questions relating to the position and role of women in society tend, sooner or later, to founder on the bed-rock of 'When did it all start?' Sexual distinction and the consequent oppression of women wanders around in search of its author through the fields of anthropology, biology, psychology, economics, cultural history, religion, sociology and so on. As we read, with partial satisfaction, through accounts of how sexually non-repressive matriarchies gave way to authoritarian private-property patriarchies, or of how man's fear of freedom or love of power made him wish to enslave others physically and psychologically (or variations on these 'alternative' socio-economic or psychological accounts), we have an uneasy feeling that the answers are somehow more accurate than the question. In other words, more or less every type of explanation contains some truth. What is wrong, or why can't they be fused to provide a comprehensive picture?

We can see the same dilemma reflected in the practical politics of feminism: women seem to be abused in every sphere, on every level; the attacks must be, in some measure, commensurately random and chaotic. Is it the economic position of women as the worst-paid workers, the social destiny of wife- and mother-hood, or the ideological attitudes to women as Adam's rib, baby doll, 'a bit of skirt' that must take precedence as the worst offender – and again which came first?

It seems to me that 'why did it happen' and 'historically when?' are both false questions. The questions that should, I think, be asked in place of these, are: how does it happen and when does it take place in our society? From this last question we can then go on to ask if, within the terms of our explanation, there are 'universal' features that would enable us to understand the comparable position of women in other cultures and in other historical epochs. In other words, we can start by asking how does it happen, *now*.

It is, I think, ultimately, this search for historical origins that mars what is probably still the most influential work in the field: Engels's *Origins of the Family, the State and Private Property*. Despite its great importance it is his preoccupation with the question of 'when did it start' that makes the inaccuracy of Engels's anthropological sources relevant.

Engels orientated his analysis around the changing nature of work, man's conquest of nature and his sophistication of techniques. The accumulation of wealth and the consequent demand to ensure inheritance are the by now familiar centre points of Engels's theory of the declining status of women. His stress on the respect paid to women in primitive societies where polyandry matched polygamy and jealousy was virtually excluded by being irrelevant, his statement that mothers have the power to choose and reject chiefs in matrilineal societies, and his overall contention that the subjugation of women was no natural subordination, have all been a source of hope for socialist feminism from the date of their first reception.

That woman was the slave of man at the commencement of society is one of the most absurd notions that have come down to us from the period of Enlightenment of the eighteenth century.[1]

Yet, in Engels's account, woman was the first slave – within civilization – and women the first oppressed group. The end of matrilineage was the world historical defeat of women; prior to this what he calls the 'natural' division of labour had been non-exploitative. However, there is an aspect of Engels's theses that is usually overlooked by revolutionary optimists, and it is an aspect that allies it far more closely with Freud's apparently opposite hypothesis than anyone cares to contemplate. Monogamous marriage, inheritance and the first class oppression are – for Engels – also coincident with civilization. Patriarchy and written history are twins. The group marriage that precedes it takes place under conditions of savagery, the pairing family of

1. F. Engels, *The Origin of the Family, the State and Private Property*, 1884, *Selected Works*, Lawrence & Wishart, London, 1958, p. 481.

barbarism. The freedom of women is pre-historic, pre-civilization.

Freud's search for origins led him to invent the myth of the totem father slain by a gang of jealous brothers who then fairly shared out the women. For Freud this civilization is then, by his own definition, patriarchal. Though he shares with Engels an interest in anthropology, his stress is nevertheless on the history of the different ideologies within culture; so, for example, his task is to explain goddess cults in patriarchal societies. Freud's civilization is not limited to written history and in this he would, therefore, have differed from Engels. For Freud, human society, whatever the level of its culture, is civilization.[2] It certainly seems that all known societies, despite matrilineage, accord the power of the law to men. But Freud too, finds a 'prehistorical' place for matriarchies. A further comparison can be drawn between Freud's and Engels's accounts: in the individual, as Freud depicts it, 'the world historical defeat' of the female takes place with the girl's castration complex and her entry into the resolution of her Oedipus complex – her acceptance of her inferior, feminine place in patriarchal society. As Freud believed ontogeny repeated phylogeny, his reconstruction of the general historical situation would thus match Engels's. The power of women ('the matriarchy') is pre-civilization, pre-Oedipal. Thus even the most seemingly diverse analyses – such as those of Engels and Freud – agree that *civilization* as such is patriarchal, and this gives their accounts an underlying similarity.

However, Freud's stress on ideology rather than social history enables us to interpret his search for origins in a somewhat different light. On the whole it seems fair to say that Freud's work in *Totem and Taboo* must be read as mythology, not anthropology. The myth Freud proposes amounts to an assumption of how mankind 'think' their history. He has deduced this from present-day mental structures on the basis of their 'eternal' nature – but it is also the way in which men *must*

2. It was fashionable when Freud was first working to distinguish between culture and civilization (for example, this was a favourite theme of Karl Kraus's). Freud rejected this distinction: they were one and the same thing.

believe it happened if they are to live according to the dictates of society. In other words, the story tells us about the present, but, in an important way, in this respect, that is not so very different from the past. The hypothesis of *Totem and Taboo* is complementary to the Oedipus myth – it fills in its lacunae, giving us a myth that had not previously been coherently articulated by the elegant pen of a Sophocles. Just as the story of Oedipus, according to Freud, took its effect from its appeal to fundamental, universal motifs in the human mind, so the great revenge stories (as, for instance, in the major Elizabethan dramas) likewise play on the rivalry, violence and jealousy inherent in the process of assuming one's human-ness. The actual totem meal – a familiar primitive rite – enacts the infantile urge to devour, and fear of being devoured, but the historical narrative Freud elaborated to account for this also enacts it. Infantile phantasy, 'primitive' tribal rites, 'invented' historical accounts, psychoanalytical reconstructions,[3] are all the same thing – each an explanation of the other on a different level.

Although Freud gave his work here, in part, an evolutionist or developmental structure – just as initially his ontogenic observations about individuals were made in terms of 'stages' and ages (the latter usually wrong, and certainly unimportant) – it is quite evident that he viewed the work of psychoanalysis itself as another kind of myth and this suggests that even his anthropology can sustain this interpretation. Thus, for instance, in writing of Schreber's paranoiac delusions, he offered the following rumination:

... I have no motive for avoiding the mention of a similarity which may possibly damage our libido theory in the estimation of many of my readers. Schreber's 'rays of God', which are made up of a condensation of the sun's rays, of nerve-fibres, and of spermatozoa, are in reality nothing else than a concrete representation and projection outwards of libidinal cathexes; and they thus lend his delusions a striking conformity with our theory. His belief that the world must come to an end because his ego was attracting all the rays to itself, his anxious concern at a later period, during the process of reconstruction, lest God should sever His ray-connection with him, – these and many other details of Schreber's delusional structure sound

3. Constructions in analysis re-tell man's essential myths.

almost like endopsychic perceptions of the processes whose existence I have assumed in these pages as the basis of our explanation of paranoia. I can nevertheless call a friend and fellow-specialist to witness that I had developed my theory of paranoia before I became acquainted with the contents of Schreber's book. It remains for the future to decide whether there is more delusion in my theory than I should like to admit, or whether there is more truth in Schreber's delusion than other people are as yet prepared to believe.[4]

This final strange rider serves as a fascinating commentary on Reich's later work: clearly a delusion but not invalid therefore. Reich's theories were private delusions; they did not acquire the status of myth, but no less, and indeed disturbingly comparable to Schreber's, they could be classified as 'endopsychic perceptions' of the libidinal processes. There is truth in both Schreber's and Reich's 'delusions', it is just that the framework is wrong: an advanced society does not offer myths to cover this sort of perception – being private, they became delusions. Except, of course, that psychoanalysis provides the myth for us – reconstitutes the dispersed unconscious elements – and offers us the theory of libido. In a yet more subtle way we have evidence once again of Reich's return to the point from which Freud started. Freud gave credit where it was due to Schreber's analysis of his own paranoia; we could likewise give credit to Reich for his projections – if it were not that they came so much after the event and by custom if not justice, priority counts for something. Reich's metaphors – the bursting bladder of masochism, the character-armour for the insignia within the ego, the cosmic rays of blue genital love – have a pertinence that came too late. It is in this sense, and not with the glibness of dismissal, that we must label Reich's a case of paranoia. Yes, but perceptively so. A private delusion for a public myth.

It is, of course, for another reason that I introduced Freud's reflections on Schreber here. Psychoanalysis makes conscious the unconscious, not only as a therapeutic technique, but also as the task of its theory. It reconstructs the unperceived, frag-

4. Freud, 'Psychoanalytic Notes on an Autobiographical Account of a Case of Paranoia', op. cit., pp. 78–9. One should also compare this with Freud's comments on hallucinations, referred to on p. 263 above.

mented and incoherent myths and ideas held within the unconscious mind, it makes them coherent and presents them as what they are: myths, representations of ideas, ideology – the word is difficult to find as each has a debased meaning. So the paranoid-psychotic Schreber, the mildly paranoid Reich, the normal man-in-the-street, share a common heritage of past, present and future which can be revealed and made explicit, or can be reconstructed in the whole form to which each suggestion, represented drive, thought or association refers. As has been said, Jung did not need to propose a 'collective unconscious' as the unconscious is already collective.

But if Freud's myth of origins tells us about how we live today, we still have to account for the universal features to which it lays claim. For our purposes here the most crucial of these are the patriarchal structure of society and its two attendant events: the anthropophagic complex (the totem meal) and the Oedipus complex. It seems to be the case that contemporary anthropology supports Freud's contention that human society in many different ways equals patriarchy rather than Engels's notion that patriarchy can be limited to strictly literate civilization. To what extent is this general observation relevant from our point of view?

2 Patriarchy, Kinship and Women as Exchange Objects

I want to make some tentative links between the myth that Freud has deduced from his analysis of the individual's unconscious and what we know from anthropological studies that confirms this. I can offer here only the most general and residual aspects of anthropological theory. Although there is considerable dispute about the interpretations made by Lévi-Strauss, it is his work that I have chosen to use, both because I like it and because, to some extent, it has been influenced by the same type of questions that I am asking here. As I am considering only such general issues as kinship, incest and exchange, in this context, the accuracy of particular anthropological observations that have been made so far would, in any case, be almost irrelevant. The outline I propose needs correction and amplification, but in the main, this will have to come from work not yet undertaken. What we need is a kinship analysis of contemporary capitalist society, for it is within kinship structures that women, as women, are situated.

Lévi-Strauss has shown how it is *not* the biological family of mother, father and child that is the distinguishing feature of human kinship structures. Indeed this biological base must be transformed if society is to be instituted. The universal and primordial law is that which regulates marriage relationships and its pivotal expression is the prohibition on incest. This prohibition forces one family to give up one of its members to another family; the rules of marriage within 'primitive' societies function as a means of exchange and as an unconsciously acknowledged system of communication. The act of exchange holds a society together: the rules of kinship (like those of language to which they are near-allied) *are* the society. Whatever the nature of the society – patriarchal, matrilineal, patrilineal, etc. – it is always men who exchange women. Women thus become the equivalent of a sign which is being communicated. Lévi-Strauss cautions against simplifying this object-status by political prejudice:

We may now ask whether, in extending the concept of communication so as to make it include exogamy and the rules flowing from the prohibition of incest, we may not, reciprocally, achieve insight into a problem that is still very obscure, that of the origin of language. For marriage regulations, in relation to language, represent a much more crude and archaic complex. It is generally recognized that words are signs; but poets are practically the only ones who know that words were also once values. As against this, women are held by the social group to be values of the most essential kind, though we have difficulty in understanding how these values become integrated in systems endowed with a significant function. This ambiguity is clearly manifested in the reactions of persons who, on the basis of the analysis of social structures referred to, have laid against it the charge of 'anti-feminism', because women are referred to as objects. Of course, it may be disturbing to some to have women conceived as mere parts of a meaningful system. However, one should keep in mind that the processes by which phonemes and words have lost – even though in an illusory manner – their character of value, to become reduced to pure signs, will never lead to the same results in matters concerning women. For words do not speak, while women do; as producers of signs, women can never be reduced to the status of symbols or tokens. But it is for this very reason that the position of women, as actually found in this system of communication between men that is made up of marriage regulations and kinship nomenclature, may afford us a workable image of the type of relationships that could have existed at a very early period in the development of language, between human beings and their words. As in the case of women, the original impulse which compelled men to exchange words must be sought for in that split representation that pertains to the symbolic function. For, since certain terms are simultaneously perceived as having a value both for the speaker and the listener, the only way to resolve this contradiction is in the exchange of complementary values, to which all social existence is reduced.[1]

Obviously in an advanced society, visible kinship structures play a much more residual role than in so-called primitive societies. Nevertheless, within any society, although the ramifica-

1. Claude Lévi-Strauss, *Structural Anthropology*, trans. Claire Jacobson and Brooke Grundfest Schoepf, Allen Lane, The Penguin Press, London, 1968, pp. 61–2.

tions may have become so complex as to mask the underlying intent, something of value is given so that something of equal value can be received in turn: the exchange is all. However, the objects of value in the kinship system that are to be exchanged are women, and those who conduct the exchange are men. Lévi-Strauss is correct to stress that the given place in a system of communication is no index of inferiority or superiority and that we must not be led astray by the false, derogatory connotations of the word 'object' either into denigrating women or labelling those who define them thus 'anti-feminist'. Nevertheless this primary sexual division is an important indicator of difference and a difference that may well be historically exploited to establish a system of deference. Lévi-Strauss suggests that there is no theoretical reason why women should not exchange men, but empirically this has never taken place in *any* human society. Such a fact again warns us against the Utopian matriarchal reconstructions. It must also make us reflect that Lévi-Strauss's repudiation of anti-feminism, while correct, is also inadequate; that is to say it is adequate as a defence but leaves the implications of the problem unsolved. Furthermore, if, as is the case, it is empirically proven that it is *always* men who exchange women, then, though the obverse is *hypothetically* possible, there must be available a *theoretical* explanation of why it does not happen.

The legally controlled exchange of women is the primary factor that distinguishes mankind from all other primates, from a cultural standpoint. That is to say that though there are crucial biological differences – upright posture, position of the thumb, etc. – the systematic exchange of women is definitional of human society. This act of exogamy transforms 'natural' families into a cultural kinship system.

Within the family both sexes already, so to speak, have each other; they naturally possess their kin in already-formed relationships. A law that merely confirmed this pattern would be futile; marriage laws and the intimately related taboo on incest are set up precisely to prevent any circular fixation at this natural stage. Undirected copulation would indicate not so much the modern fear of or desire for anarchy, as a vicious circle of repetition from which no culture could get established. The injunction against incest works two ways: you must *not* sexually possess specified members of your kin group (minimally your sister), you *must* offer them in marriage, exogamously. Society thus being based on the reciprocal exchange of values, sexual laws are therefore the equivalent of inter-human communications and coexistent with society itself. Contrary to popular belief, it is not that there is anything biologically 'wrong' with incest that is important; it is rather that the command to exchange exogamously forbids the cul-de-sac of endogamy. The subjective depth of the taboo indicates social necessity, not biological revulsion; but this is a social necessity so basic (i.e. the very basis of society) that the prohibition is experienced as immutably natural – except, that is, in the testimony of the Oedipal child who is only just learning the law.

The reciprocal exchange that marks exogamy is, however, an exchange between two people (or their representative groups) of a third item, it is not a system of barter and thus equivalence or direct reciprocity is not within its terms of reference. Again Lévi-Strauss writes: 'The reciprocal bond basic to marriage is not set up between men and women, but between men and men by means of women, who are only the principal occasion for it.'[2]

The incest taboo is the subjective expression of the need for exogamy, the objective expression is the basic kinship structure that can be perceived within all the multifarious forms that it assumes within different cultures. The incest taboo becomes the unconscious content, the basic kinship relationship remains the visible form. (The later anti-formalist Lévi-Strauss would object to this simplified distinction.) For a kinship structure to exist, three types of family relationship must always be satisfied: consanguinity, affinity and descent. The essential relationship is that between brothers-in-law (the men who exchange the women). Consanguinity is expressed in the relationship between brother and sister, affinity between husband and wife and descent between father and son. The man can give away either a sister or a

2. Lévi-Strauss, *Les Structures élémentaires de la parenté*, 1949, cited by Simone de Beauvoir in her account, 'The Early Tiller of the Soil', in *The Second Sex* (p. 96) where she discusses the implications of the situation and refutes any hopes of feminist glory within the 'matriarchy'.

daughter, the kinship structure casts down its anchor in marriage and must be perpetuated in future generations – not just for the linear survival of the race but to enable the possibility to right the upset balance between groups by giving in one generation and getting in the next. By what is known as 'the scientific principle of parsimony', the crucial elements in the kinship structure can be reduced as a minimum to the four terms: brother, sister, father and son. In our society, where the kinship system barely can be seen to regulate the social relationships, it is still important: firstly because in its internalized form (the Oedipus complex), each person acquires the laws of society, and secondly, in a negative sense: it shows us that, despite common assumption, it is not the triadic biological family that is the nucleus of society but, on the contrary, a completely different asymmetrical structure which gives prominence to a relationship entirely distinct from that contained within the two parents and their children set-up. This relationship is the avunculate – the mother's brother's position vis-à-vis her children, which will be considered in a moment. The socially non-essential nature of the omnipresent biological family is important in any discussion of possible change, Lévi-Strauss comments:

The idea ... that the biological family constitutes the point of departure from which all societies elaborate their kinship systems, has not been voiced solely by Radcliffe-Brown. There is scarcely an idea which would today elicit greater consensus. Nor is there one more dangerous in our opinion. Of course, the biological family is ubiquitous in human society. But what confers upon kinship its socio-cultural character is not what it retains from nature, but, rather, the essential way in which it diverges from nature.[3]

It is not the family but the structural relationship *between* families that constitutes the elementary form of human society; that distinguishes human society from primate groups. Furthermore, it is not what is given, but the act of exchange itself that holds any society together. A controlled act of exchange is the decisive break man makes with the beasts. It is definitional of humanity. Marriage is an archetype of exchange and can be seen to serve the exchange function by setting up a new locus of rela-

3. Lévi-Strauss, *Structural Anthropology*, op. cit., p. 50.

tionships. Ultimately what is important, then, is some legally established method of exchange and a distinction between legitimate and illegitimate relationships – within these terms, what the law establishes goes, but its expression can be extremely variable and is certainly not attached to a biological pattern which, nevertheless, it, so to speak, takes into account.

In order to establish the socio-cultural break with the circularity of the biological given of two parents and their child, a fourth term must intervene. This is where the mother's brother comes in, and he comes in with the very inauguration of society, he is essential to it. The relationship between uncle and nephew is always correlated with that between father and son: where the uncle is treated with respect, the father is regarded with familiarity, and vice versa. The former situation is a mark of matrilineal societies, the latter of patrilineal ones. The maternal uncle can today no longer be seen to function in our society; but the authoritative role of the father indicates clearly our patrilineal heritage.

The maternal brother offers his sister to his thereby future brother-in-law, within this generation he therefore acts as mediator between his brother-in-law and the latter's wife (his sister); furthermore he mediates between these parents and their child (his nephew); he thus has a horizontal and vertical role. The uncle ensures that the vicious circle cannot come again, by his intervention man cannot prey on man in rampant incest; social law is ensured. The holy (bestial) family will not reign supreme. There always has to be some other term that mediates and transforms the deathly symmetry, the impossibility for culture, of the biological family: within the kinship structure, classically this term is the maternal uncle. Lévi-Strauss writes:

... it is not families (isolated terms) which are truly 'elementary', but, rather, the relations between those terms. No other interpretation can account for the universality of the incest taboo; and the avuncular relationship, in its most general form, is nothing but a corollary, now covert, now explicit, of this taboo.[4]

The brother (maternal uncle) must give his sister in marriage and not desire her incestuously, both he and the sister whom he gives away are as close as one can get to being each other. The distinc-

4. ibid., p. 51.

tion between them is minimal and the prohibition on their union (the incest taboo) establishes that smallest of differences which is necessary to inaugurate society. At the horizontal level you cannot get nearer than brother and sister, therefore a separation must be enforced, if the circular nature of the biological pattern is to be broken in order for the movement of culture to establish itself. Leaving aside for the moment the vertical relationship of parents and children, any other relationship is further away than this one and therefore different societies can afford to dispense with other laws, or decree them as wished: this one, the recognition of the minimal distance required, is essential. The maternal uncle (the sister's brother) thus stands for the smallest possible difference.

The establishment of difference is also that which is absolutely crucial at an individual level. In other words, what Freud suggested was ontogeny repeating phylogeny, can be more accurately explained as a necessary homologous relationship between the two: one does not come before the other, they are the same event (the event of human society) expressed on different levels.

3 The Oedipus Complex and Patriarchal Society

The myth that Freud rewrote as the Oedipus complex and its dissolution epitomizes man's entry into culture itself. It reflects the original exogamous incest taboo, the role of the father, the exchange of women and the consequent difference between the sexes. It is *not* about the nuclear family, but about the institution of culture with the kinship structure and the exchange relationship of exogamy. It is thus about what Freud regarded as the order of all human culture. It is specific to nothing but patriarchy which is itself, according to Freud, specific to all human civilization.

The desires of the Oedipus complex are repressed into the unconscious. It is for this reason that the Oedipus complex is the nucleus of the neuroses and that the neuroses are the negative side of perversions which are the acting out of distorted, tabooed desires. In the unconscious lies the history of man's history that must be reacquired with the smashing of the Oedipus complex and the acceptance of symbolic castration. But while I think we can agree that the Oedipus complex, as it is *not* about the nuclear family, can certainly not be limited to the capitalist mode of production, this does not amount to saying that it does not assume particular forms of expression under different economic social systems. In our society the Oedipus complex, which is about the exchange relationships and taboos necessary for society, is *expressed* within the specific context of the nuclear family.

The proximity and centrality of the tabooed relationships within today's nuclear family must put a different load on the incest desire. Nothing is done to assist the prohibition, on the contrary, all is done to provoke the desire. It is as though the Oedipus complex of Western man were heir to the kinship structure whereby man became human, but the further mankind gets from overtly employing kinship relationships for social organization, the deeper repressed and hence more clamorous these become, for they are expressed within a context that tantalizes them. The mother and sister or father and brother you sensually cannot have are also the only people you are supposed to love. No wonder Freud found not only the dominance of unconscious desire but the prevalence of forbidden acts, for actual incest is not all that rare in our society. Psychoanalysis, in giving the analysand the myth he has lost, makes conscious the unconscious and offers him his particular human heritage, but it is in a strange context for it is one in which the mastery of the problem is particularly difficult.

Engels wrote: '. . . the determining factor of history is . . . the production and reproduction of immediate life . . . The social institutions under which men live are conditioned by both kinds of production: by the stage of development of labour, on the one hand, and of the family, on the other. The less the development of labour, and the more limited its volume of production and, therefore, the wealth of society, the more preponderatingly does the social order appear to be dominated by ties of sex . . .'[1] As the productivity of labour develops, however, societies increasingly become dominated not by sex-ties (kinship) but by class conflicts.

In economically advanced societies, though the kinship exchange system still operates in a residual way, other forms of economic exchange – i.e. commodity exchange – dominate and class, not kinship structures prevail. It would seem that it is against a background of the *remoteness* of a kinship system that the ideology of the biological family comes into its own. In other words, that the relationship between two parents and their children assumes a dominant role when the complexity of a class society forces the kinship system to recede. Many historians of the family[2] have contended that the version we

1. Engels, *Origin of the Family, Private Property and the State*, op. cit., pp. 449–50.
2. See, for instance, Philippe Ariès, who in *Centuries of Childhood*, op. cit., from his study of the history of education, literature, dress, games and iconography, charted the changing concept of childhood and contended that the two forms of relationship of the family and the line of descent are more or less mutually exclusive. The family, he claims, first comes to prominence in the sixteenth century and finally establishes itself as a small, unsociable unit oriented around a small number of children in the eighteenth century. A good deal of con-

know – the nuclear conjugal unit – really came into prominence with industrial capitalism. If – as seems likely – this is so, then, obviously speaking in rough generalizations, the move from agricultural communities to industrial complexes involved the final blow to the visible significance of kinship exchange.

There may perhaps have been a point after the (so-to-speak) surcease of kinship ties as a visible form of organization and before the success of the biological family as the ideological centrepiece of society, when neither were much in evidence. With child and female labour the order of the day, the nuclear family had small chance of establishing itself as the rationale of home-sweet-home, and daughters of working-class families were of little value for exchange. In other epochs this would also have been true for slaves and serfs, but now for the first time it is true for the masses. Under capitalism the vast majority of the population not only has nothing to sell but its labour-power, it also has nothing to exchange but this; particularly in the early stages it has nothing to inherit and nothing to give. Broadly speaking, kinship relationships are preserved as important among the aristocracy (a hangover from feudalism) and the cult of the biological family develops within the middle class. The middle class is thus the heir and progenitor of capitalism not only on the economic level but also on the ideological. The dominant class, the bourgeoisie, needs the reproduction of its labour force. The so-called biological nuclear family is the bourgeoisie's answer to the problem of repro-duction – it is imposed on the working class by various means. All humanitarian reforms were largely achieved because of the need for a higher birth and survival rate among workers. With compulsory education, prohibition of child labour and restric-tion of female labour, with the increased national wealth from imperialism, the working class was gradually able to follow the middle-class example of cultivating the biological family as, paradoxically, indeed almost impossibly, the main social unit. The biological family thus becomes a major cultural event under capitalism and asserts itself in the absence of prominent kinship

troversy surrounds this question. In England the best-known alterna-tive is Peter Laslett's *The World We Have Lost*, Methuen, London, 1965.

structures. When, within the *majority* of the population, it is no longer necessary for women to be exchange objects, then the small dominant class must insist on their remaining so – hence we have bourgeois hypocrisies about the value of the family for the working class. The taboos that establish exogamy, the various prohibitions on incest, persist (as exogamy persists) but, contained in their visible manifestations within the biological family, instead of openly expressed within a kinship system, they take on new shades of meaning. Freud was investigating (by and large) the Viennese bourgeoisie, but what he discovered was at one and the same time limited to that place and class, specific to the psychic make-up of man under capitalism, and generalizable to human culture as such. Instead of lamenting the specifics of Freud's milieu, we should rejoice – nothing could be more useful. He examined the 'eternal' structures of patriarchy in what is for us their most essential particularity: the bourgeois, patriarchal family.

Obviously, the specific context in which the Oedipus complex occurs further defines it and in our case that context – the biological nuclear family – at once endorses attitudes contained within it and contradicts it. In industrial society, if the family were not preserved, the prohibition on incest together with the already redundant demand for the exchange of women (except in the upper classes) would be unnecessary. Under capitalism, the mass of mankind, propertyless and working socially together *en masse* for the first time in the history of civilization would be unlikely, *were it not for the preservation of the family*, to come into proximity with their kin and if they did, it wouldn't matter. These are complex questions that I cannot do more than raise here. For the moment, I want to propose that with the dissolution of the Oedipus complex man enters finally into his humanity (always a precarious business). But it seems that the definition of that humanity – the differentiating instance between man and beast, i.e. the development of exchange relationships, may have become 'unsuitable' for the particular social form in which it is today expressed. Freud having shown us the heritage that we have access to only unconsciously, the next stage may be to see the importance of the contradictions between this heritage and the present way in which it is contained in the socially and ideologically reconstructed biological family. Even if this is a greatly over-simplified expression of the proposition, we can, I think, glimpse one way in which we see why the Oedipus complex is universal while the particular form used to redescribe it is specific. Hence we can see why the un-conscious, and with it the way mankind lives his humanity, is, as Freud says, 'eternal', while at the same time, the accidental and individual experiences of the subject and his particular social culture go to make it up. The unconscious is the way man lives his humanity in harmony and conflict with his particular and historically determined environment. It is why ideology persists through changing cultures, changing economic modes, while having also to be altered. If you like, it is why women are everywhere within civilization the second sex, but everywhere differently so.

4 The Different Self, the Phallus and the Father

For Freud, the learning of difference is the learning of humanity (one's human-ness). The concept of difference Freud is referring to is, in the first instance, not directly expressive of sexuality, but we shall see how it comes to be inextricably tied up with it. The theory, incidentally, contains within it an account of the predilection for one-ness represented in this book diversely by Reich, Laing and Firestone, though Laing, unlike Reich, is concerned to demonstrate how distinctions develop, so that they may be undone.

Looking back, we say with retrospective subjectivity that the newborn child experiences himself as absolute subject, indistinguishable from his world. Before any relationship with another person is established, the baby wants his sense of universal unity preserved by making sure he is attached to a crucial object, usually the mother's breast. This desire for unity with an object or a partial object and the danger of its loss, as Freud constantly stressed, is not the same as the later desire for unity with another person. (Viewing it from the angle of deprivation, the threat or practice of weaning is not the same as the threat of castration.) But, on the other hand, after the event the subject comes to interpret it in the same way as he experiences his later relationships with other objects; so that weaning, for instance, is seen through the fear of castration.

Freud records the compulsive-repetition game of his little grandson as he throws away and retrieves his cotton reel. This would seem to be the child's first attempts at repetition and mastery of the earlier experience, his representation in play of his desire for unity with the breast, whose absence he would not acknowledge. Now, however, the child, by reassuring himself of the object's return, takes cognizance of its absence. *Thus the distinguishing act is accomplished and mastered* and the object is first realized *as an object* in its absence. So, too, is the child first perceived by itself in its own distinctness in strict emulation of this presence and absence of the object (the mirror game). In a footnote, Freud confirms his interpretation that the game represents recognition of the mother's comings and goings and from this a recognition of the baby's own existence:

> One day the child's mother had been away for several hours and on her return was met with the words 'Baby o-o-o-o!' which was at first incomprehensible. It soon turned out, however, that during this long period of solitude the child had found a method of making *himself* disappear. He had discovered his reflection in a full-length mirror which did not quite reach to the ground so that by crouching down he could make his mirror-image 'gone'.[1]

What this little boy was undertaking at the age of one-and-a-half was something that could not be accounted for by the drive to attain pleasure; it revealed a tendency more primitive than the pleasure-principle and independent of it. What is being repre-sented, and repeated here, is something that the child experienced as decidedly unpleasant. Both the recognition of the separate-ness of the object and (it is the same thing) of the self can, then, only come about through the knowledge of absence. The wish for them not to be absent amounts to a wish to return things to a previous state of affairs. (We can see how, already, this accords very well with Laing's desire that we should undo the mechanisms whereby the ego is formed and whereby the self becomes a discrete self.) We can also see how the self, first gained in its image in a mirror,[2] is in its very creation con-stituted in a situation of 'alienation'. The baby, whose unified world is broken apart by the comings and goings of the mother on whom its body depends for survival, in his turn represents the terrors of this loss first with a toy, then with itself. The

1. Freud: 'Beyond the Pleasure Principle', 1920, S.E., Vol. XVIII, p. 15, n. 1. It is important also to note, as Freud points out, that the first part of the game (the loss) is played far more frequently than the second (the return) which thus confirms that it is a later acquisition.

2. Or as Winnicott (op. cit.) suggests, in the responses of the mother's face which *mirror* the baby's mood, though Winnicott omits to stress the essential feature of its impermanence: the mother's temporary absences.

self is, then, perceived *as the self* first as an object (the cotton reel) and as an identification (with the mother, in whose absence the baby had done exactly what she had done to him in his perception – the baby leaves himself and then finds himself in a *mirror*). We can see from this game that the child constitutes the other as object, constitutes himself as the other in the eyes of another for himself.

Although, certainly, there is both a schizoid and a paranoid dimension to this creation of the self in the alienated image (if there were not, how would schizophrenia or paranoia be possible?), I think Laing's account makes the mistake of supposing an already-constituted discrete subject. Laing's newborn baby, instead of being unable to distinguish himself from his world and thus having, by separation, to find both the world and himself as other, is already a clear entity merely in need of reassurance – needing, that is, to be seen. This Laingian child has an essential, pre-existent self. It is this need of reassurance that the later Laingian therapist will fulfil as he supplies the place of the good mother.[3] Furthermore, Laing's description is highly pejorative, whereas Freud here, as elsewhere, merely recognizes the paranoid and schizoid mechanisms necessary for the construction of the subject. Reich's reduction of the whole situation to a conflict (that he does not wish to take place) between the inner being of the person and the outer world, though closer to Laing than to Freud, is precisely a reduction and does not really call for further comment. Freud's child does not have the separate, pre-existent essential self that underlies both Laing's and Reich's contentions; his discrete self is set up in the moment of this recognition of absence which is the recognition of difference and which has been so importantly presaged in the first moments of life with the coming and going of the means of the preservation of life: the mother's breast. Lacan describes the Freudian situation of the child making himself in his image in the mirror thus:

> We have only to understand the mirror-phase *as an identification*, in the full sense which analysis gives to the term: namely, the transformation which takes place in the subject when he assumes an

3. Reich's therapist is urged to encourage the patient's fury and anger at the predicament in which he is left.

image – whose predestination to this phase-effect is sufficiently indicated by the use, in analytical theory, of the old term *imago*.

This jubilant assumption of his mirror-image by the little man, at the *infans* stage, still sunk in his motor incapacity and nurseling dependency, would seem to exhibit in an exemplary situation the symbolic matrix in which the *I* is precipitated in a primordial form, before it is objectified in the dialectic of identification with the other, and before language restores to it, in the universal, its function as subject.

This form would have to be called the *Ideal-I*, if we wanted to restore it to a familiar scheme, in the sense that it will also be the root-stock for secondary identifications, among which we place the functions of libidinal normalization. But the important point is that this form situates the instance of the *ego*, before its social determination, in a fictional direction, which will always remain irreducible for the individual alone, or rather, which will only rejoin the development of the subject asymptotically, whatever the success of the dialectical synthesis by which he must resolve as *I* his discordance with his own reality.[4]

Lacan, like Laing, recognizes in the situation Freud depicts a fundamental division, a divided self, or a self created in disharmony with its own reality – created, in other words, in a mirror. But Lacan's view of this is decisively different from Laing's. The child looks in the mirror and says: 'That's me', his first efforts at speech will echo this 'objectivization': 'Henry wants a sweet . . . he is going for a ride'. Only later will this 'me' be brought gradually, but never one hundred per cent within the life-span, into line with subjecthood, with the 'I' of the person. The first 'I' of the newborn baby, unable to distinguish himself from the world, is not Laing's essential self for, as Lacan elsewhere points out, though we *speak* of this baby as absolute subject of its world, it cannot really be this at all – quite the contrary. What the baby knows at this stage is, rather, the *asubjectivity* of total presence. The infant is at first not yet One, but Zero (mathematically zero is never nothing, nor is it something); for One to exist at all, two are needed, even if the second is in fact the

4. Jacques Lacan, 'The Mirror-phase as Formative of the Function of the I', trans. Jean Roussel, *New Left Review*, No. 51, Sept/Oct. 1968, pp. 72–3, a translation of a paper read to the International Congress of Psycho-analysis at Marienbad in 1949 and printed in *Ecrits*, 1966.

reflection in the mirror. Zero is not identical with itself, whereas One, like all objects, is. Zero indicates the lack, it is a situation of non-relationship in which identity is meaningless, but because it makes the lack visible, it sets in motion the movement forward. Then in the mirror game, what has been foreshadowed in the baby as Zero is re-evoked and the lack defined as absence. The lack of object forces the baby out of Zero into constituting himself as One who thus must know two, and who *acknowledges difference*. In discovering through absence his subjectivity, the baby, by the nature of the act, must for ever desire the non-relationship and non-identity of Zero. So must romantic poets and mystics: to be in a state of unity, 'at one with the world', is to be the asubjective zero from whence we came. The subject is constituted as the opposition between presence and absence, its foundation is dependent upon the discovery of difference.

The child at first does not, then, differentiate himself from others. And this essential differentiation does not happen all at once. But at the same time, the baby is fascinated by human faces and figures and he makes an initial identification with these whole and unified figures as later he is to gain his own unified image in the mirror. The baby is helpless, 'still sunk in his motor incapacity and nurseling dependency', but the image he is given of himself, through others and then in the mirror, is not helpless – on the contrary it is whole and coordinated. The mirror-image *must* be more perfect than itself – the itself that is not yet constituted – as Narcissus discovered to his cost. Because he stayed hooked on his image and couldn't tolerate its absence, Narcissus never constituted himself as subject. But these identifications with images (or *as* images) only presage the later identifications with other people. What, however, is crucial for our purposes is that the very self, the subject, is only created as a *difference*. An aspect of the self is thus in some way always only a mirror-reflection, an alienated image from which many mystical and philosophical arguments (among which we must count Laing's) would try to release us with the suggestion that we should return to the initial illusion of primordial unity: Zero that mis-thinks itself as One.

Paradoxically, then, this very wish to return is dependent on the separation having taken place; the very notion of desire cannot come into being before there is something missing, *desire* (as opposed to the baby's or animal's *need* which can be fulfilled by a real object) is never satisfiable as it relates to this absence or lack of object and what it would have must be a phantasy. The original lack of the object (the mother's breast) evokes the desire for unity and is thus the structure on which identifications will build. Both the identifications the child is to make and the object relations it is to take up are based on recognition of absence or the discovery of *difference*.

Thus the object, the subject and the identifications made can all be restated in terms of the recognition of difference. At the moment of the mirror-phase this is dual – the establishment of One by the recognition of Two – and hence circular. For instance, the baby may see himself as object, see the mother as object or see himself as object in the eyes of his mother. There is no escape, within its terms, from this reciprocity.[5] Freud discussed the dubious safety of this situation on a number of occasions, perhaps most fascinatingly in his attempt to account for the 'Uncanny' and its relationship to the issues so central here: doubling, the compulsion to repeat, omnipotence of thought, death:

The theme of the 'double' has been very thoroughly treated by Otto Rank. He has gone into the connections which the 'double' has with reflections in mirrors, with shadows, with guardian spirits, with the belief in the soul and with the fear of death; but he also lets in a flood of light on the surprising evolution of the idea. For the 'double' was originally an insurance against the destruction of the ego, an 'energetic denial of the power of death', as Rank says; and probably the 'immortal' soul was the first 'double' of the body. This invention of doubling as a preservation against extinction has its counterpart in the language of dreams, which is fond of representing castration by a doubling or multiplication of a genital symbol. The same desire led the Ancient Egyptians to develop the art of making images of the dead in lasting materials. Such ideas, however, have sprung from the soil of unbounded self-love, from the primary narcissism which

5. This dual reciprocity of mother-and-child (which is never properly broken out of in psychosis) must underlie assertions that the bond is 'natural', that women are closer to nature, cows and what have you. This is our *cultural* way of representing the animal situation. In humans even such a seemingly 'natural' moment is achieved through the ever-present retrospect of culture.

dominates the mind of the child and of primitive man. But when this stage has been surmounted, the 'double' reverses its aspect. From having been an assurance of immortality, it becomes the uncanny harbinger of death.

The idea of the 'double' does not necessarily disappear with the passing of primary narcissism, for it can receive fresh meaning from the later stages of the ego's development. A special agency is slowly formed there, which is able to stand over against the rest of the ego, which has the function of observing and criticizing the self and of exercising a censorship within the mind, and which we become aware of as our 'conscience'. In the pathological case of delusions of being watched, this mental agency becomes isolated, dissociated from the ego, and discernible to the physician's eye. The fact that an agency of this kind exists, which is able to treat the rest of the ego like an object – the fact, that is, that man is capable of self-observation – renders it possible to invest the old idea of a 'double' with a new meaning and to ascribe a number of things to it – above all, those things which seem to self-criticism to belong to the old surmounted narcissism of earliest times.[6]

The 'double' that is the first conception of the self (the mirror-image), thus becomes the menacing agency of conscience that Lacan speaks of as the I-ideal and that Laing refers to as 'murderous'. But again the apparent similarity hides the real difference; Freud's footnote describes the position that Laing adopts:

I believe that when poets complain that two souls dwell in the human breast, and when popular psychologists talk of the splitting of people's egos, what they are thinking of is this division (in the sphere of ego-psychology) between the critical agency and the rest of the ego, and not the antithesis discovered by psycho-analysis between the ego and what is unconscious and repressed.[7]

Such an interpretation is mandatory once one has dismissed, as Laing has, the importance of the unconscious.

The way out of this duality is never forever taken. Its reciprocal and circular relationships manifest themselves throughout life as the expressions of the various desires that the person has to return to things past, to restore the status quo, to retreat to a

6. Freud, 'The Uncanny', 1919, S.E., Vol. XVII, pp. 234–5.
7. ibid., p. 235, n. 2.

position of non-difference, in other words, to achieve the annihilation of the other person in whose presence one had first to establish one's own subjecthood. (The dualism appears too in psychosis.) This idea is a part of Freud's highly speculative and, at first, tentative postulation of a primary death-drive, a conservative psychical urge to restore the organism to its prior condition which in the very beginning was inanimacy. 'The aim of all life is death', or as a very different thinker, Engels, had already put it:

Already no physiology is held to be scientific if it does not consider death as an essential element of life . . . the *negation* of life as being essentially contained in life itself, so that life is always thought of in relation to its necessary result, death, which is always contained in it in germ. The dialectical conception of life is nothing more than this. But for anyone who has once understood this, all talk of the immortality of the soul is done away with . . . Here, therefore, by means of dialectics, simply becoming clear about the nature of life and death suffices to abolish an ancient superstition. Living means dying.[8]

As with sexuality and the unconscious, Freud with the death-drive started to specify and define what others long before had known, but only vaguely. We have, then, so far, two stages, and if I have reversed their order it is partly for the purposes of elucidation and partly with the intention of making clear that the situation cannot be reduced to chronological development, though clearly in the growth of the young child this is also relevant. I would like just to give a brief resumé. Freud 'discovered' the death-drive by analysing the game of his grandson, in which he first compulsively repeated the disappearance of an object/person and finally triumphantly and no less repetitiously regained it. An earlier hunch that the aim of life was death was radically transformed by his observation of this incessant, conservative game. His patients had long since been compulsively repeating unpleasant situations from their past; like everyone else, Freud knew of the 'uncanny' sensation of a fate that forces one, albeit unconsciously, into the same position time and again.

8. Engels, *Dialectics of Nature*, 1875–83, Lawrence & Wishart, London, 1954, pp. 387–8. Actually this quotation from Engels also smacks heavily of the effort to find the dialectic within the subject which I criticized in the case of Reich.

The point here is that bio-psychological considerations, with which Freud was most concerned when he first proposed the death-drive in *Beyond the Pleasure Principle*, made him suggest a dualism of drives: the death-drive which impels towards repetition and conservation, and the sexual drive which pushes forward to the production of new forms. But this dualism does not persist even at the moment of its inception for these, though in constant battle, can, because of their dialectical relationship, their total inter-dependency, also in part become attached to each other and establish a new contradiction, as in sadism, which will then in its turn enter into a new relationship with another force. Both drives are in operation (as always) in the mirror-phase. But just as the Zero of the neonate would be a trap of death if not moved out of, so too would this enclosed system of the fascination with images, doubles, dualities. It is now that we enter into the dangers of incest and the necessity of the Oedipus complex and of its overcoming.

Taking as always the boy, whose subjecthood is the concern of patriarchal culture, the third stage can be perceived and the homologous structure of all three recognized. The newborn baby who does not want to lack the breast has become the as yet scarcely verbal infant who does not want his mother's absence; what at both points has been required is to remain indistinguishable. Now this desire to be 'at one' can be expressed sexually. To remain joined to his mother he must *be* his father and the possibility of identification has already been twice heralded in the resolution of the lack of the breast and the absence of the self. But taking up this sort of position, that is attempting to occupy the place of the real father, is untenable because there *is* a real father already there or, more importantly, because the law forbids it; the rivalry is too great and thus the circularity of the dyad that the boy would preserve must for the first time be given up. In order for the boy to abandon this effort at reunion a further instance of lack-absence-differentiation is brought to bear: the possibility of the absent penis, castration. Once again the most important aspect of any object relationship makes itself felt – the *lack* of the object. The threat of castration is not, as we have seen, the same as the frustration of the actual removal of a real object – the breast or later the mother's presence, but no less than this it involves a relationship with the lack of an object. So the Oedipus triangle brings into play, for its resolution, a further term: castration. Lacan points out that there are two things that can never really be known but are always recognized: death and the father's role in procreation. It is the place of the father, not the actual father, that is thus here significant, and it is to this acknowledgement or recognition that Lacan attaches such importance. The little boy cannot *be* the father, but he can be summoned for his future role in-the-name-of-the-father. The symbolic father, for whose prehistoric death the boy pays the debt due, is the law that institutes and constitutes human society, culture in the fullest sense of the term, the law of order which is to be confounded with language and which structures all human societies, which makes them, in fact, human. This symbolic law of order defines society and determines the fate of every small human animal born into it:

> Symbols in fact envelop the life of man in a network so total that they join together, before he comes into the world, those who are going to engender him *'par l'os et par la chair'*; so total that they bring to his birth, along with the gifts of the stars, if not with the gifts of the fairy spirits, the design of his destiny; so total that they give the words which will make him faithful or renegade, the law of the acts which will follow him right to the very place where he *is* not yet and beyond his death itself . . .[9]

Before it is born the child is assigned a name and is son or daughter of — ; it has to learn to fit into this already ascribed place. Whatever the child does, whatever the specific accidents of its individual history, all take place within the larger framework of this human order. It is within the Freudian 'unconscious' that the laws of this order speak. To take it back for a moment into Freudian terms, the baby has to find its place within the unconscious system, has to struggle to establish its own individual ego, harmoniously and disharmoniously, in the order of human society that expresses itself in the unconscious, or rather, that the unconscious *is* – where id is, there must ego come to be.

Freud made a schematic statement to the effect that the system

9. Jacques Lacan, 'The Function of Language in Psychoanalysis', trans. A. Wilden, in *The Language of Self*, op. cit., p. 42.

into which he later divided mental life, the id, the superego and the ego (all of which it should be remembered are in part always unconscious) represent roughly the organic past, the cultural past and the present. This is important for it is only later that the child acquires a superego (the cultural past) and this is as a result of the dissolution of the Oedipus complex and consequently of the crucial role played by the father; it is here that the child emphatically acquires the patriarchal social order.

We are, of course, still left with the question of why human law should be embodied in the father? The father, in the context of the Oedipus complex, is not a part of a dyadic relationship of mother and child, but a third term. The self and the other of the mother-and-child has its duality broken by the intervention of this third term, one who here represents all that is essential to society – its laws. Maud Mannoni writes (in cautioning against the prevalent and fatal mistake of substituting the actual father for the father's function):

> Only the Symbolic dimension (the third element which intervenes in the dual relation of the child to the mother) can enable the subject to disentangle his words from all the snares and fascinations in which he has been lost at certain stages of his existence – to disengage them too from all the struggles for face or struggles to the death which are specific to dual situations.[10]

This symbolic dimension is only something the father represents, it is not his exclusively – thus the small boy with his gone/there game over his absent mother was allowing a symbolic dimension to enter into their relationship; through his game the child has found the symbolic mother.

We are dealing here with three difficult but closely related issues: the function of the maternal uncle, the role of the phallus (and castration), and the special nature of the symbolic father. The maternal uncle is relatively straightforward: he prevents the circularity of incest or the repetition at the level of kinship of dyadic relationships, he mediates between his sister and brother-in-law and also between generations in his particular relationship to his nephew. The phallus – I shall return to this – presents the

10. Maud Mannoni, *The Child, His 'Illness' and the Others*, Pantheon Books, New York, 1970, p. ix.

same function at another level; it, too, mediates and breaks up the possibility of incest and the dyadic trap. The privileged status of the father entering into the symbiotic situation of mother and child embraces both of the other propositions. Although there has been a great deal of refutation of Freud's suggestion, first elaborated in *Totem and Taboo*, of a primal murder of an original mythical father, the reasons which led him to hypothesize this have been in fact well appreciated and his mythology reworked by Lévi-Strauss in an attempt to preserve what is necessary within it.

Arguing from his analysis of the celebratory totem meal – the one occasion on which the absolutely forbidden is allowed and enjoyed – Freud postulated that the 'earliest' observed society, a matrilineal one, must have lying behind it a previous system. Tentatively and schematically Freud suggests that to account for the prevalence of totemism and its exogamous function (one must not have intercourse with anyone within the same totemic clan), the fraternal groups with equal rights (observable totemic systems) must one day have banded together to kill and devour the father who had kept all the women for himself. This is only a myth – only it is a very important one.

> The violent primal father had doubtless been the feared and envied model of each one of the company of brothers: and in the act of devouring him they accomplished their identification with him, and each one of them acquired a portion of his strength. The totem meal, which is perhaps mankind's earliest festival, would thus be a repetition and a commemoration of this memorable and criminal deed, which was the beginning of so many things – of social organization, of moral restrictions and of religion.[11]

We have seen from Lévi-Strauss's account that we have a universal situation in which women are exchanged: though the details that govern their mode of exchange vary, this is a fundamental fact. Within totemism there are two taboos: that against the destruction of the totem figure (the representative of the primal father) and that against incest. We can see how the one preserves the father as law-giver and the other institutes the maternal uncle as the crucial figure of the exogamous system. As

11. Freud, *Totem and Taboo*, op. cit., p. 142.

in the Oedipus complex – the particular heir to this social myth – the two taboos are: do not kill your father and do not sleep with your mother (sister). Freud comments:

> The two taboos of totemism with which human morality has its beginning are not on a par psychologically. The first of them, the law protecting the totem animal, is founded wholly on emotional motives: the father had actually been eliminated, and in no real sense could the deed be undone. But the second rule, the prohibition of incest, has a powerful practical basis as well. Sexual desires do not unite men but divide them. Though the brothers had banded together in order to overcome their father, they were all one another's rivals in regard to the women. Each of them would have wished, like his father, to have all the women to himself. The new organization would have collapsed in a struggle of all against all, for none of them was of such over-mastering strength as to be able to take on his father's part with success. Thus the brothers had no alternative, if they were to live together, but – not, perhaps, until they had passed through many dangerous crises – to institute the law against incest, by which they all alike renounced the women whom they desired and who had been their chief motive for despatching their father. In this way they rescued the organization which had made them strong . . .[12]

There are thus two aspects to the need for exogamy and its expression in totemism: the dead father and the structural asymmetry set up by the role of the brother. Of this mythologically created Symbolic father, Lacan writes:

> The Symbolic father is to be distinguished from the Imaginary father (often . . . surprisingly distant from the real father) to whom is related the whole dialectic of aggressivity and identification. In all strictness the Symbolic father is to be conceived as 'transcendent', as an irreducible given of the signifier. The Symbolic father – he who is ultimately capable of saying 'I am who I am' – can only be imperfectly incarnate in the real father. He is nowhere . . . The real father takes over from the Symbolic father.[13]

In simpler words, every time a mother threatens her child with 'I'll tell your father . . . he'll punish you', though she has in mind a real person and a real situation (which is by no means un-

12. ibid., p. 144.

13. Lacan, Seminar of March–April, 1957, quoted and translated by Anthony Wilden, *The Language of the Self*, op. cit., p. 271.

important), it is to the symbolic father behind the actual father that her words refer. The dead father of the law, who alone can say, like the Judaic God, 'I am who I am', is there, however weak or absent his real representative may be, however dominant the mother, however apparently 'matriarchal' the particular situation. And, in the last analysis, all because it is women, the *known* reproducers who are exogamously exchanged at the instigation of society.

That this mythological symbolic father is, in fact, a *dead* father has a further significance in this connection. Because of the primal murder with which Freud connects the onset of guilt, man acquires a debt for the deed done. This debt binds him for life to the law. Now all this mythology comes to rest in the more familiar myth of the Oedipus complex and the castration complex. When the little boy desires his mother and wants to murder the father who has exclusive possession of her, he confronts the two terrors of the totemic situation: murder and incest. It is here that the phallus enters to prevent murder, much as the maternal uncle enters to prevent incest. By learning that his father has the power – both to possess his mother and to castrate the child himself – the little boy, in recognizing this, pays the symbolic debt to the law of society which his father here represents. We are back once more with Freud's theory that as the castration complex smashes the Oedipal situation, so are social laws, a sense of justice, etc. set up with its replacement: the superego. We see too why castration and death are so closely linked.

Why, however, does the phallus come to hold such a privileged position? Freud referred to it constantly in terms such as 'the most precious possession': de Beauvoir and others eloquently describe its assertive, triumphant self-willed nature; but though this may be the subjective value attached to it, it is obviously a 'precious possession' for reasons beyond this. Lacan suggests that it represents the very notion of exchange itself – it is not a value in or of itself, but represents the actual value of exchange or the absent object of exchange, obviously symbolic exchange. The phallus is the very mark of human desire; it is the expression of the wish for what is absent, for reunion (initially with the mother).

In this theory the transition from need via demand to desire precisely indicates the progress of the human being from his animal status to his acquisition of his human-ness. This is in part a sophistication and in part a supplement to Freud's theory of the 'drive'. The baby *needs* food, protection, etc.; his mother then *demands* certain responses from him, as for instance in toilet training; in learning to understand the nature of his mother's demand, the child comes to desire to satisfy her desire. Desire is therefore always a question of a significant inter-relationship, desire is always the desire of the other. Need can be satisfied by an actual object; demand is *for* something whereas desire is the desire to have one's desire recognized – it is a yearning for recognition. Desire can thus be recognized but never satisfied, for, as the desire for what the other desires, it necessitates the wish to *be* the other one, or not to be different from the other one: the child desires to be what his mother desires he should be for her. He desires to *be* her with his phallus, but learns instead to be her phallus *for* her. We are back again with the inevitability of Reich and Laing's pursuit of an end to all difference and distinction – it is this end that *all* men desire for that is precisely what desire is. We are back too with the equation faeces – penis – baby. There is a further concept that must be integrated into this theory of desire; this is the notion of the lack of an object which in itself provides the very genesis of desire. At every level the relationship between mother and child is mediated by an absence or lack. We have seen this in the case of the child mastering absence with his cotton-reel and mirror game, but even before this there is the lack of the breast or whatever is needed. In its absence, need changes to demand (articulation), and if unsatisfied or unrecipro-cated, to desire. It is in expressing symbolically this essential 'lack' that the phallus features. The phallus is not identical with the actual penis, for it is what it signifies that is important. So for example, the mother who herself in her infancy has envied the penis that she lacked will find her substitute for it in the child to which she gives birth; in a sense then, she will want her child to represent her phallus, and, in turn, the child will desire to be what she desires of it . . . 'between the mother and the child, Freud introduced a third term, an Imaginary element, whose signifying role is a major one: the phallus'.[14] The phallus at this point indicates the desire of the mother (the desire for the phallus) into which the child is born; it thus constitutes a different order of experience, it represents what the child, both boy and girl, is meant to be symbolically. From the mother's point of view this is the process Freud describes as the equation: faeces–penis–child. The primary dyadic relationship between mother and child is never in itself only this, for it enters immediately into the possibility of a dialectical relationship between *three* terms: mother, child, phallus. So already, even so to speak *before*, he wants to be the father in relation to the mother (the Oedipus complex) the child wants to be the phallus for the mother or of the mother just as the mother wants him to be the final satisfaction of her own 'penis-envy'. In this way he wants to be the mother before he wants to be the father. But the symbolic father intervenes here, effectively taking over the signification of the phallus. The child wants to be the mother by wanting to be her phallus for her, but this very desire comes slap up against the function of the father – which is already to be the phallus for the mother; so just at the moment when he hopes to fulfil the desire of his mother, the presence of his father prevents him from doing this – desire is by definition unfulfillable. In submitting to the completely unreal possibility of castration the little boy acknowledges the situation and learns that one day he, too, will accede to the father's function. He pays thereby his symbolic debt to the father he has murdered in his rivalrous thoughts. So the phallus is intimately connected both with death and the symbolic father and thus with the law. In its imaginary role it too intervenes as, on a different level, do the symbolic father and the maternal uncle to break up a 'natural' situation (dyadic mother and child, biological family) and force it in a cultural direction. All bear witness to the fact that there must be an intermediary if any relationship is to move out of a vicious circle.

The situation is infinitely more complicated than this reduced and condensed version, above all because I have left out both here and in the equally abbreviated account of kinship structures

14. Jacques Lacan, Seminar of November–December 1956, quoted in Wilden, ibid., p. 186.

what really amounts to the whole framework and thrust of the theory: the importance of language. In a sense this is an inexcusable distortion of a theory but one necessitated by the specific concern: the psychology of women under patriarchy. The absence of any reference to language – the very world into which the human child is born and by which he is named and placed (man does not speak, language 'speaks' him) can only be excused by the inexhaustible number of other omissions, all of which, in that they refer to the way mankind becomes human and lives his humanity, have bearing on the formation and meaning of feminine psychology. I have really selected here only two themes: the significance of the symbolic father and of the phallus for the institution of civilization, and the fundamental part played by *difference* in the formation of the human subject. My purpose here is obviously in part polemical: I wish to counter with these arguments on the one hand, certain feminist reductions of any paternal and phallic significance to merely *male*-dominated cultures and on the other, the Reich–Laing–Firestone proposition that differences can be annihilated in the interests of harmony.

II Femininity

5 A Woman's Place

The feminist critics whose work has been discussed, and Wilhelm Reich in his early sociological writings, all praise Freud for the accuracy of his *observations* on the psychological characteristics of middle-class women who are oppressed under patriarchy. They condemn, however, his *analysis* on the grounds of its biological determinism and lament that he did not see the reality of social causation that was staring him in the face. There is justification for this attack only in so far as Freud often gave up on this question when he reached the 'biological bedrock' that underlay his psychoanalytic investigation. But what Freud did, was to give up precisely because psychoanalysis has nothing to do with biology – except in the sense that our mental life also reflects, in a transformed way, what culture has already done with our biological needs and constitutions. It was with this *transformation* that Freud was concerned. What we could, and should, criticize him for is that he never makes his repeated statements to this effect forcefully enough in the context of his accounts of psychological sexual differences. To the contrary, disastrously as it turned out for the future of the psychoanalysis of femininity, it is just at these points that he most frequently turned back from the problem, leaving the reader with a nasty feeling that Freud's last word on the subject referred her to biology or anatomy.

But clearly it was just such a taste of biology that 'post'-Freudian analysts savoured. As a criticism of this aspect of *their* work, the condemnations of Freud hold good. If any analysis of feminine psychology is to take place, it is high time that a decisive break was made both with biologism in general and with the specific contribution it makes here: that a so-called biological dualism between the sexes is reflected in mental life. Psychoanalysis is about the inheritance and acquisition of the human order. The fact that it has been used to induce conformity to specific social mores is a further abuse of it that largely has been made possible on the theoretical level by the same biological preoccupation of some post-Freudians. If anatomy were indeed destiny, as Freud once disastrously remarked, then we might as well all get on with it and give up, for *nothing* would distinguish man from the animals. But Freud made this fatal remark in the context of a science concerned with exploring human social laws as they are represented in the unconscious mind.

Both Reich and the feminist critics attack Freud for his ignorance of the determining effects of patriarchal culture, but ironically, in their own analyses, they forget exactly what they have remembered in their denunciatory rhetoric. In all the accounts the asymmetrical specific of a *father-dominated* social structure is forgotten in favour of male-female opposition with male domination. The general notion of opposition and social dualism is likewise an important feature of Laing's work. If such social dualism replaces biological dualism, circularity will be the inevitable result of the debate. The principle of dialectics is *contradiction*, not simple unity: elements contradict one another, resolve themselves, join together, and enter into further contradictions with other aspects – any 'unity' is a complex one containing contradictions. Even looking at the concept from a simplified, formalistic viewpoint, there must be at least *three* elements and the third cannot be the simple unity of the two, as Reich, Firestone and Laing (the authors who are interested in dialectics) would have it.

Freud's analysis of the psychology of women takes place within a concept that it is neither socially nor biologically dualistic. It takes place within an analysis of patriarchy. His theories give us the beginnings of an explanation of the inferiorized and 'alternative' (second sex) psychology of women under patriarchy. Their concern is with how the human animal with a bisexual psychological disposition becomes the sexed social creature – the man or the woman.

In his speculative works on the origins of human culture and man's phylogenesis, in particular in *Totem and Taboo* and *Moses and Monotheism*, Freud shows quite explicitly that the psychoanalytic concept of the unconscious is a concept of mankind's transmission and inheritance of his social (cultural) laws. In each man's unconscious lies all mankind's 'ideas' of his history; a history that cannot start afresh with each individual but must be acquired and contributed to over time. Understanding the laws of the unconscious thus amounts to a start in understanding how ideology functions, how we acquire and live the ideas and laws within which we must exist. A primary aspect of the law is that we live according to our sexed identity, our ever imperfect 'masculinity' or 'femininity'.

The determining feature of Freud's reconstruction of mankind's history is the murder of the primal father in a prehistorical period. It is this dead father that is the mark of patriarchy. In an imagined pre-social epoch, the father had *all* the power and *all* rights over *all* the women of the clan; a band of sons – all brothers, weak on their own, but strong together, murdered the father to get at his rights. Of course, they could not all have his rights and, of course, they must feel ambivalent about the deed they had committed. Totemism and exogamy are the dual signs of their response: in the totem, or symbolic substitute for the father, is guaranteed that no one else may kill him, or by then his heirs (each one of the brothers). Furthermore, not one of the brothers can inherit this father's right to all the women. For as they cannot *all* inherit, none shall. This is the start of social law and morality. The brothers identify with the father they have killed, and internalize the guilt which they feel along with the pleasure in his death. The father thus becomes far more powerful in death than in life; it is in death that he institutes human history. The dead, symbolic father is far more crucial than any actual living father who merely transmits his name. This is the story of the origins of patriarchy. It is against this symbolic mark of the dead father that boys and girls find their cultural place within the instance of the Oedipus complex.

In the situation of the Oedipus complex (which reiterates the rules of the totem and of exogamy) the little boy learns his place as the heir to this law of the father and the little girl learns her place within it. The Oedipus complex is certainly a patriarchal myth and, though he never said so, the importance of this fact was doubtless behind Freud's repudiation of a parallel myth for women – a so-called Electra complex. Freud always opposed any idea of symmetry in the cultural 'making' of men and women. A myth for women would have to bear most dominantly the marks of the Oedipus complex because it is a man's world into which a woman enters; complementarity or parallelism are out of the question. At first both sexes want to take the place of both the mother and the father, but as they cannot take *both* places, each sex has to learn to repress the characteristics of the other sex. But both, as they learn to speak and live within society, want to take the father's place, and *only the boy will one day be allowed to do so*. Furthermore both sexes are born into the desire of the mother, and as, through cultural heritage, what the mother desires is the phallus-turned-baby, *both* children desire to be the phallus for the mother. Again, *only the boy can fully recognize himself in his mother's desire*. Thus *both* sexes repudiate the implications of femininity. Femininity is, therefore, in part a repressed condition that can only be secondarily acquired in a distorted form. It is because it is repressed that femininity is so hard to comprehend both within and without psychoanalytic investigation – it returns in symptoms, such as hysteria. In the body of the hysteric, male and female, lies the feminine protest against the law of the father.[1] But what is repressed is both the representation of the desire and the prohibition against it: there is nothing 'pure' or 'original' about it.

The girl only acquires her secondary feminine identity within the law of patriarchy in her positive Oedipus complex when she is seduced/raped by, and/or seduces the father. As the boy becomes heir to the law with his acceptance of symbolic castration from the father, the girl learns her feminine destiny with this symbolic seduction. But it is less important than the boy's 'castration', because she has to some extent perceived her situation before it is thus confirmed by the father's intervention. She

1. It is the language or graphology of the body symptomatology, the traces of repressed femininity in hysteria, that the French women's liberation group, *Psychanalyse et Politique*, is deciphering. It was here in the analysis of the hysterical symptom in his earliest psychoanalytic days that, they consider, Freud stopped short. I am not sure that I would agree with the stress that I understand they put on the father's Oedipal 'rape' of his daughter, as it seems to me that the girl precisely has to learn the arts of seduction, of *winning* love.

has already acquired the information that as she is not heir to the phallus she does not need to accept symbolic castration (she is already 'castrated'). But without the father's role in her positive Oedipus complex she could remain locked in pre-Oedipal dilemmas (and hence would become psychotic), for the Oedipus complex is her entry into her human heritage of femininity. Freud always said that a woman was 'more bisexual' than a man. By this he seems to have been hinting at the fact that within patriarchy her desire to take the father's place and be the phallus for the mother is as strong as is the boy's ultimate right to do so. The bisexual disposition of her pre-Oedipal moment remains strong and her Oedipus complex is a poor, secondary affair. An affair in which she learns that her subjugation to the law of the father entails her becoming the representative of 'nature' and 'sexuality', a chaos of spontaneous, intuitive creativity. As she cannot receive the 'touch' of the law, her submission to it must be in establishing herself as its opposite – as all that is loving and irrational. Such is the condition of patriarchal human history.

With the ending of his Oedipus complex and the internalizing of the 'castrating' father as his authoritative superego, the boy enters into the prospect of his future manhood. The girl, on the contrary, has almost to build her Oedipus complex out of the impossibilities of her bisexual pre-Oedipal desires. Instead of internalizing the mark of the law in a superego to which she will live up, she can only develop her narcissistic ego-ideal. She must confirm her pre-Oedipal identification (as opposed to attachment) with the mother, and instead of taking on qualities of aggression and control she acquires the art of love and conciliation. Not being heir to the law of culture, her task is to see that mankind reproduces itself within the circularity of the supposedly natural family. The family is, of course, no more 'natural' than the woman, but its place within the law is to take on 'natural' functions. For sexuality, which supposedly unites the couple, disrupts the kingdom if uncontrolled; it, too, must be contained and organized. Woman becomes, in her nineteenth-century designation, 'the sex'. Hers is the sphere of reproduction.

This is the place of all women in patriarchal culture. To put the matter in a most generalizing fashion: men enter into the class-dominated structures of history while women (as women, whatever their actual work in production) remain defined by the kinship patterns of organization. In our society the kinship system is harnessed into the family – where a woman is formed in such a way that that is where she will stay. Differences of class, historical epoch, specific social situations alter the expression of femininity; but in relation to the law of the father, women's position across the board is a comparable one. When critics condemn Freud for not taking account of social reality, their concept of that reality is too limited. The social reality that he is concerned with elucidating is the mental representation of the reality of society.

6 The Cultural Revolution

As we have seen, Freud often longed for a satisfactory biological base on which to rest his psychological theories, and yet the wish was no sooner uttered than forgotten. From the work of Ernest Jones through to that of contemporary feminist analysts such as Mary Jane Sherfy,[1] the biological base of sexual dualism has been sought. Although there is an obvious *use* of the biological base in any social formation, it would seem dubious to stress this. For there seems little evidence of any biological priority. Quite the contrary; we are confronted with a situation that is determinately social. This situation is the initial *transformation* of biology by the exchange system expressed by kinship structures and the *social* taboos on incest that set up the differential conditions for the formation of men and women. This is not, of course, to deny that, as in all mammalian species, there is a difference between the reproductive roles of each sex, but it is to suggest that in *no* human society do these take precedence in an untransformed way. The establishment of human society relegates them to a secondary place, though their ideological reimportation may make them appear dominant.

It is not simply a question of the by-now familiar thesis that mankind, in effecting the move from nature to culture, 'chose' to preserve women within a natural ('animal') role for the sake of the propagation and nurturing of the species, for this suggestion sets up too simple a split between nature and culture and consequently too simple a division between the fate of the sexes. The very inauguration of 'culture' necessitated a different role. It is not that women are confined to a natural function but that they are given a specialized role in the formation of civilization. *It is thus not on account of their 'natural' procreative possibilities but on*

1. See Mary Jane Sherfy, 'A Theory on Female Sexuality', in *Sisterhood Is Powerful*, op. cit., pp. 220 ff.

account of their cultural utilization as exchange-objects (which involves an exploitation of their role as propagators) that women acquire their feminine definition. The situation, then, into which boys and girls are born is the same, the place to which they are assigned is clearly different. As it stands now, that place is in most important respects the same that it has always been: boys are to take over from fathers, girls are to want to produce babies. Any biological urge to do so is buried beneath the cultural demand that makes the way this wish is acquired coincident with human society itself. The technological conquest of the biological distinction between the sexes that Firestone and others recommend is redundant; in this instance, biology is no longer relevant. In an important sense, on this question, it has not been relevant since the foundation of human society. That foundation itself distinguished between the sexes.

In what way does this emphatic change of terrain affect the tasks of feminism? If we identify patriarchy with human history, the solution to the question of the oppression of women at first seems far less accessible than if we were to explore other theories. It has been suggested that we struggle for an 'ecological revolution' – a *humanized* brave new world of extra-uterine babies – or that in the power games of all men we locate and challenge the enemy. In the first proposition, technology conquers the biological handicap of women – their greater physical weakness and painful ability to give birth. In the second, a sociological analysis matches the perceived actuality of male superiority – men as such *do* have greater economic and political power and thus social equality should right the injustice. One or other, or a combination of both of these technological and sociological answers has held sway in all demands for change and all hopes for equity. Neither socialist practice nor Marxist theory in this field have been exempt from these essentially social-democratic visions.

It is no surprise that in these circumstances the feminist revolution has nowhere come about, and that women, in vastly differing ways and degrees remain 'oppressed'. Even if important details of these theories are correct, the posing of a biological problem and its technological solution or the sociological explanation of *male* domination and its overcoming (by consent or violence) are *both* at base misleading suggestions. It is the specific feature of patriarchy – the law of the hypothesized pre-historic murdered father – that defines the relative places of men and women in human history. This 'father' and his representatives – all fathers – are the crucial expression of patri-archal society. It is *fathers* not *men* who have the determinate power. And it is a question neither of biology nor of a specific society, but of *human* society itself.

Such a proposition possibly seems *more* generalized and its solution *less* available than the biological-technological and socio-logical theories. But I don't think this need be the case. Patriarchy describes the universal culture – however, each specific economic mode of production must express this in different ideological forms. The universal aspects of patriarchy set in motion by 'the death of the father' are the exchange of women and the cultural taboo on incest, but these are rehearsed diversely in the mind of man in different societies. It would seem to me that with capitalist society something new has happened to the culture that is patriarchy.

The complexity of capitalist society makes archaic the kinship structures and incest taboos for the majority of the people and yet it preserves them through thick and thin. Freud gave the name of the Oedipus complex to the universal law by which men and women learn their place in the world, but the universal law has specific expression in the capitalist family. (Anthro-pological arguments that make the Oedipus complex general without demarcating its specificity are inadequate; political sug-gestions that it is only to be found in capitalist societies are incorrect. What Freud was deciphering was our human heritage – but he deciphered it in a particular time and place.) *The capitalist economy implies that for the masses demands of exogamy and the social taboo on incest are irrelevant; but nevertheless it must preserve both these and the patriarchal structure that they imply.* Furthermore, it would seem that the specifically capitalist ideology of a supposedly natural nuclear family would be in harsh contradiction to the kinship structure as it is articulated in the Oedipus complex, which in this instance is expressed within this nuclear family. It is, I believe, this contradiction, which is already being powerfully felt, that must be analysed and then made use of for the overthrow of patriarchy.

Freud considered that 'discontent' (roughly, the sublimation and repression of desires) was a condition of civilization. It would seem indeed to be a condition, but one that Freud may well have been able to perceive precisely because it had reached a sort of 'ultimate'. Before I elaborate this point, I wish to distinguish it from one to which at first it seems to bear some resemblances. Herbert Marcuse, a Marxist who has consistently used psychoanalysis in the formation of his theories, claims that capitalist society demands a surplus repression – more repression than is needed by society in order to function. Marcuse argues that the reign of actual scarcity is all but over (or could be so), hence liberation from exploitative toil is possible; but capitalism, to retain its own nature (the exploitation of surplus-value), must create new needs, demand new 'performances' and thus institute unnecessary repression of the potentially liberated desires. It seems to me that this argument, although it welds together psychoanalytic and Marxist theory, in fact traps psychoanalysis within Marxist *economics*. In doing so it also casts, like Freud's own presentation of the progress of civilization, too evolutionary a light over the course of human history. Despite appearances and despite its important insights, this theory retains some of the worst aspects of both the sciences that it would use: an economism from Marxism and an evolutionary tinge from psychoanalysis. It is not that civilization has passed beyond the point where it needs its discontents but that there is a *contradiction* between the mode of the immediate expression-repression of these desires and the laws which forbid them as the very basis of culture. The ban on incest and the demand for exogamy howl so loudly in the contemporary Oedipus complex because they are reinforced precisely when they are no longer needed. It is only in this highly specific sense that capitalist society institutes a surplus repression; it is only the concept of *contradiction* (not that of *degree* implied by Marcuse's term 'surplus') that is of use in foreseeing any political transformation.

We can approach this proposition more concretely. Wars in no way change the basic relations of production but they do offer a different political situation and one that foreshadows the future. We can learn certain things from the last world war. Taking Britain as an example, we can see that in the period 1940–45 the family as we present it in our dominant ideologies virtually ceased to exist. In wartime the industrial employment of women was once more predominant and fathers were absent. For the first time there was planned alternative social organization to the family. Compulsory education was extended, pre-school crèches were provided, large-scale evacuation of children was organized, the state took care of food rations and ensured the basic necessary nourishment of small children and provided communal restaurants – all tasks normally left to the nuclear family. After a monumental post-war reaction, a repeat of certain of these trends is becoming visible today. With government plans for pre-school and nursery centres and the continual raising of the school leaving age, the school could rapidly become the main ideological institution into which the child is inserted. Of course such a development happens in an uneven and socially brutal fashion, but it is against such 'massifications' as the vast comprehensive school and the modern automated factory that romantics of the family and of the intimate and the private hold their own. Like the home-sweet-home songsters of the nineteenth century, they think they are looking back to a pre-capitalist golden age, but in fact they are only humming the descant. Capitalist society establishes the family in the context of its redundancy. The restoration or abolition of the family is not in itself important except as a symptom of this redundancy. It is the stress both in reactionary and in revolutionary arguments (such as Reich's) on the family and on its own contradictory nature under capitalism that has obscured the more fundamental contradiction between the specific conditions of the family and the demands of the law of human culture.

With capitalism (in its variant forms: imperialism, fascism, etc.), man reaches the limit of a historical development based throughout on class conflict. In the mass social work that man undertakes for the first time, the conditions of its own dissolution are powerfully present within capitalism. So, too, it would appear, are the conditions needed for a transformation of all previous ideology, the previous conditions of human culture. However, too often, while we acknowledge that the contradictions of capitalism as an economic system will only be resolved and released with its overthrow (and then in no straightforward manner), we forget that something similar holds true for its prevailing ideology. Why do we make this omission?

One important reason, I would suggest, is that we have tended to subject ideological analysis to economic analysis. (Although it seems to be doing the opposite, Marcuse's work is a case in point.) Or perhaps it would be more accurate to propose that the two spheres have become inextricably mingled, and theoretical progress depends not on amalgamation but on specification. However, such a commingling has still more serious consequences. Though, of course, ideology and a given mode of production are interdependent, one cannot be reduced to the other nor can the same laws be found to govern one as govern the other. To put the matter schematically, in analysing contemporary Western society we are (as elsewhere) dealing with two autonomous areas: the economic mode of capitalism and the ideological mode of patriarchy. The interdependence between them is found in the particular expression of patriarchal ideology – in this case the kinship system that defines patriarchy is forced into the straightjacket of the nuclear family. But if we analyse the economic and the ideological situation only at the point of their interpenetration, we shall never see the means to their transformation.

Under capitalism, just as the economic mode of production contains its own contradiction, so too does the ideological mode of reproduction. The social conditions of work under capitalism potentially contain the overthrow of the exploitative conditions into which they are harnessed and it is these *same* social conditions of work that make potentially redundant the laws of patriarchal culture. The working class has the power to take back to itself (for mankind) the products of the labour which are now taken from it; but no simple extension of this position can be taken to apply to patriarchal ideology. The same capitalist conditions of labour (the mass of people working together) create the conditions of change in both spheres, but because of their completely different origins, the change will come about in different ways. It is the working class as a class that has the products of its social labour privately appropriated by the capitalist class; it is women who stand at the heart of the contradiction of patriarchy under capitalism.

The controlled exchange of women that defines human culture is reproduced in the patriarchal ideology of every form of society. It goes alongside and is interlinked with class conflict, but it is not the same thing. It is not only in the ideology of their roles as mothers and procreators but above all in the very psychology of femininity that women bear witness to the patriarchal definition of human society. But today this patriarchal ideology, while it poses as the ultimate rationalization, is, in fact, in the slow death throes of its own irrationality; in this it is like the capitalist economy itself. But in both cases only a *political* struggle will bring their surcease. Neither can die a natural death; capitalism will, as it is all the time doing, intervene at a political level, to ensure their survival.

It is because it appears as the ultimate rationality, that critics mistake the Oedipus complex for the nuclear family itself. On the contrary, it is the contradiction between the internalized law of patriarchal human order described by Freud as the Oedipus complex, and its embodiment in the nuclear family, that is significant.

The patriarchal law speaks to and through each person in his unconscious; the reproduction of the ideology of human society is thus assured in the acquisition of the law by each individual. The unconscious that Freud analysed could thus be described as the domain of the reproduction of culture or ideology. The contradiction that exists between this law that is now essentially redundant but that of course still continues to speak in the unconscious, and the form of the nuclear family is therefore crucial. The bourgeois family was so to speak created to give that law a last hearing. Naturally enough, it is not very good at its job, so capitalist society offers a stop-go programme of boosting or undermining this family. It is because it is so obviously a point of weakness that so much revolutionary theory and strategy has concentrated on attacking it. But, as we have seen, its importance lies not *within* it so much as *between* it and the patriarchal law it is supposed to express. Of greater importance still is the contradiction between patriarchal law and the social organization of work – a contradiction held in check by the nuclear family.

It is at this moment, when the very structure of patriarchal culture becomes redundant, that with necessary perversity a vogue for man-as-animal comes into its own. Throughout history man has made strenuous intellectual efforts to distinguish himself from the beasts – this was always a dominant feature of his ideology; now, when the basis of his differential culture is in need of transformation, the only possible rearguard action is to consider that that culture was never in any case very significant. In the human zoo the male 'naked-ape' is naturally aggressive and the female naturally nurturative, they must regain their instinctive animal nature and forget what man has made of man. Such absurdities are a symptom of the dilemma of patriarchal human order. A symptom of a *completely different order* is the feminist movements of the nineteenth and twentieth centuries.

Under patriarchal order women are oppressed in their very psychologies of femininity; once this order is retained only in a highly contradictory manner this oppression manifests itself. Women have to organize themselves as a group to effect a change in the basic ideology of human society. To be effective, this can be no righteous challenge to the simple domination of men (though this plays a tactical part), but a struggle based on a theory of the social non-necessity at this stage of development of the laws instituted by patriarchy.

The overthrow of the capitalist economy and the political challenge that effects this, do not in themselves mean a transformation of patriarchal ideology. This is the implication of the fact that the ideological sphere has a certain autonomy. The change to a socialist economy does not by itself suggest that the end of patriarchy comfortably follows suit. A specific struggle against patriarchy – a cultural revolution – is requisite. The battles too must have their own autonomy. It seems to follow that women within revolutionary feminism can be the spearhead of general ideological change as the working class is the agent of the overthrow of the specifically capitalist mode of production. Neither contingent – women nor the working class – can act in such a role without a theory and a political practice. But there need be no order of priority here – it will depend on the conditions in which they have to take place. Because patriarchy is by no means identical with capitalism, the successes and strengths of the two revolutionary movements will not follow along neatly parallel paths. It is perfectly possible for feminism to make more intermediate gains under social democracy than it does in the first years of socialism. Nor, alternatively, because a socialist economy is achieved, does that mean that the struggle against patriarchy must cease. There is no question of either political movement taking precedence, or of either revolutionary group being mutually exclusive or even of each group containing only its own denominational membership. By this I mean that just as when the working class becomes revolutionary, people who do not actually come from the working class can make a political transformation of their own class origins and join it, so *when* the feminist movement has a revolutionary theory and practice, men too (if with difficulty) can give up their patriarchal privileges and become feminists. This is not to say that they can become members of the movement where it operates at the level of feminist consciousness any more than Marxist intellectuals can join the trade union movement which is the equivalent organization of working-class consciousness – they can merely support it in a practical fashion. I am making these comparisons only to help us situate ourselves in current debates on the left about political practice.

When the potentialities of the complexities of capitalism – both economic and ideological – are released by its overthrow, new structures will gradually come to be represented in the unconscious. It is the task of feminism to insist on their birth. Some other expression of the entry into culture than the implications for the unconscious of the exchange of women will have to be found in non-patriarchal society. We should also recognize that no society has yet existed – or existed for a sufficient length of time – for the 'eternal' unconscious to have shed its immortal nature. While matrilineages are certainly to be found, it seems as though matriarchies can be ruled out. Matrilineages only present us with a variation on the theme of the law-of-the-father. Socialist societies have had too little time on earth to have achieved anything as radical as a change in man's unconscious. And a sense of this can be read into a recent conversation between Mao Tse-tung and the late Edgar Snow. In this Mao claimed that despite collective work, egalitarian legislation, social care of children, etc., it was too soon for the Chinese really deeply and irrevocably to have changed their *attitudes* towards women. Or as he had told André Malraux: 'Of course it was necessary to give [women] legal equality to begin with! But from there on everything still remains to be done. The thought, culture, and customs which brought China to where we found her must disappear, and the thought, customs and culture of proletarian China, which does not yet exist, must appear. The Chinese woman doesn't yet exist either, among the masses: but she is beginning to want to exist. And then to liberate women is not to manufacture washing-machines.' It is with understanding how thoughts, customs and culture operate that psychoanalysis is concerned. We have to resist the temptation to neglect the analysis for a dream, for just as pre-Marxist nineteenth-century visions perceived communism as primitive communism, so too there is today a tendency to wish to see a post-patriarchal society in terms of a primitive matriarchy: the reign of nurturing, emotionality and non-repression. Clearly neither vision has much to do with the reality of the past or of the future.

Today, our specific ideology of a natural, biological family (our 'holy family') re-expresses as a repressed Oedipal saga the kinship structure to which it is in contradiction, and the problems of learning differences. Some way of establishing distinctions will always be crucial; that it should be this way is quite another question. However, in the meantime, entering into what would seem to be only a revamped patriarchal society, the little girl has to acquire, and quickly too, her cultural destiny which is made to appear misleadingly coincident with a biological one.

It is not a question of changing (or ending) who has or how one has babies. It is a question of overthrowing patriarchy. As the end of 'eternal' class conflict is visible within the contradictions of capitalism, so too, it would seem, is the swan-song of the 'immortal' nature of patriarchal culture to be heard.

APPENDIX:
PSYCHOANALYSIS AND VIENNA AT THE TURN OF THE CENTURY

Psychoanalysis and Vienna at the
Turn of the Century

In the summer of 1913 a Mrs de Castro, delegate from London to the Women's International Congress in Budapest, stopped off in Vienna for a preliminary conference. She was greatly impressed by the vitality and efficiency of the Viennese feminists and commented in her report, 'I was struck by the fact that so many of the leading spirits in the Viennese movement are evidently Jewesses. There is a very large and rich Jewish element in Vienna and they seem very enthusiastic supporters.'[1] Freud, who lived and worked in Vienna for all but the first years and last months of his life, developed his ideas on the sexual etiology of neuroses and later on feminine psychology in a city that was sexually profligate *and* was one in which for a long time there was a vocal feminist movement.[2] Neither of these factors determines the ultimate value of his concepts, they do not 'explain' them,[3] they are of interest either as corrective

1. MS Report from M. B. de Castro, No. 50/82/1118 in the suffragette collection at the London Museum, Kensington Palace.

2. I am, of course, selecting only those aspects of Viennese social life that have some bearing on the topic of feminine psychology and female sexuality.

3. In 1914, presenting his first full outline of the history of psychoanalysis, Freud wrote: 'We have all heard of the interesting attempt to explain psychoanalysis as a product of the Vienna milieu. As recently as in 1913 Janet was not ashamed to use this argument, although he himself is no doubt proud of being a Parisian . . . The suggestion is that psychoanalysis, and in particular its assertion that the neuroses are traceable to disturbances in sexual life, could only have originated in a town like Vienna – in an atmosphere of sensuality and immorality foreign to other cities – and that it is simply a reflection, a projection into theory, as it were, of these peculiar Viennese conditions. Now I am certainly no local patriot; but this theory about psychoanalysis always seems to me quite exceptionally senseless . . .' (Freud, 'On the History of the Psychoanalytic Movement', 1914, S.E., Vol. XIV, p. 39).

history or in those instances where he enters explicitly into dialogue with them in the formation of his ideas, as to an extent he does when writing about women.

Psychoanalysis is frequently rejected as the culture-bound phantasies of a man stuck in his time. Freud is 'a Victorian patriarch', in which case visions of puritan England are transposed to lascivious Vienna, or just as arbitrarily it is claimed that his nasty theory that sex was behind everything was the result of living in a cosmopolitan capital that was the fleshpot of Europe. Karl Kraus, the brilliant cartoonist and satirist whose snide lampoons Freud much enjoyed, depicted well some aspects of the fate of psychoanalysis for its originator, when he attacked it with the words: 'But since a genius does not need explanation, and since an explanation which defends mediocrity against genius is evil, there is only one justification left for psychoanalysis ... it still manages to be useful for the unmasking of psychoanalysis.'[4] Despite his attempts in his own autobiography to defend himself against such an occurrence, Freud has been personally 'psychoanalysed' by those seeking to deny psychoanalysis. In a recent lecture, Carl Schorske, a skilful critic, reinterpreted Freud's dream theory in *The Interpretation of Dreams* as Freud's compensation for personal political ambitions that were never realized; the major tenets of psychoanalysis were dreamt up to take revenge on a father and a profession that failed him; the concept of the Oedipus complex is an attempt to universalize his particular predicament. In one sense there is no reason why psychoanalysis should not be used to understand itself: *but* it only brings to comprehension unconscious or preconscious motivation; it is not a judgement or even a means of assessment; from this point of view, it leaves the person or event 'intact'. Less subtle attempts are frequently made to suggest that Freud's accounts of femininity are all the result of his authoritarian relationship to the women of his family or of his clinical practice. (Since Nazism, it has been in bad taste to reiterate the early condemnations of psychoanalysis as a 'Jewish disease'.)

Viennese sexual life, then, does not account for psychoanalysis, however Freud's reactions to it do have other interests for us.

4. Karl Kraus, *Nachts*, p. 77.

Of course these reactions are not the same as the theoretical observations made within psychoanalysis. In some ways Freud was as strong in his condemnation of repressive bourgeois morality as any of the later radical psychotherapists, and, if sometimes he may seem something of a stick-in-the-mud – as in his qualified but reiterated condemnations of masturbation[5] – Viennese conditions do offer some explanation for this attitude.

Vienna presented a familiar contrast between the restrictive morality of the bourgeois family and the sexual licence of the streets. *That* contrast was certainly reflected in the minds of Freud's patients, but it was superficial compared with the conflict between sexual desire and its repression. However, the more visible social contrast certainly interested Freud and his colleagues. On the dangers of sexual inhibition within the family Freud was quite explicit. He pointed out the damage done to both sexes by premarital abstinence: the extremely inhibiting and destructive effect of feminine sexual ignorance; the social and individual dangers of marital fidelity; the desperate inadequacy of contraception methods which, with other factors, led to – among other things – female anaesthesia or frigidity. Thus Freud condemned the practice of *coitus interruptus* as causing anxiety to whichever partner the couple decided should not reach satisfaction. Fear of pregnancy and the ill-health of the wife meant that the sexual life of a marriage (and with it a good part of the more general emotional and intellectual compatibility) could probably last not more than a few years. Freud had, indeed, many criticisms to make of monogamous marriage, and though his own was, by conventional standards, successful, one of his few remarks about it combines with an acknowledgement of his personal satisfaction his full awareness of the limitations of the institution. On the occasion of his golden wedding anniversary he commented: 'It was really not a bad solution of the marriage problem . . .'[6] For women in particular, there was

5. An interesting difference could be noted here between Reich and Freud; Reich, too, condemned masturbation – he was forced to do so by his sexual theories; Freud contrarily sought for some explanation of why it seemed to have such a deleterious effect.

6. Cited in E. Jones, *The Life of Sigmund Freud*, The Hogarth Press, 1957, Vol. III, p. 224.

supposed to be no before, after, or on the side, and on a number of occasions Freud indicated that adultery, or divorce, would save many a woman from a neurotic episode. Indeed, in 1903, he advocated that one of the most urgent and important tasks of medical science was to develop a satisfactory form of contraception. And before that he had been interested in his great friend Wilhelm Fliess's theories of periodicity because they would indicate limited fertility periods and thereby facilitate birth control.[7]

Thus, when Freud claimed that sexuality was beneath all neurotic disturbance, although he also intended something very different, nevertheless he did mean as well that sexual problems underlay neurotic outbreaks in a quite literal sense:

> It is under such conditions [sexual abstinence, non-consummation and frustration], extremely frequent in modern society, especially among women, that anxiety neurosis (of which phobias are a psychical manifestation) develops.[8]

> Several women [not satisfied with marriage and unconfident of their powers to resist other men] complained of an obsessional impulse to throw themselves out of the window, to stab their children with knives, scissors, etc.[9]

These *sociologically* oriented observations give that apparently radical dimension to his work, which is missing later. And it is at this level, too, that Freud's class awareness is at its height. For example, he discusses the fact that the working class is hell-bent on following the middle class into excessive sexual repression: he feels that a peasant or working-class girl, in particular, is still much less in danger of becoming neurotic because her pubescent sex is not repressed; it is, on the whole, as free as the adolescent boy's. The sexual habits of the bourgeoisie drive the men into immorality and perversion, the women into over-

7. Octave Mannoni (*Freud*, op. cit.) suggests a much more interesting future for Freud's interest in Fliess's periodicity – he suggests that many years later it found fruit as Freud's theory of the compulsion to repeat, part of which, as we have seen, was developed into the concept of the death-drive.

8. Freud, 'Obsessions and Phobias. Their Psychical Mechanism and Their Etiology', 1895 (1894), S.E., Vol. III, p. 81.

9. Freud, ibid., p. 76.

refinement, highmindedness and neurosis. Freud had little *parti pris*, but humanitarianism was an essential tool and inevitable by-product of his practice (later, he hoped that psychoanalysis would be freely available to all classes of the population). He vehemently castigated as completely unviable and as cruel the sexual impositions forced upon the individual by society; he was grateful as a researcher when a girl from a rural smallholders' family consulted him and allowed him to penetrate the hypocrisy and to break the taboos: 'I owed her a debt of gratitude for having made it so much easier for me to talk to her than to the prudish ladies of my city practice, who regard whatever is natural as shameful.'[10]

Once he had established the existence of infantile sexuality, Freud did not hesitate to draw the social conclusions: he emphatically believed that all children's questions should be answered honestly. He thought sexual enlightenment – or preferably, sexual openness – should greet children from as early an age as possible and he criticized the parents of his first child 'patient' – Little Hans – for stopping just short of giving the full details of sexual intercourse to their curious five-year-old. In particular, the muting of women's intellectual intelligence could be laid to a fair extent at the door of the even greater refusal in their case to give them sexual information in early childhood. Freud, of course, was well aware that telling a child about sexuality and reproduction did not solve any problems, for despite the most honest and accurate information children will believe according to their own phantasies, not according to adult rationality; it is simply that deception generates greater anxiety and an inquisitiveness bordering on the obsessional. Information should not be presented to children in obscure botanical terms of fertility as this only repeats their own myths; love should be stressed to counter their fears of violence. Grete, a young girl on the threshold of adolescence, wrote a diary which, in 1915, Freud recommended should be published. Grete, from an upper-class Viennese family, writes of the tortuous ways in which schoolgirls desperately tried to learn about sexuality. With her sister and a servant she spies on a neighbouring couple making love and when the maid tells her

10. Freud, *Studies on Hysteria 1893–1895*, S.E., Vol. II, p. 132.

that the woman will be 'torn', Grete, not understanding penetration, is scared that the woman will be crushed and battered beneath the weight of her husband and she vows never to marry; she learns of circumcision but decides that it is only the excessive cruelty of the Jews that allows such a practice, just as it is only Jews who could be shameless enough to strip naked for intercourse; she and her best friend believed that the wife 'made' the baby, but her elder sister 'enlightens' her that it is in fact the father. Through books, questions and observations, with fear and hilarity, she tries to discover 'the facts of life'; though bright at school, she cannot concentrate on her work and even her compulsive interest in sex is inadequate for, as she comments:

'. . . seeing and hearing don't take one very far. I've always kept my eyes open and I'm not so stupid as all that. One must be told by someone, one *can't* just happen upon it by oneself.'[11]

Fully aware of the dangers of deception and enforced ignorance, Freud was very liberal in his educational ideas. He supported campaigns for sexual reforms, though he distinguished his position from that of some more libertarian reformers. For instance in 1908, when Kraus's paper *Der Fackel* launched one of its major attacks on the Viennese sexual status quo, Freud, though welcoming such a move, stressed his different position: *Der Fackel* was promoting the idea of the healthy 'living out' of all desires, it wished for sexual release so that satiation could be attained, whereas psychoanalysis, Freud contended, was set only on relieving sexuality from its repression by a higher, superimposed agency; sexual control should be the choice of the individual, not the dictate of an alienating social system. In his turn, Karl Kraus found Freud's attitude reeked of Judeo-Christian notions that sex was sinful. It is at least true that where Freud was liberal in his opposition to bourgeois conventions, he was more strenuously antagonistic than some of his contemporaries to sexual corruption, to prostitution, hypocritical promiscuity and the prevalence of venereal disease.

A portrait of sexual life in Vienna at the turn of the century

11. *A Young Girl's Diary*, Allen & Unwin, 1971, p. 64.

is a familiar one; it is not essentially different from the two faces of Victorian England, though certain features give it a specific quality. Social life was still largely feudal and the practices of the nobility read more like an account of those of sixteenth-century England[12] overlaid with the more sophisticated financial customs of this banking city. Thus Lady Paget, wife of the British minister to the court of the Emperor Franz Joseph just before the First World War, commented with some surprise that the titled men who exclusively frequented the court, who had two or three regular mistresses and any number of liaisons with actresses and dancers, often drew up formal contracts guaranteeing fixed payments (equivalent to alimony) and a recognition that they had been well served by their women. When his friend and colleague, Fritz Wittels, waxed eloquent on the glory of the woman as courtesan, Freud gave him short shrift:

The ideal of the courtesan has no place in our culture. We [as psychoanalysts] endeavour to uncover sexuality; but once sexuality is demonstrated, we demand that the entire repression of sexuality become conscious and that the individual learn to subordinate it to cultural requirements. We replace repression by healthy suppression. The sexual problem cannot be settled without regard for the social problem; and if one prefers abstinence to the wretched sexual conditions, one is abstinent under protest.

The sense of having sinned which opposes sexuality is very widespread, and even the sexually free feel that they are grave sinners.

A woman who, like the courtesan, is not trustworthy in sexuality is altogether worthless. She is simply a *Haderlump* [Viennese slang for 'scamp', 'ragamuffin', 'cad'].[13]

Otto Rank, taking the minutes of the weekly meeting of Viennese psychoanalysts at which this was discussed, records

12. See Lawrence Stone's descriptions in his section on 'The Family' in *The Crisis of the Aristocracy*, London, 1965, and Thomas Masaryk's comments on the nineteenth-century period of Austro-Hungarian history: 'The underestimation of women is a sign of a polygamous society; and as a matter of fact we are still living in polygamy ...' (quoted in Capek, *Masaryk*, p. 136).

13. *Minutes of the Vienna Psycho-Analytic Society*, No. 24, 15 May 1907, New York, International Publishers, 1962, Vol. I, p. 200.

that Wittels claimed to have been dumbfounded by Freud calling a courtesan a *'Haderlump'*. Wittels's pseudo-pedestal treatment of women as sexual objects was a frequent theme of the day and one that Freud tried to explain in his psycho-analytic writings; both it and Freud's reaction to it raise the type of questions familiar to us today in discussions of porno-graphy. We should bear in mind that any eroticism is suspect in a society that degrades women.

Stefan Zweig, later a friend of Freud's, recalls his youth in Vienna at the end of the nineteenth century:

> Though I try hard to remember, I cannot recall a single comrade of my youth who did not come to me with pale and troubled mien, one because he was ill or feared [venereal] illness, another because he was being blackmailed because of an abortion, a third because he lacked the money to be cured without the knowledge of his family, the fourth because he did not know how to pay hush money to a waitress who claimed to have had a child by him, the fifth because his wallet had been stolen in a brothel and he did not dare go to the police. The youth of those pseudo-moral times were much more romantic and yet more unclean, much more excited and yet more depressed, than the novels and dramas of their official writers depict them.[14]

Venereal disease was rife and not easily curable; Zweig estimates that every sixth house in Vienna displayed a sign indicating a V.D. specialist's residence. Prostitutes were harder to avoid than find 'at every hour and at every price, and it cost a man as little time and trouble to purchase a woman for a quarter of an hour, an hour or a night, as it did to buy a package of cigarettes or a newspaper'.[15] Prostitution was hierarchized, armies walked the streets, there were the so-called 'love-quarters' where women displayed themselves in windows, upper-class procurers were above the law and demi-mondaines were able to practise without the common prostitute's licence and medical check-ups. If virginity was essential for 'decent' women, and a wife's fidelity necessary even within impotent marriages, abstinence was considered positively harmful for young men. Thomas Masaryk, later President of Czechoslovakia, recalled that when as an

14. Stefan Zweig, *The World of Yesterday*, Cassell, 1943, p. 77.
15. ibid., p. 72.

adolescent he had gone to the doctor for a small facial pimple, he was advised that a prostitute was the best cure for this symptom of superabundant vitality in the blood. Prostitutes and compulsive masturbation were a man's way out of sexual abstinence, but once the anarchic forces of sexuality were released it was feared that chaos would come again; in curing hypothetical sickness of the blood they caused actual venereal disease or new imaginary diseases. An issue of the day was whether or not masturbation produced such an illness. Freud's group considered the question, and Freud thought its deleterious effects psychological and not organic, symptomatic not causative of other problems. But Masaryk, recording the great prevalence of the practice in the schoolboys he taught in another part of the Austro-Hungarian Empire, felt it had adverse moral effects – it led to excessive, precocious sexuality and to perversion. The endless arguments read rather like the debates that surround the question of soft-drug-taking today: is it a sign or cause of disturbance; is it physically, mentally, morally or socially dangerous? Freud's position, which was both complex and interesting, was, I would say, liberal.

The intellectual contortions and psychological tensions that surrounded the question of sexuality, naturally affected the attitude to women. The savage hypocrisy of sexual life found its sublime expression either in the familiar dichotomy of goddess and prostitute or of women as glorious or hideous sexuality. If sexuality was regarded with tortuous ambivalence, so were its representatives – women. Perhaps what is unusual about this period is that this banal ideology of women took on a new life and inspired some great artists and curious thinkers. Its most notorious exponent was Otto Weininger, who claimed to have originated the concept of bisexuality. (Freud in repudiating Weininger's claim to originality here had to acknowledge his own debt, for this treasured theory, to his friend Fliess. However, Freud's and Weininger's meanings are poles apart.) Weininger exemplified the tensions of his society – a Jew who hated Jews, a man torn apart over the opposition between sexual desires and the Judaic moral codes, a man who captured the contradictions in a sexual image. To Weininger there was a fundamental and tragic conflict between the sexes, with rationalism dominant in men and sexuality in women. But the dilemma goes deeper for, in differing proportions, there are incompatible and eternally irreconcilable elements of each sex, within every individual – hence his use of the term 'bisexuality'. Of this warring pair Weininger loathed the feminine which he also regarded as Jewish. He found this too prevalent in himself, and the tension unbearable. Out of his life came his theory, out of this theory his death by suicide in 1903.

It may have been a matter of life or death whether you loathed the feminine-sensual as Weininger did or whether, like Fritz Wittels, Karl Kraus and a hundred other men, you loved it and thus secularized your creative muse and glamorized from a distance the values you would rather not live by. It may have meant suicide or great art, but the basic attitude was the same: woman as sensuality was creative or destructive, but the fundamental vision was one and the same thing. It is more or less fair to say that the attitude to women *was* the attitude to sexuality transposed on to a 'higher', even more mystified plane. Though this attitude is not substantially different from that found in other capitalist-industrial epochs, it did reach new heights with the neo-romanticism of the 1890s.

The Viennese artists of the turn of the century were heirs to the misogyny of Nietzsche and Schopenhauer. Just as the anarchic power of sexuality was dreaded, so for these philosophers was the irrational and elemental sensuality of women. But then again, irrational and elemental though it may be, so too is it natural, spontaneous, soulful; many writers, without rejecting their misogyny, turned back from Nietzsche and Schopenhauer to Goethe and his conception of the eternal feminine principle which was the source of the perpetual renewal of life and art. Within psychology, this thesis found its apotheosis in Jung's works. In writers like Kraus the feminine qualities were elevated and set against the rationalism of the male, which was held responsible for the inordinate value placed on arid technology and crass materialism – in the name of the feminine principle Kraus castigated the greed and corruption of his society. The painter Oskar Kokoschka took the proposition more literally: man passes, the feminine is the permanent life-sap, the feminine principle is not just an idea but a vital force;

so he had himself a doll made, of an ideal woman, silent and adoring, fashioned of skin and bone with real eyes. She sat beside him, the subject of some of his greatest paintings and representative of the source of all his inspiration. It cannot be said that the notion of a creative feminine principle did not serve the cause of art well, for this was an extraordinarily fertile period. Though its exposition amused him, Freud, however, would have little truck with the notion. His gallantry was more mundane.

In 1910 Gustav Mahler, whose music concentrated on an exploration of his own psychological state, visited Freud for a psychoanalytic consultation. The much-mocked diagnosis was a mother-fixation. In fact, this was no analysis but a once-only visit and Freud was only stating the obvious. It is nevertheless, whichever way one looks at it, an interesting event. Given Mahler's childhood, and given his wife Alma's assertion that he tried his utmost to make her look like his pathetic mother, with whom she independently considered him obsessed, it seems a likely hypothesis. But there is a level different from this realistic one. The notion of a creative feminine principle is obviously just a more rarefied version of the idolatry of maternity; an unresolved Oedipus complex such as Freud diagnosed would be likely to be visible in all who took their inspiration from this source. Freud's statement is both a self-evident comment on an actual situation, *and* a more intricate reflection on the psychic origin of ideas.

Freud's own relationship to the role of women in society was more down-to-earth. Though he held no exalted or debased concept, he certainly offered little hope. When, at the weekly psychoanalytic meeting, Fritz Wittels discussed an article on female physicians that he had written for *Der Fackel*, Freud analysed Wittels's archetypal ambivalence: his fear of women as sexual human beings. Wittels contended that women who had careers lost the glorious sensuality which it was their task on earth to offer. Freud shows the other side of the coin of this idolatry, but confirms from a different stance the futility of women studying. Culture (one should note he ascribes this to cultural not biological destiny) has burdened woman with a heavy share in sexual and reproductive life; for this reason she has less possibility of sublimating her sexual desires in the pursuit of learning, but she is not to be blamed therefore. Though he thought this a fact of cultural role division, Freud seems to have had no prejudice against the women who did manage to make it in the intellectual or artistic sphere: when in April 1910 a vote was taken as to whether or not to include women in the weekly psychoanalytic discussions, Freud criticized the three members (out of eleven) who opposed their acceptance as guilty of gross inconsistency. He was always most welcoming to women psychoanalysts. Lou Andreas-Salomé was the first to attend these select gatherings.

So far we have seen the situation of sexuality and femininity from the point of view of men. It must not be forgotten that although the position was very different from a woman's standpoint and that consequently women had different attitudes, male ideology was dominant and bound to determine to an extent the women's thinking and behaviour. Though feminism may have started to establish it, for most women there was no alternative non-patriarchal culture. Lou Andreas-Salomé tried to create such a culture in her own person, but what she achieved was in a sense a glorious parody of the masculine vision of women. Rose Mayreder was a contemporary and a critical sympathizer and author of a book on the women's movement taking place in Central Europe at that time; she singles out Lou as a woman who believed so fully in the meaning of the physiological differences between the sexes that she constructed a profound and independent feminine psychology thereon. A writer and analyst of talent, mistress of Nietzsche, Rilke, Tausk and many others, close friend of Freud, admired for her looks, character and intellect, Lou is impressive – but what really separates her from the living ideal of Wittels's courtesan? Is not her life the triumphant embodiment of the feminine principle, or Weininger's eternal opposition between the masculine and feminine? The feminine culture that Lou created in her person was the masculine ideology writ large: personally independent of men, she could only fashion herself within the terms of the choice this male vision offered. She was superwoman to Nietzsche's superman, the goddess of a misogynist society. Freud, who admired both her psychoanalytic work and her character, saw her as a close friend, not as an object for study, but accepting women who accepted themselves, he seemed to see no cause to criticize her for this nor for her rejection of a typical wifely and maternal role. Freud thought women's general destiny was wifehood and motherhood, but if some found satisfaction in other pursuits, he had no fault to find. Happiness was all.

Though Freud considered it a fundamental fact of human history that mankind was divided into two sexes, he did not see this as a simple opposition. When his colleague Otto Rank proposed that the unconscious was feminine (really another, this time psychoanalytic, version of the irrational creative feminine principle) Freud was emphatic in his disagreement. That he held libido to be masculine and that he considered both sexes to repress into the unconscious large parts of what is feminine are, as we have seen, different issues.

If Lou Andreas-Salomé lived the elevated status that men such as Wittels and Kraus accorded to femininity, most women were confined within the more negative aspects of such an attitude. In the autobiography of Nora Wydenbruck we have a picture of a young Austrian countess growing up in Viennese society at the turn of the century. Nora remembers being so terrified of her diplomat father that until the age of nine her life was a nightmare of fear: in her endless dreams her father appeared as an orang-outang. The victim of nervous collapses, cold-water cures and even semi-Freudian psychotherapy, she recollects that after reading Weininger's *Sex and Character* at seventeen, all the unhappiness of her life focused on a hatred of her own femininity. Later she hopes for a son who will compensate her for her female fate, but the reality of maternity only confirms her in her loathing of womanhood: 'the more I entered into the world of women, the more I disliked it.'[16] The autobiography reads like a Freudian case-book, and if the repudiation of femininity appears late-acquired and intellectually determined (reading Weininger) or socially realistic (the nuisance of her new-born baby) then we must also recall that her mother had so much wanted a son that she not only refused

16. Nora Wydenbruck, *My Two Worlds*, Longmans, Green, 1956, p. 78.

her daughter any affection but quite often thought of her as a boy. Certainly the situation was specifically culture-determined, but the 'determinism' is many-faceted, and when does culture begin?

The feminist movement grew up in such an atmosphere and, as today, its own ideology in part reflected these struggles to define femininity. In part, in its political practice, it began to change them and to institute new cultural possibilities. It seems that, at this point, feminists offered little or no response to Freud's work – his theories of feminine psychology were not yet developed, his work in general was little known. What reaction they did have was to share the prevalent distaste for his notion of the omnipresence of sexuality; idealistically they stressed that life was not so murky and childhood was vulnerable but innocent. But if they remained unconcerned by Freud, their presence and their demands were certainly a vocal part of Freud's intellectual and cultural environment. Freud was most interested in contemporary demands for women's emancipation. In 1880 he translated into German and published John Stuart Mill's essay on the subjugation of women. 'Anna O.', the most significant of the hysterical patients that he and Breuer wrote about in *Studies in Hysteria* (the particular case and its write-up was, in fact, Breuer's) was, without her pseudonym, Bertha Pappenheim, who, after the resolution of her hysterical symptoms, became a social worker and active campaigner for women's rights; she was also a long-standing friend of Freud's wife, Martha. Although Freud's letter to Martha, who was then his fiancée, about Mill's tract is full of patriarchal protectiveness (he will keep his dear girl safe from the weariness, fever and fret of the world outside the home), this is not the main tenor of his objection. To Freud, Mill is an idealist, a Utopian who shuts his eyes to the real conditions of existence. Though, as he often contends, Freud feels women's present lot should be alleviated, to call their vocation slavery because it is different from men's, as Mill does, is absurd and offensive. Freud gingerly enters into familiar romantic speculations: isn't it in fact a *more* honourable and desirable role? Some years later, speaking less intimately to the psychoanalytic circle, he stressed that Mill ignored the problem that it was impossible for women both to raise children and to pursue a career. The perspective, as was also true of a lot of feminist writings, was, of course, middle-class; as such it was realistic with the still large families and increasing shortage of servants – but such conservative realism is no justification either for a political theory or for opposition to one.

Freud considered that a woman's cultural fate of having to dedicate herself more exclusively to sexuality and propagation than did a man, meant that her psychic reactions were also more oriented to love and sensuality. It was thus harder for her to sublimate these drives in the interest of work or cultural pursuits; for this reason she lagged behind man in the achievements of civilization and power, she has had to toss away kingdoms: 'A sculptress loses her skill when confronted with the task of modelling the male body; a girl whom her teacher embraces whenever she successfully accomplishes a task, cannot achieve anything any more.'[17] The implicit message in these, his 'off-stage' remarks, is that a woman who is sexually and maternally satisfied is a satisfied woman.

But what of the large army of dissatisfied women emancipators? Freud felt that the stringent sexual mores of the day were driving them to protest. Many of their demands were just and should be answered, but the basic hypothesis of women's parity or 'sameness' with men was untenable. In this context, Freud was more lenient than most of his fellow-analysts or their colleagues. Fritz Wittels's description of 'our accursed present-day culture in which women bemoan the fate that they did not come into the world as men; they try to become men (in the feminist movement). People do not appreciate the perversity and senselessness of these strivings; nor do the women themselves.'[18] In *Der Fackel* Kraus, too, scoffed at the women's movement which to him was betraying the glorious feminine principle that women were supposed to embody. In substance Freud's argument about sexual satisfaction does not seem altogether different, but his preoccupation was with explaining not castigating a phenomenon

17. *Minutes of the Vienna Psychoanalytic Society*, No. 25, 9 October 1907, op. cit., p. 211.
18. ibid., No. 44, 11 March 1908, p. 349.

and with seeing women in their cultural and not artistically symbolic role.

Many people who lived in Vienna in the decades before the First World War looked back on the period as one of unusual tension and intensity. The death of the longest-ever reigning monarch, Franz Josef, in 1916, seemed even at the time to fore-shadow the end of the thousand-year-old empire. Introspection, death-wishes, the cult of loneliness and psychological insight, satires and comedies on decadence and immorality (e.g. Alfred Schnitzler) were certainly prevalent, and if we want to generalize, then, in retrospect, the cultural products and social life would seem suitable as the accompaniments of the decline and fall of a multi-national empire. Experimentation and novelty, of course, were also a symptom; the preoccupation with non-realistic language and the revolt against musical tonality can be singled out as examples of an urge for change and renewal. What appears ('*schein*') versus what is ('*sein*') are typical concerns, exemplified for instance in Musil's work. But Vienna was not just the capital of the largest empire and a cultural, cosmopolitan centre, it was also the most Jewish city in Europe. Zionism and modern anti-semitism were born there. The Jewish population grew to 8·7 per cent by 1910, and in a city in which newspapers had an extraordinary importance, 75 per cent of journalists were reputed to be Jewish and Jews made up 33·6 per cent of all university students. Julius Braunthal, the Austrian socialist, comments that in Vienna, where the cultures of the European East and West met, Jewish talent flourished as never before since the days of Moslem rule in fifteenth-century Granada. Jews had achieved an integration, a name and a place in Vienna that made the discrimination against them somehow even more disturbing – the tensions of pride in Judaism and a repudiation of all the semitic traits of a ghetto people are manifest in artist after artist. Pride in secular Judaic traditions (particularly humour and rationalism) and yet a refusal to be type-cast: Freud is a mild case in point. Or as Lassalle once said of himself, he hated two things, Jews and *littérateurs*, and he had the misfortune to be both.

Out of the strains of sexual life, the political contradictions of an autocratic, feudal court, a rigidly hierarchized society in a

rapidly industrializing city, from the particular tension of integrated but rejected Jewry (an overwhelming percentage of the
great artists and thinkers were Jews), came probably both
widespread neurosis and a high level of a particular type of
artistic productivity. Certainly its inhabitants saw Vienna this
way: Kraus comments over and over again on the neurotic
society, reflecting that where Prussia was a place in which one
was free to move but one's mouth was gagged, Austria was an
isolation cell in which one was allowed to scream.

Against this background, against these preoccupations,
Freud's work on femininity can be set. It is useful to know
them if for no other reason than to refute inaccurate histories,
but there are other elements than these, his reading and scientific
interests, to name the most obvious. But the prevalent sexual
situation, the attitude to femininity, the political position of
women (the feminist movement) were the factors that provided
a framework for his questions; yet the questions asked are not
the same as the answers produced. The specific conditions
probably determined some of the formulations of particular
questions, but when we come to the answers we have to ask
whether or not they stand on their own merit. There is no
doubt that psychoanalytic 'answers' do so.

Index

Figures in **bold type** indicate main references (chapters or sections). All books and articles mentioned and quoted are indexed under their titles.

About the Author

Juliet Mitchell is a qualified psychoanalyst and a university lec-
turer in Gender and Society, and Fellow of Jesus College, Cam-
bridge University. She is currently a visiting professor in
Comparative Literature at Yale University, where she is also a fellow of the Whitney Humanities Center. She has written numerous
essays in literary criticism and in the political theory of women's
oppression, and is one of Britian's foremost feminist thinkers. Her
published work includes *Women's Estate*, *Women: The Longest
Revolution*, *The Rights and Wrongs of Women*, *What Is Feminism?*
and *Who's Afraid of Feminism?* (all co-edited with Ann Oakley),
The Selected Melanie Klein (editor), *Before I was I* (edited with
Michael Parsons) and, with Jaqueline Rose, *Feminine Sexuality:
Jacques Lacan and the École Freudienne*. Her study of hysteria,
Mad Men and Medusas, is being published by Basic Books.